Race in North America

RACE IN NORTH AMERICA

Origin and Evolution of a Worldview

AUDREY SMEDLEY

Westview Press
BOULDER • SAN FRANCISCO • OXFORD

Copyright © 1993 by Westview Press, Inc.

Published in 1993 in the United States of America by Westview Press, Inc., 5500 Central Avenue, Boulder, Colorado 80301-2877, and in the United Kingdom by Westview Press, 36 Lonsdale Road, Summertown, Oxford OX2 7EW

Library of Congress Cataloging-in-Publication Data
Smedley, Audrey.
  Race in North America : origin and evolution of a worldview /
Audrey Smedley.
    p.   cm.
  Includes bibliographical references and index.
  ISBN 0-8133-0621-3. — ISBN 0-8133-0622-1 (pbk.)
  1. Race—Origin. 2. Racism—History. 3. Black race. 4. Slavery—
History. I. Title.
GN269.S63   1993
572'.2—dc20   92-25269
                                                                  CIP

Printed and bound in the United States of America

The paper used in this publication meets the requirements
of the American National Standard for Permanence of Paper
for Printed Library Materials Z39.48-1984.

10   9   8   7   6   5   4   3   2   1

To
the spirit of
my father
for all that he endured

and
for my sons
so that they will remember

Contents

Acknowledgments　　　　　　　　　　　　　　　　　　　　　xi

Introduction　　　　　　　　　　　　　　　　　　　　　　1

1　Some Theoretical Considerations　　　　　　　　　　13

"Race" as a Modern Idea, 15
Ideas, Ideologies, and Worldviews, 17
The Social Reality of Race in America, 18
On the Relationship Between Biology and "Race," 22
The Primordialists' Argument, 22
Race as a Worldview: A Theoretical Perspective, 25
Race and Ethnicity, 29
Notes, 34

2　The Etymology of the Term "Race"　　　　　　　　　36

Notes, 40

3　Antecedents of the Racial Worldview　　　　　　　41

The Age of European Exploration, 41
The Rise of Capitalism and the Transformation of
　English Society, 45
Social Organization and Values of Early Capitalism, 50
English Ethnocentrism and the Idea of the Savage, 52
English Nationalism and Social Values in the Sixteenth
　and Seventeenth Centuries, 61
Hereditary Social Identity: The Lesson of Catholic
　Spain, 64
Notes, 70

4 Growth of the English Ideology of Race in America 72

Earliest Contacts, 72
The Ensuing Conflicts, 76
The Backing of God and Other Justifications for
   Conquest, 80
The New Savages, 85
Notes, 90

**5 The Arrival of Africans and Their Decline
into Slavery** 92

The First Africans, 95
The Descent into Racial Slavery, 96
A Focus on Physical Differences, 106
Notes, 110

**6 Comparing Slave Systems: The Significance of
"Racial" Servitude** 113

The Background Literature and the Issues of Slavery, 114
The Nature of Slavery, 118
Historical Background of Old World Slavery, 119
Colonial Slavery Under the Spanish and Portuguese, 131
The Uniqueness of the English Experience of Slavery, 137
The Significance of Slavery in the Creation of "Race," 142
Notes, 146

**7 The Rise of Science: Sixteenth- to Eighteenth-
Century Classifications of Human Diversity** 152

The Questions and the Issues, 152
Classifications of Humankind, 161
The Impact of Eighteenth-Century Classifications, 167
Notes, 170

**8 Late Eighteenth-Century Thought and
Crystallization of the Ideology of Race** 171

Social Values of the American Colonists, 173
Nature's Hierarchy, 177

Dominant Themes in North American Racial Beliefs, 185
Anglo-Saxonism: The Making of a Biological Myth, 188
Thomas Jefferson and the American Dilemma, 192
Notes, 202

**9 Antislavery and the Entrenchment of a
Racial Worldview**   205

A Brief History of Antislavery Thought, 206
The Proslavery Response, 216
The Sociocultural Realities of Race and Slavery, 219
The Priority of Race over Class, 224
Notes, 229

**10 A Different Order of Being: Nineteenth-Century
Science and the Ideology of Race**   231

Polygeny Versus Monogeny: The Debate over Race
  and Species, 234
The Unnatural Mixture, 244
Scientific Race Ideology in the Judicial System, 246
White Supremacy, 250
Notes, 253

**11 Science and the Interchange of Race Ideology
Between Europe and America**   255

European Contributions to the Ideology of Race, 256
Measurement of Human Differences: Anthropometry
  and Somatometry, 258
Typological Models of Race, 263
The Measurement of "Race" Differences:
  Psychometrics, 265
The Clothing of Immigrants in the Garment of Race, 268
Notes, 271

**12 Dismantling the Cultural Construction of Race:
Twentieth-Century Transformations in Science**   273

The Rise of Physical Anthropology, 274

Franz Boas and Attempts to Transform the Meaning
of Race, 275
The Rise of Population Genetics, 283
The Rise of a Liberal Social Position on Race, 291
Notes, 292

13 **New Perspectives on Human Variation
and Some Tentative Conclusions**   294

The Decline of the Idea of Race in Science, 294
The Scientific Debate over Race: The Splitters and
the Lumpers, 297
The Ecological Perspective, 300
Monogeny Reconsidered: The Nonproblem of
Race Mixture, 302
Summary and Conclusions, 303
Notes, 309

Bibliography   311
About the Book and Author   330
Index   331

Acknowledgments

MY INTELLECTUAL INDEBTEDNESS to a host of predecessors in history and anthropology can never be repaid, especially to my professors at the University of Michigan and the Victoria University of Manchester, England. I am deeply grateful for the faith that some of the giants in their fields had in me.

Professor George Forcey in the History Department of the State University of New York at Binghamton read the entire first draft of the manuscript and offered many suggestions for revisions and improvement. He was usually right, and I offer him heartfelt thanks for such a tedious and careful job. I owe deep gratitude also for the evaluations and comments of Professors Gary Nash, Robert Berkhofer, Jack Kelso, Frank Livingstone, Colin Palmer, and Elizabeth Fox-Genovese, who allocated some of their precious time to reading and commenting on earlier versions of the manuscript. Diane Geraci of the State University at Binghamton library provided excellent bibliographical assistance for which I am most grateful. Editors and friends at Westview Press, Miriam Gilbert, Alice Levine, and Dean Birkenkamp, did a masterful job of guiding the manuscript through its many changes. In each new revision many of their suggestions helped to improve the book, and they have my enduring gratitude.

I must also give thanks to the many students who over the years have aided in the collection of an enormous amount of information. The research has taken us into so many different areas that the whole endeavor often took on the semblance of an intellectual patchwork quilt. How this quilt has been assembled is purely my own doing, however; none of my colleagues or students are responsible for interpretations, errors, or inaccuracies.

Some of the inspiration for this book came from my stay at the Radcliffe (now Bunting) Institute in the early 1970s. I will always cherish the opportunity afforded by the institute for the rich intellectual stimulation and for the friendships I developed. During my stay Professor Preston Williams of the Harvard Divinity School initiated a proposal to do an interdisciplinary study of racism in the 1980s. Working with him and other interested faculty helped to focus my thinking on the question of the origins of race as ideology and concept. He is due special thanks, as is his wife, Connie, for their hospitality and friendship.

Seed funds supporting early investigations on this topic originated from the Russell Sage Foundation. A large portion of the subsequent research was funded by the Ford Foundation.

Audrey Smedley

Introduction

M ANY YEARS AGO I introduced a new course into the university curriculum entitled "The Concept of Race in Western Thought." From the beginning, both students and I recognized a number of difficulties in dealing with the phenomenon of race. On the first day of each class, I raised the question of finding a definition of the term on which we could all agree. It came as no surprise that we never could define the concept with any degree of precision or consensus, despite the fact that publications in English alone on the topic of race probably number into the tens of thousands.

There are, indeed, few topics in Western intellectual and social history that have been subjected to as much investigation, speculation, analysis, and theoretical scrutiny as the phenomenon of race. Whether one accepts race as a God-given denouement of the complexity of an imperfect world or as a misguided conception of group relationships, race is a pervasive element in the cognitive patterning of Western thought and experience. It has been so fundamental, so intrinsic to our perceptual and explanatory framework that we almost never question its meaning or its reality.

In such nations as the United States and South Africa, in which race is the important calculus of social identity, our interactions with other individuals are influenced, whether we admit it or not, by a racial identity that we attribute to others and to ourselves. We perceive this identity as reflected in tangible and easily recognized biophysical characteristics. Indeed, the very existence of physical differences among populations is accepted as concrete evidence of race. We have been conditioned to respond automatically to the presence of certain varying physical features as indicators of race and the differences race connotes.

More important, as I document in the chapters to follow, race is seen as a part of the natural order of things, and the existence of races is believed to have been confirmed as part of nature by science and scientists. Yet the scientific record has shown enormous ambiguity on the matter of race, as well as much confusion and little common agreement among the experts on its meaning. In fact, in recent scientific treatments of race we can observe some little known but fascinating new developments.

In a 1982 article, Alice Littlefield, Leonard Lieberman, and Larry Reynolds revealed an extraordinary transformation relating to the idea of race in one subfield of anthropology. Analyzing the contents of fifty-eight introductory textbooks in physical anthropology published between 1932 and 1979, they discovered that since 1970 there has been a progressive elimination of the term and concept of race from textbooks published in the United States. This decline occurred most precipitously during the late 1970s when either the term was no longer mentioned in the texts or the argument was made by the text authors that races do not exist or are not "real." Littlefield et al. noted that although the term is still used by a minority of writers, there is less emphasis on racial typologies and classifications than on descriptions and explanations of biophysical variation. Their documentation of the lack of support for the retention of the term "race" as a scientific concept is seen by them as "dramatic" evidence of the development of a "no-race" position in the science of humankind (Littlefield, Lieberman, and Reynolds 1982, 642).

When we recall that the first textbook in anthropology defined that field as the study of "man and the races of man" (Tylor [1881] 1946) and that the "races of man" were at the heart of the development of anthropology in the United States, as they were elsewhere, it appears that either physical anthropology is defining itself out of an identity or some other more crucial metamorphosis in the wider world of knowledge has taken place.

How are we to interpret this change? If the field that had the most to do with the identification and definition of human races is relinquishing its activities and related conceptual apparati in this area, what does this mean for other sciences that have focused on "racial" differences? What does this convey to us about the nature of anthropology or science in general? Are scientific discoveries or conclusions so ephemeral or arbitrary that such a crucial concept can be so easily discarded? More important, what possible meanings or implications might there be for society at large? How can a scientific discipline overtly contradict a reality that so many of us daily experience? If scientists are no longer accepting the existence of races, does this mean that societies such as those in the United States and South Africa will ultimately give up their preoccupation with race? What is the proper approach to the study of "race relations," "race consciousness," or discrimination in the light of such a confusing trend?

The facts revealed by this study indeed stimulate numerous questions about the relationship between science and social thought, beliefs and values. The answers to such questions, however, are much less clear than the textbook trend itself. Yet the three authors just mentioned probe for explanations of this trend among social and historical facts that they mix with a strangely tendentious argument. They note, on the one hand, that the transformation could be a product of the self-correcting nature of science as it progresses; or, on the other, that it could be the outcome of sweeping changes in the American social and political milieu ushered in during the 1960s. But they opt for an explication that they consider relates more closely to certain changes in the structure of higher education, particularly to the history of the development of the field of anthropology in American universities.

In the early stages of anthropology as a discipline, they argue, the field was an elitist one, dominated primarily by men who were able to enter graduate-level training at the most prestigious universities. An unstated assumption is made by the authors that such individuals were more likely to have a strong sense of race and race differences. But, the argument continues, as anthropology began to expand into nonelite universities and the graduates of these institutions reflected less privileged sociocultural backgrounds, the content of the teaching of anthropology began to change. Teachers in two- and four-year institutions that catered to the masses, as well as textbook publishers similarly focused, began to reflect the values of the students in these institutions (Littlefield et al., 1982, 646). A parallel assumption implicit in this phase of the argument is that students as well as teachers from less privileged socioeconomic backgrounds tend to have more egalitarian and less racist values.

The correlations that the authors have found between the institutions, their students, and those who teach them are interesting ones. Their conclusion, however, especially to those who know something of the tumultuous history of race relations in the United States and of working-class racial beliefs and practices, seems strangely discordant with this larger history. The correlations may well be coincidental or a predictable consequence of changes of larger magnitude in the wider society, which, in fact, I suspect is the case. During the 1960s and 1970s there was a measurable liberalization of social values, especially the negative ones associated with racism. Since World War II, important changes that have occurred in American society have fostered more egalitarian views about races and racial differences at many levels; polls show greater commitment to equality. But the social consciousness pendulum began to swing back to cautiously conservative and less egalitarian positions during the early 1980s. Such fluctuations in social attitudes we would expect to be reflected to some degree in all sectors of society. In the past, scientists generally have been no more immune to the cyclical swings of social values, popular beliefs, and the vagaries of myths and half-truths than have other members of society.

All of this points up the fact that there are intricate and complex relationships between the scientific community and the processes that take place within it and the larger social-cultural-historical setting in which science functions. The history of science shows that events and processes occurring in one arena inevitably have consequences for the other, often unanticipated and/or unintended. For the most part, scientists cannot operate outside of the knowledge systems of their culture and the potentials inherent in them. The state of that knowledge, both technological and social, as well as perceived cultural values and needs will determine, in general, the directions along which science develops. The very queries posed by science, the methods of investigation, the configurations by which science objectifies reality emerge out of often specific cultural contexts. Feedback between the realms of science and contemporary trends in popular belief and knowledge may enhance a particular trajectory and diminish others. Thus scientific advances, experimentation, and theorizing have generally reflected not only the prevailing state of technological knowledge but also economic, social, ideological, ethical, and/or political trends (Greene 1981). The science of astronomy was stimulated in the sixteenth century by new discoveries and developments in the technology of navigation and by peoples bent on exploration and colonization of distant new lands. In the twentieth century, increasingly large-scale political hostilities between peoples organized as nation-states occur in tandem with a highly sophisticated technology capable of large-scale killing.

But some scientific discoveries or advances may also propel knowledge beyond the boundaries of hitherto socially accepted wisdom or visions of the world. The technology and experiments that allowed the recognition of bacteria as the cause of some diseases challenged many supernatural myths, transforming social habits, life-styles, and views of world realities. Since the nineteenth century, rapidly cumulating technological and scientific knowledge have emerged as major stimulants to social and historical changes, most of which have been unanticipated.

The trend away from race as a scientifically useful means of classifying human beings has to be comprehended along several dimensions.

First, both the frames of reference and the data base of science have changed dramatically. In the twentieth century most scientists have worked with definitions and conceptions of human variation specific to their disciplines; in other words, those that were confined to biophysical, biogenetic, biochemical, and other physiological factors. So any change in the scientific understanding of race must be explicable, it seems to me, in terms of developments in fields such as human genetics, biochemistry, cytology, serology, microbiology, and related subspecialties. These fields have had the benefit of tremendous advances due to highly sophisticated instrumentation for observation, identification, measurement, and analysis. Electron microscopy, electrophoresis, immunochemistry techniques, and a host of other new methods have enabled the experts to identify and measure variability in perhaps thousands of hereditary traits from analyses of DNA (genetic materials that determine our biophysical characteristics).[1] The discovery of the range and complexity of genetic variability has prompted scientists to rethink the ways by which we classify populations and to question the extent of real differences between so-called races (see Chapters 12 and 13).

Second, the wider cultural context in which science has operated for several hundred years has also been transformed, as Littlefield et al. rightly note. But this context includes much more than changes in social and ideological values accompanying the disturbances of the 1960s. Even before the twentieth century, discovery, innovation, ingenuity, and inventiveness became distinct and positive values in American culture, leading to the broadening of the range of human imagination. Change per se, progress, and growth as cultural goals prompted tolerance, especially in the scholarly establishment, for unorthodox and "trendy" thinking along secular lines. The twentieth century has brought unprecedented freedom for scientific experimentation and speculation so that the growth in the sheer numbers of researchers, their ideas, and their products in all areas has given science itself a dominant role in everyday life. This freedom has also provided science a powerful voice in social policy and political decision making. Thus a combination of liberal social values of the 1960s and 1970s, scientific advances in the study of hereditary traits brought about by new technology, a more educated public, and an ethos of change, growth, and progress may all be responsible for the no-race trend in science.

Although today these progressive scientific positions may be discordant with the public experiences and realities of race, this was not always the case. In recent years it has become widely recognized by historians who have investigated the background of the modern problems of race that past developments in the biological and anthropological sciences were invariably reflective of prevailing social beliefs and values. Science indeed played a major role in the formulation of some of the ideological components of race. This has been documented in such works as Barzun's *Race: A Study in Modern Superstition* (1965), Chase's *The Legacy of Malthus* (1980), Curtin's *The Image of Africa* (1964), Gossett's *Race: The History of an Idea in America* (1965), Haller's *Outcasts from Evolution* (1971), Jordan's *White over Black* (1968), Stanton's *The Leopard's Spots* (1960), and the recent publications of Stephen Jay Gould, especially *The Mismeasure of Man* (1981), among many others. These works reveal that, until recently, the advocacy of science has been central to the legitimization of folk ideas about human differences expressed in the idiom of race. With the no-races perspective, modern science appears to be abandoning its support of popular ideas about race.

Many scientists who today reject the idea of race as a useful biological concept tend to argue that it is a myth or an abstraction that does not correspond with the reality and complexities of human biological variation. This has been confusing to those who grapple with the social reality of "race" and the concomitant experience of the same phenotypic variation that is assumed to be the basis for racial classifications. One major reason for the confusion is that we lack a clear sense of the origins and social history of the *idea* of race. This history, it seems to me, is crucial to understanding the apparent divergence today between popular views of race and the advancing thrust in science. We need to know much more about its origin—specifically what the term race meant in those societies in which it first became a critical parameter of social identity. In addition, we want to know more about the historical forces that influenced both its origin and its meaning.

Despite referential discrepancies, the social categories of "race" are very real. To understand this, we must distinguish and separate analytically the range of actual physical diversity in our heterogenous population from the meanings and attitudes about these differences that evolved within a particular sociohistorical framework.

Race should not be seen as something tangible that exists in the outside world, which has to be discovered, described, and defined, but as a cultural creation, a product of human invention. Historical sources show that race has never been an objective scientific classification of human group variation. From the beginning of its use in the English language, the term reflected a particular way of looking at and interpreting human differences, both physical and cultural. It was intricately linked with certain presuppositions of thought held by European colonists from the sixteenth to the eighteenth centuries. During that period the word was transformed in the English language from a mere classificatory term into a folk idea. This idea expressed certain attitudes toward human differences as well as prejudgments about the nature and social value of these differences.

It is essential that we comprehend race as a sociocultural phenomenon conceptually separable from biophysical variations. This is the genesis and major premise of this book. It is not enough to argue that race is a myth because it fails to accord with any measurable discontinuity of biophysical realities. We have known for a long time that being a member of a certain "racial" category does not amount to having all or any of the physical attributes associated with that category. The first black Miss Americas in the mid-1980s were physically little differentiated from their colleagues/competitors. In the United States, people who identify themselves as African-Americans range from fair-skinned, blond-haired, and blue-eyed individuals to those with dark brown skins and wooly hair. And those who identify themselves as native Americans often share more phenotypic features with their European ancestors than with their Indian ones. Analyses of the historical construction of the idea of race will help us to comprehend these apparent anomalies.

In this work I emphasize a way of defining race that is consonant with this historical development and that continues to reflect contemporary social realities. Scholars as diverse as Alexander Alland, Jr., Michael Banton, Jacques Barzun, George Fredrickson, Ashley Montagu, Pierre Van den Berghe, among many others, have taken similar approaches, insisting that race should be treated as a sociological or sociopolitical phenomenon.[2] As an alternative way of looking at the concept, this viewpoint renders much of the disputation, controversies, and uncertainties over biological definitions of race irrelevant. Race was and is just one of several ways of perceiving, interpreting, and dealing with human differences. It is a particular worldview perpetuated as much by the continued use of the term in our daily lives and in the media as it is by the stereotypes to which so many of us have, often unconsciously, been conditioned.

As a way of imposing order on and understanding about complex realities in which one group asserted dominance over others, some Europeans chose race as the option in their creation of identities for those populations encountered and exploited in the New World, Asia, and Africa. That it brought in its wake horrendous human misery and intractable social, economic, political, and moral problems could no doubt not have been predicted five centuries ago.

In my preparation of a volume that covers so much history in a relatively brief space, I had as one broad objective the collection and organization of relevant reading materials for students in courses on the concept of race. But as I probed deeper into its history and discovered the kind of ethnological information that suggested greater need for this perspective, it seemed useful and important to appeal to a wider audience, one that has persistently demanded more information on this topic. Public lectures that I gave on the the history of the idea of race elicited great interest. So this book is not solely, nor specifically, a textbook designed for college students. I hope that it will also find a suitable berth among educated and socially conscious people who are also seeking answers to some of the inexorable problems of human relationships.

Because I planned to reach a general audience, the level of discourse does not include all of the nuances and ranges of thought and debate on any given topic, as interesting and useful as this may be for advanced scholars. The reader should also be cautioned that this is not a study of racial discrimination or racism per se nor a study of ethnic or color prejudice. It makes no assertions about biophysical differences that may exist between groups of human beings, nor does it argue that all human beings are equal. It does attempt to provide an analytic framework for the study of "race" as a sociocultural phenomenon.

In addition, this book is not designed to be a comprehensive study of the concept of race or a survey of all the literature on the topic and on related ones, such as slavery and colonialism. The universe of materials is so large that it would have been virtually impossible to incorporate everything. Even a limited attempt at such coverage would have resulted in not one but several volumes. I chose instead to delineate what seemed to be a little-explored perspective on race and to present some new insights and interpretations on United States history, while using only data sufficient to illustrate or illuminate the major points. Much of the historical materials used here are already well known through the publications of many brilliant scholars, and an interested reader would not find it difficult to flesh out greater details.

For scholars and advanced students, one of my aims is to raise new questions and to suggest new areas of research not hitherto covered by the existing studies on race. It is vital that scholars rethink the prevailing epistemological categories and approaches to their subjects from time to time. Given the events of the past half century or more and the increasing attention to ethnic and "racial" conflicts here and elsewhere, it seems that the time to revisit the question of race has come.

The people most instrumental in the development of the idea of race as we experience it in North America were the English colonists who began settlements in the seventeenth century. The book thus focuses on the beliefs, values, and social practices that the English brought with them to the colonies; these set the stage for a racial worldview in America. Under the influence of English customs and beliefs, Europeans in the United States developed and institutionalized the concept to a degree more extreme than that of any other society outside South Africa. The book therefore concentrates on the American experience and on some of the many influences that led to the formulation of the racial worldview most familiar to us.

Each race-based society (in which race is central to the social structure) developed its own unique patterns and practices, although the ideological components of the racial worldview, when clearly analyzed, were essentially similar (see Chapter 1). All have race classifications identified in law; all structure racial classifications hierarchically; all associate stereotyped behavior with each race category; and all hold, in an abstract sense, that racial characteristics are innate and unalterable.

The race system that evolved in the United States is distinctive in several ways. First, the dichotomous race categories of black and white are set and inflexible. Unlike in South Africa or Latin America, there is no legal or social recognition of a "racial" category in between ("mixed-race"); and one cannot belong to more than one race. Second, the category "black" or "African-American" is defined by any known descent from a black ancestor, thus conflating and socially homogenizing individuals with a wide range of phenotypes into one racial category. Third, one cannot transcend or transform one's "race" status; in other words, no legal or social mechanism exists for changing one's race.[3] Under the system of apartheid in South Africa, a government board existed that reassigned hundreds of people every year to different racial categories. In much of Latin America, exclusive racial categories do not exist, although descriptive terms are used to reflect the perception of *individuals* with varying degrees of admixture of Indian, Negro, and Spanish (or Portuguese) ancestry. In many areas individuals may shift between Indian and mestizo ethnic identities with ease although their physical traits do not change. And lower-status people of more negroid physiognomies may be transformed to higher social status ("whitened") by virtue of education, wealth, or professional accomplishments. In the United States, neither social class, education, wealth, nor professional or governmental or business achievements evoke a change in race identity.[4] Race is more highly institutionalized in our collective consciousness and the boundaries are more rigidly drawn. A major objective of this book is to explain this reality, the uniqueness of the race concept and ideology in the United States.

The use of limited comparative materials and data from other societies aims only to refine and accentuate the parameters of the race concept in American culture. Because of limitations of space, this effort could not be exhaustive. Space and time also prevent exploring in depth the racial worldview as it evolved in South Africa, Australia, Latin America, and elsewhere. It is important to emphasize that there is room for a great deal of comparative research on the themes introduced here.

From this standpoint the book will not satisfy everyone, for it touches only lightly on some topics and ignores others that scholars in particular fields might judge important. My hope is that people of all backgrounds will find in this work useful information and enlightening interpretations of history and social realities. Most importantly, I hope that it will introduce the reader to a more critical way of looking at the phenomenon of race and will stimulate new thinking and research about the issues and problems created by this concept.

The book follows both a chronological and thematic format. But the chronology is not rigidly bounded by precise dates, nor is it inclusive and comprehensive. It is not possible to include all levels and minutiae of information when discussing a history essentially of ideas in action. What one should understand are developmental stages in the growth of the ideas that became specific components of the racial worldview and the events and circumstances that pinpoint the hardening and softening of ideas and beliefs.

Chapter 1 introduces certain concepts, definitions, and theoretical perspectives that guide the arguments to follow. Chapters 2 and 3 recreate the antecedent historical conditions out of which elements of American racial thought were generated. Many scholars now agree that it was in the precolonial phase of English history that the seeds of the race idea were planted. Chapter 4 traces and analyzes the growth of English thought, practices, and beliefs about human differences manifest during the colonial period in North America. Chapters 5 and 6 examine the role of slavery and the processes by which enslavement only of Africans became a particular motif of English life in the New World. Chapter 6 highlights the distinctiveness of the Anglo-American variant of slavery, as it evolved during the eighteenth and nineteenth centuries, relating it to certain precedents raised in Chapters 3 and 4. Some comparisons to Latin American and Old World forms of slavery are suggested to demonstrate the significance of English practices for the structuring of the components of race ideology. Chapter 7 chronicles the emergent role of scientists (naturalists, systematists, taxonomists) and the beginnings of the scientific documentation and categorization of human differences in the eighteenth century. Certain cultural attitudes, prejudgments, and assumptions about these differences, rooted in folk beliefs, guided these earliest scientific works and dominated the classifications that resulted. In turn, science's impact on the idea of race was immeasurable, especially in fostering a detachment of the racial worldview to an autonomous realm, making possible its extension beyond the social context of its origin. Chapter 8 explores how the elements of the racial worldview coevolved and synthesized during the revolutionary era in North America, revealing the dilemmas and contradictions that slavery and the creation of the ideology of race posed for Americans.

The next chapter, 9, looks at the impact of antislavery sentiment on proslavery thought, prompting vigorous defenses of the system and a resulting entrenchment of ideas of black inferiority, so crucial to the racial worldview. This is followed, in Chapter 10, with a discussion of the intricate ways in which the concurrently developing sciences of mankind played a role in legitimizing race thinking. In the nineteenth century, some "scientific" publications virtually parodied popular thought and rising white hatred and fear in the wake of abolitionist pressure. In researching and trying to validate American folk beliefs in human differences, scientists authenticated and rationalized "race" as the taxonomic equivalent of "species," evoking a sense of the unnaturalness of black and brown variants of humankind. Scientific and other "scholarly" and popular writings were major factors in the ultimate institutionalization and dissemination of the racial worldview.

Europe evolved its own versions of race ideologies, particularly during the nineteenth century, as I show in Chapter 11, which in turn deeply affected race ideology in the United States. Eventually, components of the Anglo-American form of race ideology spread around the world, complicating and transforming ethnic conflicts. In the early twentieth century, an extreme version of this worldview culminated in German Nazi race theories and their application to other Europeans, with the horrible consequences of torture and genocide against millions. At the same time, as I show in Chapter 12, a maturing science in North America began to dissociate itself from the popular folk meaning of race under the stimulus of much new data, a greatly expanded knowledge of genetics and heredity, and a liberalizing social atmosphere induced in part by reaction to Nazi atrocities.

Developments in late twentieth-century science (Chapter 13) reveal a growing repudiation of the idea of biologically distinct races as anthropologists and human biologists are providing us with new ways of understanding human biophysical variation. Given the increasing power and role of science in revealing the "objective" world, and guiding our thoughts about it, this may represent the early and tentative first step of a major social transformation, the beginning of the end of the racial worldview in the United States and perhaps elsewhere.

Notes

1. The most widely studied and best-known genetic polymorphisms relate to diseases and to various abnormalities and immunities. Many such traits have been discovered based in hemoglobins, serum proteins (haptoglobins and transferrins), enzymes and enzyme deficiencies, and a wide variety of other proteins. See W. Bodmer and L. L. Cavalli-Sforza, 1976.

2. Earlier in this century, scholars in the growing field of sociology were among the first to recognize race as a form of social stratification. The work of such men as Robert Park and his associates and students (e.g., E. Franklin Frazier and Oliver Cox) remain of seminal interest. For a review of models and theories of racial stratification in sociology, see J. Geschwender, 1978.

3. The phenomenon of "passing," which occurred much more frequently in the late nineteenth and early twentieth centuries, is an individual and surreptitious decision not sanctioned by any social forces in the United States.

4. While he was mayor of Atlanta, Andrew Young experienced several incidents in which his low-status race classification was underscored. On one occasion he was leaving a famous New York hotel, in fancy dinner dress, when a white man handed him his keys and said, "Here, boy, go get my car." Most African-American men, including judges, university professors, actors, businessmen, physicians, scientists, and other highly trained and affluent professionals, have confronted the same type of racial put-downs, clear comments on the social status nature of race identity.

1

Some Theoretical Considerations

ANYONE WHO ATTEMPTS to write a book about race does so with much trepidation. The subject has been so widely and intensively explored that many probably believe that nothing new can be added. In the social sciences definitions, explanations, analyses, and interpretations of racial issues, meanings, problems, interactions, stratification, dynamics, prejudice, discrimination, and so forth abound. For many generations scholars have focused on the patterns of racial realities most obvious and most problematic in the United States: that between whites and blacks and between whites and native Americans. The social interactions of newer immigrants such as the Chinese, the Japanese and other Asians, Puerto Ricans, Mexicans, and even the Irish, the Italians, and the Jews have also been frequently couched in terms of race, proliferating the racial imagery imposed on the national scene. Yet we know little or nothing about the origin of the idea of race or what specific factors influenced its genesis. It does seem strange, from the lofty heights of the late twentieth century, that we know so little of this history.

To examine the sociocultural history of the concept requires a different conceptual framework from that of the sociologist whose concern is theories of race relations, or the historian who aims to document the different ways by which populations have been racially classified and the nature of their interrelationships in the past. The intellectual scope has to shift from concern about the appropriate units of analysis to ideas and their relationships and the cultural matrix within which ideological factors emerge and function.

The operant theoretical premises and assumptions of this volume will be outlined in this chapter. Like many contemporary writers, I suggest that there is indeed a meaning to the term race, but one that most experts have not really addressed. We have failed to understand this, in

13

part because we have been looking at the wrong data and in part because the inertia and myopia often plaguing the social sciences have inhibited the investigation of all of the dimensions of the subject.

The meaning of race is not to be found in the physical features of differing human populations, nor does it rest in the lists of taxa of the biological scientists. Rather than looking inwardly for some esoteric genesis, we must peel away the intricate layers of Western cultural history and look at the material conditions, the cultural and naturalistic knowledge, and the motivations, objectives, and levels of consciousness and comprehension of those who first imposed the classifications of race on the human community. It is important that we understand race as its meaning unfolded in the cognitive world of its creators and first formulators, in part because the subsequent formulations have been so ambiguous and elusive. A major goal of this book is to help eliminate some of the existing confusion about the concept and to examine analytically its constituent elements in order to understand how, when, and why they evolved together, as well as the subsequent consequences of and transformations in this synthesis.

In this chapter I first offer a historical perspective now held by many scholars who see race as a sociocultural phenomenon that appeared only within the past several hundred years. Next, I explain the theoretical context in which I conceptualize, define, and analyze the components of race. It is treated as a culturally constructed reality whose ingredients can be ascertained through historical and social analysis. It is not a unitary phenomenon but a synthesis of a number of identifiable elements that, brought together, constitute a particular way of viewing human differences. I then briefly describe the social reality of race in North American culture, emphasizing what I think are often unacknowledged realities.

Since the vast majority of people equate biological diversity with race, I next address the relationship between biology and race. To comprehend the nature and meaning of race in our society it is necessary and essential to distinguish physical diversity in the human species from culturally based perceptions and interpretations of this diversity. This is also the key to understanding recent developments in scientific views of race.

Such a position is not without its detractors, and a continuing stream of scholars in the biological and social sciences have argued that the human perception of phenotypic differences as race is universal, in a generic sense. I therefore present the arguments and a brief critique of the "primordialists," those intellectuals who would preserve the term "race" for what we might call psychosocial reasons not necessarily related to the evidence and arguments of contemporary biological scientists. The next section offers the theoretical perspective of this book, defining race as a worldview and specifying its minimal constituent components. Finally, I differentiate this definition of race from "ethnicity," a concept that has too often served to complicate the more general and profound issues of accounting for variability in both biology and behavior.

The approach of this book has been inspired in part by studies in the sociology of knowledge and in the history of ideas. Concepts such as race can appropriately be conceived as a composite of elements, each of which may have had certain distinct functions or cultural meanings in earlier times. These elements had their origins in preceding historical circumstances, events, or conditions. Race itself has become in time a shorthand method of expressing these ideas as they were conjoined or synthesized in history.

There are many other concepts open to the same sort of exploration whereby one can separate out specific components. Concepts such as *democracy, fundamentalism, evolutionism,* or *socialism* represent widespread and diffuse ideas that have become integrated into a systematic body of knowledge and thought, into ways of looking at things, and into understandings that constitute part of our cultural repertoire. Such terms thus become shorthand methods of expressing a particular worldview. *Race* is a shorthand term for, as well as a symbol of, a "knowledge system"; a way of knowing and of looking at the world and of rationalizing its contents (in this case, other human beings) in terms that are derived from previous cultural-historical experience and reflective of contemporary social values, relationships, and conditions.

"Race" as a Modern Idea

It is not without significance that many contemporary scholars have concluded that race is a relatively recent concept in human history. The cultural structuring of a racial worldview coincides with the colonial expansion of certain Western European nations during the past five centuries, the encountering of populations very different from themselves, and the creation of a unique form of slavery.[1] Expansion, conquest, exploitation, and enslavement have characterized much of human history over the past five thousand years or so, but none of these events before the modern era resulted in the development of ideologies or social systems based on race. Dante Puzzo put it explicitly: "Racism ... is a modern conception, for prior to the sixteenth century there was virtually nothing in the life and thought of the West that can be described as racist" (1964, 579). This view, although referring only to the West, clearly challenges the claim that race classifications and ideologies were or are universal or have deep historical roots.

Rising competitiveness with one another and consciousness of their power to dominate others affected the way Europeans perceived indigenous people and factored early in their methods of dealing with all aliens. Race as a mode of classifying human beings appeared in the languages of the Spanish, Portuguese, Italians, French, Germans, Dutch, and English as these groups established colonial empires in the New World and Asia and set about dealing with the heterogeneous populations of these empires. Race conceptions varied, however, among the colonizing powers. It was the English in North America who developed the most rigid and exclusionist form of race ideology, and it is on this racial worldview that this book focuses.

Reviewing this history helps us to become conscious of certain facts that, for the most part, have often escaped analysis. The peoples of the conquered areas of the New World, and the other "colored" peoples of what is now the Third World, did not participate in the invention of race or in the compilation of racial classifications imposed upon them and others. To the extent that these peoples use the idiom today and operate within its strictures, they have inherited and acquiesced to the system of racial divisions created for them by the dominant Europeans (Banton 1977). As a paradigm for portraying the social reality of inequality, the racial worldview has spread around the world, where its use often exacerbates already existing interethnic animosities (Barzun 1965).

Accepting the fact that race is a cultural construct invented by human beings, it is easy to understand that it emerged out of a set of definable historical circumstances and is thus as amenable to analysis as are other elements of culture. No amount of comparative definitions and synchronic explorations of modern race relations will lead us to more refined definitions and understandings of race. On the contrary, it is a complex of elements whose significance and meanings lie in historical settings in which attitudes and values were formed. We should be able to analytically isolate the central components, investigate their probable genesis, and determine how they evolved over time.

This approach is different from that of experts who have written about the history of the idea of race in the past. Louis Snyder, Earl Count, Thomas Gossett, and others have documented the differing definitions of races and the numerous classifications that early taxonomists invented. Such historians as Gossett, John Hope Franklin, John Haller, Jr., Gary Nash, Winthrop Jordan, David Brion Davis, C. Vann

Woodward, Carter G. Woodson, Eugene Genovese, Robert Berkhofer, Jr., Roy Pearce, George Fredrickson, as well as many other experts on slavery and race in the New World, have explored the attitudes of whites in the Americas toward peoples whom they identified as racially different from themselves. My concern in this volume is not to repeat these well-known studies, but to specify and analyze the ideological ingredients of which the idea of race itself was comprised and to identify the cultural contexts that nourished them.

Ideas, Ideologies, and Worldviews

By exploring the probable origin and history of the idea of race, dissecting it into its component elements, and attempting to relate these to their sociohistorical contexts, I am not reifying the concept or elevating ideas into a realm of absolute autonomy. Ideas should not be translated as prime movers of the cultural process, nor should they be considered as mere epiphenomena of culture. Ideas are critical, necessary aspects of culture that may vary in strength and form of expression over time and space, but invariably they meet some cultural need or advance the interests of those who hold them. From this perspective, ideas cannot even be interpreted or analyzed apart from their cultural matrices. They arise out of specific material and social circumstances and are constituted of individual and group perceptions, understandings, and decisions made by human beings who inevitably have an imperfect comprehension of the complexity of the situations that confront them. The human animal has the capacity to come to conclusions and make decisions out of self-interest, out of devotion to some abstract principle, or out of his or her perceptions of the larger interests of the group, however that is defined. Multiple individual decisions may well accumulate and become entrenched as cultural orientations that persist through time and space.

As such decisions become incremental parts of the cultural order, they reflect specific understandings of the world and its environmental and social realities. They provide explanations for, and often a means of controlling, social and natural forces. As their adaptive usefulness is realized, they become established as givens, as worldviews or ideologies, and thus institutionalized, they feed back into human thought and actions. By worldview I mean a culturally structured, systematic way of looking at, perceiving, and interpreting various world realities, a society's "weltanschauung," to use a word made popular in sociological studies. Once established and conventionalized, worldviews become enthroned in individuals as mind-sets. They may even achieve the state of involuntary cognitive processes, actively if not consciously molding the behavior of their bearers.

I define race as such a worldview. In the United States, Australia, South Africa, and in many other areas of the world, it is a cosmological ordering system that divides the world's peoples into biologically discrete and exclusive groups. The racial worldview holds that these groups are by nature unequal and can be ranked along a gradient of superiority–inferiority. My use of the term "worldview" depicts the deepseated nature of this essentially folk vision of the human species and the often unconscious processes of perception or imagery that it generates.

Race as a worldview can be understood as composed of specific ideological components. By ideologies I mean sets of beliefs, values, and assumptions, held on faith alone and generally unrelated to empirical facts, that act as guidelines to or prescriptions for individual and group behavior. The substantive ideological beliefs about human differences tended to vary in time and space, depending on the values, histories, and experiences of the colonizing powers. We can use the terms "worldview" and "ideology" interchangeably with the recognition that there is a high level of correspondence between them. I tend to think of worldview as a more systematic and comprehensive set of ideological beliefs that have an integral relationship to one another. When I speak of the concept of race, I am referring to the fundamental worldview, inclusive of its basic ideological components. The ideological elements in this worldview can be confirmed by empirical research. Where necessary, varying ideologies within different societies can be compared for their similarities and differences, as some historians do, for example, for North and South America.

Some worldviews are flexible and generalizable, capable of being diffused to and adopted by other societies. Their adaptability must be perceived by the other culture-bearers who may modify the components to fit the needs, fears, beliefs, biases, ambitions, and goals that they share. The components of race have been eminently adaptable to a wide variety of sociopolitical situations, as this history reveals.

The Social Reality of Race in America

There is a kind of intellectual or cognitive paradox posed by the abandonment on the part of some contemporary scientists of the use of the term "race," although in most Western cultures, in South Africa, and in much of the rest of the world it is taken for granted as part of folk belief that everyone belongs to a race. If modern science has not been able to produce the kind of studies that would confirm the reality of race—if indeed, as some scientists are increasingly arguing, races do not exist— then it can be legitimately asked: How can public attitudes and understandings retain the notion of their verity and the belief that science has proved their reality?

I think the facts will show that, in the general public, the fundamental belief that races exist is unaffected by contradictions or inconsistencies. We do not discard the basic patterns of thought or question the need for racial classifications when we are faced with great variation and complexity in physical traits and ambiguous realities and uncertainties about the racial identity of an individual or group. There are important reasons for the deeply ingrained sense of racial reality that we inherit as part of our cultural baggage. As I will show in the following chapters, race is the major mode of social differentiation in our society; it cuts across and takes priority over social class, gender, age, religious, cultural (ethnic), and other differences. It is essential, then, to understand race as a sociocultural reality independent of the history and uses of the concept in science and distinct from whether or not scientists can agree on a common biological definition. In this sense, race is a social principle by which society allocates desired rewards and status. It belongs, as Joel Kovel has argued, to "the regulative aspects of our culture" (1970, 26).

For some scientists to deny the existence or reality of biophysical races is to challenge, perhaps inadvertently, one of the most powerful, most deeply entrenched canons of Western thought and belief. The no-races position calls into question fundamental truisms that have been accepted for more than two centuries as part of Nature's way of arranging things. For most people, race is a given, a biological reality that does not require great leaps of consciousness or intellect to comprehend. They see it (or so they believe) in the phenotypic variability experienced in interactions with heterogeneous populations like those in the New World. Moreover, even those scientists who have taken the no-races position are very much aware of the social reality of race in Western societies. Even as they deny its existence they cannot avoid it.

There is, then, a great disjunction between the no-races position of modern scientists on the matter of biological races and the social parameters of race by which we conduct our lives and structure our institutions. Experts in many fields who have grappled with the sociology of race and race relations are not apt to find answers to the weighty prob-

lems of interracial conflict in the laboratories of modern physical anthropologists, human biologists, or geneticists. Modern scientists
investigating problems of human biogenetic variability and scholars of
social behavior are not talking about the same thing.

Reflecting this disjunction are some curious features about the semantics of race and its related terms. If, on the one hand, for the general
educated community, race has been taken to refer to biophysical variations between populations, it should be regarded as a neutral classificatory term. Yet, on the other hand, such derivatives of race as "racism,"
"racist," and "racialism" convey an agreed-upon sense of insalubrity—
prejudice, ignorance, hatred, narrow-mindedness, malice, and other
noxious defects. Virtually no one wants to be accused of being a bigot or
of practicing racism. Even members of the White Knights and Ku Klux
Klan will deny they are racists, which in the context of our culture is an
invidious appellation. There seems to be a strange inconsistency here;
we attempt to use one term in an objective, impartial, scientific way,
but its related and derivative terms are so infused with negative and
judgmental elements they cannot be functionally neutral.

We may not always be conscious of the dilemma that these subtle
contradictions reflect. But it unmasks for us a paradox that is critical to
any attempt to examine the whole phenomenon of race. The paradox
has to do with the attitudes toward and treatment of race in some of the
scholarly, journalistic, and social science literature since the beginning
of World War II and with the social realities of race that we daily experience. Stressing the concept of "sociological" or "social" race as distinct
from biological race does not obviate the dilemma. Any descriptor is
likely to lead to more confusion than clarity, in part because it cannot
deal with the complexities of the various popular and scholarly versions of race and because it adds no greater clarity or comprehension to
the problem of the perception and interpretation of human variation.

The fact is that, at the level of public consciousness, the presentation
of the no-race position by science and scientists constitutes a challenge
to our cultural worldview, to what we perceive as commonsense
knowledge, and to the kinds of relationships that large numbers of people experience. The challenge, were it to become widespread, would, in
a very real sense, negate the very structure of our society. For there is a
reality to the idea of race that is grounded in our historical consciousness and in all of our political, economic, religious, recreational, and social institutions.

Race is about status and inequality of rank in a society in which competition for wealth and power are played out at the individual level.
Any social scientist objectively observing American culture for the first

time would readily recognize patterns of behavior that reflect the important social dimensions of racial status in the United States. From our behavior alone, he or she would conclude that different races rank unequally along several dimensions and that there are specific mechanisms for maintaining separateness and inequality among them.

A fact denied by none of the experts is that race in the American mind was and is tantamount to a statement about profound and unbridgeable differences. In whatever context race comes to play, it conveys the meaning of nontranscendable social distance. This sense of difference is conditioned into most individuals early in their lives and becomes bonded to emotions nurtured in childhood. In the United States, it is expressed in all kinds of situations and encounters between peoples. It is structured into the social system through residential separation, differential education, training, and incomes, and informal restrictions against socializing, intermarriage, and common membership in various organizations, including, most visibly, the church. It is reflected in virtually all media representations of American society and in institutional aspects of culture such as music, the arts, scientific research, educational institutions, politics and political forums, businesses, the theater, television, music, and film industries, and recreational activities. It provides the unspoken guidelines for daily interaction among persons defined as of different races, especially black and white. It sets the standards and rules for conduct, even though individuals may not always be conscious of this fact.

Thus, for many, unarticulated differences between the races are profound and ineradicable. Although often the reasons given are incoherent and desultory, the underlying belief is that the differences cannot be overcome under any circumstances. This belief is unfortunately often true of some who have been the victims of racism as well as those who have not. The important point is that this sense of difference reflects the cultural construction of the reality of the racial worldview in those societies in which such differences were useful.

The reality of race rests in the uniqueness of the *attitudes* toward human diversity that it expresses. Race is a way of looking at the kaleidoscope of humanity, dividing it into presumed exclusive units, and imposing upon them attributes and features that conform to ideological and social values within the cultures that are defining the races. This may sound somewhat circular, but it is a way of stating that it was specific cultures that created the idea of race and the values about racial differences that we have inherited. Race as a cultural construct is only one way of looking at human differences.

On the Relationship Between Biology and "Race"

Stressing the cultural nature of race requires an analytical excising of the empirical reality of biophysical variation from our cognitive perspective. Yet clearly physical variations had something to do with the origin and persistence of race categorization. Perhaps the best way of stating this connection is to observe that race originated as the imposition of an arbitrary value system on the facts of biological (phenotypic) variations in the human species. It was the cultural invention of arbitrary meanings applied to what appeared to be natural divisions within the human species. The meanings had social value but no intrinsic relationship to the biological diversity itself. Race was a reality created in the human mind, not a reflection of objective truths. It was fabricated as an existential reality out of a combination of recognizable physical differences and some incontrovertible social facts: the conquest of indigenous peoples, their domination and exploitation, and the importation of a vulnerable and controllable population from Africa to service the insatiable greed of some European entrepreneurs. The physical differences were a major tool by which the dominant whites constructed and maintained social barriers and economic inequalities; that is, they consciously sought to create social stratification based on the visible differences (cf. Banton 1967, 1977, and 1988).

Today the complex patterns and combinations of genetic intermixture have transformed, indeed have increased, the biogenetic diversity that results from blending gene pools (see Chapter 12). Yet the sociocultural reality of race persists; it no longer depends substantively on the preservation of discrete biological boundaries, or for that matter on any form of phenotypic markers. We comprehend this best when we realize that western Europeans in the late nineteenth and twentieth centuries constructed their own notion of race not out of overt phenotypic differences within their populations but out of what were class and ethnic parameters. The ideology of race imputes a permanence and inheritability to differences fashioned out of cultural meanings. Phenotypic diversity still obviously exists in many societies, but the conflict between the English and the Irish, and twentieth-century German Nazi beliefs have shown that such variability is not a prerequisite for the cultural creation of race ideology.

The Primordialists' Argument

Certain deeply held attitudes tend to confuse and inhibit attempts to understand race as a cultural phenomenon with the kind of detachment that is required. Collectively, I call these attitudes "primordialist" because their proponents rely on the naive belief that it is basic human nature to be fearful of those who are different from ourselves. Many writers in the past have assumed that there is a universal human tendency to interpret physical differences among populations as somehow socially meaningful. Following this premise Thomas Gossett (1965), for example, argued that race prejudice has an ancient lineage; that it was present among the ancient Aryans of India, the Chinese of the third-century Han dynasty, as well as among the ancient Egyptians, Hebrews, and Greeks (chapter 1). In fact, he appeared to accept any historical reference to color and other physical characteristics of populations as a reference to race. Bernard Lewis has made an interpretation of race and racism in the attitudes and behavior of medieval Arabs toward sub-Saharan Africans.[2] And Pierre Van den Berghe (1967) defines race and racism sufficiently broadly so as to encompass historical conflicts between Tutsi and Hutu of the lake region of East Africa and the Fulani and Hausa in West Africa.

They are not alone. There appears to be a common tendency among many historians and social scientists to regard biophysical variations as the basis for, and the equivalent of, races and to presume that racial classifications are the norm for any society in which such variations occur. Some authors even attempt to explicate social conflict as a natural concomitant of such biophysical diversity. Thus, Edward Shils (1968) argued for the ubiquity of a connection between color and race, explaining that self-identification by color stems from a primordial need for connectedness to others like ourselves. In the same volume Kenneth Gergen (1968) speculated that skin color differences may in fact be responsible for conflict between peoples. Operating from a Freudian perspective, he argued that self-love tends to eventuate in the love of others who are like ourselves. The obverse, dislike and suspicion of those who differ from us, leads to the drawing of battle lines between physically different groups. Thus, race and racism, these authors concluded, may be natural components of the human psyche. And where certain colors are associated with negative symbols—such as black representing evil, dread, mourning, filth—and there are great differences in skin color within a population, there will be "a pronounced tendency toward strife between the light and the dark" (Gergen 1968, 122).[3]

The arguments made by some of the primordialists sound more like self-serving and self-deceiving rationalizations that stem from culturally conditioned personal bias (cf., for example, the arguments expressed by proponents of slavery during the pre–Civil War era) than objective examinations of social facts. One may look through history and contemporary circumstances and find so many exceptions that we are inclined to question such generalizations. We do know with certainty that when people are conditioned from childhood to have negative feelings about dark skin color, they will indeed respond with fear, hatred, and loathing.

This raises to the level of irony the fact that some of the world's greatest violence and the strongest and most hate-filled passions have been directed toward peoples who have been physically (and often culturally) similar, as manifest in the two world wars of the twentieth century between various European populations, or perhaps the premier example of centuries-old hate found in the Western world today, the conflict between the Irish and the English. Most of the great wars in the world during the last half millennium have had as protagonists Europeans who were, comparatively speaking, culturally similar and physically undifferentiated. The same is true of Asia and the Middle East. Moreover, there are instances in which peoples with large biophysical, as well as cultural, differences between them have come into contact and intermingled with little or no conflict. There has always been some degree of commingling, and often amalgamation, even when the circumstances were of devastating conquest (as in the example of some Europeans and native Americans). In the ancient world, the Persians, we are told, had "respect for the customs and languages of others" (Rowe 1965, 2). Alexander the Great exhorted his soldiers to mingle and intermarry with the peoples they conquered. Neither the Aryan conquests and movements into India nor the Muslim conquests in Africa, southern Europe, and throughout the Near and Far East resulted in racially structured societies. So we are not convinced by such Freudian-based arguments.

In any case, we cannot explain the phenomenon of race by reference to psychological processes that we speculate may be taking place within individuals. The structure of individual personalities comes about only within the context of cultures and ongoing social systems and the meanings, values, and proscriptions that are impressed upon individuals as they are socialized within a given cultural matrix. The idea of race is extremely complex; it cannot be understood or analyzed outside of its cultural integument. Nor is it a simple question of the juxtaposition of dissimilar human groups and the resulting conflict between them. Race and racism do not simply or necessarily follow from the mere propinquity and interaction of two peoples who happen to be physically different. As Professor Van den Berghe (1967) has also pointed out, "It is not the presence of objective physical differences between groups that creates races, but the social recognition of such differences as socially significant or relevant" (11).

I would argue that race is even more than the imputation of social significance to physical differences. For example, skin color variations in many regions of the world and in many societies have been imbued with some degree of social value or significance, but color prejudice or preferences do not of themselves amount to a fully evolved racial worldview.[4] There are many societies, past and contemporary, in which the range of skin color variation is quite large, but all such societies have not imposed on themselves worldviews with the specific ideological components of race that we experience in North America or South Africa.[5]

It is nevertheless historically accurate to recognize that physical differences were (and still are) an important and perhaps once necessary ingredient in the development of the idea of race in North America. Their existence, however, became much less critical even before the elaboration of the worldview and ideology of race that appeared in the midnineteenth century when Europeans began to extend its components to one another. Actual color and other phenotypic differences are not today crucial to the functioning of race ideology in our society, although color and physiognomy remain in the public mind as *symbols* of race differences. It is enough to know that a person identifies as a member of a particular "race" regardless of physical features.

Race as a Worldview: A Theoretical Perspective

The primary thesis of this book—and what the research has shown—is that race was, from its inception, a folk classification, a product of popular beliefs about human differences that evolved from the sixteenth through the nineteenth centuries. As a worldview, it was a cosmological ordering system structured out of the political, economic, and social realities of peoples who had emerged as expansionist, conquering, dominating nations on a worldwide quest for wealth and power. By a folk classification, I refer to the ideologies, distinctions, and selective perceptions that constitute a society's popular imagery and interpretations of the world. People in all societies comprehend the world through prisms that their cultures and experiences proffer to them. They impose meanings on new discoveries and experiences that emanate from their own cultural conditioning, which are then circumscribed by existing values.

Like all elements of culture, the racial worldview is a dynamic one, subject to oscillations in interpretation, from time to time intensified or contracted, or modified and/or reinvented in response to changing circumstances. It also manifests contradictions and inconsistencies as life experiences, various social forces, and new knowledge provoke subtle modifications in attitudes about human differences. In the United States, it has waxed and waned largely in response to economic forces that alter the conditions of labor competition.

As a folk concept, the idea of race initially had no basis, no point of origin, in science or the naturalistic studies of the times. But it was subsequently embraced, beginning in the mid to late eighteenth century, by naturalists and other learned men, and given credence and legitimacy as a supposed product of scientific investigations. The scientists themselves undertook efforts to document the existence of the differences that the European cultural worldview demanded and had already created. In their efforts to promote a valid basis for the idea of race, scientists reflected not only the biases, beliefs, and conditioning of their times, but, as in the cases of Louis Agassiz in the nineteenth century and Sir Cyril Burt in the twentieth century, they often expressed their own personal fears, prejudices, and aesthetic evaluations of peoples whom they saw as alien. That their judgments and scientific conclusions mirrored popular beliefs should come as no surprise. As John Greene (1981) has shown, science is inevitably shaped by existing knowledge, values, and presuppositions.

From its first widespread and continuous application in the English language to human populations during the eighteenth century, race was a way of categorizing what were already conceived as inherently unequal human populations. Indeed, had all human beings been considered at least potentially equal by European explorers (and exploiters) there would have been no need for the concept of race at all. People could have continued to be identified by the usual ways that had been employed ever since the first distinct groups came into contact with one another; that is, by their own name for themselves (their ethnic name), by the categorizing terms such as "people," "group," "society," and "nation," or by labels taken from the geographic region or locales they inhabited. Separateness and inequality, as we will see, are central to the idea of race.

By the early decades of the nineteenth century, the race concept in North America contained at least five analytically ascertainable ideological ingredients that, when taken together, may be considered diagnostic of race in the United States. Some were reflections of presuppositions deeply imbedded in English culture history; others were relatively new ideas that appeared with the colonial and slavery experiences but were compatible with American values and beliefs.

When combined, these formed a singular paradigm constituting the racial worldview.

The first and most basic was a universal classification of human groups as exclusive and discrete biotic entities. The classifications were not based on objective variations in language or culture, but were categories that eclipsed these attributes and included superficial assessments and value judgments of phenotypic and behavioral variations. The categories were arbitrary and subjective and often concocted from the impressions, sometimes fanciful, of remote observers. A second element, emphasized above, was the imposition of an inegalitarian ethos that required the ranking of these groups vis-à-vis one another. Ranking was an intrinsic, and explicit, aspect of the classifying process, having derived from an ancient model of the Great Chain of Being (a hierarchical structure of all living things; see Chapter 7) that had been readapted to eighteenth-century realities.

A third constituent element was the belief that the outer physical characteristics of different human populations were but surface manifestations of inner realities, in other words, the cognitive linking of physical features with behavioral, intellectual, temperamental, moral, and other qualities. Thus, what most scholars recognize today as cultural (learned) behavior was seen as an innate concomitant of biophysical form. A fourth element was the notion that all of these qualities were inheritable—the biophysical characteristics, the cultural or behavioral features and capabilities, and the social rank allocated to each group by the belief system itself. Finally, perhaps the most critical element of all was the belief that each exclusive group (race) so differentiated was created unique and distinct by nature or by God, so that the imputed differences, believed fixed and unalterable, could never be bridged or transcended.

It was the synthesis of these elements that comprised the folk concept and worldview of race in America when this term began to replace other classificatory terms and to be widely used in the English language during the latter part of the eighteenth century. The ideology enveloped in the concept was universal, comprehensive, and infinitely expandable. By the nineteenth century, all human groups of varying degrees of biological and/or cultural diversity could be subsumed arbitrarily into some "racial" category, depending upon the objectives or goals of those establishing the classifications.

Once structured on a hierarchy of inequality, different races became socially meaningful wherever the term was used and to whatever groups it could be extended. Attitudes, beliefs, myths, and assumptions about the world's peoples, developed during the period of greatest European expansion and exploitation of non-European lands and peoples, were embroidered into systematic ideologies about their differing capacities for civilization and progress.

As it evolved in the nineteenth century, race posed a new dimension of social differentiation that superseded "class" (see Chapter 9). Race offered a new mechanism for structuring society based on a conception of naturally fixed, heritable, and immutable status categories linked initially to visible physical markers. The idea of "natural" inequality was a central component of race from its inception; but few recognized this as a mere analogue of social position transformed into myth. Devout Christians saw it as God-ordained, and the irreligious rationalized the inequality as a fundamental part of "natural laws." In this same century, racial groups began to be confirmed in their inequalities by science, which cast their imagery to reflect the unquestioned verities of the dominant society's beliefs. Finally, the legal apparatus of the United States and various state governments conspired with science to legitimize this structural inequality by sanctioning it in law. Thus, the racial worldview was institutionalized and made a systemic component of American social structure.

This cultural construction of race as social reality reached full development in the latter half of the nineteenth century. After the Civil War it was utilized as a social device to transform the freed black population of the North American continent into a subordinate subhuman caste. It was further used to degrade and brutalize the native American peoples, and to establish specific social parameters for other, newer immigrants, including the Irish who had first experienced some of the elementary features of the racial worldview.

In the nineteenth and early twentieth centuries, the idea of race differences was seized upon to divide, separate, and rank European populations and to justify the dominance of certain class groups or ethnic elements. This led inexorably to the mass terror, incalculable atrocities, and genocide resulting from Nazi race ideology and practices. These events had a major impact on American social consciousness and generated growing antiracist sentiments among a populace prepared by its own ideals to combat Nazism. Also in the twentieth century, the state of South Africa came much closer to realizing and operationalizing the mandates of this worldview under its system of apartheid.

The legacy of the historical development of the idea of race has been the retention into the late twentieth century of the folk sense of fundamental differences and inequality between those peoples classified as separate races. It persists as an unarticulated reality despite recent developments in the biological sciences, which, as we shall see, have failed to confirm the existence of group differences greater in magnitude than those found between individuals. Its existence continues in large part because of its value as a mechanism for identifying who should have access to wealth, privilege, loyalty, respect, and power and who should not. And of course, for individuals, it is a powerful psychological force, providing scapegoat functions as well as a facile external means of establishing and measuring one's own self-worth. Race became, and still is, the fulcrum and symbol of a worldview and ideology that promotes an easy and simple explanation for human history and progress, or the lack thereof. Most important, it declares a kind of ordered structure to society that appears to be grounded in the very diversity created by nature.

This is the story that this book tells, but it is not an easy one to learn.

Race and Ethnicity

In previous discussions I have mentioned a distinction that requires some attention and explanation at this point. As we have seen, a fundamental dichotomy made by modern anthropologists and other scholars is that between culture and biology. We emphasize that culture is learned behavior that varies independently of the physical characteristics of the people who carry it. People who live and interact together in a common community develop life-styles, value orientations, language-styles, customs, beliefs, and habits that will differ from their neighbors. Over expansive geographic areas variations in language and culture traits may become quite noticeable so that populations may differ radically from one another even within the same political community. People who share similar culture, group identity, and language traits see themselves as distinct from other such populations. A modern way of expressing the common interests of people who are perceived by others and themselves as having the same culture is to speak of them as an ethnic group. When ethnic groups evolve values that project their own life-styles as superior to the cultures of others, we identify such attitudes as "ethnocentric" (or chauvinistic).

It is important at the outset to have a clear, heuristic understanding of the difference between race and racism on the one hand, and ethnicity and ethnocentrism on the other. These terms reflect conceptually, and realistically, quite different kinds of phenomena, and their use should be so restricted in the interest of accurate communication. It is unfortunate that the languages of the sciences, particularly the social sciences, have sometimes tended to proliferate and obfuscate meanings rather than to provide precision and clarity. Ethnicity is one of those relatively modern terms that has sometimes been hailed as a suitable substitution for race but that has also taken on a confusing plethora of meanings and nuances. Just one of the meanings listed in *Webster's New International Dictionary* will alone show how imprecise and impracticable the term can be: it refers to "racial, linguistic, and cultural ties with a specific group." Ethnicity is a quality of ethnic groups, and "ethnic" itself seems to be almost anything and everything. The automatic linkage of biology and behavior (culture) in our collective consciousness obviously precipitated the inclusion of "race" and the confusion of these very different domains.

Somewhat more sanguine about how we concatenate physical, psychological, linguistic, and cultural phenomena, anthropologists have been cautious to relate the terms "ethnic" and "ethnicity" to real, as well as perceived, *cultural* differences between peoples. Nowadays, "culture," following E. B. Tylor's inclusive and unsurpassed rendering ([1871] 1958, 1), is defined as "that complex whole which includes knowledge, belief, art, morals, law, custom, and any other capabilities and habits acquired by man as a member of society."[6] In our time, we would substitute "human beings" for "man" and emphasize the term "acquired." The point is very simple: Culture is learned, not inborn, behavior; it refers to ways of behaving and thinking that we learn as we grow up in any society. It also refers to the things we learn when we adapt to or assimilate features of a different culture. The terms "ethnic" and "ethnicity" are best used, analytically, to refer to all those traditions, customs, activities, beliefs, and practices that pertain to a particular group of people who see themselves and are seen by others as having distinct cultural features, a separate history, and a specific sociocultural identity.

On occasion we have all used certain physical attributes of individuals to speculate on their "nationality" or geographic origins as, for example, in the identification of East Indians or Asians. But physical characteristics do not automatically proclaim the *cultural* background or behavior of any individual or group. There are many people who look East Indian, but have no such ancestry or cultural background. Some Middle Easterners have been mistaken for Puerto Ricans and vice versa. Biophysical traits, then, should never be used as part of the definition of ethnicity. Every American should understand this explicitly, since there are millions of physically varying people all sharing "American culture" (ethnicity) who know little or nothing about the cultural features of their ancestors who may have arrived here from almost any area of the earth.[7]

Ethnic differences, interests, and identity are probably nearly as old as the human species. And so is ethnocentrism. Except for systems of supernatural belief and incest prohibitions, few things are as universal in human societies as the penchant for dichotomizing their worlds into "we" and "they." That *our* customs, *our* laws, *our* food, *our* traditions, *our* music, *our* religion, *our* beliefs and values, and so forth are superior to or somehow better than those of other societies has been a widespread construct, and perhaps a useful one, for many groups.

Ethnocentrism has varying manifestations, intensities, and consequences; although it may often convey an element of rivalry, it need not be accompanied by hostility. But nations and segments of modern nation-states reveal the greatest ethnocentric behavior when they are rivals for territory, for resources, for political hegemony, for markets, for souls, or what have you. Such rivalry may erupt into physical hostilities, or it may be expressed in some other, nonlethal form. It may appear abruptly and diminish just as rapidly. Or it may smolder for decades, generations, or even centuries, influencing the long-range interactions of both peoples. The important point about all cases of ethnocentrism is that it is grounded in the empirical reality and perceptions of sociocultural differences and the separateness of interests and goals that this may entail. There could be no ethnocentrism without *cultural* differences, no matter how trivial or insignificant these may appear to an outsider. (Cf. Walloons and Flemish, Ibos and Yorubas, Protestants and Catholics in Ireland, the Irish and the English, the Basques and the Spanish, the English and the Germans, Turks and Armenians, Serbs and Croats, and dozens of other situations of historical conflict that may come to mind.)

Many situations reveal the most significant aspects of ethnocentrism, that is, its fluidity or flexibility and its potential transience. In the 1940s almost every American had hostile feelings toward the Germans and the Japanese. This attitude and the feelings engendered changed in less than a generation. The transformation had nothing to do with alterations in our genetic structure. Values, attitudes, and beliefs are cultural traits and are nongenetic; they are extrasomatic, learned and transmitted through enculturation processes. Individuals and groups can and do change their ethnic or cultural identities and interests through such processes as migration, conversion, and assimilation or through exposure to modifying influences.

Alternately, racism engulfs an ideology that does not require the presence of empirically determinable cultural differences. It substitutes, as it were, a fiction and a mystique about human behavior for the objective realization of true similarities and differences of language, religion, and other aspects of culture. This mystique is bound up with biological heredity and a belief in its ineradicable bonding to moral, spiritual, intellectual, and other mental and behavioral qualities. The mystique itself is the *presumption* of cultural/behavioral differences that phenotypic or physical differences are thought to signify. It is a belief in the biological determinants of cultural behavior, a critical ideological component of the concept of race.

But because phenotypic differences in a heterogeneous society can become muddled and confused (human mating habits being not thoroughly subject to coercion) and the realities of true cultural similarities and differences sometimes penetrate its consciousness, a society predicated on race categories has to construct another fiction. This is the phenomenon of "racial essence," which is seen as ultimately determining racial character and which maintains the illusion of distinctiveness and innateness even without visible physical symbols.

Race signifies rigidity and permanence of position/status within a ranking order that is based on what is believed to be the unalterable reality of innate biological differences. Ethnicity is conditional, temporal, even volitional, and not amenable to biology or biological processes. That some biophysical and ethnic (cultural) differences have coincided in the past (and still do), for largely geographical, ecological, and historical reasons, should not be permitted to confuse us. Nor should the fact that extreme ethnocentrism and race hatred often manifest some of the same symptoms. They can, and often do, accompany and complement each other along with stereotypes that appear unabashedly racist. But ethnic stereotypes and ethnic boundaries can and do change, and much more rapidly than racial ones; ethnicity is based on behavior that is learned.

Where race is the more powerful divider, it does not matter what one's sociocultural background may be or how similar ethnically two so-called racial groups are. In fact, the reality of ethnic, or social class, similarities and differences is irrelevant in situations in which race is the prime and irreducible factor for social differentiation. The best example of this are blacks and whites in the United States whose cultural similarities are so obvious to outsiders but internally are obfuscated by the racial worldview. When the racial worldview is operant, there can never be an alteration of an individual's or group's status, as both status and behavior are presumed to be biologically fixed. Stephen Steinberg captured this reality clearly in his discussion of ethnic immigrants and racial minorities. "Immigrants," he observes, "were disparaged for their cultural peculiarities, and the implied message was, 'You will become like us whether you want to or not.' When it came to racial minorities, however, the unspoken dictum was, 'No matter how much like us you are, you will remain apart'" (1989, 42). The ideology of exclusion and low-status ranking for blacks in the United States precludes recognition of how culturally similar whites and blacks are. This is particularly true in the southern states where, except for perhaps some class differences, they share an identical culture.

Where ethnocentrism governs, a people's biophysical characteristics, no matter how similar or divergent, are immaterial to the sociocultural realities. What obtained in most of human history, and certainly throughout the ancient world, was an unarticulated understanding of these principles. It explains why so little was mentioned in ancient texts about the physical features of different groups. The ancients knew that differences of language and custom were far more significant than were mere physical traits. They also knew, despite many statements that appear to us as "racist" (some of the works of Tacitus and Herodotus, for example), that a German tribesman, or any other "barbarian" on the outskirts of civilization, could learn the language and culture of Romans and become a citizen, that is to say, that the ethnicity of a person or group was not something inborn and irredeemable; it could be transformed.

But the modern world, after the great migrations of Europeans and the intermixtures among them and with non-Europeans, experienced disorder and confusion of class and ethnicity that crumbled old patterns of social identity and division. It was in large part the uncertainties of this situation that made the idea of race acceptable and useful. Indeed, it can be argued that, beginning in the nineteenth century, many differences that were once essentially ethnic in nature and origin have become transformed and expressed in modern times in a racial idiom. Race, because its characteristics are thought to be innate, renders such differences as do exist even more profound and permanent, and thus structures a social order that is perceived as unalterable.

Although the 1960s and 1970s brought a resurgence of ethnic consciousness and the application of the term "ethnic group" to blacks and other groups, Ronald Takaki has shown that Americans have historically treated ethnic and racial groups very differently. He concluded from a study of the political statuses of different groups that "what actually developed ... in American society was a pattern of citizenship and suffrage which drew a very sharp distinction between 'ethnicity' and 'race'" (1987, 29). And he argues that it is erroneous to treat subordinate racial groups in American society as if they were merely ethnic. Race is a qualitatively different mode of structuring society.

Race represents a systematic worldview that has proved useful to some protagonists in situations of conflict and competition. It provides its own rationalization for the instigation and perpetuation of intergroup animosities, and it reduces or eliminates any potential for recognizing commonalities or for compromise. It evolved in the Judeo-Christian world as a justification for inhumanity to others. Perhaps this is why so many people are discomforted by its persistence. We can achieve a greater level of understanding of this phenomenon by looking at the molding of this ideology through history.

Notes

1. Compare Banton (1977), Harris (1968), Montagu (1969), Stanton (1960), Van den Berghe (1967), and Williams [1944] (1966).

2. See Lewis (1971, 1990), Brown (1968), Davis (1984), and Hunwick (1978) for different perspectives on this topic.

3. See also Degler's strange argument regarding Brazilian "racial" feelings especially where he assumes that negative attitudes toward darker skinned (negroid) peoples who form much of the lower classes is due to a "universality of prejudice where there are visible differences among peoples" (1971, 287).

4. In his book *Black Folk Here and There*, St. Clair Drake (1987) made a similar distinction between color prejudice and racism (8–10). Many cultures place social meanings on differences in skin color that have nothing to do with race. In Japanese history women with pale skins were aesthetically highly valued, in part because it signaled that their fathers (or husbands) were wealthy and their daughters need not work outside in the fields (Wagatsuma 1968). In contrast, white Americans often acquire deep tans to convey an aura of affluence, high status, and leisure. Drake also believed that, among other factors, negative aesthetic evaluations of negroid physiognomy affected attitudes toward Africans in many societies quite apart from mere skin color preferences or prejudices.

5. See Frank Snowden's description of blacks in ancient Greek and Roman societies (1970 and 1983).

6. This definition is frequently quoted in introductory textbooks in anthropology. See, for example, Harris (1983, 5); Swartz and Jordan (1976, 4); Keesing and Keesing (1971, 20), among many others.

7. Differences in physical appearance, the insignia of "race," are so powerful as social dividers and status markers among Americans that they cannot perceive the cultural similarities that mark them all as Americans, white and black, to outsiders. Europeans and Asians, however, not only tend to recognize the similarities but to treat such persons as part of a single ethnic category. Michael Banton (1988) noted that in studies of children of nursery school age in Sweden, children were classified according to their home languages. This resulted in some African children being classified and referred to as Swedish, a much more realistic cognition of identity than skin color. Fourth- or fifth-generation Chinese and Japanese Americans who do not speak an Asian language or

maintain elements of an Asian culture resent being mistaken for recent immigrants who have little experience and knowledge of American culture. One would think that Americans, of all people, would understand the power of enculturation and the rapidity with which ethnic characteristics and consciousness can change. But the force of the racial worldview prevents the cognitive acceptance of their implications.

2

The Etymology of the Term "Race"

I N THE FIFTEENTH CENTURY, western and northern Europeans ventured out from their geographic and historical isolation and discovered the rest of the world. Within the next five hundred years, European exploration, expansion, colonial settlement, and exploitation changed the course of human history and generated complex new relationships among the peoples of the world.

In the process of exploration and penetration into what was *terra incognita*, European adventurers encountered other peoples totally unknown to them before that time. The sometimes awesome and exotic groups had material, religious, and social life-ways alien and unexpected to the peoples of Europe. The strangeness of the peoples and their habitats challenged the imaginations of the explorers, prompting a rash of speculations and novel interpretations of the new discoveries. In order to grapple both intellectually and practically with these alien societies, Europeans imposed upon them meanings and identities that fit within their own historical understandings, experiences, and preconceptions of what the world was all about. At some time in the process they began to use the term "race" to characterize differences among human groups. Because they left little record of the source of the term, we have only a hint of the specific meaning(s) attached to it.

"Race" is found in all of the languages of European settlers in the Americas, in which it generally denoted populations of differing origins in the heterogeneous mix of peoples. However, the substantive meanings in different European languages have varied. In English the term has had nearly a dozen distinct meanings, dating from medieval times. But as a semantic form referring to human groups, the English term has a curious kind of history. Its etymology appears obscure, although most dictionary descriptions suggest that the term probably stems from the

Italian, thus assuming a Latin origin. Some British experts have debated this: H. W. Fowler ([1926] 1962) claimed in 1926 that there is no Latin term from which it is known to have descended. Noted zoologist Cedric Dover (1951) argued that it came from the Arabic term "ras" meaning "chief head, origin or beginning." From there, he speculated, it diffused into Spanish in the form of "raza" meaning a kinship group or follower of a headman. Subsequently it spread to the other Latin languages and eventually to English. In a brief reply to Dover, J. C. Trevor (1951), a Cambridge anthropologist, restated his argument that "race" derived from the Latin "ratio" in an accusative form that had similar meaning to other classificatory terms such as "species," "kind," and "nature." It came into Italian as "razza" and from there into other related languages.

Trevor added a significant piece of information, noting that the earliest use of "race" in English known to him occurs in William Dunbar's poem "The Dance of the Sevin Deidly Synnis," written in the sixteenth century, in which the author refers to "backbyttaris of sindry racis." Etymologist Leo Spitzer concurs with Trevor in his belief that the transformation of "ratio" to Italian "razza" and into modern languages was most likely the direction of development, and he mentions in passing in a footnote its "characteristic connection with animals" (1948, 160). *The Oxford English Dictionary of Historical Principles* (1933) shows no earlier date than that of the Dunbar poem. Other rare occasions of use are shown in this dictionary during the later sixteenth century in two ways: one as "a group of persons, animals, or plants, connected by common descent or origin," and the other, "a group or class of persons, animals, or things having some common feature or features" (87).

Only occasionally do we find the term used for humans during the rest of the sixteenth century. Edmund Campion (Myers 1983) did not employ the term in his descriptions of the Irish people in one of the earliest histories, compiled in 1571, although some contemporary and later writers often spoke of the "Irish race." Nor was it frequently used to refer to aliens less familiar to the English.

In fact, "race" did not appear in the English language as a technical term with reference to human groups until the seventeenth century, when it was apparently employed in several ways. One referred to the characteristics or common qualities of certain types of persons. Thus, for example, John Bunyan in *Pilgrim's Progress* referred to a race of "saints." Shakespeare, along with other writers, seemed to associate the term with the idea of the inherited disposition or temperament of individuals. Other writers conveyed the sense of a class or type of person when they spoke of a "race of bishops" or "the race of womankind."

The second usage was more incipiently technical in that various learned men, in their attempts to describe and classify different human groups, occasionally used the term interchangeably with "species" as a general mode of categorizing peoples. William Petty and a few other writers connected "races" with "generations," which we shall see was an apt reflection of its source (Slotkin 1965, 89).

The earliest Spanish dictionary, the *Tesoro de la Lengua Castellana o Espanola* of Cobarruvias (1611), specifically identifies "raza" as referring to the "caste or quality of authentic horses," which are branded with an iron so as to be recognized. But two other meanings are given: One pertains to threads in the weave of a cloth, the other alone refers to humankind. Here, "raza" is taken in a negative sense to connote some Moorish or Jewish ancestors in one's lineage (56, 57). During the period of the Inquisition in Spain, the term "raza" was sometimes applied to families suspected of heresy and to New Christians to distinguish them from the older peasant Christian community. By 1737, the *Diccionario de la Lengua Castellana* gives as the first and primary meaning "the caste or quality of origin or lineage" when speaking about "los hombres," noting only later in that same passage its earlier usage for animals and cloth weaves.

Although the data are slim, it seems that the most direct evidence of the origins and early meanings of "race" derives from the Middle Ages. It may have been a folk concept in the Romance languages (Spanish, Italian, French, Portuguese) that evidently emerged from the terms used in breeding domestic animals. Based on the materials above, its original meaning seems to have related to a breeding line of animals, a "stock" or group of animals that was the product of a line bred for certain purposes. As such, the term probably has a long history in the folk cultures of the Latin world, for human cognizance of breeding animals dates well back into early agrarian communities. In the sixteenth century Spanish writers employed the term as one of several ways of referring to new populations discovered in their travels.

During the fifteenth and sixteenth centuries, Spanish hegemony in Europe was extensive, and Spain's contacts with the English increased significantly.[1] It is quite likely that the English adopted the term from the Spanish, applying it also to New World indigenes. At that time, the Spanish pronunciation "reazza" could have been easily transformed into the English "race" in a manner consistent with other known linguistic transformations.

From the sixteenth to the eighteenth centuries, "race" developed as a classificatory term in English similar to and interchangeable with "people," "nation," "kind," "type," "variety," "stock," and so forth. By the latter half of the eighteenth century, when scholars became more actively engaged in investigations, classifications, and definitions of human populations, the term "race" was elevated as the one major symbol and mode of human group differentiation employed extensively for non-European groups and even for those in Europe who varied in some way from the subjective norm. As we shall see, of all of the terms commonly employed to categorize human beings, "race" became the most useful term for conveying the qualities and degrees of human differences that had become increasingly consonant with the English view of the world's peoples.

The identification of race with a breeding line or stock of animals carries with it certain implications for how Europeans came to view human groups. One is that the question of *species* differentiation is really left moot. The line or stock is perceived as a variation of a larger entity or group within which all individuals can interbreed. The fact of the existence of a perceived capacity for members of one line to interbreed with another or others is in itself a recognition of the sameness, the oneness of the category, and it reflects adherence to biblical authority. Second, among farmers and herders, who were perhaps the first to invent and use this term, it is well known that certain behavioral propensities are inheritable in highly inbred lines of animals. This is cognitively associated with the unmistakable observation of the heritability of biophysical features.

Following from this, a third and related implication is that value judgments are critical to the identification of the breeding line, for it is specifically for some culturally valued quality or qualities that deliberate intervention in the reproductive process has occurred. That is, qualities that the human controller has deemed desirable are evoked by the deliberate breeding of certain animals within the same population. Thus, inherent within the term "race" is a potential and real ranking and evaluation of both physical and behavioral traits. To those using the term, such ranking and judgment are real because of the known centuries of human experimentation and breeding of domestic animals. These value judgments become potentials whenever the term "race" can be or is applied to other biological forms, including humans.

Finally, unlike other terms for classifying people (e.g., "nation," "people," "variety," "kind," etc.), the term "race" places emphasis on innateness, on the inbred nature of whatever is being judged. Whatever is inheritable is also permanent and unalterable (except through calculated breeding in future generations), whether it be body size, horn length, fur length or color, or aggressiveness, fearsomeness, docility, dullness, intelligence, or any other states of being that humans attribute to their animals. The term "race" made possible an easy analogy of inheritable and unchangeable features from breeding animals to human beings.

Race, then, was not just a reasonably felicitous term that was applied arbitrarily and sporadically to indigenous peoples of other lands. This analysis shows that there were useful and important substantive aspects of its referential meaning that were already present when Europeans began to use the term as the prime mechanism for conveying human group differences. It was an eminently appropriate term for the worldview about all human differences that the English and other Europeans were beginning to evolve.

However, the English in North America were to develop and elaborate the implications of the term "race" to a much higher degree than either the Spanish, the Portuguese, or the French. The Spanish and Portuguese who settled Latin America evolved a very different perspective on human differences that did not result in the construction of rigidly exclusive "racial" groups, as occurred in North America and South Africa. Although this book cannot cover all of these situations, a few comparative references will be made to underscore the uniqueness of the Anglo-American ideas of race. What does seem clear is that there were some factors in the English experiences and circumstances of contact that predisposed this group to think of indigenous peoples in ways that varied from earlier levels and forms of ethnocentrism found throughout the world. There were new dimensions of difference added to previous beliefs and attitudes, and new ways of relating to variant human groups were instituted. We must turn to the history of the English for an investigation of this phenomenon. But in order to understand the English situation, we must examine briefly the wider context of developments in Europe during the age of expansion.

Notes

1. Commercial contacts had increased rapidly, and there was much travel back and forth, especially on the part of London Merchants Adventurers and their representatives. Some Bristol merchants and seamen settled a small colony at the major Spanish port of Seville. Intermarriages between English and Spanish royalty even led King Phillip II of Spain to rule England for several years conjointly with his wife, Mary, daughter of Henry VIII and heir to the English throne.

3

Antecedents of the Racial Worldview

ERTAIN FEATURES OF EUROPEAN SOCIETIES and their experiences during the explorations of the fifteenth through the seventeenth centuries help us to understand the source of their varying attitudes toward human differences. Some of the major influences on the development of European ideas and values were their previous historical contacts (or lack thereof) with non-European peoples; the attitudes derived from strongly held religious beliefs; a growing national ethnocentrism, particularly in England and Spain; and a generalized image of the natural and social world in terms of hierarchy. This seminal stage in the evolution of a racial worldview is reflected in the emergence of certain cultural predispositions and elements of thought in Europe during the several centuries before the late eighteenth-century revolutionary era.

For the English, some of the seeds of a racial worldview were in place long before they encountered peoples in the New World and in Africa who were dramatically different from themselves. In this chapter, after a discussion of some general characteristics of this period, we will look at several specific events and circumstances of English life and sociopolitical experiences that affected their views of other peoples. Because the English drew some of their cultural cues in the New World from the Spanish, we will also briefly consider aspects of Spanish culture that influenced certain practices toward non-Europeans in the New World.

The Age of European Exploration

In the fifteenth century the northern Europeans, and the peoples of the British Isles in particular, had a very limited direct knowledge of the world. Few of them had traveled even to the southernmost regions of the Eurasian continent, although political and commercial intercourse had increased since the Crusades. Although many influences had percolated into southern Europe from the East and especially from North Africa, virtually everything that European savants knew about these regions was encompassed within the stock of scripturally based knowledge, was draped in fairy tales and myths, or came from bits and pieces of theories derived from the newly discovered writings of the ancients. As Margaret Hodgen (1964) has emphasized, "The Renaissance and Reformation were only in part periods of dazzling enlightenment. They were streaked and furrowed with inherited ignorance, confusion, and traditionalism" (359).

During the Crusades, roughly the eleventh through the thirteenth centuries, thousands of Europeans, mostly men, had converged on the islands of the eastern Mediterranean and had attacked towns in the Near East. Those who survived the many battles and returned home brought new tastes and knowledge of Eastern cultures to Europe. Their experiences contributed to the profound social and economic changes that were already beginning to take place in Europe. Beyond the Crusaders, there were very few individuals, men such as the Polos (Marco Polo and his father and uncle), Daniel of Kiev, Benjamin of Tudela, John de Plano Carpini, and Lancelot Mallocello, who for various reasons ventured far beyond the then known boundaries of Europe.

The details of the adventures and travels of such men did not become widely known. With the general level of literacy low, communication between intellectuals, religious and political leaders, commercial travelers, geographers, merchants, and adventurers was quite random and slow, especially before the invention and widespread use of the printing press. Still, many Europeans, especially in the cities and port towns, through rumors and hearsay, heard about bizarre and extraordinary peoples and customs. The often exaggerated tales revealed to them news about the "heathen Mohammedans" and "Turks," and even stories of a fabled black king named Prester John from some strange land beyond the Mediterranean, who some historians later thought might have been the king of Ethiopia.

Southern Europeans, however, were less isolated and more sophisticated about the diversity of peoples and cultures of the Old World. The Mediterranean world itself from time immemorial had seen an intermingling of peoples from Europe, Asia, and Africa. In what are now Spain and Portugal, congeries of Islamic peoples (which included Arabs, Egyptians, Berbers, Carthaginians, Libyans, and others) had invaded from North Africa and settled as early as the beginning of the eighth century. The various waves of invaders, immigrants, soldiers, sailors, merchants, slaves, scholars, and religious leaders helped to keep viable a huge intercommunication zone. Complex networks of trade and travel not only existed among the peoples of the lands bordering the Mediterranean but also connected some of the peoples of western Africa and the Sudan zone, the eastern Mediterranean, the Saudi Arabian peninsula, East African trading cities, the Iranian plateau, and parts of India and China. Indeed, although northern Europeans tended to languish in relative isolation during the Middle Ages, this was a period of advanced development for many of the peoples of the Islamic world.

Famous Muslim travelers of this period covered even more territory than did their European counterparts. Al-Masudi traveled in India, Sri Lanka, China, Russia, Persia, and Egypt as early as the tenth century. Al-Idrisi, a geographer and cartographer of great repute, traversed throughout North Africa and Asia Minor. In the process he compiled a description of the known world and created a map that was still used in eighteenth-century Europe. He was the first of the great geographers to show that the world was round, and this in the early twelfth century. Al-Idrisi's reknown was such that he was commissioned by the Norman king of Sicily to prepare a comprehensive geography of the world.

Perhaps the best known of the Islamic travelers was Ibn Battuta, a fourteenth-century Moroccan who traveled from West Africa to what is now Sumatra and the Indonesian islands, leaving excellent descriptions of great states, from the empire of Mali in West Africa to those of India and China. What he had to say about the world was of vital importance to some Europeans, both for scholars and commercial travelers. Yet his works lapsed into obscurity with the change in the focus of attention toward Atlantic exploration. Interest in them did not revive until the midtwentieth century when scholars experienced a reinvigorated concern for Africa and for the precolonial history of its people. Battuta's understanding and tolerance of other cultures, as well as his relatively objective approach toward the reconstruction of human history, had to lie in abeyance until the era of modern anthropological and historical inquiry.

Some Europeans, nevertheless, benefited from the knowledge that Islamic scholars had about the world, from the translations that made Greek and Roman scholarship again available, as well as from the numerous elements of technology originated and/or transmitted by the Islamic world. The great scholar Ptolemy's *Geography,* with its principles of calculation by latitude and longitude, was rediscovered and translated early in the fourteenth century and generated great excitement in some circles. Even so, the knowledge of peoples and cultures outside Western Europe, for the vast majority of educated people, was acquired second and third hand and, as we shall see, was always filtered through the prism of European religious beliefs, myths, legends, and social values.[1]

Those Europeans with the most direct knowledge of the cultural and physical diversity of humankind—the peoples of Spain, Portugal, southern Italy, and the islands of the Mediterranean—had experienced a heterogeneity of peoples and cultures long before the Age of Discovery. Spaniards, particularly in the urban centers, had interacted with Africans and Middle Easterners of many ethnic backgrounds. Among their conquerors, the Moors (a term taken from the Almoravid invasion of the eleventh century) consisted of many people from North and West Africa, where the religiously inspired movement had congealed. From as far south as the Senegal River, the leaders of the Islamic jihads, or Holy Wars, had conscripted followers who were eager to spread the words of Muhammad. Swarthy sailors of Arab dhows from the coastal areas of southern Arabia and eastern Africa were seen as far north as the western coasts of France.

Columbus's epic voyage to the New World was part of an ongoing push westward for new routes to the East. Although historians have identified his voyages as among the first and most famous, there were numerous others that took advantage of new sailing techniques to venture into unknown regions. In 1494 the pope divided all of the newly discovered, yet unexplored, "heathen" lands of the world between Spain and Portugal, which provided great impetus to Spanish and Portuguese adventurers as well as to those of other nationalities. Pedro Alvares Cabral claimed what is now Brazil for Portugal in 1500. For Spain, Amerigo Vespucci explored much of Central America and Mexico beginning in 1497, and Alonso de Ojeda established a Spanish settlement in Panama in 1508. Ponce de León, Balboa, Gomés, Magellan, Cortés, de Soto, and Pizarro are merely the more well known of what was to become a vast army of "conquistadors" who explored the New World and gathered much of its riches during the first half of the sixteenth century.

Within the first century of the discoveries, Europeans had established themselves permanently in new colonies. Each group brought with them their different experiences with strangers and their different perceptions of and beliefs about the nature of humanity. It was the Roman Catholic church with its focus on the papacy, its heritage from ancient Rome, and its stress on the salvation of souls that dominated the Spanish and Portuguese settlements. But, as we shall see later, northern Europeans, especially the English, brought unique historical experiences and quite different cognitive values that governed their views of the native peoples they encountered.

The Rise of Capitalism and the
Transformation of English Society

English society in the sixteenth and seventeenth centuries experienced much turmoil connected with massive social, economic, religious, and political changes. The Protestant revolution and subsequent political developments of the sixteenth century enhanced the power of the monarchy and created divisions and conflict among the nobles, gentry, and aristocracy. In the seventeenth century two major revolutions transformed the monarchy and led to the concentration of power at the highest levels in the hands of Parliament, representing the triumph of republican ideology over the values of divine kings and absolute monarchy.

The greatest changes were economic. Historians have widely held that the sixteenth century also marked the gradual demise of feudal society and the rise of early capitalism. Capitalism evolved as a new economic system both in England and in western Europe, particularly in the Netherlands. It was complex, often drastic, and multifaceted in that it had implications for all aspects of culture and society. Dramatic and irreversible changes in social organization and values, in politics, and in attitudes toward wealth and property took place. According to many scholars, the major elements of this process were the rise of free wage labor, the separation of this labor from the land and from the means and instruments of economic production, and the transformation of both labor and land into commodities exchanged on a widening world market.[2]

It was the emergence of a "bourgeois" class whose increasing wealth was based on commerce, trade, and finance that was to leave the greatest legacy. A largely urban middle class composed of merchants in the growing overseas trade, financiers, bankers, shopkeepers, artisans, manufacturers, and industrialists who serviced them took form, eventually creating a life-style of vast material consumption and challenging the gentry and the nobility for influence in government. Some wealthy merchants obtained large estates, purchased royal titles (such as knighthoods and baronetcies), and even married some of their offspring into the aristocratic class. An entrepreneurial spirit characterized town life, and even the younger sons of the gentry, prevented by the rule of primogeniture from inheriting their fathers' estates, often turned to commerce and trade and helped to provide a veneer of polish and refinement to the rough-and-tumble competitiveness of town life.

Merchant capitalism fostered other values—of individualism, absolute private property, and the unrestrained accumulation of wealth. It was a concomitant, and a cause, of the breakdown of kinship and community ties, a process that had begun in an earlier feudal period. Feudalism had tended to associate men with particular areas of land, the fiefs granted by the king or a noble lord to a wealthy individual for his services. Lords, villeins, tenants, and serfs were bound to landed estates and to one another through personal ties and through obligations to the land and to one another. In this way generations of kinspeople had remained settled together, with tenants and serfs working the same lands.

Profound changes in the nature of kinship ties began early in England. Marc Bloch (1961) noted that, from the thirteenth century on, there was a contraction in the social recognition of kinship. Kindreds that had existed under feudalism had begun to atrophy and were slowly being replaced by much smaller families. Because of the frequency of voluntary refusal or withdrawal from the obligations of kinship, the cluster of kinsmen bound by obligations of vengeance, for example, had diminished to include only first or second cousins.[3]

Increases in trade and the development of free wage labor in the wake of the decline of feudal estates and serfdom were major factors in the attenuation of kinship ties, as individual men were forced to become mobile in order to sell their labor. Also, increasingly, protection from wealthy and politically powerful men became more important than the support of a circle of kinspeople. As the towns and cities grew and as various episodes of warfare dislocated people, some men found their only options for making a living away from their native villages and families. They then had opportunities to engage in adventures abroad (on the Continent, or in Ireland), to participate in the many wars that abounded in England and on the Continent, and for a few men, to occupy themselves in the private accumulation of wealth. Throughout the period of the Hundred Years' War, part of which was during the reign of Edward III (1327–1377), for example, English soldiers returned from France with massive amounts of plunder and loot, injecting a new sense of acquired personal wealth and inspiring in others the desire for more.

Another trend, the enclosure movement, beginning in the fifteenth century, resulted in the transformation of what were once communal lands, forests, and meadows in English villages to private property, enclosed by hedges and held in absolute possession by landowners whose objectives were the production of commodities for growing towns and greater profits. When the English learned to fence in parcels of land and the use of titles became widespread, the sense of exclusive private use of natural resources expanded and matured. Some became very wealthy as the value of these lands increased, while others, those dispersed or dislocated by the privatization of land, were reduced to abject poverty (see below).

Of great significance was the development of the use of money "in the relations of life to such an extent that it was possible to buy for money goods of any kind and to secure any variety of services" (Dietz 1932, 119). Although the English church denounced the sins of usury, hoarding, and profiteering, Dietz tells us that "worldly pursuits acquired an importance of their own, and the unity of all activity envisaged in the Christian view of life was broken, never to be achieved again" (122). Gold and silver, which could buy virtually anything, totally transformed English life.

Opportunities for acquiring wealth not only became greater from the onset of the sixteenth century, but new forms of social inequality based on acquired wealth also came into play, particularly in urban areas. Many historians distinguish this newly created property, linked with the rise of the middle class and the values associated with it, as "bourgeois property," those forms of wealth privately held to the exclusion of all others. The accumulation of private wealth became a dominant cultural value, one that was underscored by the increasingly atomistic nature of society and one that linked individuals to a new sense of social identity. As the Genoveses (1983) note, "Material possessions ... became the sine qua non of respectable and responsible selfhood" (275).

The power of the church to establish and maintain ethical and moral standards had already atrophied and begun to decline before the rise of capitalism as a way of life. Thus the pursuit of wealth by individuals was unencumbered by the demands either of kinship or of any other moral order.

For several centuries merchant capitalists involved in trading and financial institutions had been developing a collective power based on their wealth and investments in overseas enterprises. The constellation of cultural features that emerged with and surrounded the life-styles of the merchant capitalists provided some of the ideological ingredients of the continuing bourgeois revolution that brought about industrial capitalism. But some Marxists, like the Genoveses, have argued persuasively that merchant capital hindered rather than advanced economic development toward industrial capitalism. They insist that it was a conservative force that "played handmaiden to feudalism in the early overseas expansion," led to the reinstitution of serfdom in parts of Europe, and was responsible for colonial conquests in the New World and the subsequent exploitation of slave labor (1983, 6–8). Merchant capital was transformed during the crises of the seventeenth century when the feudal system was finally abolished.

C. B. MacPherson (1962) characterized the unifying political thought of English society beginning in the seventeenth century as based on a central theme that he calls "possessive individualism." He says, "The basic assumptions of possessive individualism—that man is free and human by virtue of his sole proprietorship of his own person, and that human society is essentially a series of market relations—were deeply embedded in the seventeenth-century foundations" (270). It was more than just a political theme. Its features impacted on economic, religious, and social institutions, on values, laws, customs, and beliefs about individual, natural, and civil rights, and the whole range of cultural phenomena. It was intricately linked to the English conception of property, the sense of proprietorship that extended beyond mere material matter, and its connection to the English concepts of individual autonomy and freedom.

Looking at some of the dominant political philosopher-theorists of the century who reflected and articulated the values of merchant capitalists and industrialists, MacPherson (1962) shows that freedom was equated with rights in property, with property defined in an unusual way. The basic right that any man had was the right to property in his own person, his body, labor, and capacities. A man may only alienate his labor property by "selling" it to another man, an indicator of the market or contractual nature of the relationships among men. Exercising proprietary rights in his own selfhood, independently of the will of others, gives a man freedom, and such freedom makes him fully human (264).

Among other implications of the theory of possessive individualism, MacPherson shows that it justified the appropriation and accumulation of property in land and in other resources and goods. A man is fully free when he can accumulate and retain the property of his own labor, holding it exclusively against the demands of others. MacPherson notes that John Locke's philosophy called for the right to unlimited acquisitions of property, which he defined as "Life, Liberty and Estate" (1962, 198). Government exists to protect men in the exercise of their property rights. Thus Locke made a positive value out of the unequal appropriation of most of the wealth (capital) by a few individuals, reasoning that such accumulation was a "natural right" (MacPherson 1962, 208–221). These ideas and ideals, as well as Locke's general vision of civil rights and human liberties, were transported to the American colonies in varying forms and modifications and ultimately became part of the worldviews and rhetoric of most Americans.

Capitalist ideology, then, had taken shape and form before the English turned fully to African slavery as a way of producing commodities for a world market that would make them rich. Many historians tend to agree that English culture, as manifest in its early development of a capitalist ethos, differed from most of the cultures of western Europe, which lagged behind in their development toward industrial capitalism. Most striking and emphatic about the uniqueness of the English economy and culture is the work of Alan Macfarlane (1978). In arguing that the English had ceased being a rural peasant society by as early as the thirteenth century, Macfarlane points to the atomistic quality of life already expressed in that century, manifest in its individualism and privatization of wealth. Wage labor, land commoditization, absolute and exclusive ownership of property, extensive geographic and social mobility, a decline in kinship ties and arranged marriages—all predate the sixteenth century. Primogeniture, which signifies private property in real estate, was "apparently firmly established in England by the thirteenth century" and was "widespread" even "among those at the lower levels of society" (87–88).

Macfarlane (1978) quotes from a number of medieval sources authored by foreign travelers in England that described the extreme individualism of the English, sometimes seen as arrogance, their preoccupation with their own private interests, their overbearing pride, and their suspiciousness not only of strangers but also of one another. "Combined with their self-confidence and arrogance went a mutual suspiciousness: each individual was out for himself and trusted no one else," Macfarlane paraphrases (174). Writers spoke of English wealth, their abundance of food and fine clothes, their love of freedom and independence, their pursuit of money and trade, and their lack of affection toward their children.[4] "All these writers," he notes, "clearly felt that there was something different not only about the economy, but also the personality of the English" (173).

Thus a market mentality, social interactions based on contract rather than status, and transactions governed by the laws of supply and demand had already characterized the English socioeconomic system, Macfarlane argues, even before the Protestant revolution and the emergence of capitalism. If the English were perceived as so culturally distinct by their European contemporaries long before the age of exploration and conquest, surely these cultural traits impacted uniquely on the nature and quality of their colonial experiences. Their ideologies about individualism and property guided their assault on native lands. They also helped to determine the kind of slavery that grew in North America. Possessive individualism and the near sacredness of property and property rights in seventeenth-century English culture facilitated the transformation of Africans into slave property and their concomitant demotion to nonhuman forms of being (see Chapter 6).

Social Organization and Values of Early Capitalism

At the apex of the hierarchical English social order was the monarch and his/her relatives, a genealogical reticulum of births and marriages that cut across polities and that constituted the royalty. Aristocrats and nobles were in the next tier, and these families provided the ruling class. Below this ruling elite were the gentry: large landowners, farmers, merchants, commercial agents, and wealthy craftsmen, artisans, and financiers in the towns and ports. Next came the yeomen landowners, the proper and respectable farmers. The working class constituted the bulk of the people, and they were mostly small farmers, laborers, small craftsmen, or petty traders. Near the bottom were the working poor, the unemployed or irregularly employed unskilled laborers, and finally the vagabonds, paupers, and masterless, homeless men, women, and children who tended to cluster in the poorhouses and byways of towns and villages.

Although the hierarchical system appeared rigid, there was some flexibility and movement both vertically and horizontally across social barriers. This was particularly true of the bourgeoisie in the urban centers. Wealthy merchants, for example, flourished with the expansion of overseas trade. Their political power increased along with their wealth as they competed for the attentions of royalty. They educated their offspring well and sometimes married them to royalty. But Macfarlane (1978) has also found considerable geographical and social mobility in some rural parishes as well, with a "growing cleavage between rich and poor" that often split entire families (70). Individuals left their natal homes in their teens and often never returned to their hometowns or villages.

Businesses, government, and the church had imposed on the English public the values of hard work and sobriety; and free labor, it was assumed, would work toward these goals. Such labor had been attracted to the towns and cities for burgeoning commercial, banking, and shipping enterprises. But in the sixteenth and seventeenth centuries, England experienced large population movements exacerbated by the migrations of peasants displaced as a result of the enclosure movement. There were not enough jobs for the poor. Now, through no fault of their own, the poor were without work. These conditions produced a large class of idle, "rootless" men (and women) who roamed the streets and byways of the cities and towns, scratching, stealing, and begging for food.

English propertied classes saw these people, often called "vaga-bonds," as a threat to their sense of proper social order. Their communities had long been structured in hierarchies of what some saw as clear and seemingly unambiguous statuses. Men of substance and civility were men who owned property and thus were also men who had power, or at least could wield some influence in the governance of the society. But a man without property was essentially a social nonentity, unable to undertake civil responsibilities and with no basis for exercising civil rights. Laboring men worked for those who owned property, and they were bound together by civil laws, contracts, and statutes. Thus the identity of a man in terms of his lands, stock, money, or other resources, or his attachment as a subordinate to a man with property, was a fixed part of the hierarchical system.

We have seen associated with this concept certain ideas about personal freedom. For a man to acquire property during these times of vigorous change, he had to be free to sell his labor, to acquire some semblance of education or training, to make his fortune as best he could without social constraints. A man lacking such ambitions was suspect or was considered part of the rabble that constituted the underclasses. Most men saw personal freedom as the normal status for the English, an ideology that, as Henri Pirenne tells us, had deep roots in medieval cities among the middle classes ([1925] 1952, 193). Indentured servitude became one of the main ways of linking an impoverished person to a master in order that the former might work a few years, acquire sufficient funds to establish himself, or seek his fortune elsewhere.

The greatest concern that Englishmen had was with those "master-less" men who went about robbing, raping, and looting. To the proper English they lacked some of the major qualities of Protestantism, self-control, responsibility, ambition, and thrift. Bourgeois English rigidity about personal behavior, the containment of the emotions, a sense of dignity and good taste, and submission to the rules of social propriety no doubt has a much longer history. But suffice it to say that with the development of the Protestant ethic, the autonomy of the individual was greatly elevated, and certain ideals and standards of personal behavior came to be established. Conformity to the formal rules of one's social class position was heavily monitored by one's peers, or would-be peers, and by one's betters. This contrasted sharply with the behavior of the vagabonds, looters, and "mischievous" men, some of whom were swept up off the streets of such cities as London and Liverpool and shipped off to the New World to work as bonded laborers.

Thus it was that English values about the holding and ownership of property and its linkage to a proper social and civil identity became firmly established. English beliefs about or obsession with property became so transfigured that ultimately they were conjoined with religious values. Success in the acquisition of material goods was equated with, and in some important sense confused with, rewards for the pious. The aggrandizement of material wealth seemed to confer moral virtues on individuals. It was these values that Anglican, Puritan, and other Englishmen brought with them to the New World, values that would have a long-term effect on the ways by which they viewed and dealt with other non-English and non-European groups. In the New World they elevated individual property rights to a position sanctioned by divine authority and superior to all other rights, including the human rights of indigenous peoples and those whom they bought as slaves.

English Ethnocentrism and the Idea of the Savage

Leonard Liggio (1976), in exploring the race idea and raising a more general question about the comparative differences between the English colonization practices and those of other Europeans, asks, "How is it possible to explain the fact that the English developed the most racist attitudes toward the natives wherever they expanded or established overseas colonies?" He proposes an unexpected hypothesis, that it was the English experience with the Irish "which was the root of English racial attitudes" (1976, 1). Perhaps because of the intractable and seemingly irreconcilable contemporary conflict between these two peoples, other historians have turned their attention to this long-standing belligerence for insights into the general English attitudes toward indigenous peoples and the nature of English colonial and imperial policies.[5]

Throughout the sixteenth and seventeenth centuries, and especially during the reign of Elizabeth I, Englishmen focused their attention, and a great deal of hostility, toward Ireland and the Irish people. The era was punctuated by periodic attempts to finally conquer the Irish, on the one hand, and by several major Irish rebellions, on the other. The last of the sixteenth-century rebellions (1597), which brought forth the wrath of Queen Elizabeth and the final triumph of her forces over the native chieftain Hugh O'Neill, was the climax of four centuries of repeated invasions, implacable Irish resistance, and failed attempts to consolidate English power over the western island. A brief review of this history is very instructive.

The first invasion and attempt to settle Ireland occurred under Henry II in 1169 and 1171, as part of the expansion of Anglo-Norman civilization following the Norman invasion of England. By the end of the century, most of Ireland was under some semblance of English control in the form of Anglo-Norman barons who had been given titles to Irish lands, which they ruled as personal fiefdoms. But the scattered Irish clans, lacking a centralized government, proved impossible to vanquish and control. Within a short time they had regained most of their lands and had begun the first of several great revivals of Gaelic culture that flourished from time to time throughout the thirteenth through the fifteenth centuries.

One development, however, was particularly upsetting and threatening to the nominal rulers of Ireland. Those Englishmen who had settled in Irish lands (called Old English), especially in remote areas away from the pale, intermingled with the Irish and increasingly "went native," that is, they assimilated Irish culture and language. To halt what the English saw as the erosion of civilized culture and the degeneracy of Englishmen in Ireland, the English Crown established legal restrictions forbidding Englishmen to wear Irish dress or hairstyles, to speak the Irish language, or to intermarry or trade with the Irish. These restrictions, the Statutes of Kilkenny, also outlawed Irish games, poetry, and music, apparently under the assumption that these cultural features were too seductive for young Englishmen to resist. Such prohibitions, and others, stayed in effect until the seventeenth century. But they had little consequence for the preservation of English culture, even though increasingly more Englishmen were encouraged to settle in Ireland throughout this period and to promote English culture.

The English were frustrated by their inability to establish complete suzerainty over Irish lands (some of which were in the control of Irish brigands) or to transform the natives and absorb them into English culture. Throughout the period of English attempts to subdue these lands and peoples, one ostensible objective was to spread English civilization. But the underlying reality and primary aim was the confiscation of Irish lands, the establishment of an agrarian economy, and the exploitation of native labor.

The English attitude toward the Irish, almost from the beginning of penetration into the western island, was one of contempt for Irish culture or life-styles. This was matched by intense Irish hatred of all that was English. Thus extreme ethnocentrism ensued between these two peoples early in the contact period, which is a common result of situations in which one people attempt to conquer another. But the conflict was not only based on the ethnic chauvinism of two peoples competing for political supremacy, as in the case of the many other confrontations between the emerging nation-states of Europe. The hostility between the Irish and English went much deeper. It exemplified an age-old struggle, symbolized in biblical times in the conflict between Cain and Abel, and one that has resurged many times in many places throughout human history. It was the clash between a people who were nomadic or seminomadic pastoralists and those who settled on the land as farmers and cultivated a sedentary way of life. It was a fundamental conflict between two very different life-styles, two different views of the world, two different value systems, and two different sets of problems and solutions for them.

We should understand how the incompatibility between these major subsistence patterns has led to extreme hatred and conflict in many areas of the world and perhaps early in the history of settled living. Pastoralism, an economy based on the herding of animals, is a way of life that has proved highly adaptive in many areas of the world. The basic needs of pastoral societies are herds of domestic or semidomestic animals that are amenable to human manipulation and control, grazing land sufficient to maintain the herds and provide for increases in their numbers, accessible water and salt, and strategies for protecting this highly mobile form of wealth and the requisite resources. It is a life-style that requires the human community to adjust itself to the needs of the herds. This means that cultural ways are oriented around and circumscribed by territorial mobility and the placement of highest value on and intense interaction with the animal herds.

In recent millennia, pastoralism has been sustained as a specialized way of life in areas marginal to agriculture. Yet, in many places, pastoralists seeking expansion of grazing land for their herds and farmers attempting to increase their crop production have come into conflict over land, a situation not unlike that of the American farmers and cattle ranchers of the Old West.

Although many recent studies have shown that there is a great deal of variation in the cultures of nomadic pastoral people so that it is impossible to speak of a "typical" nomadic way of life (Dyson-Hudson and Dyson-Hudson 1980), certain features have appeared both in history and in the comparative ethnographic literature that reflect common themes in such cultures.[6] Herding peoples do not recognize land or territory as having specific boundaries, nor have they evolved the concept of property associated with bounded pieces of land. The territory over which they roam belongs to all in the community. Because of their need for mobility and for often rapid movements, they usually have very little of what sedentary peoples would identify as private property. Most material goods must be portable and often disposable. Their dwellings are generally not permanent, nor do they seem to be very solid to those people who value proper houses and all the accoutrements that accompany them. Tents or other types of dwellings that can be taken apart and packed for moving are the common living quarters, but, depending on the environment, most activities take place outside. Some groups who live in relatively harsh environments and engage in seasonal migrations, like the Kazahks of northern China, may have permanent houses of sod and/or logs for their winter dwellings.

Among many pastoralists, human dependence on animal herds is virtually complete. The basic diet of milk, such substances as butter and yogurt processed from milk, meat from older animals or surplus bulls, and blood extracted from adult animals generally suffices, but may be supplemented with occasional vegetables. Skins of animals are used for a wide variety of utensils, clothing, storage containers, bedding, and so forth. Even the hoofs, horns, bones, tails, and entrails have their uses, so that little is wasted. Such usage contrasts sharply with the diet and materials utilized or exploited by farmers.

Camping units (or some other form of community unit) where face-to-face contact is possible from time to time are usually autonomous both politically and economically, operating well beyond the sphere of control of centralized authorities. When there are quarrels between units, one mechanism of resolving them is for one group to move away. More typically, however, is the institutionalization of feuding relationships, continuous and insistent conflict that separates herding units. But constant preparedness for fighting, even wholesale combat, means that nomadic herders are perceived by sedentary peoples as being militaristic and aggressive.[7] An argument has been made that this type of behavior is necessary and children are so conditioned to it because of the need to protect a form of wealth that is volatile and easily stolen (Goldschmidt 1965). It is indeed a characteristic of many nomadic pastoralists that they engage in a high level of feuding with others and that the raiding of the animals of other groups, usually to replenish their own losses, is commonplace (Sweet 1965).

One of the more striking cultural themes among virtually all nomadic pastoralists is their love for their animals, which are often accorded priority in their ideologies over love of kinspeople or wives. Some of the best known and most cherished poetry among the Arabs is that which honors or praises their animals or a particular animal. Among East African pastoralists, songs are composed to cattle, and women and cattle are expressed in folk sayings as literally substitutes for one another in men's hearts. Concomitant with this life-style is an extraordinary love of freedom of movement and a disdain for farmers who are bound to the land and who scratch in the earth for a living.

The Gaelic peoples of Ireland shared many of the habits and customs known from studies of nomadic peoples in the Old World. Because they were a herding people, cattle were their greatest form of wealth and most strategic resource. But techniques of growing crops were not unknown, and many Irish families grew some barley and oats, primarily to feed their animals during the long winter months. Farming, however, was not considered fitting for a man's major occupation. It was generally left to women. For a man, his herd was the source of his prestige and pride, and each family spent a lifetime trying to increase its herds. Like all pastoralists, they believed that their way of life was far superior to the wretched lives of farmers, valuing above all the freedom that it gave them.

English culture by contrast was ordered, structured, and controlled. Men were bound in permanent relationships of stratified ranks to one another and to property in land, houses, and commercial enterprises. The centralized governance of a strong civil state was mirrored in the hierarchical structure of the church, the parish, and the town. It was a system that provided for the preeminent values of order, stability, and security. Until the Reformation, it also imposed restraints on the freedom of individuals. What made the English culture most distinct from that of the Irish was the advanced elaboration of the jural concept of rights in property in land and the social identity and status that derived therefrom.

From the standpoint of English cultural values, Irish utilization of the land was a monstrous waste; the rich soil that their animals trampled could be put to better use cultivating grains, vegetables, and other goods to be marketed abroad and in expanding urban centers. Moreover, the younger sons of English gentlemen who had no hopes of inheriting paternal lands could earn their fortunes from great estates that would be planted in Ireland with the aid of Irish labor. Yet all attempts to force Irishmen to settle on the land were rebuffed. When the English met their intransigence by confiscating and destroying their cattle, they fled into the forests and let it be known that they preferred starvation to life as forced laborers on English farms.

Each people thus expressed the different orientations of their cultures, their different values, interests, and beliefs, and their differing ways of viewing the world. Extreme ethnic chauvinism bred of such contrasting understandings of different worlds was exacerbated by the enduring conflicts, fundamentally over land. Neither side displayed the moderating force of Christian benevolence, although both groups claimed to be on the side of God.

The contempt and hatred that the English had for Irish culture were expressed by Giraldus Cambrensis as early as 1187. "They are a wild and inhospitable people," he claimed. "They live on beasts only, and live like beasts. ... This people despises agriculture, has little use for the money-making of towns."[8] He described their uncleanliness, their flowing hair and beards infested with lice, their barbarous dress and their laziness. "They think that the greatest pleasure is not to work and the greatest wealth is to enjoy liberty." James Myers (1983) asserts that it was this inordinate love of liberty to which Giraldus Cambrensis and his successors objected, and this critique of the Irish continued throughout succeeding centuries.

At the time that Columbus was exploring the New World, the English under Henry VII in 1494 began a new policy designed to settle the Irish problem once and for all through forced colonization. Henry VIII, however, was more benign in his approach, preferring to provide mechanisms by which the Irish would voluntarily submit to his rule. But it was he who built defensive forts and established the first standing army in Ireland with the intention of ridding the fertile areas of all those who refused to submit to English rule. The colonization policy was continued by Henry VIII's successors.

Irish resistance throughout the sixteenth century enraged many of the English, who persisted in viewing the Irish as "rude, beastly, ignorant, cruel and unruly infidels" (Liggio 1976, 8). According to William Thomas, writing in 1552, the "wild" Irish were unreasonable beasts who knew neither God nor good manners and who lived with their wives and children in filth along with their animals (Liggio 1976, 8). Some Englishmen argued what was to become a familiar strain in European attitudes toward Indians and Africans in the New World during the coming centuries: that the Irish were better off as slaves of the English than they were retaining the brutish customs of their traditional culture. While confiscating Irish lands, many English military leaders, some of whom were later to be involved in the colonization of New England and the Virginia colonies, regularly killed women and children, which has prompted some historians to accuse the English of genocide.[9] Humphrey Gilbert, whom David B. Quinn (1966) called a "bloodthirsty sadist," justified this barbaric treatment by arguing that the men who fought the war could not be maintained without the women who milked the cattle and provided them with food "and other necessaries" (127). During the final years of the Nine Years' War, many of the Irish were driven off to western Ireland and their chief form of wealth, their cattle, was destroyed. Lands were taken over by the younger sons of English gentry, who subsequently set about to create an agricultural and commercial society. The Irish who remained were reduced to involuntary laborers. Under English law they were not allowed to own land, hold office, be apprenticed to any skill or craft, or serve on juries. Their principal identity was that of cheap labor.

Toward the middle of the seventeenth century, another more widespread rebellion by the Irish and by some of the Old English took place. This was followed by extremely repressive measures on the part of the English under Oliver Cromwell. According to Liggio:

> Cromwell's army in Ireland, often New England Puritan led or inspired, carried out the most complete devastation that Ireland experienced until that time. Extermination became a policy. Massacres were carried out. Prisoners of war were transported to servitude in the new English colonies in the West Indies. Ireland like New England was taken with the Bible in one hand, the sword in the other. Lord Clarendon observed that the Cromwellian policy was to act without "any humanity to the Irish nation, and more especially to those of the old native extraction, the whole *race* whereof they had upon the matter sworn an utter extirpation" (1976, 28).

The significance of this brutal treatment and the transportation of large numbers of captive peoples of both sexes to the sugar plantations in the West Indies rested upon the growing image of the Irish as something less than human, as a people whose capacity for civilization was stunted. This view took form slowly but was perhaps common among some English elite by the early seventeenth century.

Unremitting disdain for the customs and habits of the "wild Irish" is found throughout the literature of the sixteenth and seventeenth centuries. Edmund Campion, himself a Catholic, excoriated the Irish for their supposed cannibalism, their lewd marriage customs (they had trial marriages, and sometimes engaged in polygamy and free sexual behavior), their "whores" and "strumpets ... too vile and abominable to write of" (quoted in Myers 1983, 26–30). And Barnabe Rich in his 1610 description of Irish peoples, manners, and customs claimed that the Irish were educated in "treason, in rebellion, in theft, in robbery, in superstition, in idolatry" (quoted in Myers 1983, 130). In their resistance to British civilization, Rich noted that "the Irish had rather still retain themselves in their sluttishness, in their uncleanliness, in their rudeness, and in their inhuman loathsomeness, than they would take any example from the English, either of civility, humanity, or any manner of decency" (Myers 1983, 131).

The habits and customs of the Irish reminded some learned men of the descriptions of primitive peoples found in the recently recovered literature of the ancient Greeks and Romans. Doubts about the capacity of such barbaric people to accommodate themselves to civilized behavior hardened. Many men may well have come to believe a notion, first expressed in the early fourteenth century, that it was "no more a sin to kill an Irishman than a dog or any other brute." Thus there crystallized in the English mind, out of this long saga of tension and hostility, a very real image of barbarism that had concrete referents in the Irish but that could be abstracted to apply to others.

Perhaps worst of all was the heathenism of the Irish. Despite the fact of their nominal Catholicism, Englishmen could see nothing in Irish behavior that was suggestive of morality and virtue. In fact, like Campion, many tended to blame Irish heathenism on their adherence to the papal religion, albeit it was a tenuous linkage. Their alleged wildness, lack of self-control, and tendency to drunkenness and violence were all evidence of the insufficiency of Catholicism to uplift people.

This antagonism to Catholicism had its origins in the tumultuous breakaway of diverse groups from the older Roman Catholic establishment that began during the early part of the sixteenth century. Although we know of this historical transformation as the Protestant revolution, it was not a single episode in European history, but multiple defections from the Roman Catholic church for various reasons. Henry VIII was a critical figure in this revolt, and his support of hostilities against the Irish had as much to do with his anger against the pope for the latter's failure to sanction his divorce as it did with hatred for the Irish. Still, the antagonism against the Irish was compounded by an intensity of opposition to the powers of the church and by growing competition with Spain, another Catholic country, some leaders of which sided with fellow churchmen in Ireland.

At the same time, Englishmen were beginning to receive reports about the indigenous peoples encountered by the Portuguese and Spanish in their New World ventures. Interaction between the Spanish and English was intensified during this century. For a while there were close diplomatic, commercial, and political contacts between the two countries, punctuated by the marriage of Henry VIII to a Spanish princess, Catherine of Aragon, and the brief ascendancy of Phillip II of Spain to the joint possession of the English Crown by virtue of his marriage to Henry's daughter, Mary I, from 1553 to 1558. English merchants and sea captains visited Spain frequently, and English politicians and adventurers studied closely the developing colonial policies of the Spanish. Quinn points out that, for the first time, Englishmen began to regard their problems with the Irish as similar to those presented by the natives of the New World to the Spanish. They found that some of the same qualities of a barbarous and uncivilized people were attributed to the New World natives by the Spanish. Moreover, Spanish settlers were demanding laws enforcing perpetual servitude on the indigenous peoples of the Spanish colonies, a situation the English found most congenial to their own goals.

Following the successful and brutal squashing of the Desmond rebellion in Munster (1579–1583), the English consciously attempted to establish plantations in that region based on Spanish models and the principles that they perceived to be operant in both Spanish colonial settings and in the Italian Mediterranean island plantations. Again, after the final victory over "the O'Neill" in 1603, which "marked the passing of Gaelic civilization and the beginning of England's first meticulously planned effort to effect the cultural subjugation of an alien people" (Myers 1983, 8), England planned to create a colonial outpost along plantation lines. At the heart of the plantation model was the coercive exploitation of Irish labor, with the objective of "maintaining the labor force in a permanent state of inferiority to and dependence on the English settlers" (Quinn 1958, 27).

It is not surprising that the English view of the Irish was solidified by the seventeenth century into an image summed up in the term "savage." It was the invention in the English mind of the savage that made possible the development of policies and practices that could be perpetuated for gain, unencumbered by reflections on any ethical or moral considerations. The savage was first of all a "heathen," a godless and immoral creature, "wicked, barbarous and uncivil." He was lazy, filthy, evil, superstitious, and an idol worshipper, and was given to lying, stealing, treachery, murder, and double-dealing. His nomadic tendencies and presumed lack of social order or laws were the antithesis of the habits of civilized man who was sedentary and bound not only to land but also to other men by laws. The savage was a cannibal whose lust and licentiousness never yielded to the strictures of self-control, of which he was totally lacking.[10] Granted, some of the Irish had been transformed into civilized men, but for late seventeenth-century Englishmen this goal, which was an early rationalization for settlement in Ireland, became more and more remote. What did increase in the ideology and images about the Irish were the beliefs that (1) the Irish were incapable of being civilized, that the "wild" Irish, those who most vigorously resisted English hegemony, would remain untamed; and (2) the only way to bring them under some form of civilized control was to enslave them. Indeed, Irish people formed the bulk of the servile peoples who were eventually transferred to the New World English plantations during the seventeenth century (see Chapter 6).

To document and confirm the growing beliefs about the unsuitability of Irishmen for civilization, many of the Englishmen pointed to the experiences of the Spanish with New World natives. They cited Spanish practices of exterminating Indians not only as justification for policies of killing Irish men, women, and children but as an appropriate solution for those who refused to be enslaved.

In the English collective consciousness, "the savage" was thus a kind of composite of these streams of negative ideas and images that flourished during a period of much social disorder, change, and unrest. The savage came to embody all of those repulsive characteristics that were contrary and opposed to English beliefs, habits, laws, and values. The imagery induced hatred for all things Irish, which has persisted among many English people right up to the twentieth century. But it also had a feedback effect: It was of enormous convenience for those who hoped to profit from the plantations created in Irish lands.[11]

The English were not unique in their attitudes. As Hodgen (1964) has pointed out, for this period of ethnological reflection European opinion in general was "anti-savage, and strongly so" (362), an attitude that was not challenged until well into the period of the Enlightenment, which began toward the end of the seventeenth century. But such attitudes were more strongly felt by Englishmen and were instrumental in molding the English's cognitive perceptions of other conquered peoples in the New World as well as later in the Middle East, India, Burma, South Asia, and Africa. They became important subthemes to the ideology of race and in the characterization of racial differences.

English Nationalism and Social Values in the Sixteenth and Seventeenth Centuries

The consolidation of an image of the savage was a major factor in the evolution of English attitudes toward aliens. It fed into an expanding cultural chauvinism as Englishmen began to view themselves as not only distinctive from others but superior. Events seemed to propel them toward increasing nationalism and an arrogant pride in being English, a trend that had been nourished during the Hundred Years' War. The break with the Roman Catholic church in the sixteenth century was both a political and a religious underscoring of the separateness of the English polity from the rest of Europe. Consciousness of being English, not yet perceived in biological terms, flowered during Elizabethan times (1559–1603). A sense of growing competition with other

Europeans, particularly the Spanish, made them turn inward, where for some a sense of unity and purpose was found by harkening back to an ancient mythical time of greatness and glory.

Reginald Horsman (1976, 1981) points out that the myth of Anglo-Saxonism originated during this period. Depicted as a branch of a heroic and freedom-loving Germanic peoples, Anglo-Saxons were described not only as great lovers of liberty but also as originators of civilization's free institutions and equitable laws. It is worth noting, and Horsman specifically points out, that this early form of Anglo-Saxonism was not racial. It was rooted in the attempt to rationalize the existence of a pure pre-Norman church, and thus to justify Henry VIII's break with the Roman Catholic church. It was also consonant with developing ethnocentrism in other emerging states of Europe. The focus on biologically inherited "racial" features as a way of explaining Anglo-Saxon cultural institutions did not take place until the mid to late eighteenth century, a timing that, as we will see later (Chapter 8), was not fortuitous.

The unexpected English defeat of the Spanish Armada in 1588 was a major event in the eclipse of Spanish domination of the seas. It spelled the rise of this once isolated island culture, which eventually not only assumed supremacy of the seas, but became the most vigorous and successful of the competing, empire-building states of Europe. England's citizenry became increasingly united around a peculiar sense of their own English identity and superiority, which ultimately precluded the acceptance of others as equals.

A basic element in that identity was religion. The English were Christian first and, even though they were becoming highly secular and materialistic in their cultural orientation, were conditioned to that sense of religiosity that pervaded much of Europe during this time. Most important, from the time of Henry VIII on, they were predominantly Protestant, and their consciousness of an identity dramatically wrenched from the stale traditionalism of an archaic Catholicism was at its peak. Among Protestants themselves, various sects (Anglicans, Puritans, Presbyterians, and such splinter groups as the Dissenters and Arminians) vied with one another in and out of Parliament for ascendancy in political, economic, and religious matters.

The priority given to religion as a major diacritic of a person's or a people's identity in Europe is explicable in the wider framework of European history and culture. It was a time when all of Europe was undergoing tremendous social and political turmoil. One factor in this was the decline of feudalism, as we have seen. These older forms of labor bound to landed estates gradually gave way to a very different contract laborer who was for hire and, most importantly, was mobile, a fact that promoted social instability. Social dislocations also resulted from periodic pestilence and disease, going back at least to the Black Death of 1348–1350, which disrupted all lives and institutions. In the absence of scientific understanding of epidemic disease and of methods to combat it, such crises called forth supernatural explanations and supernatural supplications. No institution was more suitable to deal with this than was the church.

Then there was the sudden discovery of a whole new world drawing people into contact not only with an unanticipated paganism, but also to its lure of great wealth apparently there for the grasping by anyone with sufficient ambition, motivation, and greed. In this context, precedents for how people were to relate to one another were absent or elusive. The possibility of adventure and profit attracted men and women away from familiar forms of social control, from family, kinsmen, employers, patrons, friends, and clients, and into interaction with alien merchants, adventurers, pirates, sailors, and other strangers. The frequent anonymity of these new interactions underscored the need for a familiar identity—to which others could relate. With growing competition and protonationalistic conflicts among the various nations of Europe, Englishmen, like other Europeans, often found it critical to establish political and/or commercial alliances predicated on religious affiliation. Thus, Catholicism, Protestantism, or one of its variants was often the key to not only another person's identity, but also to how the person was to be treated.

Another factor underscoring the importance of some religious attachment was the existence of an atmosphere thick with the belief in and fear of witchcraft. Anthropologists have long observed that in times of enormous social, political, and economic disorder, of devastating warfare or of massive inexplicable natural disasters, human beings commonly turn to some form of witchcraft beliefs to help explain disaster, restore order, and regain control of their lives and of natural phenomena.

From about the twelfth century on, much more intense attention to and concern with witches and their activities took place. This seemed to reach a crescendo in the fifteenth century, as various sects began to break from the Roman church and to devise their own theologies and measures of the faith. Although all of the Protestant groups were opposed to the alleged oppressive nature of the Roman Catholic church, and especially to the Inquisition, they retained much of the underlying theological, historical, and scriptural beliefs. One of these beliefs had to do with the nature of the devil and how he manifests himself.

Christian tradition has it that the devil is the anti-Christ, the incarnation of all evil, who was in mortal combat with the forces of good in order to win men's souls. The devil had the ability to enter men's (and women's) bodies, or to make a compact with individuals to carry out malevolent aims. Thus one knew the existence of this evil force by the behavior and actions of those individuals in league with the devil. If Christianity created the devil, it also prescribed means of reckoning with this evil—through obedience and living an exemplary life, through prayer and the intervention of the Holy Mother, and, more directly, through the sign of the cross or the use of holy water. A good Christian theoretically could not be harmed by the courtship of the devil.

Reputation as a good Christian was a major protection against being accused of witchcraft. Those who were not Christian often became identified with the devil, evil, and sinfulness. This sense of identity was solidified in most of Europe and helps to explain why relationships between Europeans and the indigenous peoples whom they colonized often became so harsh and cruel. As we shall see later, when heathens were perceived to be as wicked as, or agents of, the devil, then there need be no moral restraints against brutalizing or killing them.

Coinciding with the rise of witchcraft, and a factor in the drastic social changes occurring, was the breakup of the Muslim empire in Spain and the subsequent expulsion of Jews and Moors. While the Moors made their way back to North Africa and other parts of the Mediterranean world, the Jews began a series of migrations that led some of them to other parts of Europe and to England (and some to America). The growing presence of these Jews was perceived as a threat in Europe and made Christians even more conscious and protective of their own religious identities.

Thus, in the context of a multiplicity of forces that swirled around them and often threatened their sense of security, Christians in Europe magnified the importance of religion not only as a criterion of identity but also as a source of protection, security, and comfort. For many who traveled abroad, in whatever direction, a strong religious faith had greater force even than allegiance to king, patron, or community.

Hereditary Social Identity: The Lesson of Catholic Spain

Because of the mutual influences that the Spanish and English had on one another during the early centuries of exploration and colonization, it is useful to consider those features of Spanish life and thought that may have influenced English ideologies about human differences. As already suggested, the Spanish had quite a different history and experience with human diversity from the English. Since the eighth century, the peninsula had been dominated by a civilization that was among the world's most tolerant, at least for a while. Under Muslim hegemony, Spain had experienced the formation of a heterogeneous, multicultural, multi-"racial" society. For a while, Muslims, Christians, and Jews led culturally productive lives together and had remarkably benign relationships among themselves, with some exceptions, even to the point of considerable intermarriage (Castro 1971, 499). However, with the rise to political power of some of the Christian kingdoms and with the thrust to regain Spanish territory for the Catholic church ("the Reconquest"), beginning as early as the ninth century, Jews and Muslims came under pressure to convert. Conflict ensued, and the entire social system gradually became rigidified into three ethnic-religious "castes" whose relationships in the fifteenth and sixteenth centuries were often characterized by fear, mistrust, envy, and hatred.

Some 300,000 Jews became Christian by the end of the fifteenth century, a time when the marriage of Ferdinand and Isabella had become the political fulcrum symbolizing the rise of modern Catholic Spain. Known as "conversos," these former Jewish families were rich and urban; they also constituted the largest proportion of the educated. The Moors, who tended to be concentrated in the southern regions of Spain, in Valencia, Granada, and Castile, underwent forced baptisms early in the sixteenth century, but their customs, traditions, and language (Arabic) continued intact for a while. The Moors came to constitute an underclass of laboring people who remained somewhat culturally distinct from the Spanish. Eventually, the state expelled all of the Moriscos, as they were called; some 275,000 were shipped off to North Africa between 1609 and 1614.

Jealous of the wealth, power, and influence of the Jewish families who had converted, many of whom were using their new Christian identity to advance themselves in the civil or church hierarchies, some of the Christian leaders began to question the theological probity of some conversos. Many Christians in the countryside, of peasant backgrounds, emerged as antagonists, not only to the already declining Muslim influence but also to what they believed to be the Jewish domination of trade, commerce, banking, scholarship, and the arts. In a drama characterized by intrigues, petty jealousies, and varied political machinations, opponents began to charge that some of the conversos and their descendants (the New Christians) were secretly practicing Judaism. An inquisition directed at heretics was established in 1478, sanctioned by the Catholic kings and the church. It was designed to weed out recalcitrant converts or "secret" Jews by investigating personal behavior and genealogies for the taint of Jewishness. Some of the ideas that became basic ingredients of a racial worldview were set in motion during this period of rising Christian intolerance and rampant persecution of Jews and Moors.

A major contribution to Western thought was the belief engendered by the Inquisition in the hereditary nature of social status, a theme often carried through in the extreme. Family ties were closely scrutinized to discover the "hidden Jew," and a social stigma was attached to anyone or any family that had even a remote association with someone prosecuted by the Inquisition. Although lineal descent seemed to be the avenue of heritability of social standing (vis-à-vis the church) this was not consistently observed. The result was that many Spaniards, including some non-Jews, sought a certificate of "purity" that, for a fee, would be issued by the church. It constituted a guarantee of one's genealogical purity from "any admixture of Jew or Moor" or from condemnation by the Holy Office (Roth 1964, 197–207). These "certificates of Limpieza de Sangre" (purity of blood) were not only a major source of revenue for the church, but were also vital requirements for social mobility, as certain occupations and activities were closed by law to the families of converts.

The idea that social standing is inheritable is an ancient one associated with societies in which there are class divisions, occupational specializations, and private or lineage property. Spanish folk ideology and the practices of the Spanish church and state seemed to define Jewishness and Moorishness as something almost biological, using the idiom of "blood" ties. Elaborate tests for finding social genealogical connections were incipient mechanisms for establishing social placement. And the Spanish use of the term "race," along with "castas," for both Jews and Moors bespeaks a potentially new kind of image of what were essentially ethnic (religious) differences.[12]

Americo Castro (1971) agrees that what was occurring in Spain under the Inquisition was a hardening of ethnic differences, rather than an appeal to some biogenetic reality. He says, "From the fifteenth century on, 'purity of blood' has meant consciousness of caste" (68). It has nothing to do with physical traits or "racial physical type." Yet to equate sections of the society with breeding lines of animals, even symbolically, is to suggest a kind of permanency and immutability to their social qualities that are found only in biological transmission. This attests to the great degree to which Catholic political powers, both papal and secular, were anxious and willing to separate out these populations and to eliminate the Jewish and Moorish cultural influences among them. In this way, the Catholic leaders of Spain could extend and consolidate their power over a population that was essentially homogeneous in religion and culture and uniformly responsive to imposed laws and sanctions.

But any idea of biologically hereditary social positions was contradicted by the more massive uses of conversion, essentially baptism, to eliminate the presence of Jews and Moors in Spanish society. The vast majority of those converted remained Christian, and the acceptance of these former Jews and former Muslims and their descendants as legitimate members of the Catholic community and the state is in opposition to the tenets of modern race ideology, which precludes forever the possibility of such a transformation. The apparent contradiction between the reality of the alteration of social identity, under pressure, and the notion that social identity is a concomitant of unique biological features that are exclusive and unalterable was never resolved and probably never even recognized by the thinkers and philosophers of the Inquisition.

One of the reasons for this may be that, though some of the attitudes and beliefs about the Moors and Jews were expressed in a seemingly biological idiom, at the deepest layer of reality was the more archaic sense of interconnectedness between generations, which stemmed from a peasant context. In the anthropological study of kinship, scholars have argued that kinship is a cultural creation, unrelated to actual biological realities. Human populations take the basic facts of our animal biology, sex differences and the bisexual mode of reproduction, and configure genealogical connections in a variety of patterns. We then imbue certain of these connections with moral and jural qualities. The result is what anthropologists study as kinship. The fact that kinship patterns, processes, obligations, and connections differ from one population to another is the clearest indication of their arbitrary and culturally created nature. Thus anthropologists have come to recognize that kinship relationships are best analyzed as social, sometimes sociopolitical, constructions.

Throughout most of human history and in all human societies, an emphasis on a true biological connection has been absent or irrelevant, in large part because the male role in parturition was little understood. Nor could the biological father (genitor) of a child be precisely known. It was not until the use of modern technology, beginning with the invention of the microscope, the discovery of genetic material, and the invention of electron microscopes in the twentieth century, that it has been possible to ascertain with certainty the actual biological father of any child. Yet every human society has created the role of the "pater," or social father, and has surrounded it with certain moral and jural prescriptions. In many societies, the pater is the husband of the mother, regardless of who the "genitor" is or was, and it is irrelevant that the two may not be the same. In some societies a man whose wife does not become pregnant within a reasonable time may, in fact, call upon another man to beget children for him. His (legal) fatherhood of those children is never questioned.

Adoption and the purchase of children to create kinsmen (and women) in the next generation have been widespread throughout human history, long before the industrial world order emerged. Thus genealogical descent is a jural concept that links men and women together over generations. It is only in the modern world that we have confused biological and social fatherhood, assuming the necessity of both to be the same.

This sense of kinship as an elemental social device for structuring human relations has been perpetuated, especially among peasants and poor people who have little or no property to transmit but who maintain customs of mutual obligations and responsibilities that are deemed essential for the preservation of the society. That human beings structure their kinship systems on biological models stemming from the facts of bisexual reproduction should not obscure the fundamental social nature of kinship. That we culturally create such relationships and imbue the ideologies that we build up around them and attach to them with biological parallelisms in symbols, terms, and expressions conveys a need to make them natural and indissoluble.

Although I have not seen a study of the Spanish Inquisition that expresses this, I suspect that any statute under which, for example, a man would have to prove that his grandmother was not a Jew was more a reflection of the real fact that social behavior, identity, and wealth are transmitted within the genealogical context of families than it was a belief that Jewishness actually resides in the blood. It reflected the jural dimensions of structured kinship rather than the fact of biological connection, the significance of "pater" rather than "genitor." The cognitive connection linking biology and social status did not seem to appear until the crystallization of the idea of "race" in the eighteenth century.

A clearly related aspect of the Spanish experience is the restructuring of the Spanish state as a Catholic society. The thrust for homogeneity in society by religion, certainly not by "bloodline," was one of the many ramifications of nation-state building in Europe in general.[13] Obviously, such homogeneity is best facilitated by eliminating those sects that vary from desired theology, belief, and ritual. The easiest way to make Spain exclusively Catholic was by conversion, a process totally unrelated to biology, and this is what was done.

Exclusiveness, however, is fundamental to the ideology of race, and it can only be maintained by the erection of social-cultural boundaries between populations that (1) become broad barriers against interaction between "races," (2) preclude any possibility of egalitarian relationships, and (3) do not recognize or provide for intermediate realities. Such boundaries are most effective when they can be transmuted into a biological axiom. The experience of the Spanish is suggestive in that they came very close to infusing a "racial" element into the criteria of social identity; but more important was their elevation of *religious/cultural* homogeneity to a high social value.

The Spanish brought with them to the New World many of the cultural features of the Inquisition era and infused them onto the societies created in the colonial setting. Among these were the idea of "castas," the belief that "purity" of one's Hispanic genealogy entitled one to higher social status; the fear of mixture or taint in the lineage; judicial codes, customs, and proceedings of the Inquisition; religious fervor and intolerance; and most of all the customs, practices, and traditions of medieval slavery. Many of the Spanish customs and habits of thought were no doubt picked up by the English.

Thus some of the major ingredients for the ideology and worldview of "race" were present in the thought patterns and understandings of both Spanish and English peoples during the critical period when European colonial settlements in the New World began. All of the European conquerers and colonizers turned to the use of the term "race" (raza, race, reazza). They all shared a common belief that their victims were some form of "savages," despite recognized diversity among the cultures of indigenous peoples and different conceptions of savagery in the European minds. And all of the Europeans initiated the practice of slavery, both with Indians and with imported Africans. Yet the degree to which they conceptualized and institutionalized the perceived differences varied, as we shall see later, for reasons that relate to their histories, experiences, and demographic realities. The English took the term "race" and molded it into a phenomenon unlike that of their competitors, structuring closed and exclusive groups out of the melange of peoples of the Americas. It is to the history of the English in America that we must now turn in order to examine those facets of culture and experience that led them to this point.

Notes

1. See Boies Penrose (1955) for a description of early travels by Europeans and the fables, myths, and tales concocted by them about peoples and places unknown at that time.

2. Karl Marx and Max Weber were major writers of the nineteenth century who provided theoretical paradigms for the transition from peasant feudal society to industrial capitalism. For more than a century, many historians of England have documented, interpreted, and reinterpreted the development of modern capitalism and its attendant features. The theory simplified here is fairly conventional. See, for example, Bober ([1927] 1965), Genovese and Fox-Genovese (1983), and Macfarlane (1978).

3. Most of Europe had developed a dual or bilateral system of kinship in which connections on both sides, maternal and paternal, were given almost equal recognition. A corollary and perhaps consequence of this was the absence of corporate kinship groups with stable, permanent, and exclusive membership. Instead, each generation of siblings had a circle of relatives unique to it, known as kindreds, radiating outward on both sides. Obligations of kinsmen were based loosely on genealogical closeness, with the greatest sense of solidarity between brothers, then first cousins, second cousins, and so forth. In some cases, this could be extended to sixth or seventh cousins, but at that distance (which no doubt also frequently corresponded to geographic distance) the sense of responsibility was muted.

4. See especially Chapter 7 in which Macfarlane (1978) observes that these traits of the English, described by a writer of the late fifteenth century, most certainly evolved long before that time.

5. For examples, see Canny (1973) and Quinn (1966).

6. See the section on pastoralism in Cohen (1974) and the papers in Goldschmidt (1965). Although I concur with the perspective that views cultures as open, dynamic systems, it is also true that there are persisting themes manifest over broad ranges of time in many areas of the world. My concerns here are the frequent examples of seemingly irreconcilable differences and overt hostilities that have recurred between mobile herding societies and sedentary cultivators.

7. Because of their militarism and aggression and the facility for rapid mobility, some nomadic herders have from time to time throughout history come to dominate their sedentary neighbors. In some cases, vast movements of large pastoral groups have led to conquests and to the consolidation of large new empires, as for example the migrations of Turkish peoples in Russia, the Middle East, northern India, and Persia, the Fulani in West Africa, and the Mongols in Asia.

8. Quoted in Myers (1983, 15).

9. See brief descriptions of the brutal Munster and Ulster uprisings and the eventual conquests by the British forces in Liggio (1976) and in Quinn (1966).

10. After some of their campaigns, the English pursued a scorched-earth policy, destroying livestock and vegetation so that the Irish would be reduced to

famine. It was reported that some turned to eating human flesh (Quinn 1966, 132), which confirmed the imagery of cannibalism to the English.

11. For various reasons the plantations established in Ireland were, by and large, failures, which prompted even greater interest in the New World and in the creation of plantation societies there, especially in the Caribbean Islands (see Quinn 1966, and Jones 1942).

12. Ronald Sanders (1978) makes an important point about the Spanish attitude toward and treatment of Jews. "In this notion that a certain group within society is unclean and should be quarantined we can perceive an incipient racism—still only incipient, however, since the idea remains that the uncleanness resides in doctrine, not in blood" (25).

13. Robert Berkhofer, Jr., has recognized the political significance of such homogeneity. "One king, one faith, one law," he notes, protects the political stability of new regimes in a time of religious (and secular) conflicts. (Personal communication.)

4

Growth of the English Ideology of Race in America

I N THE NORTH AMERICAN COLONIES the ideological components of race grew and flourished; the sense of exclusiveness and discreteness of group membership, the ranking of groups according to English cultural standards of Christianity and civilization, and the explanation of behavior and ranking in terms of the innate and distinct nature of biophysically defined groups evolved together, albeit at different stages. In certain specific circumstances, decisions, and events, one can identify some of the stages in this process, which are explored in this chapter.

Earliest Contacts

The first colonization attempts on the part of the English took place in the late sixteenth century. Like other Europeans, the English had acquired a taste for sugar, spices, and other goods that were imported from the East. They had been the beneficiaries of thriving sugar plantations, on Cyprus and on other Mediterranean islands, which were worked by a mixture of free and slave labor. It was a pattern of exploitation that the Spanish and Portuguese had already transmitted to the New World.

The English were keenly aware of the large colonial enterprises and of the great wealth that the Spanish and Portuguese were deriving from them. As early as 1497, John Cabot had tried to establish for England a claim to Labrador and Newfoundland. Throughout the sixteenth century English contacts, both peaceable and belligerent, with Spanish merchants increased. Some Englishmen, like Sebastian Cabot, hired themselves into the services of the Spanish.[1] An English ship under the leadership of John Rut reached Santo Domingo in 1527 to trade in wools and linen. Englishmen entered the slave trade with the first trips by

John Hawkins in the 1560s to the West Coast of Africa, during which he plundered, stole, and kidnapped hundreds of people. The Queen herself, Elizabeth I, invested in some of his slaving enterprises in 1567. Hawkins involved his cousin, Francis Drake, in some of his trips, and the latter subsequently amassed a fortune through the piracy of Spanish ships in the Caribbean and the plunder of the indigenous peoples along the way.

In Panama, Drake made alliances with a group of slaves known as "Cimarrons" who had escaped from their Spanish masters and formed communities deep in the interior. They periodically raided the Spanish settlements and helped Drake and his men to hijack caravans of Spanish goods crossing the isthmus to Atlantic ports. Edmund Morgan (1975) emphasizes the significance of such an alliance. Drake and other English adventurers, he noted, even though all had engaged in slaving from time to time, were not averse to forming unions with black Africans against the Spanish. They indeed "had cast themselves as liberators and had allied with blacks against whites. ... The alliance seems to have been untroubled by racial prejudice" (13). Drake frequently freed Indian and African slaves from the Spanish; in 1586 he arrived in Roanoke (see below) with a shipload of Indians and Negroes whom he left on the island (41–42).

By the latter part of the sixteenth century, such Englishmen as Humphrey Gilbert, John Davis, Ralph Lane, Walter Raleigh, and others were heavily involved in explorations of the coasts of North America as organizers or active explorers, from Newfoundland to Florida and the Caribbean. Some found it profitable to plunder Indian villages and/or to seize vulnerable Spanish and French ships.

In the 1580s Walter Raleigh was given a patent to plant a colony that would carry the name "Virginia" (for the virgin queen, Elizabeth). He sent out ships in 1584 to scout the area and to find a suitable place. His emissaries returned with very positive descriptions of the Island of Roanoke and its indigenous inhabitants. It was a glowing account designed to promote the colonial enterprise (Kupperman 1984). In 1585, Richard Grenville arrived on Roanoke with six hundred men. A plunderer and pirate of aristocratic background, as were many of the other explorers, he came into conflict with the Indians, which he resolved by burning an Indian village and adjacent cornfields. When he departed for home he left behind a party of one hundred men to explore the area around Roanoke. Upon the arrival of Francis Drake the next year, all of the surviving men chose to return home, thus abandoning the project.

Again, in 1587, a new set of potential settlers, this time including women and children, arrived on Roanoke. John White, selected as governor, returned to England for supplies after a few weeks. According to Carl Sauer (1971), he left a colony of "would-be settlers who knew nothing of the country. ... The innocents were left on Roanoke Island; their governor who had experience of the country sailed home for supplies and left them to face an indefinite time in ignorance and inevitable need" (264). By the time White attempted to reestablish contact with the infant colony, in 1590, there was no sign of the "innocents." The little settlement was lost, presumably exterminated by Indians, although there remains the probability that some of the English were simply merged into existing Indian populations (Sauer 1971, 253, 301; see also Kupperman 1984).

The history of these earliest contacts between the British adventurers and the native populations of the coastal regions of the Americas is of interest because of the nature of the relationships, however tenuous, that were established between them. Historians point out that in the first Roanoke Island expedition, the inhabitants not only approached the newcomers without any overt manifestation of fear or doubt, but actually welcomed them with open arms. The native peoples were described as "very handsome and goodly people, and in their behavior as mannerly and civil as any of Europe" (quoted in Sauer 1971, 252). Throughout the six weeks of that first stay the Indians were hospitable; the guests were entertained with "all love and kindness." Most revealing was the report that "we found the people most gentle, loving and faithful, void of all guile and treason, and such as lived after the manner of the golden rule" (252). The Indians brought food daily to the visitors. If there ever was a universal primordial reaction of fear toward strangers, the indigenous peoples of the Americas had never heard of it.

On the second Roanoke expedition, the Indians again came to the aid of the English. But when some of the English colonists began to help themselves to food in the fields and in storage areas, to traverse into areas of Indian lands that were not open to them, and to generally ignore Indian rights and customs, the latter began to withdraw support. Many even decided to flee from the strange ingrates who made such arrogant demands of them.

Ronald Sanders (1978) suggests that a division between two types of colonists was discernible on that expedition: "those, on the one hand, who were inclined to resort to force as soon as possible in the resolution of all problems with the Indians, and those, on the other, who clung to the ideals of gentleness and carefully cultivated friendship that had been advocated by humanists back in England" (233). Ralph Lane, whom Raleigh had appointed governor of the colony, was a leader of the pro–force-and-violence contingent; it is not surprising that he, like Raleigh, had dealt with "savages" while doing military service in Ireland.

The earliest settlers at Jamestown in 1607, which became the first permanent English settlement, also found the Indians unexpectedly generous, kind, and curious, willing to enter into amiable trading relationships, to teach the colonists what they needed to know to survive, and to learn from them. Thus all the settlers had reason to form positive views of the Indians. According to Gary Nash, "There is much evidence that the Indians provided the food that kept the struggling settlement alive over the first winter" (1972, 134). Nor were the English the only ones to experience the initial warm hospitality of Indians. The Dutch who settled a fur-trading station in Albany in 1614 and the French who had established relations with the Indians of Quebec and in the St. Lawrence River area had all engaged in amicable relationships with the Indians and had peacefully promoted trade.[2]

Yet the English consistently distrusted the Indians, interpreting their generosity and friendliness, potentially at least, as trickery and deception. This distrust seemed to reflect ambivalent feelings that were never resolved during the first years of colonization. Europeans simultaneously maintained two contradictory views of the Indians that had been formed even before they sailed to the New World (Berkhofer 1978; Bidney 1954; Hoover 1976; Kupperman 1984; Nash 1982; Pearce 1953). On the one hand, there was a relatively benign and positive attitude inspired by the writings of such Spanish travelers as Columbus and Giovanni da Verrazzano that depicted the Indians as civil, honest, uncorrupted, generous, and noble.[3] It was a view that was buttressed also by the missionary zeal of some Puritans, with its stated objective of eventual conversion of the natives and their assimilation into Christian society. This was indeed the genuine and sincere goal of many of the settlers, as Alden Vaughan has emphasized (1965). It was also the view of those whose main purpose was trade and/or exploration to find a northwest passage to China.

This benevolent view later came to be symbolized in the stereotypic phrase "the noble savage," an image that became more pronounced in the literature of philosophers and other intellectuals in Europe, especially during the eighteenth century, than it was in the thoughts of the colonists. It had its roots in some of the descriptions of and attitudes toward Indians held by many early missionaries beginning in the sixteenth century, particularly by the Dominicans and Jesuits. It was a charitable, and perhaps gratuitous, apprehension of barbarous folk as being potentially moral beings, innocent and trustworthy and hungering for the word of the true god. Their conversion would provide a magnificent expansion of the Christian religion. The theological under-pinnings of this perception of the indigenes was the unity of man under the fatherhood of (one) god.

On the other hand, there was an image of Indians as fearsome, brut-ish, and depraved that persisted in many English minds. This too was based in part on the many reports of the early Portuguese and Spanish explorers that were unfavorable to the native populations. During the latter part of the sixteenth century, many pamphlets were published that "were filled with portraits of the Indians as crafty, brutal, loath-some half-men [with] cannibalistic instincts" (Nash 1982, 37). Bizarre and unexplainable customs, heinous practices, nakedness, lascivious behavior, filth, and bestiality also were said to characterize the Indians.

Gary Nash, Howard Mumford Jones, and Nicholas Canny show few doubts about another source of the strong impulse on the part of En-glish settlers to accept the more negative image of the Indians, despite personal experiences of kindness and hospitality and pragmatic reasons for establishing friendships. Nash makes a telling point. He notes that when trade with the Indians was uppermost in English minds and their services were needed in the search for a northwest passage or for min-eral wealth, the Indians were portrayed as "primitive but winsome, as ignorant but receptive individuals. If treated kindly, they could be wooed and won to the advantages of trade and cooperation." But, "When permanent settlement became the primary English concern ... and land the object of desire, the image of the Indian as a hostile savage became ascendant in the English mind" (1972, 133; see also Nash 1982, 38–41).

Karen Kupperman explains the hostility the English exhibited at Ro-anoke toward the native peoples in terms of the English theory of hu-man nature. The English felt that if they showed weakness or vulnerability, this would invite contempt from the Indians. "People of this period seem to have felt that those who were vulnerable were re-sponsible for whatever happened to them; blame attached to them as much as to anyone who attacked or cheated them. ... When one was vulnerable, the assumption was that someone would inevitably take advantage of that fact" (Kupperman 1984, 69). The use of force was thus justified, with violence as the harbinger of English strength and invul-nerability.

The Ensuing Conflicts

The contact situation soon became one of open conflicts and intrigues. In 1608 Captain John Smith burned Indian canoes and corn in order to extort food from and frighten the Indians (Hoover 1976, 18; Morgan 1975, Chapter 4). Acts of aggression against and intimidation of Indians became frequent on an individual level and a regular policy for obtaining food and other goods. According to Morgan (1975), the early Virginia settlers, an unusually large number of whom were nobles and gentry, had not come to the colony prepared to grow food for themselves, an enterprise that many thought beneath them. They preferred to beg, bribe, and steal from the Indians (Chapters 3 and 4). Moreover, it is clear that the English expected resistance, even violent resistance, to their takeover of Indian lands and resources. Some of the descriptions of the brutal and humiliating behavior of individuals toward Indians prompt the conclusion that the English were, perhaps unconsciously, trying to provoke them into a violent confrontation (Lauber [1913] 1970).

The inevitable happened. After some colonists murdered a well-known Indian leader in 1622, the Indians attacked Chesapeake colony, killing 347 out of 1,240 persons, over a fourth of all inhabitants (Morgan 1975, 101). This had the effect that perhaps most of the English unconsciously wanted and could now even verbalize. It swept aside whatever benign attitudes had been developed toward the Indians, eliminating any inhibitions about attacking and destroying their villages. The Reverend Samuel Purchas, a chronicler of this history from the settlers' point of view, expressed his relief that now the English "have the right to do virtually as they please—or rather, virtually as God would be pleased to have them do" (quoted in Pearce 1953, 7).

The colonizers' retaliation was brutal. Some tribes were completely destroyed; others were subdued and their members forced into slavery. Hoover (1976) notes that, from 1622 to 1629, settlers attacked and burned the crops of all the remaining Indian villages every summer (19). Despite intrigues and pacts with such Indian leaders as Powhatan, agitation against the Indians swept through the settlements and even reached overseas. A tract was published in London not only encouraging the instigation of hostilities toward the Indians but also calling for their enslavement (Lauber [1913] 1970, 118).

Similar brutalities greeted further Indian attacks, including large-scale ones in 1644 and another in 1676. The inexorable expansion of the colony and their superior military weaponry brought rapid decimation of the Indians. Through treachery and deceit, like William Tucker's poisoning of two hundred Indians invited ostensibly to celebrate a peace treaty, Virginians acted out their hostility toward the Indians. Many Indians died of disease and malnutrition, often induced by deliberate destruction of their fields and stores. Others fled inland farther and farther, always finding themselves threatened by incursions from new settlers. Those who remained in the vicinity of the colonial settlements were reduced to impoverished laborers and slaves, occupying the most degraded and subservient status on the outskirts of an increasingly heterogeneous society.

In the Massachusetts Bay colony and other New England settlements, overt hostilities were a bit later in arriving, but they were equally fierce. Puritan colonists who took seriously their mission to proselytize among the Indians were able to realize some success. Christian converts, however, were forced to form their own congregations and to live within the confines of their own towns, on which numerous restrictions were placed. No attempt was made to assimilate them within the social arena of the colony itself. These "praying Indians" endeavored to acquire the accoutrements of "civilization" while meeting all the demands that the Puritans imposed on them. Yet, as G. E. Thomas (1975) tells us, they found that despite their loyalty and proven commitment, "white racism and local white land hunger made their color alone an insurmountable barrier" (20, fn). Thomas here reveals the extreme English contempt for the native population. Their color and physiognomy made them visibly different, a fact that undoubtedly facilitated the discrimination that they experienced at the hands of the English. But physical features alone were insignificant as causal factors in the propagation of English scorn and abuse. The English had already learned patterns of inhumanity and contempt for others from their experiences with the Irish, a people physically similar to themselves.

When the violence did come, it was the logical outcome of the policies and practices of the Puritans. Thomas (1975) claims that "continued encroachment of their land became the Indians' main grievance and the prime cause of violence between Indians and whites" (11). There was a series of brutal confrontations between individuals that had a lasting effect on relationships between Indians and whites. Nash (1982) speaks of petty acts of violence and plunder by the white settlers (Chapters 2, 3, and 6). Sometimes such acts became provocations to additional violence, as in the case of Thomas Weston at Wessagusset in 1621. Weston settled in the area with a group of other whites who were by all accounts ruffians and scoundrels. When they ran out of food, they began to rob the Indians. When the Indians complained to the Plymouth officials, the latter simply took their complaints as a threat to the colony. Miles Standish was sent to deal with the situation. In March 1623, he and his men attacked, chased down, and murdered some of the complaining Indians without warning. This, says Thomas, became the standard response of the Puritans to any Indian resistance or complaint.

"No Indian dared raise his hand or even his voice against a white, even in defense of his life, family or property" (1975, 12).

One of the major historical confrontations was the Pequot War of 1637, the first of a series of wars that devastated the Indian populations and left the survivors in shambles. The fighting again was triggered by the actions of white men known to the colonists as renegades and exiles. After Captain John Stone, himself a violent man, kidnapped two Indians on the Thames River in 1634, he was killed by Pequot Indians. In 1636, another renegade white man was killed for reasons that the Puritans refused to allow the Indians to explain. Instead, John Endecott was commissioned to lead a Puritan force to avenge this death and punish the Indians. He burned down the Block Island Indian village and fields, and then, in violation of existing treaties, invaded the mainland Pequot territory. In May 1637, John Mason launched a major attack on the Pequot village at Mystic Fort, burning and murdering five or six hundred Indians, including women and children. The few survivors were reduced to slavery, and many of these were sold into Caribbean plantations. That there was an even more insidious reason for the attack on Mystic Fort was revealed in Mason's report: "Thus the Lord was pleased to smite our enemies in the hinder parts and to give us their land afor and inheritance" (quoted in Thomas 1975, 15).

Perhaps the most vicious and brutal of all the battles was Matacom's War of 1675. As in the other conflicts, the basic issue was that of the land rights of the Indians, in this case, the Wampanoag and their sachem, Matacom. The Indians' complaints about white incursions led to meetings with the Plymouth leaders, as a consequence of which the Indians were forced to give up some of their arms. After three Wampanoag Indians were sentenced to death on trumped-up charges and after a white youth killed another Indian, some of Matacom's people attacked the village of Swansea.

When the war started, it involved Indians on both sides, in part because of traditional enmity between some of the tribes. But what made it so much worse, aside from the extensive involvement of so many different Indian groups, was the fact that it led the colonists to turn against the Christian tribes who had started as their allies. Christian Indians were trusted no more than were the "heathens." The uniformity with which all Indians were perceived reflected the growing racism of English attitudes. Eventually most native Americans were forced onto restricted reservations, the very first for any of the North American indigenous peoples.

Even after cessation of the major battles of Matacom's War, the violence continued. Considerable raping and kidnapping of Indians continued, and hundreds of captured natives were sold to areas as far away as the West Indies (Lauber [1913] 1970, Nash 1982). Remnants of some tribes fled north to the French territories, where they received better treatment at the hands of a very different European ethnic group. The rest scattered throughout the northeast, never again to reestablish their traditional culture and social lifeways. Friendly Indians were confined to reservations, and bounties were offered for the scalps of "hostiles," a practice that continued throughout the first half of the eighteenth century.

Many U.S. historians have emphasized that some of the early Puritan settlers made a genuine and sincere effort to convert and civilize the Indians, and that their motivations and strivings were essentially magnanimous. They stress the role of such men as Roger Williams who held quite liberal views about the potentiality for creating a heterogeneous, multicultural society in the New World. But Berkhofer, Morgan, Nash, Pearce, and Thomas provide overwhelming evidence of an essentially self-serving, brutal, and aggressive people who devised all types of strategies for justifying their inhumanity toward the native populations, and who seemed to have few ethical or moral compunctions about their actions.

In summing up this era and the complex realities of the earliest American settlements, any reviewer of the literature is impressed by two factors. One is the degree to which religion and God were used as justifications for both the colonization activities and the barbaric maltreatment of the Indians. The second is the intriguing similarities between the conquest and colonization of Ireland and the attitudes engendered during this process and the subsequent colonization of the New World with its associated prejudices toward the Indians. Both factors require further exploration since they figure so prominently in the creation of racial ideology.

The Backing of God and Other Justifications for Conquest

From the very beginnings of English excursions into overseas exploration and trade, the rationale most frequently expressed was that the venture was sanctioned by God. John Hawkins, the earliest and most successful of the English slave traders, once led an expedition of slave ships with names such as *Jesus of Lubeck* and *John the Baptist* (Wright 1965, 9). Not only were ships commonly given names with biblical references, but virtually all also had clerics aboard to bless the expedition. Leaders of expeditions invariably referred to the Lord's blessings and special care for them, his children, in their ships' logs.

Without question, military dominance of the English and their success in ultimately destroying the Indians and their cultures were seen as God's will, no matter how brutal and insensitive the actions and no matter the innocence of the Indian victims. A high degree of self-righteousness and arrogance characterized the religious beliefs, particularly of the Puritans. Offshoots of the Protestant Reformation, they had evolved a sharply focused sense of the nature of salvation and what was needed to achieve it. Their theology relinquished the vast majority of souls on earth to be damned forever. Only the select few would ultimately enter the glorious kingdom of God. These were individuals who adhered strictly to Puritan ideals of proper behavior and laid claims to personal salvation through faith. Knowledge of Christ, including a personal relationship to him, were prerequisites. In their strict division of the world into the saved and the damned, there was no explicit, or intrinsic, requirement for tolerance and understanding of others. Nor was there any commitment to humanistic values that might have inhibited or curtailed the excessive cruelty dispensed to the damned. Instead, the Puritans developed the very convenient belief that all sinners, witches, and savages who opposed the word of God deserved the atrocities inflicted upon them. They were a fitting retribution for their opposition to the civilizing efforts of Christianity.

In the New England area, many settlers rejoiced at the extraordinary reduction of the Indian population from epidemic diseases. John Winthrop, who led the colony in the 1630s, wrote that the smallpox epidemic of 1617 was God's way of "thinning out" the Indian population "to make room for the Puritans." Later, he recorded that the Indians "are neere all dead of the small Poxe, so the Lord hathe cleared our title to what we possess" (quoted in Nash 1972, 136).

According to Louis B. Wright (1965), it was the preachers of England who "induced in public consciousness a sense of mission, a feeling often not put into words but nonetheless strong, that Englishmen had a destiny overseas" (151). These preachers, both Anglican and Puritan, had a powerful influence on the colonization process. From their pulpits and in their publications, they exhorted the public to become involved in the colonization of the New World, a region seen as a new Canaan. And the commercial companies and promoters of colonization encouraged the clergy to advertise their schemes.

The English clergy themselves were motivated by a number of considerations, all of which were highly publicized at the time. Chief among these was their desire to thwart the further spread of Catholicism. The success of Spanish proselytizing in the New World was well known; and nothing irked the Protestants so much as the idea of Spain winning the battle for new souls. Economic and political competition with the Spanish intensified these feelings of religious antagonism. The defeat of the Spanish Armada had made the planting of English colonies all the more pressing.

Another important reason for ministerial preachments had to do with the increasingly large numbers of the poor and unemployed who roamed the streets and byways of English cities. Several lines of reasoning led clergymen to advocate the exportation of these "vagabonds" to the new colonies. As educated men, they concluded that England was facing a problem of overpopulation, and there was a need to do something about this demographic situation. Moreover, unemployment was acute in many areas, and existing charitable institutions were hard pressed to provide sufficient services to an expanding impoverished class. The clergy saw colonization as a way of siphoning off an excess of able-bodied workers and putting them to useful labor in the plantations overseas.

Exhortations to send the poor and unemployed off to the colonies should be understood within a wider framework of English, and specifically, Puritan beliefs. Seventeenth-century preachers, we are told, "looked upon idleness and consequent poverty as moral iniquities" (Wright 1965, 152). Those virtues most valued in the Puritan life-style were work, sobriety, thrift, diligence, and honesty. An idle or lazy person would be lacking in all of these traits. Thus, poverty, immorality, and sloth were bound together in the Puritan mind as evils that had to be overcome, if necessary by forced labor. Hoover claims that the Puritans created a new class of evil people, the poor who were seen as "being wicked and outside the bonds of society" (1976, 31). So colonization would not only relieve the poverty at home, but, by putting sinful, idle men and women to work, it would also restore them to the true and proper values of religion and improve their characters.

Finally, Wright (1965) argues that many English clergymen, who "were almost unanimous in supporting colonization in America," (86) were motivated by a sincere desire to save the souls of the heathens of America. They were convinced, and convinced others, that God had commanded them to go forth and preach the gospel. There was no better setting in which to do this than among the indigenes of newly discovered lands. However, this missionary zeal peaked in the early stages of settlement, as we have seen. The Puritans and their church leaders soon concluded that if the savages could not be saved from themselves, their extermination would be a worthy enterprise in the sight of the Lord. This notion of a God-given right to mistreat others, especially for private gain, runs through much of Western culture, and after the emergence of capitalism it became especially acute in North America.

When they were not invoking God's blessings or permission for their mistreatment of the Indians, the colonizers had other rational and pragmatic arguments of particular use for co-opting native lands. One was that the Indians did not make proper use of the land "and thus could be justly deprived of it by the more enterprising English" (Canny 1973, 596). Such an argument, we have seen, was invoked to force the Irish off their lands. A more pervasive argument was the ancient one of the right of conquest. This was often linked to the religious position and rationalized that since God had chosen the English to find these new shores, he must have wanted them to possess such bountiful land. Conquest was thus God's ordained plan; it was he who had led them thence. The Puritans as God's "chosen people" were responsible merely for carrying out his will.

Though God's supposed will should have been enough, an even more secular and philosophical argument was also proposed, one that derived from some knowledge of the codes of laws of the ancients. John Winthrop expressed this in his reasoning on the Englishman's rights to land. There are, he declared, two types of rights that God has given mankind: natural rights and civil rights. Natural rights were held by all men including those who lived in a state of nature, holding land and resources in common. But when some men began to enclose parcels of land and hold them separate from others, to have a settled habitation on it, and to use domesticated cattle to improve the land, then they acquired civil rights to the land. Since the Indians had not done these things, they gained no civil rights but retained only natural ones. And, since clearly the English had developed superior modes of utilizing land, they enjoyed lawful civil rights that inevitably took precedence over natural rights. Under this argument, superior "civilized" people had legitimate cause to seize land, as long as they left sufficient areas for the "uncivilized" to exercise their natural rights (Thomas 1975).

Partly because of the myths of origin that Americans created for themselves, too few of us have sufficiently noted the cruel and barbaric treatment that the English imposed on the Indians, although the evidence, largely from the pens of the colonists themselves, is overwhelming. The incidents described above—in no way exceptional—attest to extreme and callous brutality and to a policy of treachery and deceit that seems hardly consonant with the English history of concern for the rights of mankind, and even less with England's image of itself as the most "civilized" of the European nations.[4]

Some historians have labored hard to explain this seeming paradox. Although we might accept Nash's psychologically oriented argument that the dehumanization of the Indian was "one means of justifying one's own inhumanity" (1972, 137), this is a somewhat circular or teleological explication that does not reveal much as to underlying causes. Nicholas P. Canny's (1973) explanation follows in a similar vein and is very close to that of Winthrop Jordan (1968). Both refer to the insecurities and uncertainties of the English, and of their need to know who they were in a rapidly changing society and in a setting in which they constantly felt threatened. More evident than such psychological needs, however, were the drives to achieve power and control, to establish and maintain political, economic, and social dominance, all of which arose from an English sense of moral and cultural superiority. The Indians, said Morgan, "presented a challenge ... to their image of themselves, to their self-esteem, to their conviction of their own superiority over foreigners, and especially over barbarous foreigners like the Irish and the Indians" (1975, 89).

Christian values regarding humane behavior (the Sermon on the Mount, the Golden Rule, the Ten Commandments) had little impact on the minds, the morals, and the consciences of the settlers. Jordan gives a brief analysis of the kind of Christianity that developed among the English after the Protestant Reformation. He shows that it was "altered in the direction of Biblicism, personal piety, individual judgment, and more intense self-scrutiny and internalized control" (1968, 40). The English came to evaluate and judge themselves according to their own individual interpretations of the scriptures. The older institutional and external constraints of Catholicism were replaced with a less certain and more nebulous sense of personal responsibility and control.

Such inner controls, however, were virtually antithetical to the spirits of adventurism and greed for wealth that characterized the English in the seventeenth century and later. English colonists were caught up in a dilemma that might have evoked massive ambivalence, leading to a catatonic inability to take action. Instead, or perhaps because of this, too many of them in the New World opted for the path of moral and ethical duplicity, hypocrisy, and the priority of aggrandizing wealth at no matter what cost. A self-serving moral order had replaced the constraints once exercised by the institutions of family, kinship, class, community, and church. It was not merely self-control that the new settlers sought, it was control over others and over potentially advantageous situations and resources. Jordan's (1968) discussion of an age driven by the twin spirits of adventure and of control euphemistically glosses over this reality. But Morgan's (1975) description of the ruthless, cold-hearted, and avaricious men who led or participated in the Virginia colony leaves us little room for doubt.

The New Savages

The seemingly gratuitous violence and brutality of the English settlers are, in fact, incomprehensible without reference to our second factor, which reaches beyond religion. This is the wider historical context of the five hundred years of conflict with the Irish and the patterns of violent interaction that it had generated. David B. Quinn, Nicholas Canny, Leonard Liggio, Gary Nash, and other historians have emphasized the significant parallels between the English attempt to conquer and colonize Ireland and their subsequent expansion, exploration, conquests, and colonization of North America and the Caribbean.[5] What appears obvious is that the motivations, objectives, and rationalizations of individuals, many of whom were involved in both Irish and American colonial enterprises, were essentially the same. The one generated interest in the other; as Quinn (1966) suggests, "Ireland in a real sense turned English minds toward America" (106). Ireland also provided the standard of comparison by which other foreign societies and cultures would be judged.

The identity of a large number of individuals involved in both the Irish conquests and the colonization of the New World would suggest similarities of purpose and methods even if there were no written records of such. As Liggio (1976) notes, "Many with experiences in Ireland had been active in the plans for the colonies in America and their experience with the natives of Ireland was an important part of the heritage which they transferred to the treatment of the natives of America." He adds that "more than forty members of the Virginia Company had an interest in Irish conquests and the colonization of Englishmen in Ireland" (28). Among the names most familiar to Americans are those of Sir Walter Raleigh, Lord de la Warre, John Cabot, Humphrey Gilbert, Sir Richard Grenville, Lord George Carew, and Sir Francis Drake.[6]

Patrick O'Farrell (1971) tells us that the English early established a habit of violence in the attempted settlement of Irish affairs (6). Moreover, the sense of a religious mission, the rightness of their cause as justification for their violence, was also a part of the ideology driving the Irish conquest. The English takeover of lands from the Irish and the Indians followed much the same methodologies, strategies, and consequences. Forced removal of those who resisted, justification of their removal in the name of conquest, the presumed "legal" rights of cultivators over nomads, and religious motivations characterized English encounters with both peoples. Howard Mumford Jones (1942) points out that "the doctrine that the only good Indian is a dead Indian first took shape in the belief that the only good Irishman is a dead Irishman" (454). Lord Essex's slaughter of the entire population of Rathlin Island in 1574, about six hundred people, had its parallels in the New World, for example, in the killing of the inhabitants of Mystic Fort in 1637. The rationales for such brutality were virtually the same. Canny (1973) quotes a letter from Barkley about Essex's final solution, "how godly a dede it is to overthrowe so wicked a race the world may judge: for my part I thinke there canot be a greater sacryfice to God" (581). Finally, the belief that the Indians were incapable of civilization and therefore merited no attempt at redemption, which took rapid root after the hostilities at Chesapeake Bay in 1622, stems directly from the Irish experience, especially the ruthless developments of the late sixteenth and early seventeenth centuries.

Many factors thus influenced English perceptions and reactions to the Indians. English interaction with the Irish, guided by their desire for expansion, greed for land, and an extreme ethnocentric view of the superiority of English laws, customs, and religion, had generated in their cultural perspectives a clearly focused view of savagery. By the end of the sixteenth century, O'Farrell tells us "the English image of the Irishman was that of a savage" (1971, 25). And the Indians of the Americas, particularly as their very presence became an impediment to similar English aspirations, could be perceived as being very much like the "wild Irish." Such a transference of symbolic references was probably inevitable, in part because, to the English, there were some deeply disturbing similarities.

Both the Irish and the Indians seemed to lack shame in that they went about naked with little care as to the visibility of even their "most private parts." Both were polygynous, and the combination of nudity and plural marriages was interpreted as stemming from sexual immorality. Their way of life was viewed as disorderly, without government or laws, and most important of all, with no concept of private property. They were perceived as nomadic peoples who did not appear to make use of the bountiful land that God had given to them. Additionally, they both resisted, often ferociously, the attempts on the part of the English to civilize them. What was thought to be their obsessive love of freedom, carefree life-styles, and brutish customs and habits were galling to the civilized English. Perhaps the worst blemish of all was their refusal to accept the civilizing blessings of Christianity, preferring instead to worship idols, spirits, and devils. Such inability to grasp the saving grace of the only true religion was inexplicable to the English mind.

There was one feature, shared by both the Irish and the Indians, that perhaps generated the greatest frustration for the settlers. For some strange and powerful reason, English people who were captured by the Indians, like those who in early years had been seduced into the ways of the wild Irish, tended to find the life-styles of these savages irresistibly attractive. Captured whites, given the opportunity to escape, time and time again opted to stay with their Indian hosts and families rather than to return to civilization.[7] After Queen Ann's War of the early eighteenth century in which six hundred white women and children had been captured, less than 30 percent ever returned to the white community. Most refused to be repatriated, either by staying with the Indians or by going over to the French.

The curious attraction of Indian life raised a question, still posed later in the eighteenth century. Quoted by Dwight Hoover (1976), it went, "Why, given the choice, did the converted Indian always revert to savage ways, while the converted white, given the taste of savagery, so seldom wanted to return to civilized society?" (43).[8] For many, there was an answer that stirred fear in their hearts; the Indians, like the Irish, were in league with Satan in the quest for human souls (Pearce 1953). Thus it was that an emergent negative and fearful image of the savage in North America was solidified among the English very soon after the first settlements.

Robert F. Berkhofer, Jr. (1978) has argued very skillfully that "the Indian" is an invention of white men. In literature, art, science, and philosophy, every variation of "the Indian," whether ignoble, noble, or degraded, was contrived in the minds of European settlers and continues to influence the way we think about native Americans. I have supplemented this analysis by showing that what facilitated this homogenization of such diverse peoples into a negative construct in white minds was the preexistence of a powerful cultural image of the "savage." English culture may have been more relentless in the preservation and perpetuation of this image than were the cultures of other European colonizers, for reasons which have to do in large part with prior experiences attempting to conquer Ireland.

Many strands of English life and thought converged in the seventeenth century. English attitudes and beliefs about the nature of savagery provide us with our earliest glimpse of the elementary features of a worldview soon to be structured around the term "race." The conclusion that some populations were too savage to ever undergo redemption or conversion would become the standard attitude. The ready relegation of both Irish and Indians to the lowest status of human beings underscores the many parallels. It most pointedly reveals the impact of an inegalitarian philosophy that had survived the Middle Ages and the Renaissance, before its reemergence as a major ingredient in the elaboration of the ideology of race.

Given the circumstances, one has to wonder about the English consciousness of who they were and about the substantiveness of their design for the future of the American colonies. The English could not tolerate the diversity manifested in Irish culture on the other side of the Atlantic. The growing intolerance in the Puritan movement—with its base in Calvinist doctrines that allocated privilege, profits, and saintly status only to the pious few and condemned to damnation the vast majority of virtually all other human groups—did not augur well for the plural society that some had envisioned. Surely there was no reason in the colonies to assume that conversion of the Indians, another "savage" people, would or could result in their happy assimilation into English life and society. Whether Anglican, Puritan, or Catholic, the English kept themselves apart for the promotion and protection of what they perceived as their own ethnic interests and superiority.

Some of the rudimentary elements in the synthesis of the idea of race thus appeared early in the American experience. They were transferred to the New World in the minds and hearts of the English, and were further strengthened, fertilized, and given vastly expanded meaning in the context of English interaction with the native peoples of North America. It was no longer a question of just the one group of savages, the "wild Irish"; now there was emerging in English minds a generic, ever more monolithic, category comprised of many groups. The existence of this category not only buttressed the English people's sense of their own identity as a member of a superior nation, but its contrasting features provided them a measure of their own worth. It further led them to construct social attitudes and policies that would become institutionalized as part of a broader worldview.

The Puritans were a proselytizing people more than most Christian groups. Their missionizing activities, however, never led them to assimilate converted natives into their communities. One can perhaps explain the introspective and defensive Puritan reactions in part because of the stresses and tensions of their lives both in England and after transplantation into the New World. They were a people beleaguered, perhaps not only by their own self-doubt, but also by external factors already generating tremendous social change over which they had little control.

This was a period when, as we have seen, the old social order was giving way to new social forms; an era of growing trade and urbanization, of the disintegration of older institutions, of the decline of the church and its influence, especially in the frontier areas, and, most particularly, of the breakdown of older class structures. Many of the "vagabonds" and "masterless men" of England came (or were brought involuntarily) to the Americas in search of adventure and fortunes, and the Puritans had a difficult task keeping these men, who tended to wander to the frontiers, within the bonds of civil society. For many, then, Puritanism provided a new moral universe and a social doctrine that would help to reestablish an orderly world in which the religious community would monitor and discipline the more extremes of individual behavior. Through hard work, piety, self-restraint, service, and obedience, people could achieve salvation as well as worldly success.

As they tried to reestablish self-restraint and discipline, they recoiled from the overwhelming temptations of their external world. But the turning inward and the control, the dogmatic assertions of righteousness and the attendant intolerance, bigotry, and fear of the unknown, which led to the witchcraft trials of the 1690s, for example, were somehow incompatible with the simultaneous thrust for individualism, adventure, and independence of action that seemed required in the colonial situation. Moderation and uncurtailed greed are fundamentally opposite qualities of temperament and training. The older, more pristine Puritan values died rapidly as the colonists began to justify their overweening avarice under the guise of furthering the scheme and purposes of a God who favored only them.

Early colonial society in Virginia lacked the self-imposed moral or religious controls of the Puritans. It was a motley crew composed of too many men who were unwilling to work and who lived by begging, stealing, and extorting food from the Indians. The colonists had to enact harsh laws merely to force settlers to contribute to their own survival (Morgan 1975). They were a brawling, rough, aggressive lot, given to strong drink, gambling, and fighting among themselves. They were vicious, brutal, and often sadistic to one another, and especially to their servants. But they were also Englishmen who cherished their freedom, learned to seek profits in the growth of tobacco, and soon found themselves in even greater demand for labor.

It was into this evolving context that the first Africans were introduced a little over a decade after the settlement of Jamestown. Fifty years later, the Africans and their descendants were being submerged into a form of servitude that had hitherto never existed in the Old World. The slavery that the English colonists instituted in North America particularly was very different in certain basic features from that which the Spanish and Portuguese had inherited and transmitted to those areas of the New World that came under their control. English slavery was intimately connected with their preexisting conceptions of human differences, of property rights, and with many other aspects of English culture and history that we have just seen. Slavery provided the foundation for the magnification of human differences that they came to express as "race." It is to this story of the coming of the Africans and their enslavement that we next turn.

Notes

1. John Cabot (Giovanni Caboto), an Italian adventurer, navigator, and explorer, was originally employed by Venetian merchants, but moved his family to London about 1484. After Columbus's success, he was employed by the English king Henry VII to explore new territories, and he took possession of what is believed to have been Newfoundland in 1497. His son Sebastian was a cartographer to Henry VIII and later received several commissions in the Spanish navy, subsequently making a number of voyages of exploration for Spain. He thought of himself as an Englishman, however, and upon returning to England he accepted a naval post under Edward VI. He spent the rest of his life in England as governor of the Merchant Adventurers, during which time he helped to establish trade between England and Russia.

2. According to Olive Dickason (1979) all American Indians shared a common reaction to Europeans. They welcomed them and sought by means of diplomacy to make accommodations with them (182).

3. Columbus often wrote quite positively about the Indians, although on his first landing, he captured a number by force and speculated on their value as slaves.

4. I recognize that it is somewhat of an illusion to equate "civilization" with humane behavior and attitudes. One only has to look at modern warfare and its capacity to kill tens of thousands of people in a single attack, and brutally maim hundreds of thousands more, and at the growth of techniques of torture (most of which no "primitive" society would ever imagine) to realize that there are unmistakable parallels between the development of civilization and humankind's continuing inhumanity to others of our species. Nevertheless, it is a popular belief that still informs the behavior of a great many people in the West that, as civilized people, we exhibit a level of humane concern for others that is not apparent in those societies who lack our Judeo-Christian values. What is particularly disquieting about all this is that there are millions of ordinary Americans who subscribe deeply to these values, but they tend to elect as their leaders men and women who can be ruthless, callous, and indifferent to human suffering and for whom such verbalized values are merely techniques of politics.

5. See also the works of Howard Mumford Jones (1964 and 1942). Nicholas Canny's article (1973) contains a very useful short summary.

6. The common class interests of these men and others are illuminated by the kinship links between them. Gilbert was a half-brother of Walter Raleigh. Both were cousins of the Carews and the Grenvilles. Some of them and their

immediate ancestors had contacts and investments with Italian merchants and in the sugar plantations of the eastern Mediterranean. They all shared the vision of overseas colonies with large plantations on cheap land, worked by cheap native labor. Liggio (1976) notes that when they were frustrated in their attempts to colonize Ireland, they turned their attention to America (13). Gilbert, Raleigh, and Grenville took part in the suppression of the Munster rebellion, 1579–1583, and Gilbert particularly, who was noted for his use of massacre as a military strategem, was among the first to articulate the policy of extermination of native peoples in both Ireland and America.

7. In most Indian cultures, warfare had a different cultural meaning. It was not fought with the primary purpose of killing as many of the "enemies" as possible. In many so-called primitive tribal societies around the world, wars were usually terminated when a warrior was killed, a number of men were hurt, the day came to an end without much bloodshed, or the men simply tired of the fighting. Captives taken in wars were more likely to be adopted into their captors' families than tortured and killed, a fact that Hollywood Wild West moviemakers seemed to have rarely learned.

8. Hector St. Jean Crevecoeur, a Frenchman who lived for many years in the colonies, offered an interesting and insightful answer to this query. "There must be in their (Indian) social bond, something singularly captivating, and far superior to anything to be boasted of among us; for thousands of Europeans are Indians, and we have no examples of even one of those Aborigines having from choice become Europeans" (quoted in Nash 1982, 279–280).

5

The Arrival of Africans and Their Decline into Slavery

T HERE WERE AFRICANS and men of mixed European and African ancestry on the ships that came with Columbus and on many of the ships of later conquistadors, merchants, pirates, and immigrants. Many were descendants of the Africans brought back to Portugal and Spain after trading forays along the western coast of Africa in the midfifteenth century. Others descended from the Almoravid invaders of the eleventh century and from later immigrants. Most had been baptized and were accepted as part of the Christian community. There may have been a few who were African-born, men with sailing expertise who were taken aboard ship when Columbus stopped to rest and refuel at Ceuta on the coast of West Africa. It is said that Pedro Alonzo Niño, the pilot of one of Columbus's ships, was a Negro. According to J. H. Franklin and A. A. Moss, Jr.,

Thirty Negroes, including Nuflo de Olano, were with Balboa when he discovered the Pacific Ocean. Cortes carried blacks with him into Mexico, and one of them planted and harvested the first wheat crop in the New World. Two accompanied Velas in 1520. When Alvarado went to Quito, he carried two hundred with him. They were with Pizarro on his Peruvian expedition and carried him to the Cathedral after he was murdered. The Africans in the expeditions of Almagro and Valdivia saved their Spanish masters from the Indians in 1525.

... They were with Alarcón and Coronado in the Conquest of New Mexico. They accompanied Narváez on his expedition of 1527 and were with Cabeza de Vaca in the exploration of the southwestern part of the present United States. One of the outstanding Negro explorers was Estevanico, who opened up New Mexico and Arizona ... and prepared the way for the conquest of the Southwest by the Spaniards.

Africans were with the French in their explorations of the New World. ... When the great conquest of the Mississippi Valley was undertaken by the French in the seventeenth century, Negroes constituted a substantial portion of the pioneers who settled in the region. Around 1790, Jean Baptiste Point du Sable, a French-speaking black, erected the first building in a place that came to be known as Chicago (1988, 30–31).[1]

The documentation of the number of people who were of African ancestry in the exploration of New World territories represents a major departure from the usual image of "the discoverers" of the Americas conveyed in the public media and in traditional educational institutions. But this should be understood and explicated in the light of the next sentence in Franklin and Moss's work: "Negroes did not accompany the English on their explorations in the New World" (1988, 31).

This is a point of critical significance, particularly when we look at the manner in which history has been written by English-speaking peoples. It is also at the heart of major historical debates over the origins of American slavery and over differences in the "racial" attitudes and behaviors between the Europeans who settled in North America and those of Latin America. Of the major European colonizing nations, only the English had not had substantial experience with people of color prior to settlement in the New World. Although the English public had heard about Africans, there were very few encounters with black persons before the midseventeenth century.[2] The Portuguese had established trading relationships with West Africans as early as the 1440s, and there had been Africans in Spain and Portugal at least three centuries earlier, but the English did not begin to interact directly with Africans until well over a hundred years later.[3]

Like other Europeans, they went to Africa primarily as traders and engaged in business transactions with native leaders or their representatives. During the reign of Elizabeth I (1558–1603), when the English turned increasing attention to overseas enterprises, a few men became involved in the slave trade long before the institution of slavery was actually established in North America. John Hawkins organized three raids into Africa for slaves. On one occasion alone he stole over three hundred Africans. Like John Cabot and Sir Francis Drake, he also pirated Spanish ships carrying slaves. Before the English established their own trading connections, this was a favored source of slave merchandise. Such activities must have encouraged a callous indifference to the slaves as human beings and increased the perception of the Africans as mere cargo, like cattle, horses, and pigs. The attitudes toward Africans and the treatment of them by slave traders were probably shared among all nationalities and mirrored the hard-hearted nature of the enterprise.

Francis Drake met Africans in a somewhat different context, as we have seen, when he allied with the Cimarrons against their former Spanish masters. Throughout Central and South America, escaped slaves became known as fierce fighters, and in the competition between the various European states for colonial possessions, these men and women would lend their support to any group that promised them their freedom. Drake was thus in a position to have a positive image of some Africans as allies and potential confederates in settling the New World.

Aside from these experiences, knowledge of which filtered into communities both in Europe and the Americas, English people had other, quite vague, impressions of Africans. Negative images undoubtedly predominated; Englishmen rarely had positive or sympathetic attitudes toward those who were not English. Some early seventeenth-century writers made comparisons between the Africans and the Irish (Quinn 1966, 26–27). Throughout the rest of the century there was a general sense that the Irish, the Africans, and the Indians were all more or less savages.

Winthrop Jordan (1968) made the point that when the English did begin to interact with Africans in overseas trade, it was not within a context "which prejudged the Negro as a slave" (4). They were just another type of humankind, albeit black and with curious languages, religious beliefs, and other cultural features. Some reports show that the natives were initially judged to be both civil and hospitable; the earliest records do not suggest the more virulent image of savagery that was to come much later.

On the one hand, those advocates of colonization who held a utopian view of the potential New World colonies, where different kinds of people lived together in peace and harmony, must undoubtedly have had a benign attitude toward the Africans and the Indians, without much prejudgment as to their potential for civilized behavior. Under the first colonization schemes of Walter Raleigh and Humphrey Gilbert, for example, the first English colony (Roanoke) in North America was to be populated with Indians and Africans freed from the Spanish. On the other hand, there was clear ethnocentric bias against the habits, dress (or lack of), customs, and beliefs of the Africans, and subjective negative responses to their physiognomy. Yet the first English traders, like their Latin predecessors, evinced unmistakable cognizance that they were dealing with people from well-organized sociopolitical systems, people who were sophisticated and intelligent.

In the broader historical context of over one hundred years of enslavement of Indians and Africans by the Portuguese and Spanish, it was reasonable to expect that the English would show little reluctance to

ultimately accept Africans as slaves. Other Europe?
used them, and they were known as productive wc
glish did enter the commerce, their North Americ
onies not only became major importers of Afri/
traders eventually dominated the slave trade u:
1807.

The First Africans

The first Africans were introduced into the North American English
colony at Jamestown in 1619. They were part of a "cargo" of people sold
from a Dutch ship that had been trading along the Virginia coast. The
little Jamestown colony thus found itself the beneficiary of a new set of
laborers for which its settlers had had no previous preparation or experience. In the New England colonies, a few African slaves were introduced as early as 1633; they were in Connecticut by 1639 and in New
Haven by 1644. In none of these areas were their numbers very large,
and there is little information or agreement on their precise status.
Many historians now agree that the Africans were fitted into already existing roles as servants serving the normal period of indenture, four to
seven years. The term "slave" was rarely used for them during those
first decades. At the same time, historians have noted that varying degrees of servitude were recognized by the English, although the distinctions between them were not very precise.[4]

For the rest of that century, a small but steady stream of Africans
were brought into the mainland colonies, particularly after the development of the tobacco industry. In 1670 Virginia still relied for most of its
laborers and servants on imports from England. Sugar plantations requiring massive labor had developed in the West Indian islands after
about 1640, and the number of Africans imported there increased rapidly from midcentury on. The French, the Spanish, the Dutch, and the
English were busily establishing plantations in the Caribbean Islands,
while competing and fighting among themselves. Those who were successful came to rely on African slave labor.

On mainland North America, beginning in the midseventeenth century, major social and economic transformations began to take place
that eventually obliterated the uncertain status of Africans and their
descendants. Through the passage of various laws, Negroes, as they
were called, were separated out from other servants and gradually reduced to the status of permanent hereditary slavery. A date frequently
noted by historians to mark the first official recognition of permanent
slave status in law is 1661, when the Virginia assembly passed an act

.ng a servant who ran away with a Negro responsible for serving the
.e of the Negro slave (Morgan 1975, 311). But North American slav-
ry was not the result of a single law or even sets of laws, but numerous
acts, decisions, and habits that over time became codified into the legal
framework of colonial society.

These changes continued into the early eighteenth century and, in
the process, produced a system of bondage that was unique in human
history. Its primary distinctiveness rested on the fact that such slavery
was reserved exclusively for black Africans and their descendants. This
was a critical step in the evolution of the social construction of race. In
the next section we will look a bit more intensively at this process.

The Descent into Racial Slavery

There is a tradition in U.S. history that rightly connects race and racism
with slavery and thus focuses upon the relationship of the two peoples
who were most entangled in that institution, Africans and Europeans.
The inerrancy of the historical linkage between slavery and racism in
North America has to be recognized, although, as we shall see later,
there is no intrinsic relationship between the two. Nevertheless, much
of the historiography of the twentieth century has centered on the issue
of which came first, racism or slavery.

One school of thought has argued that it was the slave condition itself, especially the debased status of the slave, combined with the physical differences in the population of masters and slaves, that generated
the negative attitudes of racism and subsequent social discrimination.
Alexis de Tocqueville ([1831] 1945), one of the earliest external chroni-
clers of the American experience, observed in the 1830s that slavery
had given birth to what he saw as "immovable" prejudice against the
Negro (359).[5] He was followed in this view by most historians of the
slave period.[6] The implication of this position, not always apparent to
scholars, was that without slavery race and racism might not have occurred. Another school of thought holds that a kind of racial antagonism was present from the beginning of English contact with Africans.
And the institutionalization of racial discrimination, including the separation of blacks and whites both spatially and socially, preceded the establishment of slavery. The arguments on both sides are compelling,
and they can be illustrated by the works of several scholars.

In the late 1950s, Carl Degler (1959–1960) raised the question of
causal priorities again and proceeded to suggest evidence that, in all of
the English colonies, "discrimination against the Negro preceded the
evolution of a slave status and by that fact helped to shape the form that

institution would assume" (62). The institution of slavery, he argued, came to mirror the discrimination that had occurred from the first contact with Africans on American soil, and "in so doing, perpetuated it" (66). Likewise, Arnold Sio (1964–1965) argued that "discrimination against the Negro occurred before the slave status was fully defined and before Negro labor became pivotal to the economic system" (304).

More recently, Winthrop Jordan (1968, 4–20) offered an expanded version of this view. He attempted to explain or rationalize English attitudes and behavior toward Africans by suggesting that the very blackness of Negroes was, on first contact, sufficiently traumatic to ensure the development of bias toward them. Their skin color apparently rarely went unnoticed, and he feels that the frequent comments on this characteristic were a measure of the impresssion that it made on the English. On this feature alone, Africans contrasted strikingly with the English, who were one of the lightest-skinned peoples of Europe. He speculated that the "powerful impact which the Negro's color made upon Englishmen must have been partly owing to suddenness of contact" (1968, 6). He added that the English experience with Africans was "markedly different from that of the Spanish and Portuguese who for centuries had been in close contact with North Africa and had actually been invaded and subjected by people both darker and more highly civilized than themselves" (6).

Jordan saw as the basis of English hostility that the concept of blackness in the English language conveyed predominantly negative images. In this respect, the English language and culture helped to predispose its carriers toward prejudice against Africans. On the one hand, black meant filthy, evil, vile, sinister, ugly, fearful, and deadly. It was the color of mourning, "an emotionally partisan color, the handmaid and symbol of baseness and evil, a sign of danger and repulsion" (Jordan 1968, 7). White, on the other hand, was the color of beauty, virtue, purity, goodness, wonder, and perfection. It is Jordan's belief that these contrasting elements in the meaning of these color terms insinuated their way, perhaps subliminally, into English thought and became incipient molders of the English attitude toward and evaluation of the Africans.

Degler (1959–1960) agreed with Jordan that the English had a cultural predisposition, derived from their values about the color black, toward a negative view of African people. He argued, "From the 1630's up until slavery clearly appeared in the statutes in the 1660's, the Negroes were being set apart and discriminated against as compared with the treatment accorded Englishmen, whether servants or free" (53). Even though the term "slave" was rarely used, the actual practice, according a distinct and lower status to Negroes, was already in place. For some Negroes, he continued, the reality of their servitude already amounted to slavery in that they served for life.

These authors cited examples of white men who were whipped or penalized in some other way for consorting with Negroes, or "lying with a negro"; or they received differential sentences for the same crimes. They noted that Virginia and Maryland quite early passed laws that prohibited Negroes from bearing arms, imposed separate punishments for Negro and white servants, required Negro and Indian women to work in the fields, and taxed Negroes separately. There is evidence that lifetime permanent servitude was established for some Negroes and their offspring even before the existence of laws permitting it. And they account for the frequent incidences of higher prices paid for Negroes over white servants as evidence of the practice of keeping blacks in servitude for life. Thus it was not the economic need for slaves alone that explains the inferior social status accorded to Negroes even before slavery was instituted.

Other historians have argued that the position of the first Africans in North America was never so clear; it was in fact somewhat ambiguous. There is not sufficient evidence in the available sources to declare for certain that all Africans were from the beginning kept separate and apart from the white population. Oscar and Mary Handlin (1972), among prominent historians, have presented considerable evidence and logical arguments for the position that the first Africans were not slaves. "Slavery," they said, "had no meaning in law; at most it was a popular description of a low form of service" (26). They point out that Africans were brought into a society in which large numbers of people were unfree to some degree, so that the lack of freedom of Africans was not at all unusual.

We have already seen that among the many indentured servants, some of whom were the "wild Irish," were other kinds of bonded labor and some laborers who were permanent. Indian slavery had commenced within a few years of the early settlements and the first conflicts with the pilgrims, and many people were held for life. Although their numbers were not large, slaves were found throughout the early colonies. That they were heathens and were conquered in a just war was put forth as vindication for such treatment. Because of variations in the condition of bonded servants of European background and variations in the treatment of Indians, there were many degrees of servitude. Not only immigrant servants, bound to a stated number of years of service, but convicts, vagabonds, orphans, illegitimate children of all "races,"

and debtors were frequently bought and sold and even referred to occasionally as "slaves."[7]

George Fredrickson (1971, 1981) believes that Jordan's argument on
the psychological reaction of the English to the blackness of the Africans is too speculative and without much strong evidence.[8] He finds little to suggest that the first Africans were treated any differently from
other servants. All were subjected to the same discipline and general
conditions of life. The fact that some blacks gained their freedom, acquired property, and suffered little or no discrimination is indicative
that they were not set apart from all others in their station until the
1690s. Heathenism and captivity, Fredrickson claimed, made people
enslavable, not the pigment of their skin (1981, 73). If this was the case,
it did not last long.

Edmund Morgan (1975) agrees that the initial status of blacks was not
permanently fixed at the lowest social level. They seemed to suffer no
greater debilities than white servants or freed whites. After their terms
of service, many blacks gained their freedom, and apparently had no difficulty in acquiring property or even voting. Some became landowners
or entrepreneurs and commanded the respect of whites because of their
success. They engaged in trading and other commercial activities and
had business dealings equally with whites. Some black men of substance even acquired slaves of their own. Most were able to experience
the same degree of civil rights, with access to the courts and police protection, as did Europeans (154–157).

Early references to blacks reveal little clear evidence of general or
widespread social antipathy on account of their color. Some records
show a fairly high incidence of cooperation among black and white servants and unified resistance to harsh masters. They sometimes escaped
from bondage together, or collaborated in insurrections, especially in
the English Caribbean Islands. Both Liggio (1976) and Morgan (1975)
suggested that in the 1660s and 1670s the ruling classes in the island
plantations were more afraid of a general uprising of servile classes and
landless poor than of any threat presented by the Negroes per se. Intermarriage between black and white servants was not unusual and was
apparently accepted, perhaps with some social disapproval. Laws enacted against them may have had other motivations than antipathy toward physical differences (Fredrickson 1971, Nash 1982). The
disagreement over the status of blacks before the impact of slave laws,
certainly before 1660, is not easily resolved on the basis of available evidence.

Jordan's (1968) own final analysis obviates the question of causal primacy. "Rather than slavery causing 'prejudice,' or vice versa," he avers,

"they seem rather to have generated each other. Both were ... twin aspects of a general debasement of the Negro. Slavery and 'prejudice' may have been equally cause and effect, continuously reacting upon each other, dynamically joining hands to hustle the Negro down the road to complete degradation" (80). There is probably unerring accuracy in this.

The customs and practices of imposing permanent slavery on Negroes thus only gradually developed. In Virginia, in the critical years between 1660 and 1700, a number of statutes and regulations were passed restricting some of the rights of blacks, establishing servitude for life, limiting their rights to bear arms and to hold certain property, and providing penalties for interracial marriage or fornication. Both Virginia and Maryland systematically and step-by-step enclosed blacks, both bond servants and free Negroes, in a tightening vise of legal restrictions, the most telling of which were the prohibitions against private manumissions during the 1690s. North and South Carolina followed suit in the early decades of the eighteenth century. By 1723 the right to vote was ultimately denied to all Negroes in the southern colonies, free as well as slave.

Little is known about the legal treatment and social position of blacks in New England during the early decades of their presence. Except that there were both bonded servants (slaves) and free blacks, there were few documented laws or statutes that differentially affected them. Their skin color had seemingly little effect on opportunities to obtain training and employment, rights to police protection, access to courts and to justice, and to some level of participation in the political system.

Yet in the 1650s, some New England colonies enacted laws prohibiting Indians and Negroes from serving in the militia. This was the earliest of a number of legal restrictions affecting blacks and Indians alike. In the 1680s there came more regulations of a confining nature applying to Indians, Negroes, mulattoes, servants, and apprentices. The equivalence of these categories may be misleading, for the laws and statutes may have been differentially applied. Nevertheless, they do seem to reflect a perception of a common identity among these categories and a clear intent to exclude these groups from the privileges and responsibilities enjoyed by Europeans.

The major restrictions on Negroes in all of the colonies had fully emerged in the first decades of the eighteenth century, when manumission was made more difficult or impossible, curfews were imposed on these same classes of persons, and property and marriage regulations operated to separate Negro slaves from free persons and other servants. Although there were far fewer slaves in New England, and the economic value and need for slavery in this region have been questioned, every colony passed laws defining "the Negro" as a subordinate and differentiating blacks from others.

Nash (1982) encapsulated the process of transforming Africans into chattel slaves in a powerfully succinct manner:

> In rapid succession Afro-Americans lost their right to testify before a court; to engage in any kind of commercial activity, either as buyer or seller; to hold property; to participate in the political process; to congregate in public places with more than two or three of their fellows; to travel without permission; and to engage in legal marriage or parenthood. In some colonies legislatures even prohibited the right to education and religion, for they thought these might encourage the germ of freedom in slaves. From human status, slaves descended to property status (151).

The question has been legitimately raised as to why, after forty years of relatively indifferent or indecisive social treatment, the English colonists found it necessary to impose permanent bondage on Africans and their descendants. The enslavement of the native populations was comprehensible in the context of the conquest situation, in which historical precedent shows victims reduced to forced labor. Both the Indians and the Irish were people whose lands the English coveted and confiscated. But the Negro as slave did not fit into this classic mold, and this may help us to understand the early ambiguity of the Africans' relationships to the dominant white community.

Overtly the English really had little reason to compare the Africans with the Indians except in their powerlessness. Africans were neither native to the Americas, nor were they enemies captured in war and thus the target of the enmity or belligerence of their conquerers. Moreover, by English criteria of the requisites for civilized behavior, Africans met at least the basic ones. They were all farmers, and some were artisans and craftspeople adept in a range of skilled activities from blacksmithing and goldsmithing to brick-making, carpentering, weaving, and leather-working. Some undoubtedly came from areas of highly organized state societies and were accustomed to social hierarchies and obedience to positions of legitimate power. The English consequently had no reason to see in the Africans the same image of the "savage" whom they had interpreted in earlier contexts as an impediment to their progress.

The answer to the query, Why Africans? is complex and perhaps best understood in the broadest historical context, encompassing economic and material explanations along with those cultural-historical ones that are so important in human lives, but, under recent fads of scholarship, much too often ignored. What seems absent from the calculations of many recent historians of this phenomenon is the recognition and inclusion in their analyses of the historical penchant that Englishmen had long displayed toward extreme ethnic chauvinism, independently of any contact with Africans and Indians. Certain conditions presaging a negative evaluation of Africans were present even before Englishmen arrived on the coasts of North America.

In the sixteenth century the English had evolved belligerent and/or competitive relationships with virtually all other groups with whom they had any contact. Their animosity and willingness to treat others in an inhumane manner has already been documented in the description of the relationships established with the Irish and the Indians. Even before the settlements in the New World, they had developed, as we have noted, a view of the world as composed of unequal groups, at the bottom of which were the "savages." This pattern of treatment of non-English people included not only the long-standing conflicts with other Europeans, but a culturally induced belief in their own superiority, which already bordered on racism, and which shortly would be fed by a newfound and sometimes fanatical Anglo-Saxonism. What seems strange is that most of the English did not immediately identify the Africans as wild men or savages. It was not until the eighteenth century, at least in the written record, that widespread English attitudes toward Africans mirrored popular evaluations and stereotypes of the Irish and Indians. The same negative language and antiprimitivistic characterizations of savagery that had been used for the Irish and Indians were then widely applied to Africans and greatly amplified in the next century.

Consider the circumstances of English expansion. Faced with rich and abundant lands, what was lacking for their successful exploitation was the labor to fully cultivate or explore them for minerals or other forms of wealth. Following earlier precedents, the settlers in all regions attempted to coerce the native populations into the kind of controlled labor that they perceived would be most profitable. When the Indian population proved to be insufficient and ineffective as slaves (see below), the English next turned to importing impoverished men, women, and children from the streets of Liverpool and Bristol, or rounding up peasant Irishmen and Scotsmen conquered in warfare from British territories and shipping them off to provide labor for the early settlements, especially the sugar plantations in the West Indies. In fact, the wholesale shipment of Irish people into servitude in the New World became an acceptable option for dealing with them. The English knew that slavery was not illegal under international laws. So it did not matter who the slaves were as long as they were not proper Englishmen, Protestant and civilized.

Englishmen were involved in the Irish "slave trade" to the West Indies beginning in the late 1620s, long before they became the major carriers in the African-Atlantic trade to the New World. The largest numbers were brought in during midcentury when Oliver Cromwell had instigated his scorched-earth policy against the Irish; the choice as he saw it was to exterminate them or expel them.[9]

Throughout this period there was no reason to predict that the African-Atlantic trade would ultimately supplant the white "vagabonds," "destitutes," and convicts with an unlimited cargo of black labor. Moreover, it did not matter that the English had no immediate experience, or recognition, of slavery in British law. As a human institution, slavery was widely accepted as legal and appropriate for some people. For the English plantation-owner, what was needed was a docile work force over whom he had absolute authority, who could be put to work for no more than minimal keep, and thus could be treated as a piece of property or other livestock. This was what the English attempted to put into practice, even before the Africans figured significantly into the equation, for they had already established a plantation system with separate and miserable servant housing, poor food, whippings for punishment, and forced labor in gangs.

Morgan's analysis of the early Virginia colony provides the kind of cultural-historical context out of which we can better grasp the process of transformation to a slave society in the Chesapeake region. Unlike in the New England colonies, Englishmen in this rough disorderly world set out to exploit other men, including one another, with few scruples about it. The colony consisted of a large number of rebellious and unruly young men, freed after serving their years of indenture and on the make. But Morgan claims that in fact there were fewer opportunities for them to make their fortunes than history has portrayed, and they formed an unhappy cadre of idle, restless drifters who caused more than a little trouble and embarrassment to colony leaders. Eager for action, frustrated by those who tried to control and exploit them, they were more than willing to rebel against the colony's elite. The tragedy was that they took out their frustrations on a population relatively easy to hate with impunity, the Indians, who became the scapegoat for their ire. The substitution of slaves for servants, Morgan tells us, gradually eased the threat posed by unruly, aggressive freed servants, driven by greed for land and contemptuous of authority (Morgan 1975, 308). A clearly demarcated category of slaves allowed freed servants opportuni-

ties for realizing their own ambitions and for identifying common interests with those holding wealth, privilege, and power.

Several unanticipated developments led to the preference for Africans as laborers and, indeed, the fashioning of the institution of slavery
for Africans only. In the West Indies as well as on the mainland, quite
early in the contact period, Europeans began to realize that the native
populations were a poor source of potential labor. For one thing, the Indians had little or no immunity to Old World diseases that Europeans
brought with them. Ordinary children's diseases and respiratory infec-
tions from the common cold to tuberculosis had a fatal impact on the
indigenous populations, many of whom succumbed rapidly or became
weakened to the point of incapacity. In fact, between disease and warfare, the native population was drastically reduced and, in some cases,
as on the Caribbean Islands, eliminated entirely. Moreover, the remaining Indians were on their own territory, and often individuals or groups
would escape and disappear into the hinterlands. In most cases, these
runaways would never be recaptured, and this posed a major problem
for their masters. Enslaved Indians had communities of support among
their own people, and the threat of Indian attacks to recapture their
own tribespeople was constant. Besides, Indians were dealt with as
whole societies, not as disconnected individuals who had no social
identity other than that provided by the owner/purchasers. Trading and
other agreements, although often breached by Europeans, also acted as
a bar to wholesale enslavement of Indians.

Added to this was the fact that except in some of the southeast regions, none of the Indian groups represented large populations. The native peoples of the North American eastern coasts, especially, were
thinly scattered, so that even when conquered, they did not supply sufficient labor to meet the demand. Finally, most of the natives of the regions settled by the English were food collectors or simple
horticulturalists. Although the eastern woodlands and southern Indians grew some food crops, their techniques and customs did not allow
for substantial surplus production. When some southeastern tribes,
such as the Creeks, Cherokees, and Choctaws, did take up settled farming life-styles, they were able to establish treaties with the whites,
which prevented efforts to enslave them. On the tropical islands where
Europeans established plantations, food cultivation was little known
among the native populations who first succumbed to the ravages of
disease and warfare.

English willingness to use fellow Europeans as forced labor in the
West Indies was not an insignificant precursor of their massive involvement with African slaves. As we have seen, European servants came

under the same restrictions as all servants and slaves, and they often were treated worse than others.[10] The Irish particularly were a rebellious lot. Their comparatively high linguistic and cultural homogeneity allowed them to plot mutinies and insurrections, in several of which they were successful. Often they went over to the side of the French or the Spanish in their battles with the English, an alliance also experienced in Europe and based on their common Catholic faith. Support from these coreligionists was often critical to the success of some rebellions. That they were threatening to the English is witnessed in the report that "English officials armed their black slaves rather than trust the Irish" (Liggio 1976, 29). But adding to the angst of the plantation managers and owners was the fact that the Irish, whom we have already seen to have been primarily pastoralists, knew nothing about intensive agriculture, the tropical environment, or techniques for the cultivation of tropical plants. "Not unlike the Indians to which they were so frequently compared, the Irish, as the English had constantly said, would not submit to the kind of agricultural work which feudalism had demanded. The Indian tended to escape or die; the Irish either resisted work discipline, tending toward idleness, or they rebelled" (Liggio 1976, 30).

There were other factors about the Irish that diminished their value as a totally controllable and powerless labor force. Individual Irishmen could also escape and blend in with the free white population in the ports and other towns, especially on the mainland. Plantation owners and managers soon learned that the expense and difficulties of retrieving them were not worth the bother. Planters also thought of the Irish as having a dangerous nature. Irish servants frequently engaged in drunken brawls and thus quickly gained a reputation for aggressiveness and violence. Predictably, they would turn on their masters. Liggio has concluded that Irish servitude became either useless or a burden to the planters. "The Gaelic insurrections caused the English to seek to replace this source of servile labor entirely with another source, African slaves" (1976, 29).

White indentured servitude was never certain or predictable. For upward of seventy years it had been the dominant source of labor, but it was self-limiting. The treatment of European servants was subject to criticism abroad, and economic and social developments in Britain soon diminished the supply. White servants were products of European cultural values, and many knew, even though some were convicts, that certain laws protected them in their servitude. In the latter part of the seventeenth century the numbers of newly arriving indentured servants began to diminish as part of a general population decline in England. They were never again significant in the exploitation of the colonies either in the West Indies or in mainland North America.

The advantages of African labor over either the Indians or the Irish were made very obvious to English plantation-owners in the seventeenth century as they had been earlier to the Spanish and Portuguese. The supply of African slaves increased to meet a growing demand for labor, and the costs to the planters of purchasing a slave for life soon fell below that of European servants. Perhaps more striking, revealed from the records of the early West Indian planters themselves, was the fact that the Africans initially were considered a civilized and relatively docile population. They had knowledge of and experience with tropical cultivation and were used to discipline, one of the hallmarks of civilized behavior, as well as working cooperatively in groups. The Africans were also in a strange land, with no place to hide and no powerful European friends and allies to support them in their cause.[11] Of equal importance, they had natural immunities to Old World diseases, an ecologically adaptive feature shared with their masters. Many Africans thus survived, despite the brutal circumstances of their transport and their lives, and they produced the tobacco, sugar, indigo, cotton, rice, and many other crops that generated the great wealth realized by Europeans in the New World.

A Focus on Physical Differences

There is, or should be, no doubt that the Africans' physical differences facilitated their reduction to the kind of servitude that the English had long wanted and that agricultural circumstances demanded. The visibility of Africans made it possible to structure the demarcation point of permanent slavery solely on the basis of color. Captured Africans, removed from any possible source of aid and comfort, thrown together with others who did not share their language, culture, or religion, were the most vulnerable of all of the subordinate populations, even if they did not have the vast difference represented by the physical badge of color. Yet it is interesting that the justification for their reduction to such base slavery did not hinge initially on this physical difference. In fact, English arguments for participating in the enslavement of Africans rested on the same issues of religion and "savagery" that they had applied to the Irish and the Indians. So the colonists convinced themselves, and others, that the Africans deserved the status of slave because they had lived in sin and savagery in Africa. Indeed, many colonists of the seventeenth century believed, or vindicated their actions with the belief, that enslavement was a major step toward saving the souls of the Africans.

Nevertheless, consciousness of the physical distinctiveness of dark-skinned Africans along with their social vulnerability became a core component of English thinking about their own social and economic predicament during the late seventeenth century, especially in Virginia and Maryland, when sources of white servants declined. English traders entered the slaving business, lowering the costs of importing Africans whose numbers increased rapidly. The singular identification of dark skin with slave status progressed just as rapidly. Jordan believes that "by the end of the seventeenth century dark complexion had become an independent rationale for enslavement" (1968, 96).

However, complexion alone was not put forth as a primary justification for slavery. The growing imagery of human differences was much more complicated. Dark skin color soon became a symbol of savagery and heathenism and all the other negative features that these terms connoted in the English worldview. The image evolving in the English collective consciousness, not yet fully articulated, was that the Africans were different in a way that transcended all other modes of ethnic differentiation. As the eighteenth century wore on, their savagery became intrinsic and terminal.

Permanent lifelong slavery, inherited from parent to child and relegated solely to Africans and their descendants, was not a single political decision made in a moment's time by men who were conscientiously creating a new institution. Jordan portrayed the process as an "unthinking decision" growing out of the desperate need for labor, the increasing availability of Africans from numerous traders, and the already existing subtle associations of blacks with slavery in Latin America (1968, Chapter 2).

Edmund Morgan (1975) suggests that, from the standpoint of the English in Virginia, they did not have to actively enslave anyone, "they converted to slavery simply by buying slaves instead of servants" (197). Indeed, they often placed the blame for slavery on the English government, which permitted the traffic. Yet it is quite evident that the colonists felt the necessity of concretizing their practices and the customs developing around them in law by passing dozens of statutes and regulations that hemmed in the Africans with increasingly tight restrictions. The English in Virginia, as in Maryland, South Carolina, and other colonies, actively passed numerous laws separating out Africans for special treatment and institutionalizing permanent hereditary slavery for them and their descendants. Although these acts contradicted prevailing English laws governing servants and their treatment, it is obvious that the Virginia planters expected no reaction from the English government. The Africans were different; they were heathens and they were already slaves, it was argued, and to some they were a "brutish people" whom English laws need not protect (Morgan 1975, 314). Thus it became easier to think of them solely as property purchased for an obvious good.

Black slavery in America, it should be emphasized, was an important economic institution. It was profitable for both the traders and for those whose wealth was acquired from the labor of slaves.[12] But colonists of all sorts, slave-owners and nonslave-owners, did not seek to maintain slavery merely for economic reasons. It became also, and predominantly, a social institution, a mechanism integral to the structuring of the social system. It evolved simultaneously as a relationship of dominance and power and as a form of conspicuous consumption for the socially ambitious. Whites yearned after the plantation life-style with its comforts, graciousness, elite mannerisms, and luxuries. Even if its economic efficiency declined or was subject to question at times, the structural relationships and social functions persisted and strengthened in the eighteenth and nineteenth centuries. Historians who have treated American slavery as only an economic institution, a mode of production, have often ignored or failed to perceive the importance of this social-cultural factor. It was this latter reality that prompted the greatest resistance to ending slavery, as Southerners and other proslavery advocates recognized that the social dimension in all its complexity was critical to what they saw as their way of life. This will be discussed further in Chapter 9.

The process of creating this new slave system, at the domestic level, at the plantation production level, and at the level of legislated decisions and public policy, was cognitively connected to existing physical differences between those who had the power to enslave and those, lacking power, who were enslaved. The English, like other Europeans of this era, had always found it easy to treat the poor and powerless with contempt and indifference. When indelible physical differences were linked to such victims, the situation literally called for exaggerated degradation of all who bore such features. Thus even African-Americans who were ostensibly free were demarcated from the rest of society and demoted to permanently inferior beings. Multiple decisions made in the individual treatment of powerless blacks resulted in and enforced attitudes of contempt and denigration focused on the blackness itself.

Conscientiously moral human beings, however, do not conventionalize such habits of thought and behavior without a rationalizing ideology. Even as laws were enacted and customs created, the colonists were inventing ideologies to mirror, explain, and justify them. After all, they told themselves in the beginning, Africans had been slaves in their homelands and, ipso facto, were accustomed to much worse treatment. They were heathens and wracked with sin. How much better to be slaves in Christian colonies where hard work would purify their souls and prepare them for Christian worthiness? It was in this manner that Africans soon became the new savages. Almost imperceptibly the status of "the Negro" in the gallery of interacting populations in the colonial world was lowered below that of Indians, most of whom were, after all, formally free. Indians gradually receded as the most savage creature; by the latter half of the eighteenth century a primitivistic view of Indians, elevating them more as "noble savages," began to take hold in North America. A subtle reshuffling of the existing ranking system was taking place.[13]

In summary then, during the process of advancing slowly along the road to a full-scale slave society, English colonists gradually, and perhaps unconsciously, developed a unique and subtle ideology about human differences. As they were creating the institutional and behavioral aspects of slavery, they were simultaneously structuring the ideological components of race. The practices and customs of black slavery thus helped to form the basis for the racial worldview.

By the latter part of the eighteenth century we see "race" appearing not merely as a subdivision of interacting populations in the colonies, but as (1) an intellectual construct about human differences and power relationships, and (2) a novel and unprecedented quality introduced into the structuring of social status. This was the only slave system whose rationale became uninhibitedly and exclusively racial. By increasingly limiting perpetual servitude to Africans and their descendants, colonists were proclaiming that blacks would forever be at the bottom of the New World social hierarchy. By keeping blacks, Indians, and whites socially and spatially separated and enforcing endogamous mating, they were making sure that visible physical differences would be preserved as the premier insignia of unequal social statuses. In this way they institutionalized exclusive group membership and paved the way for later rationalizations of group distinctiveness in terms of natural, inbred inequality. Even free persons of African ancestry were diminished and degraded to what some have called a "pariah" caste. Thus the creation of this new dimension of social difference went beyond the mere transformation of those who were already slaves. It helps us to understand the autonomous nature of "race" itself, how it developed as an essential quality and came to persist as a form of social identity independently of slavery (see Chapter 9).

On this point, we should again emphasize that there is no *intrinsic* relationship between slavery and the development of race and racism.

Many find this difficult to comprehend, in part because the American experience has so dramatically intertwined the two in our historical memories.[14] But as will be shown in Chapter 6, slavery existed long before race and racism. Whether race ideology could have evolved without black slavery is another question future scholars will no doubt explore.

Although we must separate conceptually the idea of race from slavery, for our present purposes we must acknowledge that historically the circumstances of black slavery provided the fertile soil out of which the English ideology of race evolved. It is in these unique components of North American slave practices and beliefs, especially as they evolved in the eighteenth century, that we penetrate to the core of the race idea. In the next chapter we take a closer look at the institution of Anglo-American slavery.

Notes

1. In the sixth edition of his famous work, written in conjunction with Alfred A. Moss, Jr., Franklin refers to the works of Leo Wiener and Ivan Van Sertima, two scholars who have argued that Africans were in the Americas before the explorations of the Spanish and Portuguese. Since these theories and evidences offered by these historians have not been accepted by most scholars, Franklin notes that the "traditional story of the coming of Africans to the New World remains essentially unchanged" (Franklin and Moss 1988, 30).

2. There were a few Africans in England following the wars with Spain in the late sixteenth century who served primarily as personal servants to traders, military men, and foreign diplomats. They were concentrated in London and other port cities.

3. Although Colin Palmer (1976) acknowledges that there are no comprehensive statistics on the number of African slaves in Spain in the sixteenth century, he records that "in 1565 there were 6,327 slaves in Seville out of a total population of 85,538" and states that a majority were probably Africans. He notes further that Antonio Dominguez Ortiz claimed that there were about 100,000 slaves in Spain at this time, not all of whom were Africans (6). The Almoravids (followers of Ibn Yasin, a Muslim holy man residing in Sijilmasa) who conquered Spain during the last quarter of the eleventh century, and the later Almohades, included large numbers of supporters from the Senegal River area of West Africa (see Rotberg 1965, 39–40). See also Hitti (1953, 540).

4. See Nash (1982) and Handlin ([1948] 1957). David Brion Davis (1966) notes that "not only did slavery and serfdom coexist and overlap, but medieval jurists tended to confuse the two conditions" (48). Jordan (1968) claims that there was a measure of precision in the English concept of "slave" but it has not been well analyzed. He argues that for most, English slavery denoted a complete loss of freedom, akin to the loss of one's humanity, and to treat a man as a slave was to treat him as a beast (54). Morgan (1975) in his detailed study of the Virginia col-

ony gives convincing evidence that servants in Virginia were generally degraded and treated as things. "Virginians dealt in servants the way Englishmen dealt in land or chattels" (128). White servitude, he claims, came closer to slavery in the tobacco fields of Virginia than anything hitherto known by the English (296).

5. Tocqueville ([1831] 1945) had an amazing clairvoyance about the American experience. Writing about democracy and the potential for revolutionary fervor after his 1831 visit to the United States, he noted this: "If ever America undergoes great revolutions, they will be brought about by the presence of the black race on the soil of the United States; that is to say, they will owe their origin, not to the equality, but to the inequality of condition" (2: 270).

6. The classic work of Eric Williams ([1944] 1966), for example, declares unequivocally that "slavery was not born of racism: rather, racism was the consequence of slavery" (7). He believes that the initial reason for slavery was economic and was unrelated to the physical features of the black population.

7. In 1547 a statute was passed in England inflicting slavery upon "vagabonds" and "runaways," but it proved unenforceable and was repealed in 1553. Laws of this sort contradicted the trend toward personal liberty that increasingly characterized English society (Jordan 1968, 51).

8. Similar values and associations for the colors black and white are shared by other European cultures. This raises the questions of how significant were initial English reactions to skin color differences and what such differences might have meant in the English interpretation of social status without slavery.

9. Louis Ruchames (1969) cites H. N. Brailsford's description of the aftereffects of the civil war of 1648 in which he speaks of "the systematic sale of prisoners, Welshmen, Scots and Englishmen, to serve as slaves in all but name in the plantations of Barbados and Virginia" (7).

10. Part of the larger ethical position of Protestants was a deep-seated and irrational hatred of the poor. In their view, idle men were also evil and sinful and, of course, likely to be criminals. This accounts for the jailing of poor and destitute individuals, the establishment of poorhouses and workhouses under government sponsorship, and the harsh treatment and unmitigated exploitation of such persons. This attitude provided a legacy that weaves throughout U.S. culture down to the present time.

11. In many parts of Latin America and on such islands as Jamaica, some Africans escaped and founded remote villages replicating their African homelands. Known as Cimarrons to the Spanish, they frequently posed threats to Spanish settlements, often attacking supply stations and wagons, as well as the local militia. See Palmer (1976) and Bowser (1974) among others.

12. Some recent publications have criticized Eric Williams's main theory that slavery generated the wealth for the development of modern industrial capitalism. Scholars may debate the point indefinitely, but when the export crops of tobacco, sugar, cotton, and so forth produced by slaves generated the greatest wealth, it is legitimate to raise the question of what the alternative may have been. In any case, social policymakers aiming at eliminating racism might consider the fact that when history finally gives the African slaves their due, that is, emphasizes the real contributions of their strength, skill, and

knowledge to the building of the United States, we will have made a giant step toward transforming racial attitudes.

13. A good illustration of this subtle change is found in Thomas Jefferson's work on the state of Virginia. He staunchly defended the Indians' abilities while simultaneously diminishing those of Negroes. Jefferson was among many who held out the possibility that the Indian might ultimately be assimilated into colonial society. This was never considered an option for the Negro.

14. It is interesting that Moses I. Finley (1968a), writing on the topic of slavery for the *Encyclopedia of the Social Sciences*, felt it necessary to include a section on color prejudice, so closely bound together are these topics in the American mind.

Comparing Slave Systems: The Significance of "Racial" Servitude

THERE CAN BE NO DENYING the fact that some of the distinctive features of slavery in the English colonies had a direct relationship to the development of their ideology of race. One cannot explain American social structure and contemporary relationships without reference to the former enslavement of African-Americans. Race ideology emerged during a period of intensified slavery; it formed its roots in North American attitudes toward slaves.

We should understand that slavery was an essential social institution with deep roots in Western history, not a mere aberration in the historical unfolding of Western society. Our present-day democratic and egalitarian ideals have not persisted as untainted virtues of the West since ancient times; they are of very recent venue and, ironically, have been afforded to us principally because of the wealth created by slaves.[1] In the eighteenth century, slavery represented the epitome of inegalitarian and inhumane values at a time when social forces in the Western world were striving toward individual freedom, representative government, equality, and social justice.

It is arguable whether the components of race ideology could have been created without slavery. Indeed, historians of the Americas have explored and debated the linkage between race and slavery for over half a century. Much of the historical discussion has focused on the explanation of differences between Latin American and North American experiences of "race" in the context of their presumably different slave systems. Because of the importance of this background literature, we will examine briefly these findings in the first part of this chapter.

Alternately, since slavery existed without "race" for several thousand years, a broad look at slavery as a social institution seems useful so that we can determine which features represented the general characteristics of all slave systems, and may be found anywhere, and which reflected the developing components of "race" in North America. Because we know so little about the topic, I explore the probable origins and nature of slavery in those areas of the Old World (Europe, Africa, and the Middle East) where cultural precedents for much of New World slavery were set.[2]

Then, looking at the institutionalization of slavery in the Spanish and Portuguese (Latin) colonial settings, I note some areas of continuity in the customs, laws, beliefs, and practices these groups brought with them to the New World that persisted irrespective of phenotypic differences within these populations. At the same time, I briefly delineate certain features that may be useful diagnostic criteria for comparing, evaluating, or classifying slave systems. Some historians have already used such features for assessing analytically how different systems of slavery vary from one another and the implications of these differences.[3] I then look at the uniqueness of English attitudes and beliefs, noting how these practices differed from those in Old World slavery as well as its versions in Latin America.

In the last section, I address the problem of the significance of North American slavery and its contributions to the idea of race. Data support the argument that it may not have been so much the differences in the *forms* of slavery evolved in the New World, but the *particular cultural attitudes of the varying European colonizers toward human differences before landing on American shores* that may best explain developing ideologies of race during and after the slave era.

The Background Literature and the Issues of Slavery

Frank Tannenbaum (1947) was one of the first scholars who probed the differences between North American and Latin American slavery. Although he noted that Africans were brought nearly everywhere into the New World, he was struck by the absence of patterns of racial discrimination and clear-cut racial categories in those areas that came under Portuguese and Spanish hegemony. Indeed, in most areas extensive intermating had resulted in complex mixtures of Indian, African, and European genetic elements in the populations, and physical boundaries were blurred or nonexistent. Hypothesizing that differences in the slave systems between North and South America were responsible for the variations observed, Tannenbaum presented evidence that Latin areas had high rates of manumission, that freed slaves were not barred from participation in the larger society, and that there were no legal barriers to manumission or to intermarriage.

In searching for explanations of such different patterns of group inter-action, Tannenbaum argued that cultural-historical differences in the backgrounds of the colonizing Europeans were responsible. In the Span-ish and Portuguese territories, these were the paternalistic structure of Latin society, the church, and its insistence on the moral personality of the slaves, the previous experiences of slavery in the Iberian Peninsula, and the heritage of Roman law tempered by Christian ethics. These and many other elements of Latin culture protected Negro slaves and pre-vented the loss and abuse of their human personalities and rights, he ar-gued.[4]

Stanley Elkins ([1959] 1963) continued and extended the Tannen-baum thesis. Concentrating on variations in the systems of slavery, Elkins noted numerous differences in the slave laws of the Latin and En-glish regions. He found that nothing—not laws, customs, church, or state—inhibited the plantation-owners in English colonies from total dominance of slaves and their transmutation into chattel. Latin slav-ery, however, was circumscribed by traditional institutions; the author-itarian personal interest in the colonies shown by Spanish monarchs, the church with its numerous overseers of moral behavior, and the slave laws themselves were protective of the moral personality of the slaves and of their legal rights. Some of his conclusions were that Latin slavery was less harsh and oppressive than British slavery and had fewer debilitating consequences for the slaves once freed.

Reaction to the Tannenbaum-Elkins theses stimulated much new re-search, especially on comparative slavery among European colonists, and inspired debates among scholars on such questions as which sys-tem of slavery was more severe, what impact different socioeconomic conditions had on slavery, and how to assess the qualities of slavery in different eras. Revisionist scholars rejected the notion that North American slavery was more brutal and exploitative, pointing out that it was only in the North American slave colonies that Africans expanded their populations by natural reproduction, whereas slaves on planta-tions in the Latin areas died out or failed to reproduce. Many scholars attempted to prove that there were greater similarities than differences in the realities of slavery in all the New World colonies.[5]

Yet, as Peter Kolchin (1982) noted in his review of recent comparative studies (72), scholars have not been able to totally deny Tannenbaum's observations that there were and are significant differences in race rela-tions. North American race categories are limited in number and so-cially rigid, even though phenotypic traits vary enormously within each category. South American "racial" terms are not race categories at all, but tend to be descriptive of multiple variations in phenotype that presume random miscegenation and a range of ancestral mixtures in individuals. In North America, distinctions in attitudes toward and treatment of people in different race categories were institutionalized and rendered uniform by law in the South.

Criticizing and often contradicting the cultural-historical explanations, recent scholars have posed alternative answers for the differences in Latin and English patterns of slavery and race relations. They point to the circumstances of contact, demographic realities, the nature of the economies developed, differences between rural plantation areas and urban centers, and other economic-ecological factors. Some scholars feel that these factors alone, and not previous cultural orientations or values, may best explain differences between Latin and North American forms of slavery. Other scholars do not deny the significance of cultural traditions, but believe that the arguments for the greater importance of economic and demographic factors are more persuasive (Nash 1982, 156–160). Nash cites such evidence, explored in recent primary studies, as the labor demands of different crops, the ratio of blacks to whites and males to females, the availability of new slaves through trade, and tropical diseases as critical factors in the treatment of slaves.

Economic circumstances and ecological features are clearly important determinants of human actions and decisions, as many studies in cultural and human ecology have shown. And these must be factored in as critical to any analysis. But neither the colonial settlers nor the people they conquered and/or enslaved were totally deracinated individuals. We cannot ignore the fact that values and ideologies are strongly perdurable aspects of culture. People adapt to new situations with the cultural equipment that they have. Prior values, habits, norms, customs, and beliefs function to guide and control people's behavior even in alien and unusual circumstances. The degree to which Latin American slavery reflected some Old World traditions and behavior patterns is a case in point. The Iberian explorers brought with them knowledge of slave customs steeped in Mediterranean history, laws, and attitudes. The continuity of such elements of Old World culture can be identified not only in New World slave codes and laws but also in many actual practices.

First, Old World slave systems all acknowledged the slave as an unfortunate but nevertheless human being. There are few societies outside North America in which the basic human status of all those in a slave category has ever been denied or even questioned. As we shall see later, North American science, and even the courts, provided a battleground for just this question in the nineteenth century (see Chapters 10 and 11). And the practical consequences of scientific decisions on the problematic humanity of blacks reverberated throughout the United States in the unqualifiedly demeaning, deliberately humiliating behavior of many whites toward blacks and Indians.

Second, there are specific features that exemplify the degree to which the dominant society understood and accepted the fact of the slaves' humanity. A complete analysis of these most common features would be far more elaborate than can be outlined here. But such features might well be used in combination as diagnostic tools, or as a baseline for discussing the transformations in slavery in the New World that brought about what some historians see as a new institution in North America (e.g., Curtin 1977, 10). These features will be briefly identified and discussed in the next sections.

A third and final point is that levels of brutality and harshness are not necessarily indications of whether slaves are considered human. The acceptance of the slave as another human being did not inexorably lead to amelioration of the slave condition or even diminish the levels of brutality sustained in any given society. Much scholarly energy and time have been expended debating the issue of which system was harsher, the Latin or the English. The question, however, seems moot and irrelevant since examples of extreme cruelty as well as humane concern and treatment can be found in all systems. In any case, we may never have enough comparable evidence to assess the levels of cruelty or severity found in any system.

History demonstrates, furthermore, that we humans have never needed to invent slavery in order to brutalize and dehumanize one another. Modern warfare and internal oppression, torture, mutilation, and murder provide abundant evidence of our penchant for brutalizing one another, even when free. Humans exhibit the greatest cruelty when they have the uncurbed power to do so, when individuals perceive some extraordinary psychic or material benefits from sadistic behavior, and when mob or group actions override individual judgment and sensitivity. Slavery satisfies all of these requisites and more, and the situation may be exacerbated when there are ethnic differences between slave and free. Interethnic hostilities and pejorative stereotypes of one another are fairly constant group experiences. But brutality need not have ethnic boundaries, as we all know. Moreover, it is a fact that owners of nonhuman property (e.g., pets) may treat their horses, dogs, and cats with a great deal of tenderness, love, and care, especially those living in close conjunction with them. In the North American colonies slave children were often treated very kindly, literally as pets, while simultaneously considered subhuman. And many owners held their slave property as much too valuable to mistreat them. In other words, levels of violence and brutality alone are *not* the best indicators or measures of the dehumanizing qualities in slave systems.[6]

An anthropological perspective does not attempt such a difficult, indeed impossible, task of evaluating severity even if all data for making such judgments were available. This approach seeks only to specify the substantive areas in which institutions manifest similarities and differences. But first we must establish the common features, or baseline similarities, of Old World slavery by briefly examining its nature and history.

The Nature of Slavery

Slavery is only one of a number of forms of servitude that are predicated on unfree, controlled labor. It is easier to characterize or describe slavery than to define it in some universally useful manner. Although a great deal of work has been done in the past four or five decades, scholarship on comparative slave systems is still in the fairly early stages of research and theory development. This research has shown, however, that the diversity of forms of servitude and the customs associated with them have been considerable; a wide range of practices, beliefs, norms, and values have been subsumed under the rubric of "slavery." Sometimes the dissimilarities among societies have been so great that they inhibit making generalizations acceptable to all scholars. Different scholars emphasize differing aspects of slavery, and they often disagree on how to translate terms in other languages into concepts meaningful for comparative study. The result is that there is only limited and somewhat tentative agreement on the empirical dimensions of slavery contrasted with other forms of servitude.[7]

Nevertheless, slavery has generally been defined as an institution in which some persons are legally owned by other persons just as a piece of property is owned. The slave exercises no will of his or her own, theoretically, but submits to the authority and domination of the master. Customs and laws in slave-owning societies permit the slave to be bought, sold, given away, inherited, bequeathed, used to pay debts, or used in any other way that personal property can be used. Thus the essential quality of slavery everywhere has been that an individual is defined legally as a thing, a piece of property owned by another, and physical force and/or some other form of coercion is the chief mechanism for maintaining this fiction.[8] The power of the master-owner over the slave may vary in time and space but it has always been one constant, and usually inviolable, fact.

But the slave is also a human being with all of the attributes of consciousness, sensitivity, and thought that characterize free persons, and this is where the fundamental contradiction unfolds. All slave-owning societies have had to deal with the paradox expressed in the question, How can a human being be both a person and a thing?[9] Throughout history, societies have had several different ways of trying to resolve this problem or of at least coping with the glaring contradiction that it masks. I argue in this analysis that "race" evolved in the Judeo-Christian society of North America in large part as one way of dealing with this dilemma, by defining Africans and their descendants as something less than fully human, or a different and inferior form of human being from whites.

Slavery has sometimes been treated as if it were solely an economic institution, with emphasis on the productive activities of slaves. My analysis focuses on what I consider to be the most important aspect of all such systems, the social and human relationships. Whether or not systems of slavery are or were productive and profitable (as has been debated in studies of Greco-Roman and in some periods of American slavery) is not relevant to this analysis. It is the consequences of slavery for human social systems and social relationships that matter; in this case, the manner in which it contributed to the concept of "race" and the postemancipation relationships between racially defined populations. There are elements of personal power and dependency, of social identity and consciousness, of prestige, status, and social distance, of religious belief, morality, ritualized interactive patterns, and many other factors that cannot be subsumed under a limited vision of slavery purely as an economic institution. Like all human institutions, slavery has to be comprehended within a wider context. To this end, we need to examine, albeit briefly, its history and the ways in which the institution has functioned over time.

Historical Background of Old World Slavery

Slavery (in its fundamental sense) originated in societies that were essentially kinship-based; that is, kinship structures, institutions, values, beliefs, and ideology were dominant forces in the social system. The chief organizing principles were those of kinship; it was the foundation not only of a person's identity, but of his/her social, political, economic, and ritual status in society and his/her relationships to others. This was true even in the civil societies of Rome and Greece where social identity came nearest to the concept of citizenship, a form of identity essential to modern nation-states and viewed as a contractual relationship between the state and the individual. The *pater familias* was the head of the Roman lineage or family; its members derived their social status, property, and identity, and thus a large element of their "citizenship," from their relationship to him. Such was the power and responsibility of the pater that he "had the right to life-and-death decisions about his own children" (Curtin 1977, 4).[10]

In all such societies, the kin group, whether it was a large aggregate encompassing thousands or a small lineage of ten or twenty persons, or something in between, was the basic unit sine qua non of the sociopolitical system. Without a kin group to support and fortify him, a man was essentially a nonentity. Even the poorest peasants were enmeshed in a complex of relationships of which the vortex was the kin groups that socialized them, told them who they were, provided guidelines and sanctions for their behavior, and determined the course of their future lives. Genealogical ties, regardless of their biological accuracy, were a network of links that bound individuals (most importantly men) to one another and specified their rights, privileges, powers, immunities, and obligations.

In the urban city-states of the ancient world, in kingdoms and chiefdoms throughout history, kinship underscored the political-jural relationships of peoples and groups. The element of kinship as the universally recognized mechanism by which the most significant political relationships were established and maintained has been well established by anthropologists. All civil societies before the modern nation-state of the industrial world were in many ways elaborations on the principles of kinship. It is important to establish this point early since slavery is best comprehended minimally as a nonkinship relationship, institutionalized in societies in which kinship provided the central principles of organization, particularly at the community or local level. As Paul Bohannan (1963) has observed, "Slaves are essentially kinless people" (180); indeed, he claims, the institution of slavery itself is antikin. Patterson has likened this condition to one of social death.[11]

We will probably never know exactly when and where slavery first arose as a new concept of human relationships. Evidence indicates, however, that it came about only after the establishment of a mature farming way of life, with large stable populations, and an emphasis on the aggregation of property and wealth. Such societies had already evolved groups and statuses that were unequal in their command over goods and services and in the degree of social-political power that they could exercise. By the time of the first records on slavery, there were already small city-states with stratified social systems incorporating many specialists, such as farmers, herders, fishermen, traders, metal workers, builders, carpenters, butchers, priests, administrators, bu-reaucrats, military men, and so forth. Differences in economic func-tions had given rise to social distinctions and to the further tendency to rank these different occupations and positions. Moreover, power and privilege had become politically concentrated in the hands of specific functionaries. Slavery arose, then, in inegalitarian societies in which the concept of one person having power over others was already devel-oped.

Another characteristic of these societies was that some form of com-pulsory labor was also recognized. We know from many anthropologi-cal studies that in developed chiefdoms (an early stage of centralized governance) community members were required to allocate a portion of their labor or produce to the chief, his retinue, and household. Young men, for example, who constituted the members of age-grade organiza-tions (age sets) were required to clear land, footpaths, and roads, build bridges, erect granaries and other semipublic buildings, and serve in the armed forces. This was customary and expected, and there were few or no options permitted from such service. Other types of what we would call coerced work have also been documented. What we should bear in mind, however, when we look for comparative materials is that these were societies in which there was no wage labor as we know it (a phe-nomenon of early capitalism). All labor, voluntary or compulsory, was invariably compensated through the reciprocal processes inherent in preindustrial economic systems in which kinship values prevailed.[12]

Trade was a source of much of the wealth and the basis of political de-velopment of most ancient kingdoms. As various groups came into greater competition for trade and for strategic resources and raw materi-als, many of them also came into open conflict. Hostilities led to small- and large-scale battles, and eventually there came a time when one of the consequences of this warfare was conquest, the takeover of whole communities and the subjugation of their people. It was without doubt in answer to the problem of what to do with these "foreigners" that slavery developed. The first recorded instances of slavery represent the slaves as products ("booty") of war. And warfare was to remain through-out much of human history a major source of slaves (Finley [1960] 1968b). Slavery was an alternative to extermination.

Slave men and women could be put to productive work, augmenting the resources and wealth of their masters. Those with special skills were more valuable than plain laborers. Women could be used as do-mestic workers, as prostitutes, or to bear children, adding more workers for their masters. Both domestic and industrial enterprises benefited from this unpaid labor, who needed only to be fed and clothed with minimal material comforts, often produced by themselves. Slaves thus liberated free men and women from productive tasks. They also became a source of prestige to the wealthy and powerful; owning slaves was a symbol of status and affluence, a form of conspicuous consumption.

Several other factors facilitated the conquering societies' treatment of alien human beings as objects, property, and beasts of burden. First of all, from the earliest settled Neolithic farming way of life some ten thousand to twelve thousand years ago, when units of people and demarcated pieces of land became associated together, property relationships factored into all human relationships. In such societies groups of people formed by kinship principles came to be identified with property, and specific kinds and pieces of property became symbols of social relationships among and between individuals and groups.[13]

In probably all human societies, some aspects of persons have been interpreted as exchangeable for some form of property. Bridewealth is a recognition of the fact that women have value as wives. Prostitution is an ancient institution that focuses on a woman's sexuality as a thing of value, in other words, exchangeable for some other form of property. Children were and are frequently pawned, sold, and adopted via the exchange of some valued good. And, of course, wage labor is a prime example of the exchangeability of some facets of human beings, their time, skills, talents, abilities, strength, senses, and attention, for property. Yet, the differences are clear; under most forms of slavery, the total person becomes a complete commodity, and the exchange is mostly involuntary and often permanent.[14]

Second, in kinship-based societies, particularly in which the kin group is a corporate, estate-owning entity, an ethos already exists expressing the value that both individuals and groups have rights-in-persons over their members and one other.[15] This means that individuals belonging to the kin group, and the group itself through its representative or headman, can make demands of its members and can dispose of them according to their judgment of what is best for the group. This is manifest in the high degree of control and power that kin groups exercise over members' behavior in such transactions as the arranging of marriages, the adoption, sale, or pawning of children, the allocation of labor and resources among members, and the imposing of penalties for wrongdoing. The group may also make demands for expenses accompanying all rites of passage (births, puberty ceremonies, marriages, deaths) and other ritual occasions. Some of these rights are exchangeable, as in virilocal marriage in which men of one kin group relinquish certain rights over their daughters or sisters, "giving away the bride" to another kin group. In most societies, before the imposition of state-level laws protecting the individual, kin groups had the sole power of life and death over their members.

Slavery evolved, then, in traditional societies in which the concept of "rights-in-or-over-persons" was part of a nexus of understandings, customs, and beliefs about human relationships.[16] The extension of some of these values to the resident stranger(s) was probably an inevitable outcome of the adjustment of the host society to the presence of unfree strangers in their midst. There is of course a theoretical if not always pragmatic distinction between rights in people as property and rights-in-persons, a point that Miers and Kopytoff (1977) do not address (11). But the notion of power and rights over others clearly forms the backdrop for the transformations that gave rise to slavery.[17]

As strangers, the conquered aliens had no kinship ties among the conquering group, and thus were not a part of the ongoing social system.[18] Although the norms, etiquette, and values of kinship and community demand that proper behavior be accorded to all members of one's own society, there were certainly in the early stages of its development no laws, customs, or religious proscriptions that governed the treatment of aliens as booty of warfare. As "enemies" who were no longer a threat, and no longer free to pursue their old way of life, captive persons were without any viable position or status in the new setting. Their very existence, as Patterson (1982) has noted, was as an option to physical death. In the absence of any previous experiences as guideposts, an avenue was open for the creation of a whole new system of relationships, new attitudes, customs, habits, and patterns of interaction. The conquering people, given unrestrained power, could theoretically formulate their own policies and laws, to suit their own purposes, and from the standpoint of their own group or self-interest alone.

It was probably at the juncture in which decisions were made about how to treat these marginal human beings that variations in the institutionalization of slavery must have begun to take place. The variables that influenced the developing system related to the economic and sociopolitical complexity of the host society, to the nature of the domestic situations (in which most slaves were placed), to already existing customs governing the behavior of persons in the stratified society, to the economic factors of production and distribution, and perhaps to a host of other features as well. It is impossible at this stage to know this precisely. What the evidence shows, however, is that certain trends began to develop, many found within the context of quite different societies. One of these was the habit of absorbing individual slaves into the masters' kin groups.

Most preindustrial or peasant societies valued large kin groups for the prestige, protection, and power that they provided. Beyond normal reproduction, one of the chief ways of enlarging one's kinship unit was to incorporate other individuals through adoption and/or marriage. This process was particularly frequent in those situations in which there were few slaves, in which the economy could not sustain or had no need for slave labor, or in which there were slaves with unusual talents or skills. Throughout Africa where traditional slavery has been found, there is considerable evidence of the frequent absorption of unfree persons into the kin group of the conquerers (Miers and Kopytoff 1977; Watson 1980). In many societies, including the ancient Mediterranean states and the Muslim world, this absorption became an important device for freeing slaves. Once kinship had been created, obviously the slave status no longer existed.

In a different context, in which agricultural and manufacturing activities could be enhanced through additional labor, slavery was institutionalized as pure labor, and there grew a demand for slave labor on farms and plantations, in mines, manufacturing industries, and commerce, as well as in the domestic setting. Since warfare and conquest are unpredictable ways of obtaining slaves, other mechanisms appeared for filling the demand. Slave raiding and trading are described early in the literature of the Mediterranean and Babylonian peoples. Phoenicians and Greeks raided for slaves along the Mediterranean coast and inland as far as the Danube River and the coasts of the Black Sea. In Asia Minor, where some of the largest trading centers developed, records show that there were Syrians, Germans, Thracians, Greeks, Jews, Egyptians, Ethiopians, Arabians, Persians, Spaniards, and North African peoples sold in the slave marts. In Roman times, the Greek islands were a favored source of slaves, but many came from what is now Spain, France, Germany, and the British Isles. The Germans raided their neighbors and the people along the Black Sea area to obtain captives for Muslim lands.[19] Once the trade in slaves had been established, it became an end in itself as a source of wealth for merchant entrepreneurs.

Slavery subsequently became a very flexible institution that could be molded to fit many kinds of social exigencies. As such it was perceived as essential and necessary. There were many poor but free men, for example, who could barely eke out a living in the farmlands and towns. So it soon became a custom for men who had become impoverished to sell themselves or their children into slavery. Men would voluntarily enter into servitude for a period of time to work off their debts, after which they or their family members would regain their freedom. Debt slavery became quite common and was widely recognized as an accepted variant of slavery. In addition, slavery as punishment for crimes committed by free men evolved as a way of dealing with miscreants. Individuals were sometimes sentenced to enslavement for a given period of time or for life, and might be sold away into some foreign land as an extreme form of punishment. And, of course, persons identified as enemies of those in power were sometimes ambushed, captured, and sold away into slavery as a way of dealing with political dissidents. Debt slaves, dissidents, and criminals were usually (but not always) of the same ethnic group as the slave-owners, a fact which may have tended to modify the nature of slavery itself. Moreover, these groups enlarged the numbers and sources of slaves and further entrenched the institution into the existing sociopolitical system by making it more of a functional necessity.

From their beginnings, the Roman Catholic and Byzantine churches were major slave-owning institutions, as had been their ancestral pre-Christian temples of the ancient world. They were also major forces for improving the conditions of the slaves and frequently manumitted some of their slaves, often with the purpose of incorporating them into the clergy. Some of the high church officials, including popes, were descendants of slaves or were themselves born into the condition of slavery. There were state-owned slaves, often men of great training who kept the books, prepared documents, and wrote and even administered the laws. There were industrial slaves who worked in the mines and craft shops and local factories, and finally the largest category of all, the domestic slaves owned by families. Many states of ancient and medieval times used slaves as part or all of their military forces. Slaves were even appointed as leaders of the armed forces. Some of these military leaders achieved greatness on their own and were able to gain their freedom because of their exploits and successes.

Most of the ancient and medieval states depended to a greater or lesser extent on slave labor for some facets of their economic production or trade. Not only was slavery extensive in the Old World, but the slave trade also continued throughout the Mediterranean, the Indian Ocean, and the Black Sea areas up to modern times. David Brion Davis (1966) points out that the "great Mediterranean slave trade reached its peak in the fourteenth and fifteenth centuries" (58). Christians enslaved Muslims and Muslims in turn captured and enslaved Christians. Davis tells us that Swedish merchants traded captive Russians down the Volga and Dneiper River valleys along with furs and wax. Merchants and nobles of old Russia saw the export of slaves as a principal source of wealth. Men from Genoa and Venice established slave-trading posts in ports along the Black Sea coasts, where they did a thriving business. "Tartars, Circassians, Armenians, Georgians and Bulgarians flowed into the markets of Italy and Spain" (Davis 1966, 58).

At the height of the Muslim empire, some of the caliphs of Baghdad, then the political and religious center of the Islamic world, were importing tens of thousands of slaves, many from Spain, a few even from the Far East. When sugar production was established on islands in the eastern Mediterranean, a new impetus was given to the slave trade and a new structuring of slaves in plantations took place, despite the fact that slavery was beginning to decline in western Europe. Slavery was thus an institution that was not only widespread in the Old World, but it was intertwined with virtually all aspects of culture: political, religious, economic, and social. Just as in Old Testament days, it was recognized as a necessary, normal, and proper component of the social system. There were those who condemned the immorality or brutality of slavery, but did not question or object to the legality of the institution.

Yet slavery was never considered a "nice" institution, even by those who believed it to be right and proper. The fundamental dilemma of slavery has frequently intruded into human consciousness. This is evidenced in the fact that in its development some men felt the need to attempt to justify it. They were bothered by the disturbing reality of treating people as objects and took great pains to rationalize this paradox and make it acceptable to themselves and others.

Early in the history of the Greek city-states, slaves were thought of as normal human beings who had the misfortune of being taken into slavery. Later there evolved the belief that some occupations were only fit for slaves and that conquered peoples were suited only for servile tasks. Greek ethnocentrism depicted all alien peoples as barbarians, uncivilized, and deficient in governing themselves. Like some Englishmen two thousand years later, some Greek apologists for slavery argued that it was just, legitimate, and proper that the Greek states should enslave barbarians and provide law and order throughout the Mediterranean world. In this context, it was the superiority of Greek institutions of government, not the biological superiority of Greek people, that was the issue and rationale. And in Rome, those persons who accepted the Latin language, customs, and laws ceased being barbarians and could be accepted ultimately as full citizens of the state.

Much has been made of the fact that some Greek philosophers, notably Aristotle and Plato, formulated the argument that there were individuals who were "natural slaves." But it is important to realize that this categorization, although sometimes referring to specific ethnic groups, was a general statement about differences of personality and abilities among individuals, specifically what these philosophers thought was the power to reason. It was applied to other Greeks as well as to non-Greeks (Cuffel 1966).

Independent of the attempts to rationalize slavery, and much more frequent in expression, were the periodic efforts to improve the conditions of slaves. Perhaps because it was viewed as part of the natural order of things, the morality of slavery was not widely questioned until the rise of antislavery sentiment in Western culture in the eighteenth century. During the most oppressive periods, such as in Rome under the Republic several centuries before Christ, the power of masters over their slaves was tyrannical. The slave had no civil position and could be punished, or even killed, by the master with impunity. Industrial slaves working in mines received the harshest treatment of all. They were frequently beaten or worked to death, and they were merely replaced by newer slaves who could be cheaply purchased. The sheer brutality of such conditions inspired pressures to ameliorate the slaves' situation. But it was not just a reaction to the harshness of the treatment of slaves. Some men soon realized that slavery appeals to the most base, corrupting, and degrading of human inclinations. Both free people and slaves are brutalized under slavery, and each suffers a loss of freedom and of human sensitivity and compassion. The unchecked power of the masters sometimes led to unspeakable cruelty, and no one was exempt from the consequences.

There were other factors providing a dynamic social tension that periodically served to curtail or inhibit the abuse of slaves. Practical self-interest led slave-holders to moderate their behavior, if for no other reason than that one cannot get good work out of a skilled and intelligent man or woman if he or she is treated merely as a "thing." Many of the slaves of Roman times, for example, were highly educated, well-trained Greeks and Egyptians. In so many instances, the masters soon recognized the superiority of the slave. This helps to account for the fact that in different areas and in different circumstances, the treatment of slaves and other unfree labor varied enormously.

The fact is that no matter how ruthless and brutal may have been the practices in different stages or time periods of slavery, inevitably the slave-holders could not ignore the humanity of the slaves. But recognizing people as human beings is not tantamount to showing kindness and compassion. (From the standpoint of contemporary moral values, anchored in humanitarian ideals, all forms of slavery are tyrannical, brutal, and oppressive in that they deprive other human beings of their basic freedoms. This was not always the case: The moral arena in which evaluations and judgments are made today differs greatly from that of antiquity.)

A variety of customs, habits, and conventions developed affecting the sale and treatment of slaves and the relationships between slaves and their masters and other free persons. Some of these soon became codified in bodies of laws, like those found in the codes of Hammurabi of Babylon, eighteen centuries before Christ. In societies without written literature, these were part of a large oral repertoire of customs and traditions that were handed down from one generation to the next and maintained as general guidelines for behavior.

These ancient bodies of laws, customs, legal precedents, and traditions recognized the dilemma of people being defined as things. Lawmakers, writers, and philosophers grappled with detailed guidelines on the fine points of cases in which distinctions had to be drawn between the slave as property and as human. One distinction, expressed in the law codes from Augustinian times to those of Justinian, was that between *ius gentium* (law common to all people) and *ius naturae* (natural law). The law of nature, some Romans argued, declares that there are natural rights inherent in mankind that cannot be denied under slavery. The law of nature makes every man an equal. When the law of nature comes into conflict with civil laws or laws of property, it is the law of nature that must prevail. Thus, law codes, although dominated by considerations of the owner's property rights, provided an out by which the human rights of slaves could be given precedence over the property rights of masters.[20]

The Justinian code expressed existing standards of Roman law and thought at a time when slavery was being gradually transformed into a new type of servitude, villenage or serfdom. Historians disagree on the distinctions between the conditions of serfs and of slaves, but they do agree that both institutions continued side by side in many parts of Europe until the fifteenth century and even later in some places. Slavery and serfdom declined and became extinct in western Europe gradually from the thirteenth century, although Jordan (1968) notes that laws relating to villenage as a form of unfree labor remained "fossilized" in the English legal system (50).

Slave codes, customs, and actual practices reflected the degree to which societies were willing to give cognizance and priority to the human rights of slaves. Of significance for this study is the fact that, prior to the eighteenth century, there appears to have been no society that categorically denied the humanity of slaves in law and social beliefs, even when the treatment of them appeared most brutal.[21] That is, no society felt the need to rationalize slavery by denying that slaves were fully human. Virtually all societies viewed them as unfortunate, inferior, and powerless, although their statuses varied widely.[22]

Scholars from Tannenbaum on have identified some of the pragmatic social features that are indicative of the society's recognition and acceptance of the slave as a human being. These include the possibility of manumission, the right to marriage or some form of connubialism, the right to hold or own property (and to use it to purchase freedom), access to training or education in some skill, and some form of special rights or protection for slave women and their children by their masters or by other free men. These are the most frequently found customary rights permitted to slaves in Old World societies and were sometimes expressed in the written law. It should be obvious that these rights or privileges were not all equally and fully available to slaves in all societies and at all times. But evidence shows that they were accepted as normal aspects of slavery in the Middle East and Africa and in Greco-Roman times throughout much of the Mediterranean.[23] It is not clear whether such rights were always protected under the law, given the perversity of human behavior, but they reflect, it seems to me, the dynamic nature of slave systems and attempts at the resolution of, or compromise between, the property rights of slave-owners and the constant reminders or assertions of the slaves' humanity (Barrow 1928).

Slaves have had other rights accorded to them, such as the right to seek legal redress from cruel and unusual punishment, the right to be sold to another master, the right to some degree of physical and social mobility within the slave status, the right to enter into contracts and to conduct businesses, and the right to religious instruction and to worship the gods of the dominant society. These rights were probably less commonly implemented in the Old World than the previous set of rights, but it is significant that they are also found in the literature on Latin American slavery at various times and places (see Bowser 1974, and Rout 1976, among others).

Of greater importance is the fact that Old World slavery never developed as "racial" slavery, although the potential ingredients were there.[24] Peoples of all physical variations and ethnic groups were subject to enslavement since ancient times. The only restrictive custom was the prohibition against enslaving one's coreligionists: Christians theoretically did not enslave other Christians, nor Muslims other Muslims, a situation likely honored more in its breach than its observance.

In the Iberian Peninsula, dark-skinned Africans arrived as part of the Muslim conquests, as we have seen.[25] But slavery had existed here since Roman times and by the end of the fifteenth century comprised such varied peoples as Armenians, Bulgarians, Circassians, Greeks, Jews,

Lebanese, Syrians, Russians, and even other Spaniards (Bowser 1974). Peoples from sub-Saharan Africa were not unknown in this medieval world; some records of Africans who were traded in Portuguese and Spanish ports reach back as early as the thirteenth century (Rout 1976, 4), but many were certainly there before. Snowden has documented the even more ancient presence of dark Africans in the Greco-Roman world (1970, 1983).

After Portugal established trading ports along the West African coast beginning in the 1440s and Turkish forces conquered Constantinople in 1453, effectively cutting off trade with Black Sea ports, slave traders turned to West Africa. This increased greatly the numbers of African slaves bought during the latter part of the fifteenth century. The Portuguese initially monopolized the trade to West Africa, supplying spices, ivory, gold dust, skins, as well as slaves to Europe. Lisbon and Seville evolved as major trade centers. Of the estimated one hundred thousand slaves in Spain during the latter part of the sixteenth century, many were of African origin, including some who were descendants of the Moors (Palmer 1976, 6). They were primarily domestic slaves, but also served more public functions as soldiers, laborers, porters, and trash collectors. There were also free people of African background in the Iberian Peninsula, so dark-skinned, negroid-looking people were not unfamiliar to the Spanish and Portuguese even before they began direct importation of Africans to the New World colonies in the early sixteenth century. Herbert Klein (1971), speaking of the intimate contacts between the Spanish and African peoples, claims that "the Iberian peoples had long accepted the individuality, personality and co-equality of the Negro." They had mixed freely in slavery with all other Europeans, slaves and free, and "there was no reason for the white Iberians to conceive of these Africans as anything but normal human beings" (141).

Leslie Rout, Jr., (1976) notes that more female African slaves were imported than male, and they functioned as domestic workers and concubines. "As a result, a number of mulattoes were to be found in al-Andalus (the Muslim term for Spain), and several of them allegedly enjoyed positions of importance in the national aristocracy and bourgeoisie" (14, 18). Thus we perceive customs and practices already in place involving not only slavery but also patterns of interaction with diverse human populations that subsequently would appear in Spanish America.

Certain codes of law had systematized and distilled many characteristics of Old World slavery as they were manifest in Spain and Portugal. *Las Siete Partidas*, a body of legal and moral principles enacted in Castile in the thirteenth century, governed slavery in Spain, and like its predecessor, the Justinian codes, it placed restrictions on the behavior of both masters and slaves, decreed appropriate punishment for offenses, and specified the rights and entitlements of slaves. It provided, among other things, for the manumission of slaves and for the recognition of the rights of slaves to marry, to earn wages, to have instruction in religion, and to be protected and represented in courts of law. The continuity of slavery in the western Mediterranean meant that its customs, practices, beliefs, and habits were already established precedents for the New World conquerers. These precedents formed part of the cultural knowledge that was transmitted to the New World by the conquistadors and others. Elements of *Las Siete Partidas* were carried across the Atlantic and instituted in the New World colonies under the supervision and sanctions of the Crown and the church. They were designed to serve as guidelines for the legal regulation of slavery among both indigenous peoples and later imported ones. However, such historians as Magnus Morner, Colin Palmer, and Leslie Rout, Jr., have warned that strict supervision of the relationships between masters and slaves in the New World context could hardly have been very efficient, and it is likely that adherence to *Las Siete Partidas* was very minimal in many areas. They suggest that local laws enacted to deal with particular circumstances often superseded or contradicted the laws of the Crown or the colonial governments.

Nevertheless, *Las Siete Partidas* and the decrees issued from the monarchy and backed by the Catholic church provided standards and guidelines for slave-master relationships as reflected in Old World customs. If nothing else, they were reminders of the human personality and the inviolable rights of the slaves and undoubtedly protected them in many instances from excessive brutality and abuse. In the structure of colonial society, representatives of the Crown and members of the church functioned to monitor the behavior of slave-owners, and these men often had considerable power especially in the towns (Klein 1971). But custom and habit more than anything probably functioned to provide adherence to the tenets of slave laws.

Colonial Slavery Under the Spanish and Portuguese

Unlike the English settlers, the Spanish conquered New Spain (Mexico) and Peru with armies of men and established an elaborate colonial bureaucracy that eventually controlled huge territories encompassing large numbers of indigenous peoples. Under instructions from the Crown and mandates of the Catholic church, they set about immediately not only to impose their laws on the heterogeneous populations within the regions under their control but also to convert the Indians to their religion and monitor their moral behavior. Their primary aim as conquerers, however, was to exploit the wealth in gold, silver, and precious stones so abundant in the Aztec and Inca worlds.

Cortés set out to conquer Mexico in 1519, and within a decade Pizzaro formed a company in Panama to explore the wealth of Peru. According to Bowser (1974), "blacks figured in all the expeditions undertaken by the company between 1524 and 1528" (3). In 1534 Pedro de Alvarado sailed from Guatemala with two hundred blacks in his company to claim some Peruvian territory. After the conquest of the Incas, when the followers of both conquistadors came into conflict and civil war ensued, blacks were important in the battles on both sides. "Even more significant was the role played by skilled Africans in the supply of the royal army. Black artisans were employed to manufacture harquebuses, swords, and lances, and an African woman was commissioned to supply the force with rosaries" (9).

These first Africans to come to the New World, having been brought from the Iberian Peninsula, were already Hispanized—that is, acquainted with Spanish language and culture. Although most were probably slaves, some were free men and women serving as retainers and employees of the conquistadors or church officials. When Africans served outstandingly in battles or as scouts, they were often given their freedom along with land and some other booty of war, much as in Old World slavery.

Bowser (1974) claims that Africans in Peru "profited by the free-and-easy atmosphere of the conquest period to gain their freedom" (273). And many more, he points out, came as free men on their own. They soon became an important component of coastal towns. All of this suggests that in the early years of colonization the life-style that developed was much more like that of the Old World ports and cities, including the ease with which individual slaves could purchase or attain their freedom by virtue of their services.

Initially it was the Indians whom the Spanish planned to use as slave labor in the mines and in food cultivation and provisioning. Colonial settlers everywhere used the argument of the conquest of indigenes in "a just war" to justify their actions (much as their northern counterparts would later do). But within decades the decline of the Indian population from disease and maltreatment by their Spanish overlords became disturbing to the Spanish Crown and threatening to the labor supply. By 1550 the Crown outlawed Indian slavery, although subsequent patterns of wage labor, using the mita system by which Indian districts or provinces had to provide laborers, and the organization of large haciendas reduced most remaining Indians to impoverished peasantry under the nominal protection of the Crown.

As the Indian population declined, a growing demand for labor resulted in decisions to import more Africans who had already demonstrated their viability within the tropical zones.[26] Beginning in about 1518 the Crown allowed slaves to be imported directly from Africa; these formed a new category of slaves ("bozales") who initially spoke no Spanish and were not yet acculturated to the European way of life. After the establishment of the African-Atlantic trade, Peru and Mexico received the bulk of the slaves brought during the first two centuries of Spanish colonialism (Palmer 1976). And it was in these territories that the dominant patterns of New World colonial slavery were first established. The numbers of African slaves increased steadily throughout the first part of the sixteenth century and much more dramatically after 1580 when the Spanish and Portuguese empires were united under Philip II and Spanish ships became directly involved in the slave trade.

Colonization and interaction among the Spanish, Africans, and Indians differed in many ways from the patterns later established in the English colonies. Demographically, the number of Iberian colonists in any area was never very large, except in a few cities. In most rural areas, not only did native peoples outnumber their conquerers and their followers and slaves, but in certain regions, the slave population eventually equaled or surpassed that of the Europeans, who were concentrated in the cities.[27] Spanish efforts to govern and control the regions of the two major viceroyalties, with capitals in Lima and in Mexico City, entailed strategies that either kept ethnically distinct populations separated or pitted some groups against others. Whenever Spanish officials dealt with Indians, for example, they armed their black slaves, who always came with them. In addition, the Spanish in both areas frequently passed laws that attempted to prevent contact between the bozales blacks and the Indians in order to protect the latter from alien and sometimes heretical (such as Muslim African) influences and to preclude any possible unity among them.

All conquered regions came under the direct control of the colonial administration, involving both church and state, and the administrative bureaucracy was spread widely and thinly over all territories.[28] This meant that in towns, mining settlements, agricultural plantations, and rural districts a Spanish minority governed an increasingly heterogeneous society. The social structure that the Latin rulers envisioned and tried to achieve was one in which clear status differences among the visibly distinct populations could be retained for the organization and efficient governing of the colonies. Their vision followed the model of estates that had been developed in Spain under the Catholic kings in which a system of "castas" distinguished Jews, Muslims, and Christians. The idea of castas was transmitted to the New World colonies, but the term itself came to be used to specify people of "mixed blood," the mestizos, mulattoes, "zambos" (African-Indian), and various subsequent mixtures among these. The social structure was further complicated by class and status divisions and internal rankings within the European, Indian, African, and mixed groupings.[29]

A variety of civil laws were passed to keep the Africans, Indians, and mixed bloods apart. They were often separated by residential areas and to some extent by the kinds of occupations opened to them. Sumptuary rules placing prohibitions on dress, occupations, and access to the military, universities, and hospitals and imposing restrictions on marriage were repeatedly promulgated. But efforts to enforce these laws were ineffectual or only weakly attempted.

Since both the Spanish and their slaves were predominantly male and the slaves identified with the Spanish as conquerers, both turned to Indian women for sexual partners. In Mexico, Palmer (1976) relates frequent complaints were lodged throughout the sixteenth century against Africans who absconded with Indian women and often mistreated and intimidated Indian men with whom they worked in the mines or on haciendas. In Peru similar processes took place. Blacks assumed a position of superiority over Indians and often forced the latter to serve them. The Crown imposed harsh penalties on Africans who mistreated Indians, attempted to prevent sexual relations between slaves and Indian women, and tried to bar blacks from carrying arms (Bowser 1974, 154). The government appointed an Indian agent (corregidor de indios) to protect the Indians and prevent contact with black slaves. Despite official government policies, none of these numerous efforts at social control worked. The African slaves preferred to mate with or marry Indian women since their children would be free, and Spanish men exercised their dominance as conquerers by mating with both Indian women and their female African slaves. This sexual intermingling among the different populations began early and continued right through the colonial period and beyond, following customs very like Old World slavery.

On occasion intermarriage with Indians was encouraged by the Crown, as when Spanish men were pressured to establish strategic marriages with high-status Indian women. On other occasions local attempts were made to prevent the mixture of peoples because of the confusion of statuses entailed. But none of the Latin colonies passed laws, as did the North Americans, strictly prohibiting intermarriage on pain of legal penalties. The church was responsible for more than a few marriages because it periodically forced Spanish men to legitimize their unions and their children by Indian, mestizo, and mulatto women (Klein 1971). As in the Old World, marriage was considered a normal state for a man and woman. Colonial laws permitted slaves to marry, and both custom and the Catholic religion pressured slave-owners to recognize such marriages.

Well before the eighteenth century, "miscegenation," says Leon Campbell, "had caused racial lines in Peru and elsewhere to become hopelessly blurred" (1973, 324). But it was not "race" that was blurred; it was the biophysical variations that the Spanish had tried to use to structure a society in a hierarchy of social categories. In Peru, Campbell asserts, the hierarchy placed Spaniards on top, mestizos next, then Negroes, and below them the large mass of "Indians" who retained much of their culture and communities.[30] With the confounding of physical distinctions, new social criteria for signifying status had to be adopted. And these allowed for a certain fluidity in the social hierarchy so that some wealthy castas could purchase certificates of "whiteness" and children could be registered at birth in higher social strata for a fee (Campbell 1973). Wealth and/or occupation alone was often the catalyst of change in casta identity and further complicated the social statuses of mixed groups (Morner 1967; Rout 1976). Moreover, some physically recognizable whites also sank in status as their fortunes declined.

An important feature of these societies was the number of Spanish or high-status men who recognized their children by Indian and African-descended women.[31] Bowser (1975) notes that "sexual contact between Spanish men and African women was widespread and persistent throughout the colonial period" (347). These preferences of Spanish males were observed earlier in Spain (Rout 1976, p. 14). Their children were frequently freed, often provided with education and/or training, bequeathed estates or some form of wealth, and permitted to hold significant roles in the colonial hierarchy. In a process of "whitening" some mestizos and mulattoes were allowed to inherit the social status of their European fathers, despite the even greater burden of illegitimacy in some cases. Whiteness or being of "pure" Spanish ancestry, because it symbolized the conquerers, represented the pinnacle of the social system.

In both Mexico and Peru "whiteness" was a social category that provided numerous privileges and advantages, and families in this numerically small upper crust continued to preserve as much of their declared "purity of blood" as possible. But it is clear that the elite assimilated considerable numbers of mixed persons. At the same time the great masses of indigenous people absorbed both Spanish genes and those of the Negro population, so that in most of Peru and Mexico the combination of distinctive African negroid physical characteristics virtually disappeared as they were blended into the dominant mestizo population.[32]

Similar processes took place in Brazil, where a genetically mixed population soon came to predominate, particularly in the northern state of Bahia. Both Pierson (1942) and Degler (1971) describe a colonial society sensitive to the multifarious intermixtures of peoples and offering special benefits and higher status to mulattoes. The "mulatto escape hatch," as Degler called it, allowed those of mixed backgrounds to function in the interstitial areas of the economy, to have training and skills not available to freed blacks, and to achieve levels of political and social status closer to that of whites.

In all of the Latin areas, the European colonists not only recognized the intermixture of peoples, but also allocated distinct names to the various combinations and attempted to utilize their gradations within the social structure. Rank often came to depend on how much Spanish or Portuguese ancestry was manifest in one's phenotype, even though early in the conquest period negative connotations were associated with castas, primarily for their supposed illegitimacy. The social hierarchy, however, was a complex one, not easily fitted within parameters familiar to North Americans. Prejudice and discrimination against individuals with dark skins, reflecting descent from slaves, characterized all of the Latin colonies in various forms and intensities. The value hierarchy ensured the persistence of color preferences, which were exacerbated in the postcolonial period. What some have called a "pigmentocracy" emerged slowly, according to Morner (1967), and became more rigid as the colonial system matured. Black, Indian, white, and every mixture among them became not "racial" classifications but synonyms of individual social rank. As a consequence, before the end of the colonial period, in the nineteenth century, some degree of fluidity had allowed mixed persons to achieve high status, wealth, and even fame, and poor whites declined in status. As Emilia Viotti da Costa (1977) and others have revealed, "the society was in fact structured according to criteria of wealth, rank, color, and legal status" (297). She continued by saying that in Brazil, "money and status could change black, or at least mulatto, to white" (298).

In summary, the documented evidence from a variety of sources on Latin America suggests that whereas minute physical variations and admixtures were recognized and used for an ideology of social inequality, they were not homogenized and translated into specific, exclusive, and distinct groupings. And even the names and categories supplied that tried to represent every possible ancestral combination were not associated explicitly with stereotyped behavior or institutionalized as dogma about innateness. Continued reproduction of genetically mixed people ensured that easy boundaries could not be drawn on physical traits alone, and individuals shifted about within various social strata on the basis of criteria other than what would have been considered "race" in North America. Instead, the criteria were markedly varied and included education, social class, family background, occupation, and wealth—as well as color and physiognomy. Moreover, as da Costa also tells us, in Brazil, blacks, slave or free, had a wide variety of personalities reflected in literature and in the minds of dominant whites. Their image was never relegated to the "Sambo" or "Nat" that dominated white minds in nineteenth-century North America (Fredrickson 1977; da Costa 1977). We would expect this to be true also throughout Spanish America.

The fundamental question raised by extensive miscegenation, and its social recognition in the Latin colonies, is whether the attitudes and practices of discrimination against dark-skinned or more negroid-looking people are reflective of the existence of "race" and "racism." Campbell (1973) implies that in Peru there was racism without race due to the fact that visibly clear-cut, nonoverlapping, exclusive groups did not and could not easily have emerged. When we recall that exclusiveness is a major component of race in North America, as we here define it, the query rises to central importance.[33] We need new conceptual tools and a more refined vocabulary to denote these differences.[34]

The Uniqueness of the English Experience of Slavery

All forms of colonial slavery bore numerous institutional similarities in the use and treatment of Africans as slaves. Historians have argued in recent times that every colony differed in some respects from others, whether Latin or English. Plantation societies, whether in Brazil, on the Caribbean islands, or in the southern United States, and whether producing tobacco, sugar, or cotton, were more similar to one another than to urban areas; it was on plantations that slaves everywhere worked hardest and received the most inhumane treatment. Urban centers tended to also manifest, inter alia, similarities in the kinds of work that slaves did and in personal relationships to slave-owners and other free persons.

But there were differences that reflected the colonizing powers' varying historical experiences with human heterogeneity and with older forms of slavery and the cultural strategems devised in the past for coping with these realities. In other words, the differences between English-American and Latin-American slavery relate most directly to the retention of Old World customs and habits in the Latin areas, irrespective of the physical diversity in the population.

On the important issue of manumissions, for example, we have seen that there were always substantial numbers of free blacks and mixed peoples in the Latin colonies, and no laws prevented the emancipation of slaves. On the contrary, the laws and customs of the Iberians assumed that freedom was the natural and normal desire of human beings, and moral pressure was put on those recalcitrant slave-owners who denied freedom to their slave(s) when it could be purchased. According to Bowser (1974), the principles of Las Siete Partidas "viewed slavery as a necessary evil, as a transitory condition that did not alter or diminish the nature of the slave" (273). Thus manumission was not only possible but, at least in Peru, the old Roman peculiam (property earned by slaves) was restored to provide slaves a means of income (Bowser 1974, 278). Spanish American practices relating to the purchase of freedom, Bowser further tells us, were "more liberal than that envisioned by the Partidas" (1975, 343). Moreover, several historians have noted, Latins did not fear their freed slaves. Although most were poor, large numbers of freedmen worked in important crafts and professions. Many were mulattoes who did not identify with slaves or blacks.

In North America, numerous legal and customary prohibitions made private manumission difficult or increasingly impossible from the late seventeenth century up to the Civil War period. North Americans everywhere feared the consequences of freeing large numbers of slaves, a fear that peaked in the first half of the nineteenth century, when, as will be argued, "the Negro" was becoming viewed and defined as subhuman, or a species apart.

North American slaves had no refuge from, or any rights to redress against, cruel or unusual punishment. Nor could they sue through the courts and request to be sold to another master, as was often the case under Old World slavery, and as was sometimes found in the Latin colonies. In North America, from the eighteenth century on, outside of the northern colonies, slave marriages were not considered legitimate or legally binding on the master, nor was there institutionalized religious pressure to recognize them. It was an arbitrary decision on the part of an owner to permit slaves to enter into any form of connubialism. There was indeed no acceptance of the need for affective relationships between male and female slaves. On the contrary, slave women were thought of only as workers or breeders and concubines at best. The slave codes gave the master complete discretion in the matter of separating "husband" and "wife" or mother and child and gave virtually total control over the welfare of the slaves.[35]

It was in the matter of female slaves and their children by their masters or other white men that North American racial slavery contrasted most sharply with the practices and customs of the Old World and with the slavery of the Latin American colonies. Historical records from the biblical times of Sarah and Abraham to the laws of Islam show that it was customary for a woman slave who had a child by her master to be protected from further sale and even to be allotted heightened status within the household.[36] It comes as no surprise that "Brazilians and foreigners alike acknowledged that the offspring of unions of masters with slave women were accepted as part of the family" (Degler 1971, 234). Nothing prevented Portuguese or Spanish settlers from recognizing their children by Indian or African women except their own personal inclinations and values.

This was not so in North America, although miscegenation manifested itself early in the history of the colonies, and, by the first part of the eighteenth century, "mulatto" offspring constituted a sizeable and recognizable demographic reality, albeit nothing like that in Latin America. There was no customary provision for a slave woman's security or for that of her children, nor did the system permit a change of her status under law. Indeed, North Americans obfuscated the facts and denied any separate social recognition to offspring of "mixed" parentage. Such children were not permitted by law or custom to be liberated, to be acknowledged by their fathers, or to be claimed as their heirs. In very few instances in the south or north did the mulatto descendants of white slave-masters have legal access to the status or property of their fathers, even on those rare occasions when they were emancipated, a clear indication that the ideology of race superseded other status dimensions.

The economic and social implications of this prohibition (or taboo) on paternal recognition have been far-reaching. The North American black population today derives an average of about 30 percent of its biogenetic ancestry from Europeans, due initially to the matings of masters and slave women.[37] When we remind ourselves that it was not the poor whites who owned slaves, and the latter produced enormous wealth for their owners and for the nation as a whole, then the demands made during the 1960s by some black groups for reparations do not seem quite so specious.

This critical difference in the attitudes of Latin and North American slave masters and the general society toward their offspring by slave women cannot be explained fully by the demographic and economic facts adduced by recent scholars who relate the frequency of sexual unions with Indian and/or African women to the ratios of white men to white women. In the Latin colonies, men came to explore and exploit the land and people for wealth and generally did not bring their women with them. Consequently, it is argued, they established sexual liaisons with Indian and African women. Because of their fewer numbers, European men in the Latin colonies often elevated their children by these women to freedom (and freed other blacks) in order to fill "the innumerable petty jobs, the interstitial work of the economy, that the constraints of slavery would not permit the slave to perform and that white men were insufficient or unwilling to man" (Degler 1971, 44).[38] In contrast, the argument continues, English men came with greater numbers of their own women, whose higher position and greater influence in English society made it possible to thwart any recognition of slave children (232).

Yet Nash (1982) reminds us that until about 1620, white women were generally unavailable in Virginia. And English males still took "little recourse to Indian women" (276). He cites a contemporary of this period who thought the English men were "imbued with a false delicacy ... and could not bring themselves to sleep with Indian women" (276). Nash finds it difficult to believe that such squeamishness characterized the generally lower-class English men, and argues that the cause probably lay within the Indian community, which felt no need to give up their women.

But the overall patterns of European relations with Indians tell us a somewhat different story. In the early sixteenth century, both the Portuguese and the French cultivated alliances and cooperation with the Indians. They sent boys and young men to live with the Indians and learn their languages (Dickason 1979, 189). All of the Latin peoples assimilated some Indians into their communities, although sometimes attempting to separate them residentially and by occupations. They vigorously converted them and transmitted to them their language and life-styles. The English, however, systematically excluded Indians from the very beginning. Nash says of the English, "the general lack of red-white sexual intermingling forecast the overall failure of the two cultures to merge" (1982, 278).

The Latin colonies, in contrast, produced and incorporated large mestizo populations, out of which came many outstanding cultural and political leaders. Not only was there genetic fusion but also the syncretism of Indian, Latin, and African cultures was extensive. Talented mestizos and mulattoes were co-opted into the elite Latin community, many holding professional and skilled occupations. Of the English, Nash states, "But in colonial America the half-Indian, half-white person, usually the product of a liaison between a white fur trader and an Indian woman, remained in almost all cases within Indian society [and] were the most alienated of all people from white society" (1982, 279). What Harris (1964) called the "rule of hypo-descent," whereby children were accorded the lower status of their mothers, obtained in the cases of both Indian and black mixed offspring among the English (56).

We have seen that some scholars have argued against the importance of previous cultural attitudes of Europeans in determining their patterns of colonial interaction (Nash 1982, 284). But we are reminded of the Statutes of Kilkenny that forbade intermarriage of English settlers with the Irish and the general English cultural predisposition, seen in earlier chapters, to keep themselves apart. It was not primarily the presence, or lack, of English women that generated English men's indifference to their children by nonwhite women. Nash comes much closer to the truth when he states that English men objected not so much to sexual relations with dark-skinned women, but to conferring status on them "by accepting such intermingling as legitimate or by admitting its product to white society" (1982, 284). It was exclusion from English society that was the goal. The Portuguese and Spanish were also protective of their statuses but they never erected exclusive categories and were not so rigid in their proscriptions.[39]

It seems, then, that the worldview of Latin colonists was from the beginning very different from that occupying the minds of the English, because of their varying experiences with human diversity. The Latin colonists accepted Africans in a wider variety of roles, from free men of diverse social statuses to the lowliest of slaves, just as they had in the Old World. With the passage of time and increased importation of Africans, they came to associate dark skins with the status of slaves, but the correspondence was neither precise nor comprehensive. In the nineteenth century, Latin Americans came under the influence of the race ideology of North America. But because of extensive intermixture of peoples, among other historical and cultural factors, it was impossible to incorporate all of the ideological components of race as they had developed in North America.

Because of their inability to structure phenotypically based separate and exclusive groups, none of the other components of race were institutionalized in Latin America as formidably and as widely as in the United States. The ranking and inequality were (and still are) heavily predicated on social factors, including income, education, inherited wealth, language, occupations, and life-style, which long predated the tricontinental mixing of peoples. This is so despite the retention of linguistic evidence suggesting phenotype-based categories. Postcolonial developments reveal clear preferences for "whiteness," in emulation of European and American values, but the race concept was never so rigidly and firmly established in the Latin colonial world as it was in pre–Civil War North America.

All of this suggests the need for rethinking and reformulating our understanding of attitudes toward human differences, not so much in terms of "race," using a lexicon specific for the North American situation, but in more precise terms derived from comparative studies of the ideological components in the worldviews of different societies and at different stages of their development.

The Significance of Slavery in the Creation of "Race"

What the English were developing, concurrently with slavery, was a new criterion of status, the idea of race, whose rationale could be situated in the "natural divisions" of humankind. But these divisions were not historically recognized as natural *and* as relatively insignificant as they were in the Old World. Instead, they were compounded into autochthonous taxonomic population units and ranked so that the lowest acquired questionable human status.

The imposition of subhuman status, within the slave context, required the denial of any recognition of the human rights of the slaves. Nash (1982) portrays this phenomenon in terms of "the psychological compulsion to dehumanize slaves by taking from them the rights that connoted their humanity. It was far easier to rationalize the merciless exploitation of those who had been defined by law as something less than human" (151).

That "something less than human" is the critical element. The institution of slavery facilitates the dehumanization process in a logical manner by posing the contradiction that a human being is simultaneously both a piece of property, a "thing," and a person. This permits emphasis on the property element and the prioritizing of the rights of owners to their property. It also allows gross subjugation and brutality on a large scale, while obviating the possibility of guilt. The dynamic tension inherent in this dilemma has always in the past provided fluid space for preserving the human rights of slaves. American slave-owners, however, steeped in English legal history and traditions regarding the overarching importance of property and its connection to individual liberty, reversed this trend. They never came to accept fully the concept of slaves having natural rights that might supersede the property rights of the master. When they confronted the age-old dilemma of slavery, they chose to emphasize the slave as a piece of property first and foremost. It was the strongest and most successful assimilation of human beings to property that has ever been made.

The evidence for this is clearest in the numerous judicial decisions that fortified property rights. It is also found in many of the laws that were enacted after the turn of the eighteenth century, especially in the fugitive slave laws, the various legal codes controlling the movements and behavior of slaves, and the lack of specification of slaves' rights in any of the relevant legal documents. It is manifest unmistakably in the customs and social habits that developed governing the treatment of slaves and the interactions of slaves and masters. However, before complete assimilation could be accomplished, as Nash so clearly recognized, the slave had to be defined first as a creature who was not fully human.

There were, as we have seen, already existing tendencies in English culture that promoted or ensured this cognitive transformation and provided a kind of cultural validation for it: a hierarchical view of the world; the pseudoscientific/religious notion of the Great Chain of Being; and an extreme form of ethnocentrism emanating from long antagonistic relationships with other neighboring groups. The English had an elaborate conception of what "savagery" was all about, the most important feature of which was its "subhuman" status. We will recall that, in the late sixteenth century, some Englishmen were beginning to believe that the "wild Irish," their prototype savage, were inherently inferior and could never become civilized. In parallel with the enhancement of black labor as the only viable and suitable labor force that could be totally controlled in the context of colonial development, the Africans were increasingly fitted into the mold that the Irish had once occupied in the dreams of the Sidneys, the Gilberts, the Raleighs, and likeminded others. It was fortuitous for the English that (1) the new labor force happened to be not only culturally different but also physically distinct and not easily mistaken for any of the other populations in the new colonies; and (2) the African-Atlantic trade provided an unlimited supply of this labor.

Several observations should be made indicative of the complexity of the processes taking place and of the dynamic nature of the interplay of ideological beliefs impinging on these processes. One is that it was ironically the context of a developing Christian world that virtually required the transmutation of the Negro's human status. Christianity was a doctrinal religious movement that emphasized humanitarian and spiritual concerns over material ones. Certain sectors of Christian European society throughout the centuries were progressively elaborating and expanding on the themes of Christian brotherhood, human rights, and the elevation of the good of the many over the privileges of the few. Euro-Americans were virtually all exposed or conditioned (at one level and to a greater or lesser degree) to the virtues of selflessness, charity, compassion, and brotherly love. Within their own communities, certain standards of social behavior, shared systems of etiquette and politeness, shared attitudes toward proper social graces, all exemplified, at least minimally, the Judeo-Christian values governing human interactions. Theoretically, those who failed to adhere to the Ten Commandments and to the Golden Rule, to treat others as they would like to be treated, would experience divine retribution, if not here on earth, then in the other world. Such a sanction was strong in a world in which religious faith was still a significant aspect of a people's social well-being.

But greed and the great drive for accumulating wealth, which were the engines of the new economic order, required increasing deployment of forced labor and a callous indifference to human suffering. The pyschological and physical violence against other human beings that is inherent in the use of forced labor called for some justification that would inhibit or assuage any guilt, for guilt was an interloper and an obstacle to the spirit of a growing capitalism. Donald L. Noel (1972), in answer to his own query why exploitation should cause racism, answers, "It does so, paradoxically, only if the values of the exploiting society are such that its members have misgivings about the justice of their actions" (164).

Given the degradation of slavery, it took only a minor cognitive transition to focus on the obvious physical and behavioral differences between Africans and Europeans and for the Europeans to reach the conclusion that Africans were somehow not quite human like themselves. With this conclusion, all moral and ethical problems receded, and there remained only the pragmatic ones of selective perception, in other words, the obliteration from one's daily experience of any consciousness of the slaves' human qualities. Since the new definitions depended upon the very visible differences of the blacks, this psychological mind-set had to be extended also to those free blacks whom one might encounter. This accounts for the growing patterns of behavior and their corresponding attitudes, deeply humiliating and degrading, that were shown to all blacks, especially in the southern United States. However trivial, every act symbolically had to remind both masters and slaves, whites and free blacks, of the subhuman status of the blacks. It also explains the increasing focus on the physical attributes of "the Negro" as we have seen.

This concern for the physical differences of blacks was to grow and intensify throughout the eighteenth century. It attracted the attention of learned men, and future scientists, even as it was evolving as the basis for social, political, and economic discriminations. Jordan (1968) notes that there was a rapid growth of interest in the "anatomical investigations of human differences" in both America and Europe toward the end of the eighteenth century (xiii). Two things are striking about this development. One is its indication of the direction that rationalizations of slavery were beginning to take. The other is the degree to which it coincided with the heightening of antislavery sentiment in both England and the colonies and with the independent mushrooming revolutionary spirit on both sides of the Atlantic. As will be seen in Chapter 9, the growing antislavery movement was an inadvertent catalyst for the final synthesis and elaboration of those elements represented in the popular culture explicitly by the term "race."

We can conclude that slavery was seminal to the creation and development of the idea of race in the North American colonies. First, it gave the colonists, individually and collectively, the unrestrained power to create their own savage. They fabricated and imposed their ancient image of savagery over an easily distinguishable, and powerless, category of people, making it possible to view them as subhuman. Second, since slavery always exacerbates cultural-behavioral differences between the free and the enslaved, black and white behavior grew even more divergent, especially on those plantations where slaves were forced to survive under brutish conditions. When people were treated like beasts, they inevitably behaved accordingly. The slavish, cringing behavior forced on the slaves, the stumbling and awkwardness, the inability to remember simple directions, the feigned ignorance or ill-health, all were postulated as innate. This belief was then used as justification for the further indignities and brutalities of slavery. It was a cycle that more deeply imbedded the idea in the white mind that behavior and biology were conjoined and inseparable.

Third, it enabled the colonists to maintain "the Negro" as a separate and discrete social category, regardless of slavery, imposing laws that preserved their distinctiveness. Although some miscegenation occurred, it was nowhere near the degree of genetic mixture of African, European, and Indian people found elsewhere. Legal prohibitions against intermarriage and fornication, along with the rule of hypodescent, meant that the pigmentation and physiognomies of original populations could be preserved intact, for the most part, and thus used for the critical function of maintaining easily perceived social categories. Fourth, slavery facilitated the establishment and maintenance of unequal social rank even after emancipation. It created gross cultural differences between whites and blacks and left the latter as a largely illiterate population without property or status and ignorant of prevailing political and economic processes. Because of its unequivocal linkage of social identity to physical characteristics, all people could easily be conditioned to such inequality. The ranking was implacable and permanent. All whites, regardless of social status, income, education, occupation, or social refinement, would always be on top and all blacks at the bottom.

The next step in the crystallization of racial reality took place in consequence of the contributions of learned men who responded to the public's interest in the great physical diversity of human populations and its implications. The rise of Western science coincided with the great colonial enterprises of western Europe and particularly with the structuring of a slave society in North America. Variation in human populations was a natural subject of investigation for educated people. They were soon to provide the public with the scientific evidence and rationalizations that it needed to articulate this diversity in a manner that suited European interests and cultural values. In doing so, science and scientific "truths" became critical to the ideology of race. We will see the beginnings of this process in the next chapter.

Notes

1. See Morgan (1972, 1975) and the works of W.E.B. DuBois ([1935] 1985, 1965), who was one of the first to recognize this connection.

2. Curtin (1977) notes that "the popular image of slavery is still pretty well confined to slavery in the United States, an image dominated by *Uncle Tom's Cabin* and textbook accounts of the cotton kingdom and the Civil War" (3).

3. The effort here has to be very brief and not at all exhaustive. We need much more research that attempts to systematize comparative studies.

4. Tannenbaum was not the first to note and investigate this phenomenon. Sir Harry Johnston's book, *The Negro in the New World*, pointed out that travelers in the past had often observed differences in treatment and conditions of slaves in Latin and English areas. Many writers and travelers had pronounced Latin American societies, especially Brazil, as free of racial discrimination. See for example Pierson (1942).

5. See Davis (1966), Degler (1959–1960, 1970, 1971), Harris (1964), Lane (1971), Mintz (1961), Morner et al. (1982), Noel (1972), Sio (1964–1965), and Skidmore (1972) among others.

6. Eugene Genovese's award-winning study (1976) argues that Southerners did recognize the human personality of the slave, and this was manifest in the paternalism of the master-slave relationship. But there are many circumstances that reveal some telling truths about what owners really thought about blacks. For example, if slaves were accepted as human, why the shock, anguish, and feelings of betrayal, which "reverberated across the South," when the "most trusted and pampered slaves" promptly deserted them after the Civil War (Genovese 1976, 98)? Slave-owners appeared to have expected the loyalty of dumb animals and not the most human of all desires, to be free, which they would certainly have accorded to themselves.

7. For much of the material that follows, I have relied primarily on Davis (1966, 1975); Degler (1956–1960, 1970); Elkins ([1959] 1963); Finley (1968a, [1960] 1968b); Morner (1967); Morner et al. (1982); Patterson (1982); Tannenbaum (1946); Watson (1980); Westermann (1955); and various articles from Foner and Genovese (1969); Miers and Kopytoff (1977); Mintz (1974); Noel (1972); and Rubin and Tuden (1977). But the reader should be aware that there are other works on slavery too numerous to mention here.

8. A definition that is at greatest variance with the classic ones of Finley (1968a) and others is offered in the remarkable study of Orlando Patterson (1982) in which he attempts to identify the "constituent elements" of all systems of slavery. Patterson defines slavery ("on the level of personal relations") as "the permanent, violent domination of natally alienated and generally dishonored persons" (13). It is a definition that might well apply to others, as, for example, poor blacks in the South after Reconstruction and convicts and prisoners in certain well-known circumstances. Patterson also characterizes slavery in ways utilized by other scholars. Domination and powerlessness seem to merit his greatest emphasis, but he also claims that slavery was tantamount to social death in that the slave has no social status or human ties beyond his identity as an extension, and property, of the master. In the end, Patterson analyzes all slavery as a relation of human parasitism (Chapter 12) in which the slave's dependence on the master for all that he is and does is in some existential way countered or matched by the master's dependence on the slave, not only for his labor but for the honor that accrues to him as the owner and master. Honor and social death, however, are not clearly empirical and therefore not easily documentable qualities.

My concern, of course, is not the commonalities of all slave systems but those features that differentiate one from another. The Patterson work, however, provides enormous amounts of information and great insights into slavery in general.

9. The most articulate and important exploration of this problem in recent literature is the work of David Brion Davis (1966). See also his study of slavery during the revolutionary war period (1975) in which he discusses among other things the "remarkable shift in moral consciousness" (41) that ultimately helped to bring about the end of slavery.

10. Wiedemann claims that "slaves were seen as similar to children; they were addressed as children" (1987, 25). See also Hopkins (1978), Watson (1987), and Weaver (1972).

11. Bohannan (1963) has a good brief discussion of this point (179–183). Most experts have recognized this aspect of slavery. It is critical to understand what the absence of genealogical links means in such societies. See Finley (1968a and [1960] 1968b).

12. For elucidation of these points and discussions of the issues, one should see some of the classic works in economic anthropology. A good collection in a single volume is Dalton (1967).

13. See Gluckman (1965), especially Chapter 2, for insightful understandings of the role of property in tribal and early state-level societies.

14. Finley (1980) argues that the uniqueness of slavery "lay in the fact that the labourer himself was a commodity, not merely his labour or labour-power." This meant that he had "total loss of control over his person and his personality" (74–77).

15. See the discussion by Miers and Kopytoff (1977) about "rights-in-persons" as it is applied in the African case in which the question of defining slavery has been the center of some debate.

16. Here, I am extending the argument from the African materials, but Chinese, Arab, and Indian kinship structures from many areas had similar controls over their members.

17. Curtin (1977) follows Kopytoff and his predecessors in identifying slavery as the "legitimate exercise of a bundle of different rights over another person" (4) and speaks of it as a form of social control. It was just one of "many kinds of bundles of rights," he notes.

18. In the Introduction to their book, Miers and Kopytoff (1977) provide a brief discussion of the issue. Their notion of the marginality of the slave is well taken, but it is questionable that such slaves were considered "non-persons."

19. The term "slave" as used today comes from "Slav" a term applied by Muslims to prisoners captured by the Germans from among the Slavonic tribes of northern Europe and sold to the Arabs (Hitti 1953, 525). Davis (1966) also points toward a German origin, with the term "sclavi" applied to foreign slaves to distinguish them from slaves of German ethnicity (68). These are not inconsistent propositions since Arab dealers may well have picked up the term from their German partners in the business.

20. It is this understanding that may fundamentally be responsible for the contradictions between the firm identification in laws of the slave as property, and social practices that recognized slave marriages, income/property (peculiam), education, training, and so on. See Barrow (1928), Buckland (1908), Hopkins (1978), and Watson (1987), among others.

21. Early in the conquest period, some Spanish conquistadors and some Englishmen questioned the humanity of native Americans. Largely because of the advocacy against Indian slavery of Bishop Bartolomé de Las Casas, Pope Paul III, as early as 1537 declared that the Indians were fully human with souls worthy of saving.

22. As in all human institutions, there are always exceptions that render the making of generalizations extremely difficult. Power has to be ascertained within specific contexts. Throughout the Middle East, Muslim North Africa, and much of the rest of Africa, many individual slaves held great political, economic, and social power, sometimes by virtue of being appointed as military or political leaders by their masters, sometimes as a result of revolts against existing political systems. Well-trained or educated slaves sometimes exercised more power than their masters. In Muslim history, many sons of slave mothers ascended to the high positions of their fathers. (See Campbell 1974, Cuffel 1966, Hitti 1953, Rotberg 1965, among others.)

23. The most obvious exception to the custom of slave marriage was the large number of eunuchs created in many slave systems, a condition designed to preclude marriage and procreation. In Africa master-owners were expected to provide male slaves with wives as a normal condition for all men.

24. See M. Campbell (1974), and Cuffel (1966). In his 1980 book, Moses Finley "insists" on the term "racism" to characterize Greco-Roman slavery because, he claims, slaves were considered barbarians and aliens in ordinary discourse, and ancient writers rationalized that they were inferior by nature (118–119). But his certainty is undermined by an earlier discussion in which he asks us rhetorically to contrast the fate of freed slaves in Rome with that of freed blacks in America (97). A Roman freedman "automatically acquired Roman citizenship" and his descendants suffered no stigma. For Finley the difference was obvious.

25. As Snowden (1970, 1983) has well documented, negroid peoples have interacted with southern Europeans and Near Easterners in the Mediterranean since ancient times. They were frequently found in the military forces of the Arab-Muslim world from Spain and Morocco to India (Hitti 1953). However, the intermixture of peoples in the Mediterranean never led to an ideology of race or institutionalized color prejudice.

26. Indians forced into labor for the Spanish began to be perceived as being "weak and of little strength" (Palmer 1976) so the demand for black labor was made known early in the sixteenth century. From 1501 the Crown periodically allowed some black and mulatto slaves to be sent to the colonies. In 1517 Las Casas sent his famous request to the king for African slaves to be substituted for the Indians, which he later regretted.

27. See the tables (11 and 12) of population estimates published in Palmer (1976) for the Mexican regions in about 1570. Comparable data for Peru seem not to be available, but Bowser (1974) reports that after 1593, during the height of the African slave trade, the population of Lima (the capital) "was half African and remained so until 1640" (75).

28. All of the Spanish territories were organized under political divisions called viceroyalties and were governed by a viceroy from a capital city. Mexico City was the capital of New Spain, which included what is now California, New Mexico, Arizona, and Texas, as well as most of Central America. There were also territories called "captaincies general" ruled by special governors theoretically responsible to the viceroy.

29. Men born in Spain of old Christian backgrounds set themselves above those Spaniards born in the colonies ("creoles"), and wealth and titles distinguished individuals within the colonies. Among Africans, those acquainted with Spanish culture and language functioned in roles superior to African-born blacks unacquainted with the language and culture (bozales), among whom were also ethnic divisions. And free blacks held higher status still, with wealth, occupation, and residency as other social dividers. See Morner (1967); and Rout (1976).

30. Bowser (1974) earlier asserted that "the black man rapidly came to occupy an intermediate position between Spaniard and Indian rather than the place beneath the Indian to which the law had consigned him" (7). Some free Africans had Indian slaves or employees. The rapid increase in the "mixed" population resulted in many mestizos, mulattoes, and other combinations often settling into Indian communities. What came to define "Indianness" was not biology, but culture and language. The same is true of "mestizoes." By living in the cities, speaking Spanish, and worshiping in the Catholic church, Indians often changed their category of identity. See Morner (1967).

31. See Bowser (1974, 1975), Morner (1967), Palmer (1976), and Rout (1976), among many others. Some historians disagree on the extent and nature of this phenomenon, but none denies its existence, despite the evidences of discrimination against such illegitimate children.

32. Small pockets of more or less negroid-looking peoples have remained in largely isolated areas of such Latin American countries as Peru, Chile, and Venezuela. Recent literature suggests that, as a result of the civil rights and "black power" movements in North America, a consciousness of "blackness" as a biosocial category has emerged in Latin America. It appeared among some of the predominately negroid peoples in Brazil's lower economic classes within which, as elsewhere, most people are of mixed genetic background and do not identify themselves as black unless they show very little mixture. See the articles in Fontaine (1985) and Graham (1990).

33. "Racial" prejudice as opposed to color preferences against blacks or negroid-looking people, in particular, in Latin America increased in the nineteenth century in direct proportion to the numbers of Europeans immigrating to these areas who brought with them an evolved racial ideology. In the twentieth century, increased interaction with and influences from North Americans amplified and intensified the racial ideology of the "white" upper crust. Brazilians were vulnerable, says Thomas Skidmore, to European theories of innate biological differences among people, in part because of their own feelings of inferiority vis-à-vis Europeans (quoted in Graham 1990, 10). Space does not permit exploration of the diffusion of the race concept from North America, but this is a fertile territory that needs extensive investigation. See also Knight (1970), Drake (1987), and the other essays in Graham (above).

34. Michael Banton (1983) has suggested several schemes for making these distinctions, derived in part from Charles Wagley, an anthropologist who has studied in Latin America. They suggest that racial identity in North America is based on ancestry; in Central America, on sociocultural status; and in Brazil, on

appearance (19). Although there may be merit to such a scheme, it may not reflect all the complexities of the varying ideologies about human differences prevailing in these regions.

35. Richard Sutch (1975) has addressed one of the "seeming paradoxes" in the comparisons of American slavery with other systems. Blacks in the American South, he claims, "seem to have been better cared for in terms of food, living conditions, and medical attention than slaves in other systems. Yet the American slave, unlike his counterparts in most countries was stripped of his humanity" (174). Most North American slave-owners regarded their slaves "solely as capital assets, no different in kind from acres of land, from farming implements, or from work animals" (173). Like all capital goods, they best met market conditions for profitability when they were in good condition and could be sold for high prices. In addition, particular slave-breeding plantations may account for some of the good care and the high rates of reproduction of North American slaves.

36. Under the code of Hammurabi of Babylon, if a slave woman bore a child by her master, she could no longer be sold away, and she and her child were set free upon his death. If he called the child "my child" during his lifetime, that child could share equally in his estate. Among the Muslims, the slave woman became "umm walad" (mother of children) and like her Babylonian sister, her position was made secure. She "could neither be sold by her husband-master nor given away and ... at his death was declared free" (Hitti 1953, 236).

37. See Glass (1953). Estimates of non-African genetic mixture in the ancestry of African-American populations have varied considerably. See also Reed (1969), and Goldsby (1971).

38. Although it appears reasonable, this explanation does not account for the fact that slaves in other societies performed the petty jobs, the many highly skilled crafts, and all of the ranges in between. I suggest that Latin slave-owners freed their slave offspring because this was the known custom from biblical times on, and there was no reason (no legal prohibitions or social pressures) not to do so. For a fuller discussion of sexual relations in the Latin colonial setting, see Morner (1967).

39. The English in the West Indies islands, Jamaica, and Barbados demonstrated a pattern more similar to Latin customs because of special circumstances. Some were absentee owners, and the managerial staffs who ran their large plantations were not encouraged to marry. The result was sexual intermingling with black and mulatto slave women and the production of a mixed population, some of whom achieved freedom and privileges through their paternity. See Fredrickson 1981, chapter 11.

7

The Rise of Science:
Sixteenth- to Eighteenth-Century
Classifications of Human Diversity

E VEN AS MULTIPLEX PATTERNS of slavery were evolving in all the New World colonies, attitudes toward human group differences were shifting and flowing, buffeted along by a wide range of individual and collective experiences. The knowledge, attitudes, and understanding of learned men were also changing and congealing. By the end of the eighteenth century, a whole new body of intellectual endeavors termed "science" had begun to emerge as a distinct domain of Western culture. Science grew in large part out of curiosity of and concern about the different kinds of human beings. As will be shown in this chapter, it came to play an important role in defining human groups and the relationships among them.

The Questions and the Issues

We have already seen that from the beginning of European expansion and colonization questions were raised about the identity of the indigenous peoples of the New World. Speculations about their human status became particularly critical after Magellan's discovery of the Pacific made it clear that the Americas were really a new world and not some easternmost outpost of India. Men of scholarship and learning, adventurous sons of the wealthy and well-born, antiquarians, theologians, missionaries, sailors, merchants, traders, and scholars communicated with one another over the mysteries of the new discoveries.

When they were not marveling at the wealth of Montezuma or speculating about El Dorado, Europeans ruminated about the place of the strange new natives in their model of the world. Were they children of

Adam and Eve as were all the peoples hitherto known to Europeans, or were they products of some separate creation? If they were to be accepted as fully human and products of God's creation, from which of the ancient peoples identified in the Bible were they descended? Were they, despite their savage ways, moral beings who could submit to the influence of the church and be saved? How does one account for and explain the naked savages within the confines of religious-based theories of natural history? If God indeed had formed human beings in his own likeness and if all human beings are descendants of Adam and Eve, how can differences of language, culture, and physical characteristics be explained? Such questions were intimately implicated with some of the crucial scientific, historical, philosophical, and moral issues regarding the nature of humans in general, and their place in the natural scheme of things. The European conception of humankind had been framed within culturally specific and thus limited knowledge systems of their own societies. It could hardly have been other than Eurocentric. God had created humankind in his own image, but the image was European. Any deviation from the European model was subject to interpretation, and there were limits to the flexibility of such interpretations.

Italian scholars of the Renaissance were among the first to have an interest in newly discovered peoples and to speculate on the origins and present circumstances of native populations. A fifteenth-century nobleman and merchant, Alvise Cadamosto, made several trips to Africa in the 1450s and wrote one of the oldest descriptions of the regions and peoples of Senegal, Gambia, and the Canary Islands, one that is still used by scholars for its ethnographic and historical materials. Another Italian, Pietro Martire (Peter Martyr), who was in the employment of Ferdinand and Isabella, began a systematic collection of all the reports from the men who first sailed to the New World, starting with Columbus, in 1493. Martyr was able to see the merchandise and other materials that they brought back with them and even to interview the native people that had been captured and presented to the court. His works were published in the early sixteenth century, and they were made readily available to other scholars and to the Roman Catholic church.

According to John H. Rowe (1965), Martyr had a special interest in the peoples brought back by Columbus on his first voyage. From them he collected a short vocabulary of Taino Indian words, becoming the earliest European to record a New World Indian language. Later scholars have noted the tolerant attitude that he took toward the customs, body decorations, and physical traits of those he described. It was as if the range of diversity on these matters was perfectly acceptable and expected. Rowe claims that Martyr inspired explorers of the New World to make notes on native customs (18).

The educated people of the eighteenth century looked to such Renaissance literature, as well as to revived descriptions of the customs and institutions of ancient times, for comparative materials. A scattering of writers of antiquity, among them Herodotus, Megasthenes, Vitruvius, Tacitus, Strabo, and Pliny the Elder, had provided brief descriptions of peoples on the peripheries of the then civilized world. Although most of these works contained subjective assessments of "barbarians" and their customs, they did provide points of reference for some Renaissance thinkers who felt compelled to identify modern savages in some known historical context, to "clothe savagery with documentary significance" (Hodgen 1964, 354), by showing their similarities to peoples of antiquity. Increasing attention to cultural and linguistic diversity generated not only speculations about origins, but also the development of methods of collecting materials and studying them, reflecting the rudimentary beginnings of the "sciences of man."

Until the nineteenth century, the major source of knowledge and explanations of the world and its complexities were the biblical interpretations and inferences made largely by men of the church. To be sure, the Enlightenment period in Europe, which spanned most of the eighteenth century, produced scores of men who objected to the often dogmatic positions of the church and who sought to free scholarship from its restrictive doctrines. This period is well known in Western history for the rise of naturalistic explanations, for confrontations between science and theology, and for the advances in empirical research and experimentation that are at the heart of modern science. It was through the efforts of men who dared to question theological positions and assumptions that the growth of Western science took place. By the mideighteenth century, science was well on its way to becoming a full-blown and distinctive ingredient of Western culture.

We should be very clear, however, about the nature of science and its position and functions in Western culture. Both naturalistic and supernaturalistic knowledge as well as the application of this knowledge to the resolution of human problems and the explanation of world realities are found in all human societies. Throughout human history, naturalistic knowledge—the pragmatic information and understandings that peoples have about the world around them and the practices they undertake to modify that world—and supernatural beliefs have been intertwined. Naturalistic knowledge is supplemented by the culture's supernatural explanations for things and events that are otherwise inexplicable. A farmer may, for example, inform a visiting anthropologist that it is the will of the gods that the crops on a farm failed this year and will simultaneously confirm that a reduction in rainfall or that infertility due to exhaustion of the soil were the proximate causative factors. For the peasant farmer both explanations are valid and inseparable; after all, it is the gods who control the rain and the wind, the qualities of the soil, the pests that threaten the crops, and even the goats who nibble and kill the seedlings.

Western science arose, gradually evolved, and became self-consciously dissociated from religion and other supernaturalistic perspectives, but only after much conflict and debate between the advocates of the new science and the theologians. It became a peculiar epistemology arising out of a distinct philosophy about the acquisition and manipulation of knowledge. Enlightenment writers saw science as an endeavor emanating from man's rational mind, unfettered by superstition or blind emotion.

Contemporary science comprises those ways of knowing and understanding that theoretically exclude the supernatural and the mystical; that is, science is based fundamentally on empirical knowledge, independently and objectively acquired through normal human sensory faculties or through mechanical techniques. It is guided by a body of concepts, formal procedures, particular rules, methodologies, and perspectives that carry the presumption of objectivity and neutrality. We are conditioned to view it as a separate sphere of culture and its findings as products of strict empiricism and rigid procedures.

Yet from its beginnings, certain theologically based assumptions and propositions survived undiluted in scientific thought. These assumptions related to the underlying cosmological and ideological themes of European cultures, specifically those values, beliefs, and "revealed" knowledge about God, nature, the world, and humankind. In its early stages, the Judeo-Christian idea of a single creation and the Noachian explication of human diversity were some of the main survivals of biblical thought in science. Their persistence was based on unquestioning acceptance of the scriptural representation of human beginnings; but they also reflected the church's pragmatic commitment to the spreading of Christian doctrines.

The Book of Genesis provided a divine explanation of human origins as well as the main impetus to proselytize. In one broad episode of creation, God (always identified as male) gave life to man, located him in the Garden of Eden, provided him a female mate, and charged him to be fruitful, to multiply, and to subdue the earth. God also cautioned Adam, this first man, in obedience, admonishing him that he could eat all of the fruit of the garden except that of the tree of knowledge of good and evil. But the reality of sin intruded in the form of a snake who tempted Eve (the woman and rib-mate of Adam) to eat the forbidden fruit. She found it so delicious that she shared it with her mate. Subsequently Adam and Eve fell from the grace of God and were banished from Eden for their disobedience.

One aspect of this story had extraordinary relevance to those who grappled with the identity and meaning of the "savage" peoples of the colonies. In their state of ignorance before they tasted the fruit exposing them to knowledge of good and evil, Adam and Eve were naked, innocent, and unashamed. But after eating the banned fruit, they not only became conscious of their nudity but also experienced shame. Thus nudity in the Judeo-Christian world became associated with a state of sinfulness, of the condition of Adam and Eve after the Fall, and a sign of their disobedience of God's commands. In earlier chapters, we saw how this cultural value about nudity prompted the English particularly to develop hostility and contempt for Irish and native American peoples, and to see in their absence of clothing reflections of the original sin and of bestiality.

Generations later, the descendants of Adam had multiplied on the face of the earth, but they had also become wicked and corrupt in the eyes of the Lord. Repenting his creation, God decided to destroy humankind and most of life on earth. But Noah, a descendant of Adam, had found grace in the eyes of God who determined that he, Noah, along with his sons, their wives, and representative couples from the animal and plant world would be saved from destruction to renew and replenish the earth. In a covenant with God, Noah built an ark for his family and assorted living things, and in it they rode out a massive storm of forty days and nights that destroyed every other living thing.

After the flood, the descendants of Noah prospered and proliferated. They formed the new nations of the earth, all of whom spoke one language. But, not content with things as they were, the ambitious descendants decided to build a city and in it a tower so tall that it could reach into heaven. For reasons not clear in the biblical text, God was not pleased with this, recognizing apparently that the children of man would not be restrained in those things "which they have imagined to do" (Gen. 11:6). So he descended from the heavens, confounded their language (gave them plural languages that were mutually unintelligible), and scattered them upon the face of the earth (Gen. 11:7–9). He called the tower that they had erected Babel, and from then on the term has been used to refer to situations in which there is a confusion of languages and an inability to communicate. This passage was interpreted, allegorically if not literally, as the source of the origins of different peoples, languages, and cultures.

The vast majority of peoples known to Europeans before the Age of Discovery could be fitted into some scheme of descent, following the genealogical figures of the Bible. Thus Shem, one of Noah's sons, was the ancestor of the Shemites (Semites), and Japheth was the founder of lines that lead to Christian Europeans. Later Ham came to be interpreted as the founder of the darker skinned peoples known to the Hebrew tribes, the Cushites and Canaanites and others not always fully identified. The task of scholars concerned with origins was to trace which of the three sons of Noah gave rise to various other ethnic groups. Central to the paradigm was the idea and Christian ideal of the universality of the fatherhood of God and the brotherhood and oneness of humankind deriving from the single creation.

We should not underestimate the influence of biblical theology and the interpretations of world history and relationships provided by the church. Until the second half of the nineteenth century, only a minority of men, and even fewer women, were literate, much less well educated. Virtually all, nevertheless, were familiar with the basic tenets of Scripture, so that even those in the natural sciences operated from the same widely held presumptions of human origins. Among the literate elite as well as the larger populace biblical passages were taken literally as unerring explications of contemporary events and conditions and moral righteousness. The "truths" extracted from scriptural sources were considered infallible and were rarely questioned before the eighteenth century. The Scriptures were the authoritative source of information about the world and everything in it. As Malefijt (1974) has aptly summed up, "Whatever God had wanted man to know about nature and society was revealed in the Scriptures, and whatever was not so revealed was intended to remain hidden" (25).

Renaissance writers, under the influence of the materialistic and naturalistic approaches of the ancients, developed a healthy skepticism about scriptural explanations. By the sixteenth century a few writers, such as Paracelsus and Giordano Bruno, began to speculate on the possibility of more than one creation. Such skepticism reflected the broadened horizons of European learning during the early era of exploration and colonization. From the sixteenth century on, one trend of scholarship followed a trajectory that increasingly veered away from orthodox explanations of natural phenomena toward material and secular ones. This movement paralleled the growth of a natural philosophy that required and emphasized objective, empirical studies and the search for the causes and origins of natural phenomena in elements of the environment.

Some explanations for the aboriginal inhabitants of the New World reflected the dynamic tension and antagonism between those who espoused religious or biblically based explications and those who sought answers in natural history and/or rational deductions from empirical evidence. After a 1537 papal bull was issued, which declared that the Indians were fully human and also descendants of Adam and Eve, numerous theories were generated tracing Indian ancestry to some biblical tribes. The wanderings of Noah's offspring became a major concern of many biblical authorities, and their speculative theories were proportionately numerous.

One of the most popular theories was that the natives of America were descended from the ten lost tribes of Israel. Toward the middle of the seventeenth century this theory was strengthened by the writings of a Jewish scholar, Menassah Ben Israel, who published a book in 1650 about how the Indians had arrived in the New World and the customs that they had in common with Old World Jews. That same year Thomas Thorowgood published *Jews in America*, in which he listed more than fifty traits that were similar in Jewish and Indian cultures. He also identified what he thought were some linguistic similarities. This theory was widely accepted and continued to be reflected in later writings, such as those of James Adair, its major proponent in the eighteenth century, and in the Book of Mormon.

Hugo Grotius, one of the most learned men of Europe and the Swedish ambassador to Paris, denied that Indians could be lost Jews. In 1642 he claimed that the Indians of North America were descended from Scandinavians who had crossed Greenland and reached the Americas. On the basis of the negroid sculptures found there, which predated Europeans, he decided that the peoples of the Yucatan-Mexico-Guatemala region were of African origin. He also noted the existence of Indian legends that spoke of a black god, as well as other similarities to West Africans that had been observed by Columbus and later travelers. The Indians who lived in the Peruvian Andes had arrived from China, according to Grotius's theory, and again he based this on both physical and cultural similarities.

Robert Comtaeus argued that the Indians were offspring of roving Phoenicians. He tried to prove that the Phoenicians were direct descendants of Ham, one of Noah's sons, whose lineage had been cursed for Ham's failure to avert his eyes when he came upon his father lying naked in a drunken stupor. Comtaeus's argument notably provided justification for the subjugation and enslavement of the natives by the

Spanish as the proper fulfillment of Noah's curse. This was also an argument later grasped and exploited by many of the English, as we have already seen, to rationalize perpetual enslavement of Africans.

Closest to modern ideas about the origins of native Americans was that of Laetius in 1643 who not only rejected Grotius's theory but argued that the Indians were migrant Tartars, because of their similarities in body structure, complexion, and other physical characteristics. He noted such features as the absence of beards, the custom of shaving heads, and the worship of one creator god along with fire, sun, light, water, and earth. He observed that both peoples were nomadic and made implements of bone and stone, were unclean in their eating habits, and often descended to cannibalism. South American Indians, he thought, might have Carthaginian and Hebrew origins, an assumption he rested primarily on their "higher" levels of civilization.[1]

All of these speculations, it will be observed, derived from understandings, accurate or not, of *similarities* among these peoples. These are in dramatic contrast to some writers of the eighteenth century who concentrated almost solely on human *differences*, with a perspective reflecting changed times and hardening social inequalities.

Understandably, it was the speculations of men like Isaac de la Peyrere that most disturbed the wider world of learned men. Peyrere was a Calvinist from Bordeaux, and in 1655 he argued, like Paracelsus and Bruno before him, that multitudes of people had been created before Adam who was the founder only of the Jews. The chronologies and events of the Bible, he believed, did not refer to Gentiles who existed prior to the special creation of Adam, but only to the Jews and their lands. Moreover, God did not destroy all of the peoples of the earth in the flood, merely the adulterate Jews. Grotius called Peyrere a madman, and many publications made similar attacks. The French Parliament ordered his books to be burned and he was imprisoned. Forced by the church to recant, he spent the last years of his life in a monastery. In this he was more fortunate than Bruno, who had been burned at the stake for his heretical beliefs.

A strange twist to the rigidity and restrictive suppositions of Christian establishment thinking, however, can be found in the works of some of the early missionaries, particularly those in the Spanish and French territories. In 1534 a remarkable man, Ignatius of Loyola, a learned monk in Italy, had founded the Society of Jesus, a religious order of adventurers and crusaders, missionaries and teachers, who later came to be known as Jesuits. The men of this order became some of the most esteemed thinkers of their times, and the most active. Ignatius trained his emissaries to learn as much as they could about the peoples and cultures in the lands where they went to proselytize. Coming to the New World in the mid-sixteenth century, they worked among the Indians, often providing support and comfort in their dealings with their Spanish rulers. These monks carefully recorded everything they saw or experienced, and their reports, brought together under the title *Jesuit Relations*, constitute some of the earliest ethnographic descriptions of the natives of the New World. In some cases, they preserved all that we know about cultures now virtually extinct; that of the Caribs is an example. Seventy-three volumes of the *Relations* were published between 1610 and 1791. The reports, in many cases, were unusually objective and comprehensive, especially on religious beliefs, rituals, and the daily lives of the people.

For the Jesuits, there was no question but that the Indians were fully human and that God had arranged for their discovery in order for the church to save their souls. Whether descended from the lost tribes of Israel or from some more remote branch of the human family described in the Bible, they were amenable to the ministrations of the gospel. This vision of the human family had a lasting impact on future scholarship. Jesuit writings, covering most of the Catholic territories, served as source materials for the theories of Hobbes, Locke, Rousseau, Montesquieu, Voltaire, and other writers of the Enlightenment and as a model for the "noble savage" image.

Meanwhile, the authoritarian hold of the Catholic church over men's minds began to decline with the Protestant Reformation and the breakaway of various sects from the mother church. In the wake of much political upheaval in Europe, widespread civil wars, numerous schisms and factionalism in both church and state, the power of the church was greatly diminished. The rise of merchant capital and significant changes in class structure brought new social forces into power. An accelerating quest for knowledge resulted in the rapid formation of private schools and academies, learned societies, and universities, many of which arose spontaneously in the colonies. Increasing wealth permitted some young men to devote their lives to research and writing, much of it on the amazing new discoveries in areas opened to European exploration. The writings and publications about aboriginal peoples proliferated, gradually acquiring more scientific tenor.

Even so, commitment to the idea of a single creation persisted with virile strength even down to the present. Scientists as well as nonscientists adhered tenaciously to the belief, not just as a fundamental element of religious faith, but for its philosophical significance in giving meaning to human existence. Rudimentary speculations on the possibility of multiple creations aside, the dominant religious and philosophical themes of the Age of Discovery made all the newly discovered peoples part of the great human family.

Belief and faith are highly adaptable to the varied conditions under which different elements of society operate and even to massive changes in these conditions. In turn, scientific minds have been able to embroider and elaborate diverse theories to make them compatible with basic cultural themes, such as the descent of all humankind from a single origin. This was particularly evident in the earliest attempts by scientists to identify and classify the then known variety of human beings.

Classifications of Humankind

In the early stages of the development of science, the most fundamental operation was the collection of data and their subsequent examination, description, and arrangement into categories according to certain explicit principles. This became a vogue in the sixteenth century with respect to newly discovered territories. Those persons who accumulated and often published data on the flora and fauna of strange lands and peoples were often known as "naturalists." Others were writers, geographers, and curiosity-seekers who simply wanted to inform a widening circle of literate persons about the wonders of foreign lands.

Many persons acquired material objects from cultures around the world, forming collections that became the bases of the great ethnographic museums of modern times. Others accumulated descriptions of alien peoples and their customs from travelers, commercial men, missionaries, geographers, and adventurers. The arrival of the printing press in the midfifteenth century had greatly aided the sorting and organization of descriptive materials and their dissemination. Based on these collections, enormous compendia of natural phenomena were published. Some of the men involved became known as classifiers and systematists, noted for organizing specific sets of data into logically comprehensible schemes. This was the beginning of a new trend in which the collecting activities were deliberate and were organized for systematic study of data in order to provide answers to fundamental questions. A scientific perspective on the world's realities thus began.

Detailed descriptions of little-known animals became common, especially during the seventeenth century. The accumulation of these data prompted learned men to attempt a comprehensive recording of all of the world's known creatures, establishing in the process the first steps toward a comparative perspective. Often such men, trained in physiology and anatomy, achieved significant understanding of the physical attributes of diverse animal forms. They were particularly challenged by the discoveries of nonhuman primates. The first published account of what we now know as the chimpanzee appeared in 1641, the orangutan in 1658. Reports of baboons and other Old World primates appeared soon after, and interpretations of who and what they were multiplied within the primate lore drifting about Europe and America.

Edward Tyson, an anatomist sponsored by the Royal Society of London, studied the morphology of various primates during the 1690s, including a "pygmy" sent from Africa. He was the first European to demonstrate great similarities in musculature and skeletal structure between humans and the great apes. The pygmy we know now to have been a chimpanzee, but his error had critical significance. He speculated that his "pygmy" was a form that had been created on the "Scale of Being" halfway between monkeys and true men, thus establishing a kind of "missing link" theory even before the development of evolutionary paradigms in biology.

This work shocked the scholarly world of the late seventeenth and early eighteenth centuries, for few were prepared to accept such unassailable human affinity to the apes. Only a short while before, Andreas Vesalius had been denounced by the church for suggesting such a relationship. Yet, by the latter part of the eighteenth century, scientific thought, especially in England, had not only accepted the notion of a relationship between humans and apes, but had also placed human beings within a larger natural scheme that included nonhuman primate forms. The idea of kinship between humans and apes was also taking shape in popular thought, but, as we shall see, with a somewhat different objective and motivation.

Taxonomic systems for the world's flora and fauna multiplied and so did efforts to classify human groups. Giordano Bruno and Jean Bodin in the late sixteenth century attempted an elementary geographic arrangement of populations using skin color. Bodin's color classifications were purely descriptive, including such neutral terms as "duskish colour, like roasted quinze," "black," "chestnut," and "farish and white" (Slotkin 1965, 43). Bernard Varen and John Ray in the middle of the seventeenth century placed then known human populations into categories according to stature, shape, food habits, and skin color, with brief descriptions of other peculiarities. All the early taxonomists used classificatory terms such as "types," "varieties," "peoples," "nations," and "species." Occasionally the term "race" was employed, revealing as we now know the influence of Spanish-language usage in the colonial experience. We have already seen that prior to the eighteenth century terms like "race" and "species" were sometimes used by learned persons in a loose generic sense that was roughly synonymous with "kind," "type," and "variety" (Chapter 2). Furthermore, none of the terms referred, specifically or exclusively, to biophysical characteristics, even though such features were normally a part of the general descriptions.

Francois Bernier, in an article in a French journal in 1684, was perhaps the first to propose a classificatory system that emphasized physical traits, using skin color, hair form, and "general appearance" (Slotkin 1965, 94–95; Jordan 1968, 217). His four classifications were "Europeans," "Far Easterners," "Negroes" (blacks), and "Lapps" (whom he thought had faces like bears and were "quite frightful") (Gossett 1965, 32). William Petty considered the different types of mankind, using "species" as a generic term, and raised only a minor query as to whether they had all been created at the same time. He did not establish a classificatory scheme for the various populations, observing merely that "'tis very possible that there may be Races and generations of such; since we know that there are men of 7 foote high & others but four foote" (Slotkin 1965, 89). "Race" here is used with reference to inherited physical traits after the fashion of Spanish references to breeding lines. Many other writers similarly connected "races" with "generations."

Modern classifications of human populations began with Carolus Linnaeus, a Swedish botanist, who in 1735 published *Systemae Naturae*, the first version of a vast classificatory scheme. For the first time Linnaeus included humankind, not only within the larger classification of all living things, but also in specific relation to the apes and monkeys. Linnaeus, considered the founder of scientific taxonomy, originated the binomial nomenclature still used today that denotes all living forms by "genus" and "species." He grouped human beings with the higher primates, under the order "Anthropomorpha," and divided the genus "*Homo*" into four basic varieties—*Europaeus, Americanus, Asiaticus,* and *Africanus*.

Like most scientists of the eighteenth century, Linnaeus had a precise understanding of "species," which was distinguished from "varieties." Species were distinct primoridal forms dating from creation that remained essentially the same throughout all time, but varieties were clusters within a species that had acquired superficial changes in appearance. Species were fixed and unalterable in their basic organic plan, but varieties reflected changes caused by such external factors as climate, temperature, and other geographical features. It was the general and widespread belief that all humans were members of the same species because they descended from a common original ancestry and were capable of intergroup mating and reproduction.

In later editions of his work, Linnaeus elaborated on his classifications of both apes and humans. Significantly, and like classifiers before him, his descriptions of the four human groups indiscriminately mixed physical features with supposed traits of character, disposition, and behavior, features we would see today as specifically cultural. His groups were

Americanus: reddish, choleric, and erect; hair black, straight, thick; wide nostrils, scanty beard; obstinate, merry, free; paints himself with fine red lines; regulated by customs.
Asiaticus: sallow, melancholy, stiff; hair black; dark eyes; severe, haughty, avaricious; covered with loose garments; ruled by opinions.
Africanus: black, phlegmatic, relaxed; hair black, frizzled; skin silky; nose flat; lips tumid; women without shame, they lactate profusely; crafty, indolent, negligent; anoints himself with grease; governed by caprice.
Europeaeus: white, sanguine, muscular; hair long, flowing; eyes blue; gentle, acute, inventive; covers himself with close vestments; governed by laws.

Linnaeus had several other categories for human types that included *"Homo ferus,"* or wild men, and *"Monstrosus,"* a category that lumped together a miscellany of exotic peoples such as "dwarfs" and "large, lazy Patagonians." He accepted popular myths regarding the existence of "Troglodytes," a nocturnal humanlike creature who lived underground and hunted only at night. The tenth edition of *Systemae Naturae* in 1758 classified the latter in the genus *"Homo,"* noting that they were also called *"Orang outangs."*

Linnaeus's commingling of physical features with behavioral and psychological traits shows the growing influence of a certain type of thinking, which presumed that each species had qualities of behavior or temperament that were innate. Like all his European contemporaries, Linnaeus acquired the vast majority of his data from the writings, descriptions, commentaries, speculations, musings, opinions, and beliefs of travelers, explorers, traders, missionaries, plantation-owners, and the like with experience of the New World, parts of Africa, or Asia. Their perceptions of "savages" with their accompanying interpretations and fantasies flowed into the scientific establishment and fueled its speculations.

The works of such men as Tyson and Linnaeus brought home to a world of increasing complexity and confounding realities the extraordinary similarities between human beings and apes. The existence of such creatures, first known to Europeans from early traders in Africa, had mystified them. Learned people, looking back to classical literature, could now recognize descriptions of apes in the writings of such early naturalists as Galen, Pliny, and Aristotle. Their writings, although showing how fundamentally similar morphologically were the apes and humans, inspired questions about the souls of the apes. They also invited skepticism about the images in which God had created humans and about the similarities of apes, humans, and God. Greene (1959) notes that many scholars, like Linnaeus, did not have living specimens to study nor did their classifications rest on reliable descriptions of primate forms.

Such intense work with weak sources led the reigning experts to disagreements. They argued over the classifications of nonhuman primates as well as those of human groups. Once the human-primate connection had been made, the materials often gravitated toward a fusion of human and apelike qualities, evoking paradigms that suggested a continuum. On several occasions Linnaeus confessed difficulty in distinguishing the Troglodytes, Satyrs, and Pygmies from real humans (Greene 1959, 185). Drawings from the late eighteenth century show deliberate distortions to make some great apes appear human.

Scheidt (1950) credits Louis LeClerc, Comte de Buffon, with introducing the term "race" into the lexicon of the natural sciences (1749), although clearly the term was used by trained scientists before Buffon. Moreover, his use of the term was not significantly different from the term "variety." His varieties included Laplanders (or the Polar Race), Tartars (or Mongolians), Southern Asiatics, Europeans, Ethiopians, and Malays. Buffon, however, was less interested in classifying than in explaining the varieties of humankind, whom he saw as a single species. He offered a modern theory of human diversity:

> Whenever man began to change his climate, and to migrate from one country to another, his nature was subject to various alterations. ... The changes he underwent became so great and so conspicuous, as to give room for suspecting that the Negro, the Laplander and the White were really different species, if, on the one hand, we were not certain, that one man only was originally created, and, on the other, that the White, the Laplander and the Negro, are capable of uniting and of propagating the great and undivided family of the human kind. Hence those marks which distinguish men who inhabit different regions of the earth, are not original, but purely superficial (quoted in Slotkin 1965, 185).

Buffon thus had reasoned that climate was the "chief cause of the different colours of men" and that foods, soil, air, and the earth's topography have an influence on the form of the human body. A third area of causation was that of culture, habits, customs, beliefs, and practices that he speculated must have affected physical features. Such naturalistic elements then were the prima facie causes of human differences. Buffon concluded: "Upon the whole, every circumstance concurs in proving, that mankind are not composed of species essentially different from each other; that on the contrary, there was originally but one species, who after multiplying and spreading over the whole surface of the earth, have undergone various changes by the influence of climate, food, mode of living, epidemic disease, and the mixture of dissimilar individuals" (Slotkin 1965, 185). Slotkin holds that this relatively modern sense of race, which converges with much of twentieth-century usages, originated with Buffon. But belief in the natural, environmental causes of human variation was widespread among the learned people of Europe during the eighteenth century.

Toward the end of the eighteenth century Johann Blumenbach, a professor of medicine in Germany, emerged as the most important of the classifiers for later scientists. Between 1770 and 1781, he proposed the division of humankind into four, later five, "varieties" associated with the major regions of the world. These five (Caucasian, Mongolian, Ethiopian, American, and Malay) came to be widely accepted by the educated community and continue in use today. Like a majority of scientists, Blumenbach worked within the single-origin (monogenetic) framework, holding to the biblical version of human creation. The unity of the origin of humankind is either explicit or implicit in all of these cited works. The groups named, however, were not considered equal, except in a general spiritual sense; their ranking along a scale determined by their distance or closeness to "civilized" status gained currency during the late eighteenth century, becoming a premier feature in the comparative sciences.

On this score, Blumenbach was responsible for promoting a major and familiar theory of the monogenists, the argument that *degeneration*, caused by climate, food, and living habits, accounts for the external differences between human groups. Although not a new idea, Blumenbach's sophistication and reputation elevated it to a fundamental deterministic principle of science. His theories of causation were thus similar to those of Buffon and others, proposing external environmental factors as responsible for the state of civilization of different human groups.

To his credit, Blumenbach emphasized the difficulty of setting boundaries between human populations, observing that the varieties of men blend "insensibly" into one another (Slotkin 1965, 189). Here he recognized a reality that Americans rarely expressed, or even perceived, with the notable exception of a few men, such as Samuel Stanhope Smith who, as a faithful monogenist, maintained steadfastly the potential equality of all men. Such thinking suggested a kind of arbitrariness about human classifications that contradicted the trend in the United States toward establishing rigid and exclusive categories.

Nevertheless, all seventeenth- and eighteenth-century scientific classifications were burdened by the heavy weight of ethnocentrism, or cultural chauvinism, and by subjective judgments on the physical features of non-Europeans. Blumenbach, for example, like the vast majority of his contemporaries, believed that the original human form was that of European whites. To him, they were the most physically attractive of the varieties of humankind. If God had made humankind in his image, this surely was the variant he would have chosen. Blumenbach selected the term "Caucasian" for this classification because he felt that the women of the Caucasus region in Russia were the most beautiful of all Europeans. Value judgments about other human groups varied insofar as they departed from this ideal. Blumenbach was not alone in his willingness to impose his aesthetic judgment on the physical features of different peoples. Buffon and Linnaeus had done so, as well as many others. It was part of the general cultural values of the European world that people with black skins, thick lips, and wooly hair compared unfavorably with white skins, straight hair, and narrow features. This was acceptable scientific commentary in the eighteenth century, clearly demonstrating the degree to which scientists shared the cultural values and preconceptions of their times (Greene 1981).

The Impact of Eighteenth-Century Classifications

The consequences of these classifications were long-ranging and perhaps unanticipated, with implications that went way beyond the immediate taxonomic problems.

1. They gave an aura of permanence and rigidity to conceptions of human differences. Once you classify something, you set it irretrievably in time and space, with a tendency to be transmitted to others as a fixed and unalterable entity.

2. The categories, as drawn up, accepted unquestioningly the linkage of physical characteristics with behavioral ones, along with such psychocultural features as temperament, disposition, and moral character. Such fusion, we have seen, was a trend in the general popular thought of the times; hence it documents the growing strength of this

component of the racial worldview in the minds of both the classifiers and their readers.

3. The classifications easily lent themselves to hierarchical structuring, fostering an impression of inequality among the different groups, with the most positive and progressive cultural features associated with Europeans and the least positive ones associated with those called "savages." This clearly fit well with the still expanding racial worldview and accorded with social, economic, and political realities.

4. Finally, such classifications by such reputable and highly reknowned scientists (naturalists) as Linnaeus and Blumenbach made humankind part of the natural order of things. They thus legitimized as "natural" and God-given the inferior qualities ascribed to non-Europeans and helped to justify their lower positions in world societies. In other words, they tended to provide the scientific sanctions and scholarly credibility for prevailing popular images and stereotypes of non-Europeans.

All of the scholars who produced classifications of human groups, we will be reminded, were Europeans. None had extensive experience with diverse human groups, except for Bernier; most had never even seen a "savage." Nor, it bears reiterating, were the sources of materials on which they based their classifications impeccable. They came not from trained researchers, but from ordinary men preoccupied with other interests and purposes. They came from the writings and verbal descriptions of men operating from a position of dominance: slave traders, sailors, slave-owners, merchants, and others who were sometimes the social equals of the systematizers. Today, such descriptions of the "dispositions" and habits of "savages" strike us as at best naive. But the reality is that to the eighteenth-century mind "Satyrs," "Troglodytes," "Giants," and "Dwarfs" were very real populations. So was the still evolving belief in the innate foundations of all human behavior.

To their credit, most of the classifiers accepted the principle of the unity of the human species, if for no other reason than adherence to scriptural requirements. Most also expressed a belief in the potential improvement of savage peoples that was consonant with Enlightenment ideas about environmentally induced change and human progress. That the human animal was plastic, flexible, and capable of progress was not in doubt.

However, toward the end of the century, polygenesis, the theory of multiple creations, reappeared, emerging from its subordinate role among philosophical theories. Among the learned people of Europe who suggested that the major variants of humankind were separate species, created at different times, was the French philosopher and dramatist Voltaire (1694–1778). Not a scientific researcher, but an opponent of the dogmatic positions of the church, Voltaire simply believed that the differences in physical characteristics, as well as the "state of civilization" of Africans and Indians, were sufficient evidence to categorize them as species distinct from Europeans. He thought of black Africans as mere animals who mated with orangutans.[2]

Voltaire, more than most of the Enlightenment writers, was an "establishment" man. He lived in England for several years and became an admirer of English laws and concepts of property and their linkages to freedom. He also invested heavily in commerce and trade, which he saw as the lifeblood of a free society. He thus had vested interests in maintaining the colonial system and the slave trade. Voltaire's influence, on both sides of the Atlantic, was powerful among the educated classes. Poliakov observes that "no writer of the Enlightenment had as many readers—or as important ones—as Voltaire" (1982, 56).

Voltaire was joined in his view of separate origins of the races by Henry Home (Lord Kames), a Scottish jurist who also wrote about a great variety of topics and was widely read on both sides of the Atlantic. Kames scoffed at Buffon's definition of species in terms of their mating behavior and reproductive isolation, denied that climate was responsible for the great variations in biophysical characteristics, and insisted on fundamental and primordial differences of innate behavior, as well as overt physical traits, as indicative of species distinction. His *Sketches of the History of Man*, published in 1774, was looked upon, even by some monogenists, as providing authoritative arguments for the separation of the races. His pronouncements on the inferiority of blacks and Indians could have been received by both monogenists and polygenists without disturbing their respective positions on human origins. But within a little over a half-century after the publication of Lord Kames's work, a new group of writers and scientists began an unparalleled debate in science over the very questions raised by Voltaire and Kames.

The questions must be posed. Why, after over a century of Africans, Indians, and Europeans (and various mixtures of the three) interacting in the American colonies, should there have been any problem about the classifications and relationships in nature of these three originally separate human groups? What was there about the nature of the relationships to prompt such energetic attention to questions of classification and difference? Was it merely a product or by-product of the growth of science, or were there deeper, hidden meanings in the desperate attempt to ascertain the different places in nature of various peoples? Before we take a look at the debate on human origins that raged in the midnineteenth century, we should examine other thoughts about human differences emerging in the late eighteenth and early nineteenth centuries. These were thoughts that reflected popular opinion, but they also portray growing differences in the social roles that different populations in the New World were playing.

Notes

1. See Hallowell (1960), an excellent source on these early theories; Slotkin (1965), has a wide range of readings covering this period.

2. Despite his progressive and tolerant views on other matters, Voltaire, according to Leon Poliakov (1982), was strongly anti-Jewish as well as antiblack (56).

Late Eighteenth-Century
Thought and Crystallization of the
Ideology of Race

B Y THE END of the eighteenth century, the constituent components of the race idea had reached a kind of critical mass. A variety of beliefs about human differences had emerged and now became fused together, both in the popular mind and in scientific thinking, to form an internally consistent cosmological system. As a folk system of thought, it represented a way of looking at the world's peoples that reflected the cultural values of expanding European polities and the relationships that Europeans engendered with indigenous populations in the process of expansion. "Race" thus became a potentially comprehensive worldview evolving out of and compatible with the power relationships, political goals, and economic interests of European colonizers.

The syncretism of scientific and popular perspectives on human variation should not surprise us, not only because of the rudimentary nature of all science at the time and the lack of a positive and objective epistemology, but also because scientists generally came from a class of people who had vested interests in the profit-oriented activities of overseas enterprises. They also shared the same religious axioms and ethnocentric orientations as their peers. Except for some Enlightenment writers, scientists were not likely to have open-minded or detached perspectives, or to be critical of the overseas activities and empire-building of their own nations. Cultural relativism had not yet fully developed as a guidepost for understanding other human groups. A Blumenbach, Linnaeus, or Buffon could not function with self-conscious independence of the aesthetic, social, and moral values of their cultures, nor could they assess the descriptive materials on which they based their classifications with a critical eye. Thus there was nothing neutral, objective, or scientific (by modern standards) about the elements bound together in the idea of race.

Because ideas may evolve slowly, absorb and lose additional ingredients, and shift over time and space, it is impossible to identify at what precise juncture a fully evolved racial worldview became part of Euro-American cosmology. During the eighteenth century, new trends in social and scientific thought were germinating as a result of technological, demographic, economic, and political changes. A crisis in relations with the English government resulted in the birth in the American colonies of revolutionary social philosophies, radical conceptions of the nature of government's relation to its citizens, and, ultimately, the American Revolution. Within the same period, concerns about the moral rightness of slavery periodically arose, reaching a crescendo during the war era. In the wake of accusations of colonists' hypocrisy in owning slaves while advocating freedom, a hitherto insignificant rationale for black slavery—the argument of the Negroes' natural inferiority—was planted in American social thought, synthesizing irretrievably with existing presuppositions about human differences. With this synthesis, race ideology and the racial worldview came into existence. By the end of the century, its basic features were already intact; but the social implications and wider ramifications were to reach fruition in the nineteenth century.

In this chapter we examine the historical and cultural matrix in which this transformation took place, identifying those aspects of North American thought that were most relevant to this worldview. American society in the pre- and post–revolutionary war era was in a state of great economic and social flux, with diverse religious and social movements reflecting a search for order and stability. This may help to explain why the American vision of the world permitted for many total displacement of any comprehension of the moral dilemma of slavery in a free and democratic society. The contradictions in American ideology coexisted without much trauma, as if they occupied separate spheres of the mind and never connected at any level with each other. One level of ideology rejected undemocratic divisions of class and ancestry; the other prefigured individual and group identity and unequal placement in society on the basis solely of "race."

Beginning with a discussion of significant social values in the colonies, we next look at the emerging hierarchy of races, specifically the status ascribed to Indians and blacks. We then focus on certain other features of North American ideology: the idea of races as separate and exclusive groups, the linkage in white minds of the slaves' blackness and their degraded condition, and the beginnings of racial determinism in explaining history and culture. Next, we examine the function of the Anglo-Saxon myth in the construction of English identity and its transmutation into an ideology of innate white superiority. Finally, we examine this era of Jeffersonian influence and ideals for the representative and somewhat transitional role that Jefferson himself played in the cultural construction of race.

Social Values of the American Colonists

Ever since the Glorious Revolution (1688), when James II was overthrown and prevented from reestablishing absolute monarchy, English society and its offshoots in the Americas had experienced a sense of people power unexcelled in any previous era of European history. The people power, however, was limited to the middle classes and gentry who opposed the unlimited power and privilege of monarchy. They were able, through the restructuring of Parliament and the establishment of political parties, to carve a voice for themselves in government and business affairs. The vision of a people having a role in their own governance was a novel paradigm about society. Its roots rested deep in English history, but its eighteenth-century philosophical manifestations lay in the writings of such men as John Locke, whose idea of government as a social contract became a useful political device to opponents of royal despotism. It was a philosophy highly compatible with the rough-and-tumble individualism, aggressive competitiveness, and volatile ambitions of the American colonists.

The history of the peopling of the North American colonies by Europeans in the eighteenth century was often one of flight from repressive authoritarianism, resistance to legal and religious constraints, and a striving for freedom of expression, thought, and action. Self-determination, along with efforts at self-discipline, provided the dynamic tension in the life-styles of the colonies. The Calvinist ethos, shared in varying degrees by all the Protestant groups, undergirded much of the process of expansion. A widely held belief in the autonomy and rights of the individual was strengthened and expanded. Hard work, ambition, thrift, and perseverance were the qualities that brought success. And success was measured by the acquisition of property in land and slaves. Individual freedom and unimpeded property rights were bound together in the American mind, reflecting the persisting theme of possessive individualism. It, too, prevented planters from comprehending the moral arguments against slavery.

The restlessness that prompted the push westward to the Mississippi after the end of French dominion (1763) in the Midwest could only find expression among a people who felt themselves liberated from political and social restraints. Nathaniel Bacon's rebellion against the Virginia governor in the late seventeenth century was an early example of extreme individualism and contempt for authority that was to characterize so much of eighteenth-century behavior. It also exemplified a cultural predisposition to uninhibited ambition and recklessness that continues to the present time. The aim of most immigrants was to make their fortunes, and the American frontier was where many sought it. An extreme outcome was that expansion westward created lawless frontier areas from Michigan to Louisiana where every man was a law unto himself and the exploitation of others was a common phenomenon. The bourgeois ideology of early capitalism, indeed a history of highly individualized social and political conflict and attendant values, had predisposed many of the English to thinking of all those beneath them, and even of their equals, in a competitive and exploitive manner. Many saw nothing wrong in impoverishing others while enriching themselves. And they had already institutionalized the rationalization that the poor and powerless get what they deserve. Rapid social mobility, unbridled greed, and social instability had a powerful impact throughout the colonies.

One source of traumatic social disturbances was the almost sudden appearance of a series of religious revivalist movements called the Great Awakening. Beginning about 1740, itinerant evangelists preaching doctrines of rebirth began spreading rapidly throughout many of the colonies, attracting large numbers of people in a mass movement that reflected a personal searching for stability, order, salvation, and inner contentment. Charismatic fundamentalist preachers appealed widely to the masses, who were quickly drawn to the near hysteria and emotionalism of the events. Their preaching tended to be antiestablishment and thus gained the attention and sympathy of small farmers, ordinary laborers, and petty tradesmen. Some preached a "radical egalitarianism" (Nash 1982, 220), excoriating the extremes of wealth and poverty. They also frightened into conformity large numbers of people with their descriptions of hellfire and damnation. Those who were swept up in the movement split from their Anglican, Presbyterian, or Congregationalist backgrounds and formed new congregations, the largest of which were the Southern Baptists and the Methodists. These latter were democratically run organizations, composed predominantly of the working class and the poor. They were thus among the first populist movements functioning well without traditional elite leaders.

In the coastal towns a small elite class of landowners, merchants, planters, and traders had already emerged. Although their life-styles varied from region to region, they had common pretensions to influence and power. An older gentry and the newly rich were distinguished from the small farmers and servants by their wealth and life-styles. They or their representatives in the colonial assemblies controlled the finances, made the laws, and often enforced them (Morgan 1975).

In the Southern colonies, particularly Virginia, the most influential men were those descendants of early planters who owned many slaves and could afford lives of leisure and travel. They had the time and the fortunes to dabble in politics, read the classics, send their children to school in Europe, and emulate its aristocracy. Although they were upright and often sanctimonious supporters of traditional values, they were also molded from the wellspring of individualism. Most importantly, they had close supporters and associates among the smaller planters, whose interests they also claimed to serve.

These large plantation-owners were powerful enough to become serious opponents of British colonial policies. They resented, among other things, taxation and control of exports and imports and interference through numerous and vexatious laws in their business enterprises, particularly the arbitrary setting of the price of tobacco and attempts to regulate the slave trade. In their confrontations with England, the ideology of republicanism developed to promote their cause had been inspired by John Locke's view of liberty and society. Every man, they argued, had the right to life, liberty, and property. Liberty was construed generally as freedom from governmental interference in private lives. Property was construed, as we have seen, as an inalienable right equated in its profundity to life itself. Government should exist, the colonists insisted, only to protect people in the exercise of their proprietary rights and from foreign invasions. When government goes beyond such mandates, it becomes tyrannical and oppressive.

These were political and social values with which even the poorest landowners (or would-be landowners) could identify. All concurred in the belief that the man who owned his own land had the God-given, natural right to protect it. In this freedom, with responsibility, he was the equal of every other man with property. In this, and in other economic matters, the small landholder recognized common interests with the large planter. A growing republican philosophy bound them together, especially as opposition to English policies grew. Edmund Morgan noted that they were equal in another way, of which most had daily reminders. They were not slaves. Republican equality, Morgan claimed, rested on slavery, at least in Virginia (1975, 381). Indeed, it rested on more than that; it rested on a growing racial stratification, for it was infinitely easier to perceive equality with members of one's own "natural" category, or so people were told.

Despite obvious differences in wealth and standing, eighteenth-century white Americans proudly envisioned their society as one "where a wealthy aristocracy did not dominate and no masses of poor whites were ground into the dust" (Nash 1982, 214). America, they thought, did not present the great extremes of wealth and poverty seen in Europe. So it was not difficult for settlers to conceive of America as a land of essentially "middling" folk who lived in comfort with sufficient food, housing, fuel, transport, and clothing so that no one faced abject penury. For Europeans, North America became the land of abundance, of wide-open frontiers, unlimited opportunity, and vigorous growth. An egalitarian value system for white males propelled both rich and poor alike toward the establishment of the democratic republic.

Certain trends of thought about Indians, blacks, and their places in nature and society illuminated this period. In thinking about these matters, European-Americans began to see themselves not so much as ethnic entities (English, Swedes, Dutch, Germans), but as a common group vis-à-vis Indians and blacks. They brought to bear long-standing folk ideas, including beliefs about savagery and savages, as we have already seen, in their assessments of social realities. Such ideas became major themes in the structuring of social identities based on "race."

One of the dominant themes was the separation and ranking of those groups whom they increasingly saw as ineligible for the powers and privileges that white men could claim. To many, the status of the Indians as a conquered and oppressed population manifesting few tendencies to transform themselves into "civilized" beings was very clear. They would ultimately become extinct with the advance of white civilization. Negroes, however, were an invaluable adjunct to the development of the colonies, but their very difference precluded their aspiring to the beneficence of white civilization; so their unquestioned inferiority had to be established, as this became the new basis for their allocation to permanent servile status.

Since the ideology promised no redemption or escape, the justification for black inferiority had to be impeccable. Vociferous arguments for the unique and lowly ranking of blacks were taken up on both sides of the Atlantic as the potential uses of these very biophysical differences became manifest. One of the first ideas propelled to front stage was an ancient one about the natural ranking of living forms.

Nature's Hierarchy

Most writers of the late eighteenth century who had anything to say about the nature of human differences operated from a theoretical/ideological assumption that governed all of the biological sciences. This was the Great Chain of Being, which we have already seen (Chapter 6) was a powerful world model of the relatedness of living forms to one another. It was a quasi-scientific, quasi-theological scheme that propounded a hierarchy of all living things from the smallest insect to the most complex animal forms. With God at the apex, human beings ranked higher than any other living forms, just below the angels. Originating in the philosophical speculations of ancient Greek writers, this notion of a natural unilinear scale along which all beings could be placed and graded, and on which they were linked together often by miniscule degrees of difference, persisted throughout the Middle Ages. It was familiar to most learned men as a speculation of interest, but not necessarily as an issue of great controversy. Although it had earlier surfaced from time to time, this element of Western cosmology was resuscitated in the wake of Linnaean taxonomy. When the concept and the principles behind it reappeared in the eighteenth century, they "attained their widest diffusion and acceptance" in quite a different setting from that of their origin (Lovejoy 1936, 183).

This paradigm of a hierarchy structured from the continuity and relatedness of all living forms found its most significant expression in its application by some authors to human groups. As a comprehensive scheme, it was used to embrace all newly discovered aborigines and those peoples already connected to the European and American polities in various ways. Despite the fact that direct empirical evidence of such a scheme was far from a reality, scientists of the day accepted without question its fundamental tenets as axiomatic. According to Lovejoy, "No history of the biological sciences in the eighteenth century can be adequate which fails to keep in view the fact that, for most men of science throughout that period, the theorems implicit in the conception of the Chain of Being continued to constitute essential presuppositions in the framing of scientific hypotheses" (1936, 227).

The "presuppositions" associated with this paradigm and undergirding the hierarchy of races in the eighteenth century governed not only the framing of scientific hypotheses, but also perceptions of data, the methodologies used, and the terms in which results were couched. Stephen Jay Gould (1983) has shown how Linnaeus's belief in the Great Chain of Being led him to expect that there would be creatures intermediate between apes and humans, hence his classification of "*Homo*

troglodytes." The attempt to establish such "missing links" also accounts for the exaggeration of the humanlike features of "pygmies" and
other apes described by Tyson, Arnout Vosmaer, Linnaeus, Nicholaas
Tulp, and others. Buffon's "Jocko" was made to look as human as possible (Greene 1959, 183). Like many other contemporary drawings of primates, it showed a chimpanzeelike creature with a benign facial
expression holding a walking stick. Gould notes also how Tyson's use of
the comparative method owes much to his commitment to the idea of a
Chain of Being (1983, 22). Later in time, but in an analogous fashion, the
ideas of human cultural evolution and progress stimulated the development of the comparative method in sociocultural anthropology. The
method helped to buttress and confirm a hierarchy of cultures that
could be ranked or graded along a variety of dimensions from savagery
to civilization.

Such grandiose and comprehensive schemes as the Chain of Being
function as unquestioned assumptions about the nature of the world,
and since virtually all people of science are conditioned to them as part
of their earlier enculturation, they rarely become hypotheses requiring
testing or proof. On the contrary, they insinuate themselves into the
thinking patterns of scientists and lay people alike as accurate models
of world reality. They can be maintained for long periods of time unaffected by either training or empirical research, both of which may tend
to reinforce the prevailing worldview. The result is that scientists can
be compromised in their levels of detachment and degree of neutrality
until a revolutionary new paradigm supersedes the existing one.[1] In the
case of the placement and gradations of human groups on the Chain of
Being, social, political, and economic realities had already decreed the
ranking system. Thus, the preexistence of a grand theoretical scheme
that was already a part of folk culture and was consonant with these realities provided the model for the ranking, and affirmed the naturalness
and the God-given nature of the inequality of human groups.

The Status of the Indian

Eighteenth-century thought turned to the physical characteristics of
the Indian as well as of the black population. By midcentury, most of
the Indians of the East Coast, from Maine to South Carolina, had either
died of disease and warfare or been reduced to pitiable remnants on the
outskirts of white civilization. Native Americans continued to pose a
problem, however, in the frontier areas, where white expansion was dis-
placing them and causing much social turmoil.

The apparent unwillingness of the Indians to either transform themselves culturally or to submit to the depredations of white settlers and

traders came to be interpreted by many as evidence of an inferior racial character. In some areas a growing stereotype of the native as addicted to alcohol, wantonness, wildness, and violence and given to despair helped to perpetuate the conviction that the Indian was unassimilable. As with Negroes, white Americans looked for explications and justifi- cations for their practices and policies in what they thought were the intrinsic characteristics of Indians themselves.

Roy Pearce claims that in the American mind of the revolutionary era, the Indian was a "symbol for all that over which civilization must triumph." He was not a person but a type, not a tribesman but a savage (1953, 73). Drunken, diseased, and degraded, he was headed for inevita- ble extinction under the advance of white civilization. It was this view with its foregone conclusion that governed most of the relationships that the new United States government and its citizens had with the In- dians. Because they were savages (the stereotype held that all Indians were nomadic hunters and gatherers), they had no right to exist on lands that God had given to white men.

After 1785 the Continental Congress established a policy for distrib- uting lands in western territories to white farmers. Although these were lands still occupied by Indians, it was widely assumed that white advancement was inevitable. The ideals of republican government re- quired widespread ownership of property, since only with property in land could white men realize democratic and egalitarian principles. "Property was connected with life and liberty because its ownership was the surest guarantee of those other inalienable rights" (Berkhofer 1978, 137). A new Indian policy had to be created that would deal with the implications of this reality. Ostensibly the policy protected the in- terests of the Indians, with the objective of civilizing them. But the un- derlying and contradictory belief was that such an aim was hopeless. Thus "treaties were made, and boundaries were set by the new Ameri- can government; and treaties were promptly broken and boundaries disregarded by frontier citizens who had little respect for their govern- ment and less for what Hugh H. Brackenridge termed in 1782 'the ani- mals, vulgarly called Indians'" (quoted in Pearce 1953, 54).

Toward the end of the century, many other tribes beyond the Appala- chians had been forced to surrender their lands as settlers pushed west- ward, but not without sometimes fierce resistance. In some cases, land was openly and violently expropriated from such groups as the Dela- ware, Chippewa, Shawnee, and Ottawa because many of them sided with the British in the conflict with the colonies. In the Southeast, only the "Civilized Tribes"—a loose confederation of Creeks, Choctaws, Chickasaws, Cherokees, and Seminoles—had been able to retain some degree of identity and autonomy. But they held twenty-five million acres of land in what is now Georgia, North Carolina, Tennessee, Alabama, and Mississippi that they had farmed since early in the century. And there were increasingly large numbers of white settlers and land speculators who coveted this land (Hoover 1976).

Although a few whites believed that the native Americans of the Southeast could be assimilated into white society, others preferred not to wait for such a process to occur. Many thought that these Indians would simply die out, as had previous groups. After the Louisiana Purchase in 1803 greater attention was focused on the southeastern Indians who as sedentary farmers had absorbed much of the cultural trappings of whites. But some had refused to give up aspects of their tribal culture, with the result that suggestions for dispossessing them of their lands were frequently made. Of the public leaders who had opinions about the future of the Indians, Jefferson was the first to suggest that they be forcibly removed beyond the Mississippi River, prognosticating a new policy brought to fruition after his death.

As Hoover (1976) and others have convincingly argued, the Indian Removal policy was instigated by white fear and, especially, by greed (83). Despite numerous treaties before and after the creation of the Indian Department in 1787 under the federal government, most of which were designed ostensibly to protect the rights of Indians, their days were numbered.[2] The policy of separation, so intrinsic to the ideology of race, was easily reconciled with white avarice and ambition. The expulsion of most Indians from territories east of the Mississippi was eventually accomplished following the passage of the Indian Removal Act in 1830 under President Andrew Jackson who held the "generally accepted view" that they should be settled in the Great American Desert, "which white men would never covet since it was thought fit mainly for horned toads and rattlesnakes" (Tindall 1988, 423). Between 1830 and 1844 "some 70,000 Indians were removed from their homes in the South and driven west of the Mississippi River" (Takaki 1987, 63). In the hardship and brutality of the process nearly one-third died.

Meanwhile, interest in Indian mounds and earthworks, the discovery of other material remains of Indian origin, and the publication of various studies of Indian languages engaged the attention of a number of scholars. Mounds found in the Ohio and Mississippi valleys were a particular topic of discussion because of the suggestion by Noah Webster and others that they were constructed by Ferdinand de Soto. A debate ensued about the origin of the mounds and the seemingly superior cultural remains found in them. This curious development was an early example reflecting the limitations of the mind-set of "race." A great many persons in the white community quite readily assumed that the "savages" of America could not have descended from the "obviously" superior peoples who had created such antiquities. So the question of who were the Mound Builders occupied the attention of professional archaeologists and other learned men and women into the twentieth century. It is one of the earliest examples of the intrusion of "racial" thinking into the reconstruction of history.[3] Moreover, it is a telling moment in which we see the direct manufacturing of the new mode of viewing history—in terms of racial accomplishments.

We must remember that nascent views concerning the incapacity of "savages" for achieving the levels of progress of civilized Europeans date back at least to the Irish-English conflicts of the sixteenth century. The continuity of this rationalization made it a prominent part of the ideology about human differences. Once "race" became the major mode of thinking about group differences, history received its simplest (and most distorted) explanation for all human achievements. Thus any society composed of "inferior races" lost the potential for social, economic, and political advancement in the minds of whites. Cognitive perceptions and understandings of the nature of cultural differences were reduced to a single causative factor—"race." The future of the native peoples of North America was thus predetermined within the context of white expectations about their behavior and development. Because by the nineteenth century the Indians were a totally conquered and powerless race, white expectations were never very high.

Black Inferiority: The Lowest of Them All

As early as 1680 in the colonies, Jordan notes, the Reverend Morgan Godwyn attempted to refute an allegation that Negroes were not truly human (1968, 229). What had prompted this speculation was that both the apes of Africa and the African peoples had been discovered by Englishmen at about the same time, and, in the minds of some imaginative travelers and writers of tall tales, the two had been subtly linked together. In some circles, it was held that ape males and black females in the wilds of Africa sometimes copulated together (Jordan 1968, 236). The English were obviously titillated by the presumed lewdness and promiscuity of Africans, and this imagery has persisted up through the twentieth century.

Jordan believes that the "handful of assertions" that Negroes were not truly human were not advanced seriously (1968, 231) largely because of the strength of Christian tradition. Humans differed from beasts in that they had speech, were capable of rational thought, and possessed souls waiting to be saved. The Negro was indubitably human, but this did not prevent the growth in the eighteenth century of the perception that blacks were closer to the apes than to other human groups. As the barbarities of slavery progressed, it was easier to seize upon any speculations about the physical resemblance of Negroes to apes to diminish the humanness of the slave.

Belief in black inferiority expanded and increased during the eighteenth century; it came to be expressed in a variety of forums and among some men who had quite legitimate claims to scholarship and erudition, as we have already seen. Edward Long, a planter for twelve years in the West Indies, published a volume entitled *History of Jamaica* in which he revealed a doctrinaire set of beliefs about Africans that Jamaican and other English planters accepted as explicitly and as tenaciously as they held to biblical history. First published in 1774 in England, sections of Long's book attracted greater attention in the United States after they were reprinted in 1788 in the *Columbian Magazine*, which also published excerpts from Jefferson's writings. Long's book was designed primarily as a justification for slavery in this Caribbean island. Although at first a minor voice, it later had major influence on Southern proslavery thought.

Long's scenario for black slavery was one of the first popular ones that incorporated some of the speculations and the language of the developing sciences of humankind. He argued that the Negro was a separate species from white men and described their physical differences in terms that made it appear they were closer to beasts than to humans. Instead of hair, they have a head covering of wool, "like the bestial fleece." They differ also in the "roundness of their eyes, the figure of their ears, tumid nostrils, invariable thick lips, and general large size of the female nipples, as if adapted by nature to the particular conformation of their childrens mouths" (Slotkin 1965, 209). The lice that infests their bodies are black and they have a bestial or fetid smell.

It was, however, in the faculties of the mind that the Negro showed the greatest disparity. "In general," Long argued, "they are void of genius, and seem almost incapable of making any progress in civility or science. They have no plan or system of morality among them ... it being a common known proverb, that all people on the globe have some good as well as ill qualities, except the African" (Slotkin 1965, 209). He then went on to rank the Negro and the orang on the Chain of Being in a position intermediate between man and the lower primates, stating, "That the oran-outang and some races of black men are very nearly allied, is, I think, more than probable" (210). The gradation rises from monkey to ape, to orang, to the Guinea Negroes; "and ascending from the varieties of this class to the lighter casts, until we mark its utmost limit of perfection in the pure White" (211).

Long's characterization of the Negro was a subjective exegesis, harboring folk stereotypes that became a significant part of the American heritage. In his view, "the Negro," in addition to being devoid of intellect, was given to excesses, lacking in moral restraints, and prone to idleness and thievery. Dwelling on what he thought were the lascivious and rapacious tendencies of this creature, Long averred that it was the Negro's uncontrolled sexuality that was most troublesome, a quality that made him most like a beast. In his assertions about the Negro's affinity to the ape, or "oran-outang," Long played up the theme of the male of a lower species having a "passion" for the female of a higher form. "Ludicrous as the opinion may seem, I do not think that an oran-outang husband would be any dishonour to an Hottentot female" (quoted in Jordan 1968, 490). The simile of an ape male passionately embracing a black woman was not lost on white society, which showed a growing, but baseless, fear of black male rape.

In Europe important new dimensions to the consideration of who the Negro was in the natural scheme of things were added by the works of a number of scholars involved in the study of the morphology and physiology of apes and monkeys. The distinction between the two was not as clear as it is today. Such men as Arnout Vosmaer, Comte de Buffon, and Peter Camper attempted to work out the relationships between the variously described primates, the "Pongos," "Jockos," orangs, and others. Camper, in studying the skulls of diverse primate forms, invented the facial line and the facial angle, which measures the degree of prognathism, or forward projection of the jaw vis-à-vis the skull. He made a lasting contribution to studies on race by showing that there was a gradation in the angle between apes and humans and "a marked analogy between the head of the Negro and that of the ape" (Greene 1959, 190). It was left to others to follow the implications of this "scientific" finding and to promote the conclusion that the Negro was a separate species, halfway between a European and an ape.

Ever since Isaac de la Peyrere, a minority of men had continued to believe that the major groupings of humankind represented distinct species. Among the notable and influential men of the eighteenth century, as we saw in Chapter 7, were the philosophers Voltaire and Lord Kames. They provided not scientifically based arguments but what they thought were rational ones for the separation of blacks and Indians as distinct and inferior species. Both reasoned, on the basis of differences in physical features, that there must have been unique creations for the three or four major races. It was the Negro, however, who provided the significant foil against which the contraposition of the white appeared immeasurably superior. Said Voltaire of Negroes, "They are not capable of any great application or association of ideas, and seem formed neither for the advantages nor the abuses of philosophy" (quoted in Gossett 1965, 45).

The Scottish philospher David Hume was among the first to suggest, in 1748, what was to become in the nineteenth century a dominant theory of history. "I am apt to suspect," he said, "the negroes, and in general all the other species of men (for there are four or five different kinds) to be naturally inferior to the whites. There never was a civilized nation of any other complexion than white, nor even any individual eminent either in action or speculation. No ingenious manufactures amongst them, no arts, no sciences" (quoted in Jordan 1968, 253). He believed that even the most primitive whites, like the ancient Germans and the Tartars, had some eminent qualities that redeemed them. The only rational explanation for these striking differences was that "nature had ... made an original distinction betwixt these breeds of men" (253).

The works of these European scholars were widely read by the educated American public. Scientists, philosophers, and people of letters in both North and South converged in their thinking, particularly about the nature of the Negro, and the causes of his inferiority. So great was the distinction between whites and blacks that evolved in the collective consciousness that toward the end of the century a major controversy began taking shape, comprehending both public sentiment and scientific speculations. This was the great debate between the polygenists and monogenists over the origin and taxonomic status of "the Negro," which received inordinate attention for several decades in the midnineteenth century. The debate became the central focus of developing sciences in the United States and involved biologists, anatomists, physicians, antiquarians, politicians, social theorists, and others. We will turn to this controversy in Chapter 10.

One perceives during the mid to late eighteenth century a tremendous acceleration in the thrust to magnify the differences between blacks and whites. As Jordan (1968) notes, "a few men ... were so intent over distinguishing Negroes from whites that they proceeded to invent the facts they were unable to discover; they claimed variously, that the Negro's blood, brains and skull were black. Cornelius de Pauw announced in 1770 that the Negro had dark brains, blood and semen" (249). The term "race," with its basis in heritability and descent, cohered as the symbol of all those differences. Although it may have appeared ill defined, its cognitive correlates were increasingly specific and tangible in the mental images held by whites.[4]

With the writings of proslavery individuals, and even some who were antislavery but viewed "the Negro" as a being apart, we see the nearly complete transformation of "the Negro" into a subhuman creature. This grotesque monster, more ape than human, was perpetuated as much in the writings of learned men as by members of the white public whose repugnance toward blackness was increasingly fueled by such writings. In the eyes of many whites, both North and South, the Negro had been transformed into a degraded and contemptible creature by the turn of the nineteenth century (see Fredrickson 1977).

Dominant Themes in North American Racial Beliefs

The major themes and constituent components of North American race ideology came into clear relief before the beginning of the nineteenth century.

Races as Exclusive Groups

The element of race that holds that different human groups constitute separate, discrete, and exclusive entities, differing in important qualities from other groups, was fashioned from earlier antecedents in the folk practices of the English. One may see its elemental nature in the policies of the first colonists who segregated "missionized" Indians in their church congregations and who established separate villages for converted Indians. It is also evidenced in statutes that forbid intermarriage, prompted perhaps by the desire not to confuse distinctions of social status between servile and free populations. But such exclusiveness and insularity was an established custom in English culture. In Chapter 3, we saw that the English, from the thirteenth to the sixteenth centuries, fulminated against a practice that they found both menacing and malignant. This was the habit of proper Englishmen settling in Ireland and going "native," taking on the language, customs, dress, hairstyles, and general behavior of the "wild Irish." Just as aggravating and incomprehensible were the same processes occurring with the natives of America. Why was it that white men, women, and children were so attracted to the Indian way of life that, once exposed to it, many refused to return to civilized society?

The facts, as we saw earlier, are suggestive of a disquieting uncertainty and apprehension about the English sense of their own identity. The posing of this question by writers of the colonial period implied another query, suggesting deep-seated doubt about the value and worthiness of English culture. It may be that the more threatening this reality, the more attenuated the sense of self and society, the more rigidly insular and introspective they felt it necessary to become. Could it also be that the burning need of the English to associate themselves with property and power was, in part, a desperate effort to construct and preserve a sense of self? Both Winthrop Jordan and Margaret Hodgen infer that Englishmen may have had a psychological need for the "savage" to affirm their own virtues and as a symbol of what they must not become.

Certainly by the eighteenth century the English sense of exclusiveness and superiority was counterpoised against what in white minds was its new antithesis: the blacks, the latest savage. In some writings the characterization of black slaves was strident with vehement hate, and an almost pathetic contempt is shown in the exaggerated homogenization of blacks. Why so much investment in the degradation of a people whose only function was to enhance the power, wealth, and prestige of their masters? Was it merely to prevent intermixture and the consequent threat of confusing social ranking?

The English created a new savage by the dehumanization of Africans during the process of establishing slavery. The irrational logic of human minds, even in the most brilliant of thinkers, might have unveiled a parallel: Was there a fear that they might also become like this latest, and final, savage? Does this help to explain the need on the part of Anglo-Americans, given over a hundred years of this evolving slavery, to progressively exaggerate the differences between themselves and the black slaves whom they could not avoid? And could it be that one factor behind all of the puffery and prating of race ideas was an enormous English self-doubt?

Racial Determinism

The idea that *biological* variations account for differences of *cultural* behavior did not appear suddenly in the eighteenth century. An incipient sense of biological concomitants, if not determinants, to human behavior is found in a few of the early writings and philosophical and scholarly musings of people who were among the intellectual leaders of the seventeenth century. William Petty (see Chapter 7), for example, was perhaps only a bit ahead of his time when he wrote:

> And what difference is between the Bulke of one Man & another, seemes to mee to bee also in their Memories, Witts, Judgements & withall in their externall Sences.
> I say that the Europeans do not onely differ from the aforementioned Africans in Collour. *They differ also in their Naturall Manners, & in the internall Qualities of their Minds* (quoted in Slotkin 1965, 90, my emphasis).

We have to assume that Petty was probably expressing an opinion that was extant among some elements of the plantation world. Writing at a time when the English were becoming more involved in trade with the African continent, he was aware of the variety of English reactions to the cultures and peoples of Africa. And since these early (and later) traders were hardly men guided by sympathetic considerations of cultural differences, their descriptions of Africans, both written and verbal, were often colored by highly subjective impressions and preconditioned modes of thought, some of which found their way into the classifications of eighteenth-century systematists.

The most negative descriptions of alien peoples up to the middle of the eighteenth century were frequently expressions about the unattractiveness of their physical features, a clearly subjective assessment. Bernier described Asians as having flat faces, a small squab nose, and "little pig's-eyes long and deep set." His Lapps were "little stunted creatures" with "thick legs ... very ugly and partaking much of the bear," and the blacks who live at the Cape of Good Hope were different from the rest of the Africans. "They are small, thin, dry, ugly, quick in running" (quoted in Slotkin 1965, 95).

By the mid-eighteenth century the considerably greater experiences of Europeans in trade and colonization had led to far more complex perceptions and evaluations of non-European peoples. Variations in material cultures, languages, and beliefs among peoples of the colonized territories were often recognized. But the myriad of impressions reaching the European mind could only be processed and comprehended in terms of antecedents within its own culturally prescribed sets of meanings. And there were existing categories, imprecise and value-loaded, that could be employed not only to identify all newly discovered sociocultural realities but also to give meaning to, and literally "read," the panorama of humanity.

The terms "barbarian," "heathen," and "savage" had been invariably applied to most non-Europeans, from Africans to Turks, Chinese, and Indians. These were ethnocentric terms that reflected the most striking contrasts with the Europeans' views of themselves as people who were both Christian and civilized. All of these terms had in common the implication of the inferiority of the cultures of non-Europeans. Until the eighteenth century no clear connection had been made between the biophysical features of the different human groups and their specific cultures. That is, no causal link was assumed to exist between their differing physical characteristics and their habits, customs, beliefs, values, and behaviors. If anything, the extrinsic nature of cultural behavior should have been recognized, since both Indians and blacks had long been observed to learn Spanish or English or Portuguese (and sometimes all three) and to be able to function as cultural beings in European contexts.

Earlier in the century some scholarly writers had begun to speculate on the material causes of cultural differences and to pose cultural/historical theories about the reasons for certain practices, beliefs, and developments. The beginnings of cultural evolutionary thought had already made an appearance in the literature of men such as Jean Lafitau, Condorcet, John Hunter, and others. It has already been noted that the idea of environmental causes for human differences had long precedents in the sixteenth-to eighteenth-century writings of such Europeans as Montaigne, Thomas Hobbes, Rene Descartes, and William Temple. Such theories of external causation persisted in Europe, albeit in limited circles, into the nineteenth century.

However, a central ideological component of race, hereditary determinism, was soon to take precedence over other explanatory models, especially external, environmental, or material explanations of human history and cultural diversity. This new causal theory appeared in the writings of a number of scholars from the latter part of the eighteenth century who, without hesitancy, linked physical features with cultural behavior. What emerged was a comprehensive ideology with the capacity to inform all understandings and all queries about the nature of human groups everywhere. It was manifest in an expanding consciousness, and a widening interpretation, of all cultural-historical features as due to "race"—a process that Marvin Harris and others have called the "biologization of history" (1968, Chapter 4). It obscured all possible perceptions of similarities among individuals and groups and distorted the meaning of behaviors that in modern times we have come to understand as part of our universal primate, and human, nature. By the midnineteenth century, racial determinism was a dominant ideology; it had become the central key to the interpretation and explanation of all human achievements and failures.[5]

Anglo-Saxonism: The Making of a Biological Myth

In Chapter 3 we saw that sixteenth-century Englishmen, partly to justify the break from the Roman Catholic church, sought a new historical identity that could rival the glories and accomplishments of the Romans. Turning to the tribal histories of pre-Roman and pre-Norman times, they fabricated as part of a national identity a myth of an Anglo-Saxon people who had a pure religion and free political institutions. The invention of distinguished ancestry was not merely a political action of Henry VIII's followers, but was part of the broader pattern of cultural chauvinism, intolerance, and ethnic conflicts that accompanied nation-state building in Europe from the sixteenth to the nineteenth centuries. During this period, Englishmen solidified their identity as Anglo-Saxons, further distinguishing themselves from the Celts, Vikings, Normans, and others who also had composed the melange of peoples in England.

The Anglo-Saxons, it was said, had developed advanced political institutions before the Norman conquest. They were a "freedom-loving people, enjoying representative institutions and a flourishing primitive democracy" (Horsman 1976, 388). Scholars spent lifetimes researching this history and concluded that their Anglo-Saxon ancestors had derived the excellence of their social system from German forebears. Glorification of the German past became a prelude to the history and greatness of the Anglo-Saxons.

Scholars like Horsman and Curtis (1968) agree that such chauvinism was not initially racial, but focused instead on reconstructing the continuity of institutions. However, they both found a change occurring in the mid to late eighteenth century that transformed ideas of Anglo-Saxon ethnic superiority into a philosophy of racial superiority.[6] According to Horsman (1976), "Not until the 1760s and 1770s did a variety of new tendencies foreshadow a shift in emphasis from the continuity of free institutions to the inherent racial traits which supposedly explained them" (1976, 390). It is no mere coincidence that this transformation paralleled the rise of racial ideologies on the North American continent.

There is, it should be noted, a theory that racial ideas in Europe may have evolved independently of those in North America, with origins quite distinct from English sources. Jacques Barzun (1965) and Hannah Arendt ([1951] 1968) observed the germination of racial thought in the works of Count Henri de Boulainvilliers (1658–1722), a French nobleman and apologist for the aristocracy. Barzun (1965) noted that Boulainvilliers's writings, published in 1727, were widely read in England because of his connections with the freemasonry movement (19). Boulainvilliers argued that the noble classes of France were not originally Gauls, but Germanic Franks who, after conquering inferior natives, had established themselves as the ruling class. They derived their laws, pride, individualism, and love of liberty from their Germanic ancestors. They ruled by the right of might, and Arendt ([1951] 1968) claims that in Boulainvilliers's representation they, like all racists, were antinational, having more in common with other ruling castes than with the French people (43).

Boulainvilliers's diatribe against the native Gauls, whom he saw as peasants and slaves, was a political tract, designed specifically to promote the interests of one class over the others. What concerns us here is the fact that both he and the proponents of Anglo-Saxonism in England based their claims for the superiority of the Germanic peoples on a single source. This was the second-century Roman historian and early anthropological writer Tacitus, whose essay on the German tribes represents one of the few recognized ethnographic descriptions of what was then a primitive people in Roman times.

Tacitus had praised the Germans as a simple, crude people who lived uncomplex lives, adhered to pure values, loved freedom, practiced monogamy, and were courageous and warlike. Tacitus's purpose in extolling the simple virtues of German culture was to contrast their pure and unadulterated lives to the corruption and decadence of Rome, the sophisticated, civilized state whose evils he abhorred. Those who mined his work to prove Germanic purity and superiority tended to ignore his less flattering characterizations of Germans. He claimed that not only were they very warlike, but they also hated peace and would always find some occasion to continue fighting. The warriors despised work, opting to sleep or lie about idly when off the battlefield. They gave blind obedience to their chiefs, and had an ignoble passion for gambling and drunken fights. Large, awkward, rough, with hair the same color as their reddish faces, Tacitus observed that they clothed their ugliness with the skins of wild animals.[7]

Nothing in Tacitus's descriptions of the Germans matches or resembles the diagnostic features proposed here for recognizing the modern idea of race. Roman writers, like others, were not reluctant to make ethnocentric or subjective assessments of the "barbarians" they encountered. The primitive German tribesmen were, in fact, the first of the "noble savages" whom "civilized" peoples have frequently viewed as living pure and idyllic lives. They were not, however, the stuff of which ideologies of racial purity and superiority can be made.

The highly embroidered Germanic myth, nevertheless, had a tenacious following both in England and on the Continent. It became in the nineteenth century the crux of the Nordic myths of Count de Gobineau and Houston Stewart Chamberlain, who easily assimilated it to contemporary race thinking. The twentieth century was to find the greatly enlarged Germanic myth transferred full-blown in Nazi notions of racial superiority.

Transatlantic intellectual discourse meant that ideas about race were transmitted back and forth from Europe to the Americas throughout the eighteenth and nineteenth centuries. Before the American Revolution, Americans conveyed their ideas about the inferiority of Indians and blacks to European intellectuals, and Europeans began to see themselves and others in similar racial terms. The influence was pervasive. Jefferson, for example, had an intense interest in Anglo-Saxonism and was well aware of the developing ideas of superior Anglo-Saxon history, religion, and language. Such was his obsession that he actually tried to learn the ancient language. He and other Americans accepted the myth of Anglo-Saxon racial purity and superiority because it was so consonant with prevailing beliefs and comforting to those whites who might on occasion be smitten with doubts over slavery.

The idea of innate Anglo-Saxon superiority was nurtured by, and became an integral part of, American racial ideologies of the late eighteenth and nineteenth centuries (Gossett 1965). It also became part of the American mythology associated with republicanism, Protestantism, democracy, laissez-faire economic theory, progress, and empire-building. The superior "racial" traits of Anglo-Saxons became a stimulus for American expansion. Indeed, the myth was at the heart of the doctrine of Manifest Destiny, by which white Americans expressed belief in themselves as a "chosen people" destined to dominate others. Over time, many non-English whites also assimilated this myth because it provided the basis for the general ideology of white supremacy.

By the turn of the nineteenth century the vision that Americans shared about human groups had taken on full racial coloration. The characterizations of racial groups suggest that the authors thought of races as homogeneous biophysical entities. Non-European races were considered to be fundamentally and intrinsically different from Europeans. There were few attempts to ascertain or establish similarities among human populations, and even the possibility of similarities was precluded by the growing belief that each race has a unique racial character granted by God or nature.[8]

This "unique" racial character reflected the fusion in white minds of distinct intellectual, moral, temperamental, and physical characteristics. Outside of some Enlightenment writers, whose materialistic philosophies emphasized the power of education and whose influence waned by the end of the century, no significant voice contradicted this idea. Even the writings and speeches of Reverend Samuel Stanhope Smith, Presbyterian minister and professor of moral philosophy at the College of New Jersey (later Princeton), tended to associate refinements of culture among blacks with a change in their physiognomy (Gossett 1965, 40). Smith, who became president of Princeton, believed fervently in the potential equality of all men, a rare stance and one with few progeny in the early nineteenth century.

Before we go on to consider the full flowering of race ideology in the next century, it is important to recognize the dilemma that the growing concept of race posed in the context of the democratic ideals of the revolutionary era. No one reflects the emergence of this peculiarly American paradox better than Thomas Jefferson. We will examine facets of his life that are emblematic of this dilemma in the next section.

Thomas Jefferson and the American Dilemma

Winthrop Jordan in his classic study *White Over Black* (1968) rightly focuses on Jefferson to illuminate some of the problems of race and slavery that confronted the incipient new nation during the period of the American Revolution. Jefferson's life spanned not only the drama of the revolutionary era and the birth of a new nation but also the debut of a new worldview often vividly expressed in his own writings. As a young man he inveighed against slavery in powerful language, but once elected to public office he took a position as a Virginia planter that John Chester Miller (1977) describes as "utilitarian," "pragmatic," and "prudent," even once advocating the extension of slavery into the western territories (18, 37, 39).

Jefferson's life exemplifies the agonizing ambiguities and contradictory impulses that came to warp American thought. Indeed, he was central to the formulation and dissemination of American attitudes about race, as we will see. Specifically, he was instrumental in casting the whole question of racial inferiority into the arms of science. But Jefferson represented a great deal more than that. He articulated better than almost anyone else the concepts of human rights, individual liberty, and justice—an enlightened ideology diametrically opposed to the growing ideology of race. As a slave-owner, he vividly reflected and internalized these opposing forces.[9]

The questions of personal freedom, the rights of men (not women) within the state, and human liberty in all its forms and manifestations constantly occupied Jefferson, and not just because of the political conflicts with England. We see it clearly in the turmoil and ambivalence that characterized his early writings on the subject of Negroes and slavery. We are told by his biographers, and apologists, that he hated slavery with a passion.[10] But since he participated fully in the plantation slavery system, buying and selling slaves from time to time, and could not bring himself to free his own slaves, who often numbered upward of 200 to 250 on his plantation at Monticello, one has to either question the verity of this passion or speculate that it was merely the abstract *idea* of slavery that he hated.[11] He apparently never ceased believing that slavery was ultimately doomed to extinction but made few efforts to bring this about in his lifetime.

What is so striking about Jefferson on this score is that he was one of the few men who put into writing some of his anguish over the issues of slavery and freedom. Other men, like Thomas Paine, an impoverished English-born revolutionary leader, wrote brilliant and inspiring passages on the nature of slavery, freedom, and the rights of man. But Paine, who also wrote against the extremes of wealth and poverty, never owned a slave, and his soul was never scoured by a confrontation with the realities of his own duplicity and hypocrisy. Jefferson, however, faced enormous inner contradictions. His actions in many areas of politics and social affairs often seemed to give little veracity to his words. Even his written statements, especially on the matter of slavery, the Negroes, and the Indians, contaminate one another with their sophistry.

Nevertheless, Jefferson was one of the most brilliant men of the American colonies, and his writings on slavery, the Indian, and the Negro reveal much about the thinking of the times and of the men and women who, like himself, were caught up in the controversies over slavery and the rights of humankind. David Brion Davis (1975) claims that in Jefferson we see a microcosm of the conflicts permeating American culture (166). And it was these controversies and conflicts that influenced the man, swirling around him and prodding him unsuccessfully to face the world that the colonists had made, with all of its evils and its potentials for human good.

Like all men of conscience who owned slaves, Jefferson was faced with a double-pronged dilemma, one with both intellectual and moral implications. The first was that existential Gordian knot, which we have already met. Slaves were conceptualized as property and thus, in a very real sense, tantamount to a "commodity." But the slave was also a human being, a talking, walking, thinking, living organism like oneself. Although it appears that this was the source of some of Jefferson's pain and anguish, he could never confront the implacable contradiction, the monumental paradox of the simultaneity of both the animate and inanimate, personhood and commodity, consciousness and unconsciousness.

There followed from this dilemma the equally troubling problem of the development of relationships between master and slave, between free and unfree persons. The double identity raised the kind of question for which there is no logical or suitable answer: What kind of behavior is required or necessary in order to treat someone as both a human being and a commodity or thing? It was the kind of dilemma that generates ambivalence, inconsistency, and indetermination, to say nothing of confusion. Fawn Brodie's (1974) intense research into the personal life of America's third president shows that all of these qualities were characteristic of Jefferson.

As already indicated, the American option on the question of the double identity of slaves was one that gave greater weight, stature, and legitimacy to the property rights of slave-owners. Many statutes and judicial decisions clearly underscored this fact. Constant references in court documents to slaves as property, the accordance by decree and by legislative actions of absolute power to masters over this property, and the enactment of fugitive slave laws on state and federal levels for the property's recapture are just some of many examples. Despite the occasional use of the word "persons" in laws designed to control the movements, activities, and potential manumission of slaves, it is very clear that the overwhelming reality of the legal status of black slaves was as property, not as persons.[12]

Legal decisions and interpretations, nevertheless, cannot set precedents or procedures for all the actions of daily life. Jefferson, like all large plantation-owners, had to deal with a variety of workers. A few white men provided some of the skilled labor and were the managers and overseers. But most of the skilled laborers were slaves: blacksmiths, bridle-makers, carpenters, grooms, cooks, spinners, weavers, mechanics, brick-makers and bricklayers. They were distinct from the larger body of field hands and from the special group of drivers and foremen who kept the field slaves in line. A few of the slaves had reknowned skills, even in such areas as midwifery and healing, and were sometimes contracted out, with their services sold for cash. Indifference to the humanity of remote field hands may have been easy, but Jefferson, like all slave-owners, must have had to come to terms with the diverse humanity of those workers with whom he had more intensive interaction. This group included those who tended his most personal needs as well as those who cooked, washed, scrubbed, waited tables, tended the fires, spun the cotton and wool, and wove the cloth and made the clothing for the household. It also included the young woman who was to share his bed for more than two decades, who gave up a chance for freedom during more than two years with him in Paris, and who returned to slavery at Monticello probably pregnant with her first child, Tom.[13] That Jefferson often vacillated or was indecisive about matters and frequently had bouts of deep depression may have been one of the by-products of the morally duplicitous life of a slave-owner in a "free" nation.

As a political and intellectual leader in the newly independent United States, Jefferson faced tremendous pressures. Critics throughout Europe and in some Northern states confronted the nascent new nation with a damning question: How can the American revolutionists speak of liberty, justice, and the rights of man and still keep large numbers of their fellow human beings in slavery? As a young man still in his twenties, Jefferson had purchased a three-volume French edition of Montesquieu's *de L'esprit des Lois*, and he was in Paris on the eve of the French Revolution. He was much affected by the ideas of Enlightenment thinkers and especially by their condemnation of the abuses of authority and the evils of injustice and oppression. He was also aware of the growing abolitionist movement in England and in the United States, which endangered the very foundations of the new state.

Nevertheless, on the question of slavery, Jefferson shared with his fellow planters the anguishing realization that a total life-style itself was at stake. Jefferson knew as well as anyone the intractable and overpowering dependence that white planters had on slave labor. It was their belief that without the slaves there could not have been the critical commerce on which the new nation depended, nor the great wealth which was accruing in both North and South. Over 80 percent of the nation's overseas trade was in products produced by slaves: tobacco, rice, cotton, sugar, and indigo. Manufacturing, transport, banking, and ship- and road-building all benefited from the profits of slavery. More than that, white workers and small farm-owners who had no slaves had come to view the hierarchy of racial ranking as natural and redounding to their benefit.

In a very personal manner, Jefferson agonized over this unhappy dependence on slave labor and realized that his own life-style would be impossible without it. As all of his biographers recognized, he was much obsessed with the life of opulence that his status provided, even though later in life he excoriated young men for their greed and materialism. He mused that the Southern economy would be in shambles were all slaves to be immediately freed (this accounts for his belief that it might be possible to gradually emancipate the slaves). It is indeed highly relevant that, although he owned at their peak over 15,000 acres of prosperous plantations, he stayed in debt much of his life because he persistently overextended himself. The productivity of Monticello or Poplar Forest did not seem to ever reduce those debts, in part because he took on the debt responsibilities of others. He became as ambivalent and evasive about his debts as he was about the subject of freeing his slaves. One cannot help but speculate that Jefferson's economic woes may have been in part self-destructive behavior, an unconscious way of imposing punitive sanctions on himself for the preservation of a system that he claimed to abhor, but could not do without.

His ambivalence did not cease on the matter of economic dependence. He was implicitly aware of the deficiencies in the rationalization that Africans could rightly be held in slavery because they were heathens. Consequently, he was among the first to embrace, albeit tentatively, an intellectual argument that was much more devastating than any previous ones: the claim that the Negro was an inherently inferior form of human being. Jefferson found himself one of the foremost spokespersons of this view in America.

Jefferson's ideas, published materials, speeches, and actions had enormous influence over other men and women. Jordan (1968) pointed out that Jefferson's *Notes on the State of Virginia*, when published in 1787 (first published in Paris, 1785), "helped generate a lively discussion of the Negro's nature" (547). It was he, more than anyone, Jordan tells us, who framed the terms of the debate on Negro intelligence. When he first wrote this manuscript and up to the time of the American Revolution, Jefferson indeed was the only Southerner of his time to speak out publicly on the subject of the Negro's intellectual inferiority. Moreover, Jordan explained, "Until well into the nineteenth century Jefferson's judgment on that matter, with all its confused tentativeness, stood as the strongest suggestion of inferiority expressed by any native American" (455). John Hope Franklin's observation is even more damning, "From the time that Jefferson's *Notes on Virginia* was made public, Southern leaders did not hesitate to use his work to strengthen their contention that Negroes were by nature an inferior race and therefore should be enslaved" (Franklin and Moss 1988, 172).

Jefferson's famous work contained descriptions and speculations about "the Negro" that made it clear that he was equivocal, at best, about the blacks' humanity. He asserted that in memory blacks were equal to the whites, in reason they were much inferior, and in imagination they were dull, tasteless, and anomalous. Nature itself had produced a great distinction between the races, not only in physical features, but in temperament and in mental endowment. Later, he corrected the absolutist tenor of such statements and posed this qualification: "the opinion, that they are inferior in the faculties of reason and imagination, must be hazarded with great diffidence." He offered some redemption by suggesting that assessing mental ability was a difficult matter. He even conjectured an alternative explication that the "conditions" under which the Negroes lived (as slaves) may have a determining effect upon their character. Yet he was quite capable of writing later, "I advance it therefore as a suspicion only, that the blacks, whether originally a distinct race, or made distinct by time and circumstances, are inferior to the whites in the endowments both of body and mind" (Jefferson [1787] 1955, 143). Alternately, Jefferson asserted that the Negro's "moral sense" was as "fully developed" as that of whites. When he was not contradicting himself, on a number of occasions he made the prophetic suggestion that we must leave it to science to determine the true nature of the Negro's inferiority. On this matter, Merrill Peterson (1970) has offered the most revealing statement. "Many of his (Jefferson's) observations," he said, "paraded as scientific, were but thinly disguised statements of folk belief about Negroes" (262). These folk beliefs have been the very substance of the idea of race from the beginning.

Jefferson's general orientation toward liberal and Enlightenment thinking (he was a disciple of John Locke, a friend of Condorcet, and was widely read in philosophy and history) was subverted by his role as plantation-owner. As such he shared the general values, beliefs, and conditioning toward blacks that characterized this class. Born into a world in which he was surrounded by slaves all of his life, Jefferson seemed never to have considered them except as "the other." Indeed, he believed "that an indelible color line had been drawn by Nature between the two races and that this line determined the rights and liberties to which they were entitled in America" (Miller 1977, 17). To resolve the contradictions he "reached a tentative conclusion on the Negro that he knew to be indefensible morally and unproven scientifically" (Peterson 1970, 264).

George Havens (1955) suggests that Jefferson was "confused," and Dwight Hoover (1976) declares only that Jefferson "could not make up his mind," (75) either about black inferiority, intelligence, or sexual appetites. Dumas Malone (1962, 1970, 1971) rationalizes Jefferson's dilemma, preferring to emphasize his generous and humane treatment of his slaves. Fawn Brodie (1974), who has delved into Jefferson's life with microscopic candor, tells us that he was a man in deep conflict, "ambivalent not only about love but also about revolution, religion, slavery and power" (7).

Jefferson, like so many other men of his time, was ready and willing to accept the argument that blacks were a separate and permanently inferior "race" because it provided an intellectual, seemingly rational, defense of slavery and the way of life to which he was deeply committed.

After he came into public office, Jefferson personally managed to avoid much of the controversy over slavery and the questions of Negro inferiority. Though in his early years he had written scathing passages about the evils and immorality of slavery, and especially its malevolent effects on slave-owners (see Chapter 9), he never publicly condemned it after his rise to political prominence, nor did he support any of the abolitionist movements or publications. He was caught in the quagmire of growing racist sentiment as the role of the ideology of race was beginning to be focused in the minds of those leaders who were committed to the preservation of slavery in the age of revolution. Although Jefferson showed honest ambivalence and was perhaps even tortured by the reality of slavery in the land of the free, like most other men (in both North and South), he seemed ultimately able to resolve his internal conflict only by increasingly projecting the African as something subhuman.

It may never be possible to fully comprehend the workings of the slave-owners' minds. That they were able to successfully dichotomize their daily experiences and perceptions of reality and avoid confronting their own hypocrisy is readily apparent. The most tragic instances of this mental gymnastic involved the treatment of the offspring they had by black slave women. Visitors to Southern plantations were often struck by the frequency of such "mixed" offspring among the other slaves. Whether sired by the owners, the white overseers, or other white men, these children constituted a growing population. By defining the Negro, indeed creating him, as a subhuman creature, white Americans precluded all possibility of claiming such children as their own or even establishing a relationship with them on a human level. As shown in Chapter 6, this most extraordinary feature of slavery in North America set it apart from all other systems of slavery. It was a feature that carried major implications for the future relationships of all peoples in the new nation, and it was critical to constructing the exclusionist components of race ideology.

North Americans apparently found it not only socially and ideologically necessary but also easy to distance themselves from any consciousness of connectedness to their slave offspring and kinspeople. Once racial slavery had become fully institutionalized early in the eighteenth century, paternal recognition of slave children publicly became increasingly rare, virtually ceasing during the rest of the eighteenth and early nineteenth centuries.[14] The result was a rather strangely irrational social reality, of which Jefferson's own life appears to provide a fascinating example. When, during his presidential campaign, his opponents accused him of having fathered children by "Dusky Sally," Jefferson responded with silence, even though at least one alleged son was said to greatly resemble the master.[15] Jefferson's legal grandson, Thomas Jefferson Randolph, many years later admitted to an interviewer that one of the slave sons (either Madison or Eston, with whom he grew up) looked so much like Jefferson that in the dusk or at a distance he might have been mistaken for him. When asked why Jefferson did not remove these children who so resembled him from public sight by sending them to his Bedford estate, Randolph replied that Jefferson "never betrayed the least consciousness of the resemblance" (quoted in Brodie 1974, 322). (See also Malone 1970, Appendix II.)

This suggests that Jefferson had developed a mechanism for so compartmentalizing his consciousness that the dichotomy of free and unfree was totally synonymous with white and black, and the barriers between them were so indelible that he could not even recognize his own children, emotionally, psychologically, or socially.[16] In the orderly world that he wanted to create, the fuzziness of genetic mixture had no place. Apparently Jefferson could only tolerate the slave situation if he could retain the conviction that slaves, even his own children, were qualitatively different and inferior kinds of being. The ideology of race that he had created in his mind required that the white population retain its identity unthreatened by any of the uncertainties that miscegenation represented. He was no doubt aided and abetted in this philosophy, this mode of thinking, by his enormous concern (or growing obsession) with Anglo-Saxonism.

The idea of a pure Anglo-Saxon people and culture was one of the major sociocultural themes that, though it emerged independently in Europe, as we have seen, found one of its greatest areas of nurturance on the American continent. It gave added strength to the idea of racial purity and the need to protect whites from contamination by blacks. Culture and biology became so intricately interwoven that the biological processes of intercourse and reproduction were considered threatening to white culture.

Nash (1982) believes that, at a much deeper level, it was a question of power. The prohibition against interracial sex ran only one way, he notes, since sexual relations between white men and black women "were frequent and usually coercive throughout the eighteenth century" (283). White men, he argues, banned interracial marriage as a way of declaring legally that the Negro, even when free, was not the equal of whites. "But white power was also served by sexually exploiting black women outside of marriage—a way of acting out the concept of white domination. Racial intermingling, so long as it involved free white men and slave black women, was a way of intimately and brutally proclaiming the superior rights and strength of white society" (283). Thus the offspring of such unions had to be morally, psychologically, and legally invisible. Jefferson and his compatriots set the stage for the dichotomy of consciousness and the moral duplicity and hypocrisy in many areas of life that still haunt many white Americans today.

Jefferson's role in the evolution of the concept of race was that of the institutional mediator through whom popular beliefs and attitudes toward human diversity were meshed together with and confirmed by a growing body of "scientific" judgments. In Jefferson there occurred the amalgamation of pseudoscientific truths, folk beliefs, and stereotypes, and this blend was transmitted to a populace that desperately needed a way out, a new justification for the economic and social system on which they depended for survival and for their way of life. From then on, throughout the nineteenth and well into the twentieth century, science was to provide the guidelines for the ideology of race.

As the medium through which science and popular images were conjoined, Jefferson played a critical role in the growth of American science, and not just because he was admired by others for his knowledge and intellect. According to John C. Greene (1984), he was a practitioner and promoter of science in an age of seminal developments in American science. He "participated in one way or another in nearly every field of scientific inquiry, stimulating his compatriots with his ideas and researches and inspiring them with the knowledge that their efforts were appreciated at the highest level of government" (1984, xiv).

In his *Notes on the State of Virginia*, Jefferson brought together his researches on the flora and fauna of the newly emerging state. He established himself as a creditable scholar by his careful research, which included descriptions and measurements of all kinds of phenomena. He successfully defended the animals of the New World against the charge by Comte de Buffon that these creatures had migrated from the Old World and subsequently degenerated in size and vigor because of the influences of the American climate. He also defended the native population against similar charges of lacking vigor and sexual ardor. In fact, Jefferson's attitude toward the Indians, whom he thought might become assimilable, was inconsistent with his attitude toward blacks, which was a reflection of the different roles they played in his life. In the Scale of Beings, Indians clearly ranked higher than blacks. Page Smith suggests that Jefferson had a romantic infatuation with Indians (1976, 266).

As an activist, Jefferson participated in the excavation of an Indian mound, collected fossils of ancient animal forms, was instrumental in the development and distribution of smallpox vaccines, organized and provided the guidelines for the Lewis and Clark expedition, and promoted other such scientific explorations (Greene 1984). His personal library, which contained one of the largest collections of scientific works in the nation, became the nucleus for the Library of Congress. Greene claims that Jefferson became "a national symbol of interest and faith in science" (35). Because of Jefferson's centrality in the formation of American science, Greene designates this period in American life as the "Age of Jefferson."

By virtue of his great reputation, whatever pronouncements Jefferson made on moral, political, or scientific matters would have been both widely known and respected as authoritative. They would have functioned as guideposts to the thoughts of others. Whatever was left unstated and whatever was absent in his philosophy, ideals, and judgments would also have had an impact. When the author of the Declaration of Independence compromised on the ideals of the American Revolution and failed to extend his advocacy of the rights of man to the internal situation of slave labor, this did not pass unnoticed by the public.

In Jefferson's lifetime the transformation of Africans and their descendants in the American colonies into subhuman creatures was, to a great extent, completed. From the latter half of the eighteenth century on, virtually all references to blacks as well as to Indians were couched in the idiom of "race." From that time and well into the nineteenth century, the term had a consistent and well-understood meaning. Its various elements had been consolidated into a worldview that had undeviating clarity and that, in the nineteenth century, was to become total. Critical to the elaboration of the ideology of race was the central role of science. "Race" as a new and infallible truth had to await the development of a proper substitute for religion, and science became that substitute. It provided an intellectual response tailored to the needs of a materialistic, pragmatic society that had elevated greed to a holy passion and made property and the acquisition of property an unassailable and sacred right, superseding even the right to life, liberty, and the pursuit of happiness.

The entire revolutionary period, its causes, motivations, and objectives, was permeated with this prime consideration, the rights of property. Jefferson's silence on the subject of slavery and Negro rights to life and liberty, to say nothing of happiness, conveyed just this fact—the primacy of property rights among people who reckoned their wealth and status primarily in terms of two forms of property, slaves and land.

As an esteemed political leader and a chief advocate and promoter of science, he helped to introduce to the American public what was to become the supreme justification for however they chose to treat blacks in their midst. When he suggested that the question of the Negro's intellectual inferiority be put to the scrutiny of science, he opened the way to the documentation of assumed black inferiority and to the widespread acceptance of it, not only by Americans with interests in preserving slavery and the privileged positions it had brought but also by the world at large.

Notes

1. See Thomas Kuhn (1962) for one view of the processes of scientific growth. This is a view and a model that has its critics. Greene (1981), for example, poses a much broader paradigm in which he includes the importance of cultural traditions and preexisting worldviews as well as challenges to them from outside the scientific establishment (e.g., political economy) for generating new scientific theories.

2. Hoover 1976, 59. The first Indian Department was established in the War Department, under the Secretary of War, a telling comment on white attitudes toward Indians as separate nations that had to be dealt with through violent means.

3. This was brought to my attention by David Dodd, then a graduate student in the Department of Anthropology, SUNY-Binghamton.

4. Jordan (1968) claims that the term "race" at the time of Jefferson was "characterized by total absence of any precise meaning" (489). But the evidence that he himself provides in this massive work of the range of white beliefs and attitudes shows a far more concrete conceptualization of race and race differences than he would allow. Jordan even recognizes Jefferson's "axiomatic" acceptance of the model of a Great Chain of Being in his *Notes on the State of Virginia* and his even more significant adherence to the "objectively hierarchical character of natural variation" (490). My point is that "race," coming into widespread use, already referred to unequal groups.

5. The linkage of biology and behavior is one of the components of race that appears so intractable and so aggravating to physically identifiable minorities. It homogenizes all individuals in a perceptible minority category and prevents the understanding of individual differences in culture and behavior. Benjamin Franklin's admonition against such a view is just as pertinent today as it was two hundred years ago: "If an Indian injures me, does it follow that I may revenge that Injury on all Indians? It is well known that Indians are of different Tribes, Nation and Languages, as well as white people. ... In Europe, if the French who are White People, should injure the Dutch, are they to revenge it on the English because they too are White People? If it be right to kill Men for such a Reason, then should any Man, with a freckled Face and red Hair, kill a Wife or Child of mine, it would be right for me to revenge it, by killing all the freckled red-haired Men, Women and Children, I could afterwards anywhere meet with (quoted in Jordan 1968, 277)."

6. In addition to the Horsman (1976) article, see his book (1981), and see Curtis (1968).

7. From *The Complete Works of Tacitus,* translated by A. I. Church and W. J. Brodribb (New York: Modern Library, 1942).

8. The interesting exceptions were those few scholars who concentrated on the customs, beliefs, and traditions of "primitive" societies. As early as 1724, Jean Lafitau studied the kinship system of the Iroquois and others and discovered the kind of similarities in kinship terms that later anthropologists were to call "classificatory." He saw value in comparing the customs of contemporary savages with those of ancient times. Later in time, William Robertson not only recognized similarities but also suggested that they were caused by independent invention and by developments along parallel lines. Both writers were expressing the early speculative evolutionary themes of eighteenth-century anthropological thought, which presaged fully mature nineteenth-century theories.

9. It is instructive that, perhaps because they could not directly face their own hypocrisy, Jefferson and many other planters placed the blame for the origination and persistence of slavery on the English king, George III. (See Miller 1977.)

10. The classic biography of Jefferson is Dumas Malone's six-volume work under the general title *Jefferson and His Times*, published from 1948 through 1981. Another well-known biographer is Merrill Peterson (1962, 1970). John Chester Miller's work (1977) deals specifically with Jefferson and slavery. The most controversial work, and perhaps the best known, is Fawn Brodie's best-seller (1974), which has been scorned by many more conservative authorities. New books on Jefferson appear with somewhat predictable regularity.

11. There were several rare circumstances, perhaps not so unusual during those times, under which a few of the slaves in Jefferson's household were permitted to obtain their freedom. One was the proviso in his will that freed five slaves, all members of the Hemings family, which allegedly included two of his own sons by his slave concubine, Sally Hemings (whom he did not set free in his will). The earliest-known instance relates to his stay in Paris as United States representative (1785–1789). All of the slaves whom he brought with him were technically free once they set foot on French soil. But Jefferson apparently persuaded James Hemings (Sally Hemings's brother), who had learned French cooking, to return to Virginia with him in order to instruct some other servants in the preparation of French food. In return, Jefferson promised him his freedom. It was not granted, however, until seven years after his return (Brodie 1974, 303).

12. See Loren Miller (1966); also John C. Miller (1977) who explicitly observes that although black slaves were "admittedly human beings, they were also property and where the rights of man conflicted with the rights of property, property took precedence" (13).

13. Many American historians have long denied that Jefferson had such a "miscegenous" relationship with a slave. Peterson (1970) says the allegations, which came out in local newspapers at the time of Jefferson's first presidency, were groundless and scandalous. "Such a mixture of the races, such a ruthless exploitation of the master-slave relationship, revolted his whole being" (707).

John C. Miller (1977) feels that such a relationship would have contradicted the ideals by which Jefferson lived, especially his moral sense and his "loathing of racial mixture" (176). Malone (1970) concurs, and denies the relationship in several volumes, arguing that the "vulgar liaison" cannot be proved, but was "distinctly out of character" and "unthinkable in a man of Jefferson's moral standards and habitual conduct" (214).

Jefferson is a true and revered hero of the American revolutionary era and an honored founder of the nation, but he was not a saint. And he was most definitely a product of his times and his culture. Two facts about Jefferson's circumstances should be considered. One, he was a widow before the age of forty and never remarried; and there is no reason to believe that he remained celibate. Two, in all slave-owning societies, without exception, masters have taken advantage of the power relationship inherent in the roles and have engaged in sexual relationships with their slaves with total impunity. In the United States, it might have been distasteful to those who focus on the racial element, but it was a natural concomitant of slavery. Adultery was considered much worse, and historians report with little hesitancy about Jefferson's overtures to several married women. Nor have they been reluctant to expose the fact that Sally Hemings was the slave offspring of John Wayles, Jefferson's father-in-law. Thus she was a half-sister to Jefferson's own wife and was considered very beautiful. My contention is that Jefferson was human, not a sacred legend. His biographers provide abundant evidence in many aspects of his life that he did *not* in fact live according to the ideals he so eloquently espoused; keeping slaves was the most obvious and glaring example.

14. Historians have recently found evidence that "on the eve of the Civil War … some eminent white men were having not only one child by a Negro woman but several children" (see Joel Williamson 1984, 41). Moreover, Williamson claims, they tended to recognize the relationship and to will property to these children. Until 1850, the United States Census did not even count "mulattoes" (people of mixed heritage).

15. The allegations of Jefferson's paternity can never be proved, nor can the assumptions made by Dumas Malone and others that Sally Hemings's children were fathered by one of Jefferson's nephews, Samuel or Peter Carr (or both). See Malone 1970, Appendix II. The reality is that such miscegenation was a fact of life in the South and this analysis applies regardless.

16. Long after I had written these chapters, I discovered the work of Page Smith (1976) in which he observes that Jefferson had a "strange capacity for compartmentalizing his emotions" (59). Speaking of his sexual overtures to Betsey Walker, a friend's wife, Smith says that "far more than most historical figures, (he) is constantly stepping 'out of character'" (60). Smith accepts without equivocation Jefferson's liaison with Sally Hemings.

Antislavery and the Entrenchment of a Racial Worldview

T
HE RISE OF ANTISLAVERY SENTIMENT in the mideighteenth century implied worrisome doubts about the moral rightness of slavery. It prompted a reassessment of the economic and social value of slavery, moved some slave-owners to free their slaves, and inspired organized movements to end the slave trade. It also simultaneously provoked in the South a hardening of resistance to antislavery pressures and an increased tendency to denigrate "the Negro," helping to more deeply imbed the ideological components of race in American culture.

Donald Noel (1972) has suggested that the antislavery movement was the catalytic agent that conjoined "the material fact of gross exploitation with an egalitarian value system to produce racism" (163). Racism, he continued, "emerged from the 'necessity' to defend a profitable institution which was under attack because its gross exploitation of human beings was sharply at odds with emerging Western values" (165). That antislavery pressure was seminal to important transformations in ideas about human differences in the late eighteenth and early nineteenth centuries should not be in doubt. And the context within which antislavery functioned, an expanding democratic and humanitarian ideology, clearly conditioned the proslavery response. Without the pressures of antislavery, especially by the abolitionists, there might have been less need or propulsion to construct the elaborate edifice of race ideology that has been our legacy.

In this chapter we explore some of the implications of this development, further elucidating the components of the race identity imposed on blacks. Focusing on some of the main thrusts of the antislavery movement, we briefly outline its history and the diverse motivations of its participants. Following the superb, detailed analysis by David Brion Davis (1966), two major sources of antislavery thought are identified, religious inspiration and Enlightenment ideology, although the differences between them were probably irrelevant for the galloping advance of racial ideology. Many of the opponents of slavery were themselves deeply influenced by their conditioning to the growing racial worldview and antagonism to blacks.

We then examine the often extreme reaction to abolitionism of proslavery forces, delineating the realities of Southern economic, social, and psychological dependence on both race and slavery. The idea of race differences became an instrumental part of American social structure, molding values and life-styles. Southerners, including those who never owned slaves, saw race as critical to their way of life and were much more comfortable when biophysical variations clearly marked the differentiation between the statuses of free persons and slaves. They came to see free blacks as an anomaly, a contradiction of their visions of what should be the natural state of things. Antislavery endangered their perception of what was essential to their culture in part because of the very real economic changes it would entail, but also because it threatened to disrupt the status and power relationships to which many whites had become addicted. Unmitigated power permitted white racial hostility and sense of superiority to flourish with impunity. It also allowed the fabrication of a vicious and devastating image of "the Negro," one that precluded the acceptance of blacks as potential equals.

Finally, we consider the autonomous nature of the concept of race, arguing that it was created as a qualitatively unique social phenomenon. Abolitionism undergirded the development of race as a cognitive social domain distinct from other forms and patterns of social stratification because it compelled proslavery forces into an extreme defensive posture from which there was no retreat. In its uniqueness, race solidified and rigidified the social hierarchy, permitting fluidity in a class system preserved only for whites. It is argued that since the end of the eighteenth century "race" and "class" have represented separate and distinct social arenas; one is not reducible to the other, although an obvious relationship and similarities between the two domains should be recognized.

A Brief History of Antislavery Thought

There had always been some people, both in England and the colonies, who expressed varying degrees of opposition to slavery. Many were merely uncomfortable with the idea of the kind of total control by force that one human being had over another. Others accepted slavery, and even recognized some basis for it in the Bible and in the writings of the ancient Greeks and Romans, but they argued that the course of human history had advanced away from such practices. Human progress in the future would be based on free labor, which would ultimately prove more productive. Such views were influenced by the ideology of early capitalism and growing urban and industrial development in the North that depended on free wage labor.

Some critics of slavery recognized an implacable reality; that was the corrosive effect of slavery on white attitudes toward all blacks. Even Thomas Jefferson, in his painful ambivalence, wrote one of the most eloquent expressions of such sentiments.

> The whole commerce between master and slave is a perpetual exercise of the most boisterous passions, the most unremitting despotism on the one part, and degrading submissions on the other. Our children see this, and learn to imitate it; for man is an imitative animal. This quality is the germ of all education in him. From his cradle to his grave he is learning to do what he sees others do ... The parent storms, the child looks on, catches the lineaments of wrath, puts on the same airs in the circle of smaller slaves, gives a loose to his worst of passions, and thus nursed, educated, and daily exercised in tyranny, cannot but be stamped by it with odious peculiarities. The man must be a prodigy who can retain his manners and morals undepraved by such circumstances ([1787] 1955, 162).

Thirty years before these sentiments were written by Jefferson, the great abolitionist John Woolman had observed how the "wrongful enslavement of Negroes ... depraves the mind" (Jordan 1968, 274). Both Woolman and his fellow abolitionist Anthony Benezet decried how the minds of white children are conditioned to Negro inferiority. The Negroes, Benezet noted in 1762, "are constantly employed in servile Labour, and the abject Condition in which we see them, from our Childhood, has a natural Tendency to create in us an Idea of a Superiority over them, which induces most People to look upon them as an ignorant and contemptible Part of Mankind" (quoted in Jordan, 275).

They were not alone in discovering the power of such conditioning and its corrupting effect on human relationships. Speaking about the "fallacius reasoning and absurd sentiments used and entertained concerning negroes," David Cooper declared, "the low contempt with which they are generally treated by the whites, lead children from the first dawn of reason, to consider people with a black skin, on a footing with domestic animals, form'd to serve and obey" (Jordan 1968, 276). A population so humiliated and degraded, overworked, sweat-drenched and filthy most of the time, and totally deprived of any form of self-esteem, could hardly have met the requirements of "civilized" appearance and comportment. Those whose perverse reasoning denied the effects of the slave situation and environment on blacks could accept with equanimity the equally perverse belief that such behaviors and appearances were "natural" to all those with black skins.

Despite such critics, during the long decades when the institution was being solidified few voices opposed slavery, although some men like Morgan Godwyn were critical of the greed and materialism of slave-owners (Davis 1966, 369). In the eighteenth century the moral problems inherent in slavery became more acute, with antislavery sentiment emerging out of what Davis sees as a new ethic of benevolence (378). This was an era of rising humanitarian concerns, of revolutionary thought about human nature as rational and/or governed by natural laws, the application of which would lead to improvement of the human condition. As Europeans were reconceptualizing the functions and limits of government and ruminating on the nature of life, liberty, economics, and politics, they speculated on the equally critical meaning of Christian living. Sensitivity, compassion, the expansion of moral feelings, and the idea of public duty appeared as common topics of sermons and literature providing a fertilizing milieu for antislavery thought.

The Religious Inspiration

There was considerable debate over the issue of converting and baptizing slaves. On the one hand, there were those who felt that it was civilized man's obligation to instruct the heathen Africans in Christianity. Such men were disturbed by widely accepted proscriptions, dating from medieval times and earlier, against the enslavement of fellow Christians. They were matched against those, on the other hand, who were opposed to conversions, for much the same reasons. As long as the slaves remained heathen, Christian qualms about their continued enslavement would be largely abated. The strongest negative reactions to exposing slaves to religious teachings were found primarily in those states in which the largest numbers of slaves were concentrated. The New England colonists, for the most part, seemed generally to favor missionary activity and even the establishment of schools for instructing servants and slaves.

In the coastal and southern colonies where dependence on slavery was greatest, proselytizing among the poor and the servant class was perceived as a problem. When it proved impossible to control either the proselytizers or their influences, proslavery forces turned to alternative strategies. As early as 1664 some colonies began to enact laws declaring that baptism could not affect the status of the slaves or require their manumission (Jordan 1968). In this the colonists were following precedents established in Latin America where baptisms were virtually universal and the church also owned large numbers of slaves.

Early in the eighteenth century various religious groups in England and Europe, mostly Protestants and including some men and women of prominence and wealth, began to press more vigorously for the conversion of slaves. In 1701 the Society for the Propagation of the Gospel in Foreign Lands was formed, which eventually gained the support of the Church of England. Although its success was at best questionable (it found itself the heir of a large plantation with four or five hundred slaves and soon succumbed to the lure of profits), it kept the obligation to proselytize alive and exemplified the ways by which Christian duty could be rendered compatible with slavery.

Actual arguments against slavery itself appeared to surface slowly in the Christian community. The earliest and most vociferous and persuasive of all of the religious groups were the Quakers, and for the next 150 years theirs was the strongest and most consistent voice in the antislavery movement in England and in the colonies. When George Fox, the Quaker leader, began his campaign in the 1650s, he argued that slavery was inherently evil and repulsive to Christian principles. But many Quakers owned slaves or were involved in trade that was dependent on slave labor, so the response was slow.[1] Soderlund (1985) observes that it took a hundred years of deliberation before the Quakers could convince their fellow religionists to give up their slaves. Wealthy Quaker slaveholders acted to hold onto their laborers, insisting on their own benevolence as sufficient for Christian redemption. In 1776 Quakers finally prohibited all slave ownership.

During the Great Awakening, as we have seen, evangelical preachers penetrated the South and many preached against slavery. If this movement appealed to the poor, the uneducated, and the dispossessed, it was no less attractive to black slaves who found in it a soothing balm for the psychic wounds of slavery. Blacks took to the revivalistic movement with a vigor and vitality that could not be expressed in other forums. For a time, early in the movement, blacks and mostly poor whites worshipped together in open-air meetings. They shared a common experience of being "born again" with a living Christ who saw their spirits, if not their bodies, as equal in the divine light. This experience of shared rebirth may have ushered in a new and revolutionary ethos, but the implications of transforming personalized evangelical zeal into a social movement were never realized (Mathews 1980). By the 1790s white and black churches in the South began to emerge as separate and segregated congregations under the power of expanding racial ideology.

Although antislavery sentiments were expressed in tones of moral outrage, particularly by those whose views stemmed from religious piety, it should not be assumed that they reflected egalitarian views. Most opponents of slavery did not advocate the total equality of blacks, although many men such as Samuel S. Smith and Benjamin Rush held to the view of their potential equality. Products of their time and culture, eighteenth-century Americans were increasingly socialized to believe that there were profound differences between races and to accept the developing negative stereotypes of Africans.

External pressures, often only for the humanization of slave conditions, were perceived as threatening to the plantation system and caused considerable uneasiness. For one thing, the process of conversion continued to raise the question of the legitimacy of slavery itself. For another, conversion and baptism often carried in their wake a requirement for some degree of literacy in order for the converted to read the Bible. Early missionaries and educators with concern for heathen souls frequently established schools for blacks and Indians specifically for the purpose of teaching them the Scriptures. But even minimal literacy was seen by slavery proponents as dangerous to the preservation of a caste of ignorant, dependent laborers. Equally threatening of course were the subversive ideas that slaves might inculcate from written sources, including the Bible. The model of Moses leading the Israelites out of bondage was not considered appropriate for black slaves in America.

Far more fundamental was the nagging query that followed the unexpected logic of missionizing zeal. If the black slaves were capable of being converted to Christianity, would not that mean that they had souls? And if this were the case, then surely they would have to be accounted as fully human, men and women like their owners with all of the subtle sensitivities, passions, reasoning abilities, and spiritual needs of others. Some slave-owners thought, rightly as it turned out, that literacy would encourage conspiracies and rebellion among the slaves. It would give them pride and too great a sense of themselves. It would, indeed, make them more like their masters.

The slave-owners' dilemma was expressed poignantly in Jordan's words: "For if the Negro were like themselves, how could they enslave him? How explain the bid on the block, the whip on the back? Slavery could survive only if the Negro were a man set apart; he simply had to be different if slavery was to exist at all" (1968, 183–184).

Despite much initial resistance on the part of slave-owners and many of the organized Protestant churches, the majority of slaves, in time, converted to Christianity. Most became Baptists or Methodists, and some became members of the churches of their masters. The revivalist fervor of the Great Awakening era may have underscored the spiritual equality of blacks and whites, but it had little impact on the slave condition. Although many evangelists became abolitionists, others placated slave-owners who objected to conversion by arguing that the effect of Christianity upon slaves would be a mollifying one, conditioning them to proper Christian humility and willingness to serve their masters.

In any case, the black presence was no longer an alien one; there were already in many areas blacks who were descended from seven or more generations of laborers on American soil. Both the African-Americans and their masters had learned much from each other, and the very intimacy of their lives in the South no doubt led to many breaches of the customs that were designed to underscore their differences. Life in the southland for both blacks and whites had taken on an interactive pattern and rhythm that was not to be broken until the Civil War—and then, some might say, only temporarily.

It seems oddly incongruous that, simultaneously, the more culturally adjusted these populations became, the more the dominant whites focused on and emphasized their differences, even to the point of inventing some.[2] The insistence on a wide cultural gap between themselves, blacks, and Indians was a mental construct, created to provide whites with a major justification for the exploitation of these peoples. Were they to admit to any similarities, "then the entire rationale of domination and exploitation would crumble" (Nash 1982, 292).

The option to the admission of similarities was the conceptualization of the created social-cultural gap as biologically determined, in other words, as part of the different inborn natures of blacks, Indians, and whites. Proslavery Christians thus invented a cognitive protective mechanism to justify and preserve their privileged status, one that required avoiding the reality of blacks as full human beings. Dwight Dumond, observing this process, said, "The denial of emancipation by conversion to Christianity had shifted the basis of slavery from heathenism to race" ([1961] 1966, 62). In the creation of the racial domain, the moral dimensions of slavery and exploitation could be projected to a different plane, thereby acquitting Christian consciences.

Enlightenment Influences

The second source of antislavery values emerged from the maturing political and social consciousness of the English regarding the nature of freedom in a culture that claimed to greatly value the rights of individuals. English thoughts about the meaning of a free society were clearly products of revolutionary political changes over several centuries, the rise of bourgeois capitalism, and Enlightenment history and philosophy. The English Constitution (or Common Law) since the seventeenth century had been characterized by increasing emphasis on human and civil rights and by the growth of sentiments for the advancement of popular democracy and political liberty. Many English people were enjoying a greater expansion of freedom and opportunity than ever before. The constitutional guarantees that the middle and upper classes had wrenched from the monarchy were being praised and emulated on the Continent. English people in the Americas saw themselves rightfully as heirs of this tradition, although not necessarily of all Enlightenment thought.

By the last quarter of the century, some of the English took the argument against slavery to political forums, claiming that the history of the development of English laws was reflective of the unfolding and strengthening of human liberties. Slavery, they said, was a regressive institution inherently incompatible with this tradition. In 1772 Granville Sharp was instrumental in securing the judicial decision that West Indian planters could not hold slaves in England because slavery was contrary to English law. Within a few years, English Quakers began a vigorous campaign for complete prohibition of the slave trade. In 1787 the primarily Quaker British Abolition Society was organized, and its leader, William Wilberforce, led the campaign against slavery in Parliament. Such men as Thomas Clarkson spent many years gathering evidence against the slave trade in courts, anticipating that if the trade were banned, slavery itself would eventually disappear. The inexorable progression of antislavery sentiment reached its heights in England as the issue of slavery became the focal point of parliamentary debates. People from virtually all segments of English society supported the abolitionist movement.[3] Petitions by the hundreds of thousands poured into Parliament. Both traditional congregations and radical dissenters joined together in support of the cause.

Some opposition to slavery came from Enlightenment writers in Scotland, England, and France. We noted earlier that radical new currents of social thought, as well as new perspectives and developments in science, reflected a liberalizing atmosphere of inquiry and speculation. The thinkers and writers of this period appealed above all to reason, denied the traditional emphases on supernatural revelation, and created a milieu for the triumph of empiricism. Some argued for the recognition of scientific principles governing all of the processes of nature and extended this model to human societies. Many also turned to notions about the perfectibility and progress of humankind, speculating on what would become in the nineteenth century a full-blown evolutionary paradigm. Focusing on the quest for freedom from both secular authority and stifling tradition, some Enlightenment writers made a clear connection between the abolition of slavery and the expansion of English values of liberty and equality.

Influences of Enlightenment writers provided nourishment for the growth of liberal ideologies in the colonies. By emphasizing people as rational beings who should be free to make choices and decisions about their own destinies, by raising questions about democratic reforms and human rights, and by awakening intellectual thought to new possibilities, they fostered bold and novel ideas for political and social reforms. Consistent with their progressive social philosophies, most Enlightenment writers were generally opposed to slavery. Yet, as we have seen, some were ambivalent on the question of equality and expressed doubts that blacks were the equal of whites. Many also promoted the value of property rights, which inherently contradicted the accordance of human rights to slaves. Opposition to slavery was not necessarily predicated on beliefs in the natural equality of all humankind.

In the American colonies, Enlightenment thinkers gained sympathetic audience from a populace who shared their optimism and their advocacy of freedom and who strove to emulate their sophistication. When Thomas Paine set about to write his famous paean to human freedom, *Common Sense*, it was the views of Enlightenment thinkers that informed his positions and arguments on liberty, equality, justice, and the rights of humankind. Like Jean-Jacques Rousseau, Paine was against concentrations of power, privilege, and wealth in the hands of the few and the less than coincidental impoverishment of so many.[4] His advocacy of the rights of ordinary citizens, the common man, fed the spirit of revolution in the colonies and in France.[5]

Throughout the revolutionary era, Americans were sensitive to many charges of hypocrisy and duplicity. Few critics failed to emphasize the blatant inconsistency that while the colonists were struggling for freedom from English domination they were holding hundreds of thousands of people as slaves. Disturbed by the naggings of moral consciences, some people did free their slaves. For a brief few years, individual acts of manumission increased, and all Northern states eventually outlawed slavery.

When the Constitutional Convention met in 1787 to frame a new federal document, its members debated, often passionately, the prohibition of the slave trade. Antislavery advocates offered moral and practical arguments for the gradual elimination of slavery, and even members from slave states like Virginia conceded that slavery was a fundamental

evil, a canker on the body politic. But Southern opposition to emancipation was intransigent. In the end, members deferred to Southern interests and prohibited terminating the slave trade for twenty years. The
Constitution did not directly refer to slavery, but some of its provisions
tended to lend implicit protection to the slave system. Article IV, for example, provided that fugitive slaves be delivered back to their owners,
and Article I prohibited Congress from taxing slavery out of existence
(Miller 1966, 20). In fact, no Southern state would have ratified the Constitution if the convention had attempted to eliminate slavery. Men
who were ostensibly antislavery capitulated in the compromise; all
were aware that slavery was an important foundation of the American
economy and society and a major source of overseas income.

When dealing with the question of the bases for taxation and representation in the House of Representatives, an even stranger compromise was effected. Southern leaders insisted that "the Negro" could not
be recognized as a full citizen, but at the same time they sought to enhance their power in the new government. The result was that slaves
were counted as "three-fifths of all other persons" for the apportioning
of representatives. This famous clause was to haunt some leaders of the
federal government for decades as their critics castigated them for what
many saw as an ignoble definition of black people.

These actions by America's first leaders demonstrated the extreme
degree to which black slaves had come to be seen as mere property. The
close interlinking of life, liberty, and and the right to property has been
a consistent and enduring theme throughout American history. When
the country's leaders spoke of individual or private rights, they always
meant rights of property, which tended to eclipse all others. Such actions also reflected the transparent ambivalence that we saw in Jefferson, and in many other minds, about the humanity of slaves. As Loren
Miller (1966) observed, the "Founding Fathers were well aware of the
contradictions implicit in recognition of slavery in the Constitution
side by side with the guarantees of individual rights." Yet he claimed
that their glossing over these contradictions should not be perceived as
hypocrisy, for "the belief in the inferiority of Negroes was widespread
and deeply rooted" (23). Indeed, these compromises reveal how remarkably and strongly entrenched slavery had become; and so also was the
system of ranked and unequal groups embraced in the idea of race that
was evolving along with it.

The antislavery movement experienced a brief decline in the last decade of the eighteenth century. Much of its momentum had already
dwindled during the convulsions of the American Revolution. Under
pressure of British abolitionists, however, both the United States and

England passed laws abolishing the slave trade on the high seas in 1807. Now fully committed to the ending of the slave trade, the English government placed the full force of its navy into the battle against this commerce.

Meanwhile, a number of events and changing economic circumstances catalyzed an even greater commitment to slavery and to the continued dehumanization of blacks. The first was the invention of the cotton gin, which made it possible to grow and process cotton at a hitherto unimagined rate. As a result, new territories were opened to cotton cultivation. From South Carolina to Georgia and eventually westward to Texas, cotton plantations sprang up all over the South. With them came unparalleled demand for slaves as planters strove to expand production and feed the insatiable English textile industry.

Second, an increase in slave rebellions, some of which were of large scale, shocked and frightened Americans. The most dramatic began in 1791 in Haiti and ended with the stunningly successful overthrow of French dominance. This was followed by Gabriel Prosser's conspiracy in 1800, Denmark Vesey's 1822 rebellion, and Nat Turner's 1831 revolt, along with numerous others of lesser fame. There had always been slave insurrections and conspiracies, but the Haitian Revolution was the first to meet any measure of success. It had come on the heels of and as a direct inspiration from the French Revolution; its meaning intensified the atmosphere surrounding all acts of resistance. It struck such fear in the hearts of slave-owners on the mainland that it was a constant topic of conversation and caused panicked attempts to close state borders to immigrants from the island. The prospect of slaves gaining freedom, through emancipation or revolution, now seemed very real and very terrifying.

A new era of radical antislavery fervor was initiated in the 1830s when William Lloyd Garrison began publishing his famous newspaper, *The Liberator*, and the American Anti-Slavery Society was born. Opponents of slavery were now calling for immediate abolition and were prepared to take drastic actions to bring it about. The next three decades were punctuated by periodic demonstrations, public lectures and meetings, the organization of numerous antislavery groups, and widespread criticism of slavery in newspapers and magazines in the North and abroad. Dwight Dumond ([1961] 1966) claims that Theodore Weld's *American Slavery As It Is* (1838) sold more copies than any other antislavery pamphlet, more than 100,000 the first year alone. When Harriet Beecher Stowe published her famous book, *Uncle Tom's Cabin*, in 1852, it became a clarion call for antislavery action.

Such intensification of abolitionist activities often came in response to actions taken by the states, and especially by the federal government, to protect or extend slavery. Amid controversy over slavery and related stormy debates in Congress over proper constitutional interpretations of the powers of the legislature and federal judiciary, the federal government found itself unable to deal with the problem of slavery. Its actions were contradictory and often incoherent, leading ultimately to a situation that could only be resolved by violence.

The Fugitive Slave Law of 1850 when passed by Congress generated a storm of protest. It required the retrieval and return of fugitive slaves to their owners, endangering many blacks who had lived unmolested for years in free territory. What was worse, it denied the right of suspected runaways to testify on their own behalf and presumed them to be guilty rather than innocent. The abrogation of the Missouri Compromise of 1820 had a similar effect. Although allowing slavery in Missouri, the 1820 act had prohibited it in the Kansas-Nebraska territory. In 1854, the Kansas-Nebraska Act repealed the compromise, opening an opportunity for the expansion of slavery. States passed numerous laws in an attempt to control or calm the slavery controversy, sometimes later repealing them. The arguments pro and con were strident and harsh. Abolitionists continued and strengthened their demands for the immediate freeing of all slaves. And, in 1859, the irascible John Brown dramatized the conflict and the antislavery cause for all time when he was elevated to martyrdom following his unsuccessful raid on Harpers Ferry.

The Proslavery Response

Larry Tise (1987) notes that little was written or published in defense of slavery until the latter part of the eighteenth century, and each spate of proslavery writings thereafter was in response to an upsurge of antislavery activities. Toward the end of that century white slave-owners and proponents of slavery were caught in a quandary of cataclysmic proportions. With slaves in even greater demand for cotton production, yet increasingly feared and hated because of their frequent refusals to accept their degraded circumstances, the visceral reaction of slave-owners was to increase discipline and control. In this context, antislavery simultaneously forced slave-owners and those who benefited from slavery to strengthen arguments to protect and preserve the system.

In the wake of such fervor there appeared, progressively, a more virulent mythicizing in the white mind of a creature called "the Negro." Some turned again to the legend of Noah and the curse placed on Ham's descendants through Canaan. Updating an older sixth-century interpretation, they proclaimed that black slavery was merely the implementation of God's ordained punishment for Ham's transgresssions on the ark. Who could argue with God's will or his plan for the different races? Although the appeal to biblical sanctions for slavery, along with the "Christian duty" to save African souls, may have satisfied the religiously oriented, there were more pragmatic and secular arguments. Slavery was essential for the Southern economy. More important, it was a means of controlling a savage, ignorant, irrational, and potentially violent population and of bringing them the blessings of civilization. Indeed, they had been slaves in Africa and knew no other condition.

In the decades that followed the American Revolution, argues Tise (1987), Americans backed away from the revolutionary and egalitarian ideals of Jefferson, Adams, and Madison (191). Some formulated a subtle new argument that sanctified inequality and made republican values consonant with slavery. Turning to history, especially Greek and Roman, they argued that all great civilizations were built on slave labor, that inequality is normal and natural in humankind, just as it exists in nature, and that justice and liberty for all is a myth. Led largely by New England–born clergymen, many Americans came to view abolitionism as a subversive and conspiratorial movement while they extolled the benefits of conservatism and preservation of the status quo.

Just as they retreated from the liberating and humanitarian ideals of the revolutionary era, many American social thinkers also turned away from the environmentalist explanations of the early Enlightenment and began to focus more on the inner qualities, and character, of "the Negro" as a way of explaining the predicament of slavery and the existence of white prejudice.[6] Reflecting the long-standing English discomfort with differences, many whites North and South, perceiving the end of slavery, advocated forced removal and colonization of all blacks in some distant territory, along with reservations for Indians. But slaveowners were understandably not intrigued by the prospect of losing their laborers, and more rational men rejected such schemes because of the prohibitive costs to the federal government of resettling blacks in some as yet unknown territory. When confronted with the impracticality, logistics, and costs of removing nearly two million unwilling black Americans to some unspecified land, advocates of removal backed away. Nevertheless, the colonization effort reflected the concerns of those who believed that blacks represented a danger to the order, stability, and progress of white civilization. It also represents irrefutable evidence of the vast differences accorded to the Negro in white minds.

Although Fredrickson ([1971] 1987) believes that the organizers and supporters of the American Colonization Society (1817) did not promote a racial argument for their attempts to resettle blacks outside of the United States, the very existence of such a movement is testament to the powerful exclusionist forces in American social thought. Like the Free-Soilers decades later, some colonizationists exhibited a deep and abiding antipathy toward the presence of Negroes in their midst and even argued that white bigotry was too powerful to ever accept blacks.

In 1828 white Americans elected to the presidency Andrew Jackson, a man widely known to be an Indian fighter and an Indian hater (he fought in the War of 1812 and the Creek War of 1813–1814) and who was the proslavery owner of a Tennessee plantation with over one hundred slaves. He was a new type of politician, elected with a large majority of votes from the white male populace. Most states had eliminated property-owning and tax-paying requirements, and suffrage for white males was now almost universal. A humble Westerner without aristocratic background or pretensions who appealed to the masses, he thus represented a democracy of the "common man." During this era, Americans were described by European visitors as crude, unrefined, ambitious, aggressive, prudish, vulgar materialists whose great passion was money (Pessen 1985). They had no respect for tradition, for laws, for learning, or for intellectual accomplishments. Jackson was the ideal role model for this common man, inspiring a sense of identity and unity among them never experienced before. His vice president was John Calhoun of South Carolina, one of America's most powerful defenders of slavery.

During Jackson's presidency in the 1830s, conflict over slavery reached a crisis. Abolitionist pressure had forced confrontation with the problem of what to do with "the Negro" after slavery. Colonizationist proposals began to evaporate as the lines between proslavery and antislavery forces hardened (see below). White Americans everywhere feared the consequence of huge numbers of blacks set free on American soil. Many who opposed slavery in principle could see no alternatives to maintaining the institution, and there ensued a massive spurt of writings in defense of slavery.

The 1830s also saw the beginning of Irish immigration. Dirt poor, illiterate, half-starved former farmers and their families appeared in the East Coast cities and began to compete for unskilled jobs with poor white Protestants and black Americans. They soon supplanted the blacks in foundries, factories, and domestic service jobs, in the trades, and as laborers on the canals and railroads. Hostilities among all three groups festered and became violent and urban riots occurred. The Irish soon learned that, as poor as they were, the blacks were even worse off and had no political voice in the Jacksonian world, one that the Irish supported.[7] It did not take long before the Irish were acculturated to the racial worldview, and they took a proslavery stand to protect themselves from black competition.

In the meantime proslavery forces marshaled every possible logical or reasonable argument in defense of the status quo, and their arguments became even more extreme in the 1850s (Fredrickson 1987). Although both Tise (1987) and Faust (1981) observe a "remarkable" consistency in proslavery arguments from the seventeenth century on, one proposition assumed heightened significance in the nineteenth century. The most powerful argument, in an age increasingly harkening to the authority of science, was that of the natural inferiority of the Negro, with all the malevolent implications of that belief. This component of race ideology came to constitute the most enduring argument, superseding all others before midcentury and forming the basis for much of public policy and social treatment of African-Americans in the post–Civil War era. Its remarkably effective ally was the growing scientific field of American anthropology, as we shall see in the next chapter.

The Sociocultural Realities of Race and Slavery

There were three fundamental realities about racial slavery that rendered the seemingly unassailable moral and legal arguments of abolitionists virtually ineffectual, particularly in the South. One was the overwhelming dependence of white plantation-owners on black labor. Another was the fact that a whole Southern culture and social system had evolved with race and slavery at its core. In the emergence of the Southern life-style, race had added a new dimension of social differentiation to the structuring of American society, coinciding with a growing capitalist economic system. The third reality, intrinsically related to the second but separated for heuristic emphasis, has to do with the corrupting nature of personal power and the human inability or unwillingness to relinquish it.

Dependence on Black Labor

Such dependence became manifest within several generations after the first white settlements. It is well documented in literature, letters, memoirs, fiscal records of plantations, diaries, and other materials. It was most visible in the persistent demand for slaves, which increased toward the end of the seventeenth century and became all but compulsive in the eighteenth.

As early as 1645, Emanuel Downing, in a letter to his brother-in-law, John Winthrop, expressed the hope that the settlers could use Indians "captured in just wars" to exchange for Negro slaves from the West Indies. "For I doe not see how wee can thrive untill wee get into a stock of slaves sufficient to doe all our business," he opined (quoted in Davis 1966, 146). This was a revealing statement of simple clarity, and one echoed by multitudes of later settlers. Other such expressions reverberated throughout the Americas in the Spanish and Portuguese colonies as well as in North America (Davis 1966, 148–150, 164). Davis's own cautious conclusion is that, given the mortality of Indians and the blockage of traditional sources of white labor, "it can be argued that the development of the New World as a producer of tropical staples would have been impossible without African slaves" (1984, 357).

No set of events better exemplifies this ineluctable dependence on black labor than the history of the colony of Georgia. Financed by wealthy philanthropists in 1730, the colony was deliberately planned as a social experiment; its settlers were to be refugees, orphans, and convicts, often men who had been imprisoned for debts. Its organizers were also idealists, many of whom believed, as did their leader James Oglethorpe, "that a colony founded to bring relief to the distressed of Europe should not be the cause of enslaving thousands of free Africans" (Davis 1966, 166). Although this was only one of a number of reasons given for the policy, in 1732 Georgia became the first and only non-slave-holding colony.

Within a few years, however, members of the colony began to petition the trustees to alter this policy and to allow slaves. The experiment was not working. Each year they begged for relief. The white workers would not, perhaps could not, produce the food and export crops needed. Hunger, disease, poverty, and death ravished the settlement. When settlers saw the tremendous wealth being produced by slaves in neighboring South Carolina, the remedy for Georgia's predicament seemed self-evident. The colony needed slaves or it would not survive. Even the "Great Awakener" George Whitefield "was convinced that Georgia could not subsist without slaves" (Tise 1987, 21). During the long controversy that ensued, black slaves began to be illegally brought into the colony. By 1750 the act prohibiting slaves had been repealed. From then on, Georgia prospered. Even poor white men firmly grasped the connection between owning slaves and one's individual advancement along with colonial prosperity.

The Culture of Racial Slavery

The second reality, the creation and reification of race as a new form of social stratification with all its cultural integument, as we have seen, is a bit more complex to delineate, yet is at the heart of this analysis. It involved the differentiation of blacks as distinct beings, a magnification of the social distance between blacks and whites, and the formulation in the white mind of a stereotype that became a caricature known as "the niggers." We have seen that the dichotomy between slaves and free persons had become established in the American mind as concomitant with physical differences. It is on this fact that Davis (1966) concluded, "In no ancient society was the distinction between slave and freeman so sharply drawn as in America" (62). White Americans had come to express this distinction by defining blacks as a race apart and ranking them the lowest of all groups in a racial scale of being.

Once reified, that is, crystallized and rendered as substantive reality, the folk idea of race assumed an identity and an autonomy of its own, aided by the authority of learned opinion. The autonomy of any aspect of culture is, of course, relative. But ideas and ideologies, when institutionalized in the human mind, often have a fluidity and refractivity that allows persistence even in drastically altered situations. In this case, the amorphous nature of race meant that the ideology could transcend the sources of its origin, and race classifications could be logically extended to any populations in which inequality and a sense of unbridgeable differences were desirable. Such populations could be identified by color or other physical features and their relative ranks established.

In the nineteenth century relationships between whites and native American populations were changing dramatically as white dominance crippled the ability of Indians to resist their cultural encroachment. Views about the Indians also shifted as what some historians have called "romantic racialism" replaced images of bestiality and savagery (Berkhofer 1978; Fredrickson [1971] 1987; Nash 1982, 1986) and as blacks became the new savages. Indians were placed in a higher rank above blacks in the ordering system. Asians, when the need arose later, were variously located either between whites and Indians or between Indians and blacks, depending on who was constructing the gradations. In the eyes of its formulators the ranking was based on each group's presumed capacity for civilization.

There is no doubt, whatever the strength of their attitudes toward human variation, that the originators of race perceived it as a mechanism of social stratification. They argued from a simple logic. Someone had to be the "mudsills"—to do the mean, dirty, dangerous, and difficult work in civilized society—and others had to be the leaders, thinkers, planners, creators, and administrators of high culture.[8] The use of original physical differences to structure such social ranks, for those who had the power to do so, was perhaps a logical consequence of the conquest situation and of the enslavement of physically differing populations.

It was in the treatment of nonslave blacks that the element of race as the premier determinant of social position is best viewed. The free Negro contradicted the white image of those who by their very racial definition were not entitled to freedom. If slavery was the natural and normal condition of Africans and they were happiest and freest when subordinate to and in the care of whites, then free Negroes were an abomination, a threat to the social system, and a danger to themselves. In both North and South, the lives of free blacks in the late eighteenth and nineteenth centuries were surrounded with numerous and onerous restrictions. Their mobility was limited; they could not vote or hold public office in most states, own or bear arms, or testify against a white man. They had no right of assembly, except in churches, were forced to observe curfews, and often had to carry certificates confirming their free status. In both North and South the free Negro was perceived as lazy and improvident, prone to crime and general depravity, and not worthy of white respect, fair play, or justice. Simultaneously, they were also being displaced from skilled jobs in favor of white workers.

The cultural behavior prescribed by an ideology of inequality and exclusiveness meant that everywhere the rank of white was given precedence. Even where there were no strict laws of segregation, the black presence was downgraded. In religion, recreation, and economic and social life, blacks and Indians could be present only as subordinates, unseen and ignored. Only low-status occupations were open to low-ranked races, and it was inconceivable that such persons could have any role to play in public life.

For all blacks, slave and free, repeated daily humiliations and unrestrained cruelties translated into conventional behavior and were perpetuated in each new generation. It takes little imagination to conjure up the proliferation of demeaning treatment of "the Negro," and the consequent institutionalization of such practices. A variety of customs were originated and associated with the debasement of blacks. Acts of physical and psychological brutality were carried out with impunity. There should be no doubt that the degradation, dehumanization, and demeaning aspects of the slave relationship elicited from many blacks behavioral syndromes of abject subordination. On many plantations, slaves were broken in spirit and were constantly fearful of the unmitigated power of their owners and other whites over them. Lower-class whites who would never own slaves debased and humiliated both slaves and free blacks, if for no other reason than to demonstrate their own superiority and power to do so.

As they were structuring a social hierarchy based on race, white Americans instituted patterns of etiquette, demeanor, and personal address between racial populations that were to survive and become exaggerated in the post–Civil War period. The essence of racial inequality was distilled in the shuffling and subordinate behavior of blacks vis-à-vis whites, the lowering of the eyes, the avoidance behavior in public, the jocular acceptance of insult and humiliation that was required, and the deference always to white opinion. Black subservience to and control by whites was important, from the white point of view, not only to prevent riots and rebellions but also to prevent race mixture and the subversion of white racial purity, a belief that gained currency with the ascendancy of racial Anglo-Saxonism.

The overarching vision of America for most whites became that of white advancement, privilege, and homogeneity, with inferior races kept at a distance in a state of permanent subordination. To this end, throughout the nineteenth century, race hatred, fear, and contempt increased as commonplace sentiments. Numerous physical attacks on blacks, even in northern cities, attested to the intensity of race hatred instigated by those whites who felt threatened or insecure. All of the precursors of Jim Crow laws, enacted toward the end of the century, were already in place in the sense that white manipulation and control of blacks were an everyday, ongoing affair fulfilling the explicit mandate to keep the Negro in his decreed place. The culture of race placement required embroidering a social tapestry replete with little acts and nuances that formalized and entrenched gross inequality.

The Corrupting Nature of Absolute Power

In a society in which personal acts of brutality and violence are often touted as bravery or courage, or are tolerated as "human nature," unmitigated power becomes a dangerous instrument. Power corrupts, as Lord Acton observed so astutely; and absolute power is so bloating to the psyche that men and women who acquire it lose all rational perceptions and connections to reality. We have seen in this century many examples of tyrants and despots around the world who have aggrandized excessive personal power (and wealth) and become addicted to its lure. There is no redemption from the corrosive consequences of absolute power. It is an addiction so complete that people's minds become warped. They can no longer comprehend limits of any nature and too often accede to extremes of brutality, avarice, and lust. They cannot relinquish the exaggerated levels of power and privilege, nor even think rationally enough to try. This is the sickness of excessive and absolute power. It was this sickness and the seductive nature of white power that characterized the social reality of white/black relations in the nineteenth and early twentieth centuries.

Some whites reveled in their power over blacks. It shored them up, gave them the feeling of mastery and grandness, and even seduced some into unspeakable acts of cruelty and sadism.[9] Every white person, slaveowner or not, could experience the lofty feeling of not only being better than any Negro but also having power over blacks sanctioned by the society. When Jefferson spoke of the depravity that such power rendered to whites and transmitted unwittingly to their children, the "unremitting despotism," the "giving loose to his worst of passions," and the education in the "exercise in tyranny" ([1787] 1955, 346), he revealed the malignancy of such raw insensate power. He was not a stranger to the brutalizing and odious effects of absolute power in the slave situation. When he often philosophized on or contemplated solutions to the troublesome nature of power, it is obvious that he was not always limiting his musings to the national political arena.

The daily exercise of white personal power over black individuals had become a cherished aspect of Southern culture. To abrogate it by emancipating the slaves was tantamount to giving up the "Southern way of life," as the North was so frequently reminded during and after the Civil War. Wealthy plantation-owners even convinced poor whites, who had never owned slaves, that they shared in this power relationship over blacks; indeed, they enlisted poor whites in the proslavery cause. This was one issue that could and did bind together all whites. It became a cause that transcended their own cultural and class differences and is clear historical evidence of the emerging distinctiveness of the race domain and its priority over class.

The Priority of Race over Class

Events in the nineteenth century made it abundantly and irrefutably clear that race as a thing sui generis superseded and took priority over social class in its function as the dominant mechanism of social division and stratification in North America. But social science literature has been ambiguous on the relationship between race as an ideology of social division and social classes as empirical social organizational features of the capitalist system. Put simply, the thesis of this section is that race differences in identity and social position were, and are, more important than class differences in American society.

There are two major approaches to the study of social class in the scholarly literature: One is ethnographic and descriptive; the other offers a variety of perspectives that come under the rubric of Marxist. Under the first, sociological texts attempt to describe the class structures of modern society, to define their boundaries empirically, and to identify their number and functions. Scholars typically propose an array of diagnostic features for class identification, including income, education, residence, occupation, and life-styles. Income is a primary indicator of social class, and some experts establish arbitrary limits for such categories as *lower class*, *middle class*, and *upper class* based on income and life-styles. Although boundaries are imprecise, arguably flexible, and subject always to rebuttal, most people have a general sense of class differences in relation to the ability to acquire material comforts and luxury goods and to make the sociopolitical system work to one's advantage.

Marxists identify social classes as groups standing in different relationships to the "mode of production," and they interpret the formation of classes historically as a product of the introduction of private property, industrialization, and the growth of capitalism. The Marxist paradigm of industrial capitalism posits a conflict between two classes that have different relationships to the mode of production: the owners and managers of capital; and the exploited laboring class, who produce the products whose surplus value is expropriated by the owners of capital. Race and racism, say Marxists, evolved as products of the colonial stage in the development of capitalism and the social divisions attendant to conquest and imperialism. Thus such dominated racial populations as blacks and Indians came to represent special segments of the working class, subject to superexploitation and kept poor and powerless. In Marxist terms, capitalists created and used racism to keep the entire working class "divided, weak, and exploitable" (Geschwender 1987, 138). Where race is thus seen as an aspect of class and class conflict (class reductionist theory), it plays a subordinate and limited role in the social system and derives its meaning from the form and material conditions of the economy.[10]

Class analysis as a mode of accounting for race and racism is simplistic and bears little relationship to the complexities or the realities introduced by the racial worldview. It ignores or obscures the material circumstances and specific interests of the white working class that has for more than a century benefited from diminished competition from other racial groups who were barred, by custom and law, from jobs and positions available only to whites. By stressing the common exploitation that all working-class people experience at the hands of capitalists, it precludes, indeed exempts, white working-class culpability in the preservation and continuity of racism. It ignores, and sometimes denies, an important reality, that the white working class shares the same exploitative, self-aggrandizing, and oppressive capitalist ethos of the bourgeoisie and essentially the same racial ideology.[11] Few white, or black, scholars have researched or documented the millions of blatant acts of exploitation experienced by poor blacks at the hands of working-class whites, especially after emancipation, but the existence of such acts was (and is) common knowledge in African-American communities across the nation. A regular feature of black life in the South was having to put up with humiliating, intimidating, and degrading acts from working-class whites on a daily basis. Such behavior was part and parcel of the corrupting nature of unbridled power that even poor whites held over blacks as a consequence of the racial ranking and associated habits of denigration.

Although the expressions of racism may have varied, whites of all social classes adhered to the racial worldview. Joel Williamson (1984) reminds us that the radical racists of the 1890s were of upper-class backgrounds, and the Ku Klux Klan during Reconstruction was organized and led by upper-class white men. He concludes that upper- and lower-class whites "functioned, not against each other, but both against the Negro, the intermittent, sporadic, open violence of one complementing the steady, pervasive, quiet violence of the other" (295).

Class analysis cannot explain the power that race has for eliciting a sense of vast differences. This power grew from the eighteenth to the late nineteenth century to the point at which it became almost unnatural to even conceive of different races as potential equals. So strongly were Americans, and many Europeans, conditioned to the idea that the world's human population was constituted of distinct "racial" units that it became an indispensable way of looking at world realities. This helps us to understand why race became so much more important after the Civil War, whether applied to freed blacks or extended to new immigrants, such as the Chinese and Japanese or to the "little brown men" in the Philippines. After 1865 emancipation may have brought freedom from formal slavery, but it did not bring freedom from the debilities and tyranny of the racial worldview.

After the brief but promising period of Reconstruction, race separation was built into the infrastructure of American society by law and by white social preferences. In all areas of life, Americans were persuaded that the major races, black, Indian, Asian, and white, could not and should not live or work together, and certainly not as equals. All blacks were homogenized, regardless of education, training, skills, religion, income, or place of origin, into a single category. With few exceptions, so were all Asians and native Americans, regardless of differences of language, traditions, religion, education, or experience.

In contrast, class separation was temporal and situational, as so many Americans found out. White Americans grew up with the vision that any youngster who succeeds in business, politics, entertainment, the arts, or professions automatically improves his or her class status and eliminates the barriers of most upper-class institutions. Class barriers can be transcended; race barriers cannot. The poor white Southern tenant farmer who objected to his daughter's scholarship to enter a prestigious Eastern college because he heard that a black man's daughter was there knew this implicitly. He also knew that the quality of subordination that he expected from blacks was very different from the deference that he himself showed periodically to upper-class whites with whom he felt more than a democratic kinship.

During the colonial period, the discriminating features and symbols of social class became blunted and imprecise. Although the Puritan communities sought to protect themselves as an exclusive social and religious entity, and although a few of the settlers in Virginia and the surrounding colonies were able to retain their middle-to-upper-class pretensions, there were many others from the lower levels of society who aspired to status and wealth.[12] Yeoman farmers grasped at the opportunity to become plantation-owners. For some in the lower rungs of society, the former convicts, the former thieves, and others who had come as indentured servants, their potential anonymity in a new and vibrant setting was a welcome and necessary protection. Many people sought to break with their past and start anew in the colonies without the restrictions of language, name, and class origin. They learned that not only were there great fortunes to be made but also the social dynamics in the fluid arenas of expanding and bristling towns and frontier areas obfuscated older class lines. An American atmosphere vibrant with energy and the spirit of adventure made the rigidities of class for whites less relevant. In an era of assertive individualism, energy and ambition counted far more than family and proper table manners.

A new American class system based on wealth and conspicuous consumption soon emerged, supplementing older class structures that were still retained in the collective mind. Several new phenomena, however, tended to undermine prevailing class barriers and lead to a flexible and dynamic stratification system that allowed white Americans to boast about a lack of class distinctions. One was the intermingling of European ethnic groups, rare for most of the initial settlements, but increasingly more significant during the next centuries.

Scots, Germans, Irish, French, Danes, Swedes, Dutch, Belgians, and other Europeans mingled with the descendants of early English settlers. Within a few generations, intermarriages between these ethnic groups began to confound the trappings of traditional status. Thus Europeans experienced radically different social motifs at work in the New World. Land and property were still requisites of status, but breeding, ethnicity, and genealogy no longer worked against an ambitious person. White Americans came to believe that any person healthy and driven enough could acquire property in land, livestock, slaves, business enterprises, and real estate and rise up the social ladder. The American colonies were indeed a land of freedom and opportunity unlike anything that had existed for them before.

A second phenomenon was the erection of racial barriers, which eventuated in the imposition of a firm castelike quality on all blacks and Indians, condemning them to perpetual low status and enabling white society to be fluid and dynamic "without the crippling apprehensiveness that proper social ordering was going entirely by the board" (Jordan 1968, 134). This new social order placed Indians and blacks in a context from which services could be extracted but from which social mobility was made impossible. With native Americans kept at physical distances on reservations and blacks defined as functioning only in a servile status, members of white society were free to develop among themselves a strong sense of the equivalence of all white people (Morgan 1972, 1975).

A third and related phenomenon was the emergence of a new value ethic about the power and importance of the "common man." Jefferson's ideals and the entire experiment in republican government after the revolutionary war presaged an apparent commitment to an egalitarian ethos. It was an egalitarianism that included for the first time men of the working classes, but restricted to white Europeans. The fullest manifestation of this ethos was to come with the election of Andrew Jackson in 1828, inaugurating what contemporaries and later historians were often to call "the Age of the Common Man." The opening of voting and political rights to all white males further exaggerated the differences between them and the blacks and Indians who had no civil rights. Later, with the organization of the first labor unions, black Americans were excluded at almost all levels, a fact that made it possible for some employers to use them as scabs or strikebreakers, further exacerbating the divisions among all working-class people.

European ethnic divisions paled with the experience of the more powerful differences of race. Class distinctions were of far less weight than those posed by color and permanent subordination. In white minds the essential nature of blacks and Indians were of such variance that they could not be accounted as part of an even more egalitarian society; certainly they could not be assimilated into the body politic. The transformations in worldview that restricted the definition of who would be full participants in American society were confirmed repeatedly by judicial decisions, scientific researches, and legislative enactments. They were reiterated in the daily activities of whites, who affirmed in their behavior the rightness of the racial ordering system. Race came to outrank all other considerations of social valuation, superseding class and adding a totally new criterion to the ways by which societies could be hierarchically structured.

Although discernible differences in physical features were the initial criteria of racial rank, once instituted as a qualitatively different way of categorizing people the idea of race ceased to require significant overt biophysical differences. Race differences could be imputed or external symbols could be used to denote the unbridgeable chasm. Race quite simply was a matter of human inventiveness, a fact most vividly manifest when Europeans began to apply the racial worldview, and racial categories, to themselves in the nineteenth century.

Notes

1. For a more detailed study of the significance of Quaker involvement in slavery, see Davis 1966, and Soderlund 1985.

2. Until recent decades, many historians seem not to have recognized the inevitable cultural assimilation that must have taken place between people who lived in such close juxtaposition as did slaves and masters in the South. Despite the status differences, blacks and whites came to share elements of a common Southern culture. The myth that blacks constitute an "ethnic" group in the United States operates to prevent sociological acceptance of the reality of cultural similarities among blacks and whites. It is only in highly segregated Northern cities that blacks have developed unique cultural forms, in such areas as music, language, personal behavior, art, literature, and so forth. White receptivity to black urban culture forms also demonstrates that cultural assimilation is not a one-way process. Earlier in this century, it was common to find older blacks, born into slavery, explaining how much they once had to teach white folks in the South about ordinary ways of thinking and doing things. This sense of black history has rarely been captured by historians, although scholarship in this respect is changing.

3. See Walvin 1980. S. Drescher (1986) has dealt with the rise of abolitionism in Britain and argues that its causality rested in the expansion of capitalism and political liberalism.

4. The growth of moral consciousness and introspective disquietude about the extremes of wealth and poverty seems to be a little-studied aspect of West-

ern history. It parallels the development of the American nation and is at the heart of many contemporary humanitarian concerns. Rousseau, born of a middle-class background, was shocked at the atrocious inequality that saw the building of a Versailles but left peasants starving. He even had to put his own five children (by his mistress) in a foundling home because he was too poor to feed them.

5. After the publication of *Common Sense* in January 1776, over 500,000 copies were sold. His booklet "The Rights of Man," advocating aid to the poor and unemployed, education for all, a progressive income tax to be used for public benefit, and the destruction of monarchy in favor of a republic, was banned in France during the Revolution, and he was tried for treason.

6. See Fredrickson ([1971] 1987) and Jordan (1968) and their treatment of transformations in social thought in the decades around the turn of the nineteenth century.

7. For a good introduction to the culture of the Jacksonian world, see Pessen 1985.

8. See Fredrickson 1988, Chapters 1 and 13; Takaki 1987.

9. See some of the descriptions in Blassingame (1979) and in Elkins ([1959] 1963). Dumond ([1961] 1966) provides examples gathered by the abolitionists of personal acts of unbridled cruelty toward slaves.

10. Some Marxist scholars have perceived the limitations of older Marxist scholarship and have begun to modify their approaches. They have concluded that race *is* a distinct form of social division and thus not reducible to class or to analyses based on class conflict. For variations in thought on these matters, see Cox ([1948] 1959), Fields (1982), Gabriel and Ben-Tovim (1978), Genovese (1967), and Geschwender (1987).

11. The great American historian W.E.B. DuBois ([1935] 1985) recognized the superior significance of the racial divide, especially in his studies of black and white labor. And Fredrickson (1988), like other historians, taking a cue from DuBois, acknowledges the dual forms of stratification. The race hatred of poor whites had little to do with class conflict with the elite. They tended to identify with the elite and derived psychic, emotional, and often material benefits from their outbursts of violence against blacks. See also Williamson 1984.

12. According to Morgan (1975), among the first Virginia pioneers there was "an extraordinary number of gentlemen," members of the gentry and nobility and their personal attendants, who were ill-suited to the rigors of pioneer life (83–84). Nash (1982) concurs and adds that "almost nobody" came from the top layers of European society during the eighteenth century (201). Jones (1964) points out that a whole class of the American elite disappeared when the Loyalists returned to England during the revolutionary war period (316). The implications are that there was greater homogeneity of class status among early English-Americans than perhaps realized, and the later emergence of a new and fluid class structure with an egalitarian ethos may be in part a product of this lack of rigid class differentiation.

10

A Different Order of Being:
Nineteenth-Century Science
and the Ideology of Race

$\mathcal{S}$HAPING SOCIAL THOUGHT in the antebellum period were numerous writers, social activists, politicians, and clergymen from all parts of the country who vigorously projected a conservative proslavery stance. For their expanding arguments on human differences and inequality they turned to the authority of science. It was thus not mere coincidence that at the height of the abolitionist movement in the 1830s certain scientific developments occurred that provided greater legitimacy to the folk beliefs identified in Chapter 1 as the ideological components of race. The next decades saw the emergence of an American anthropological establishment, dedicated to the investigation of race differences, that grew in prestige and power as the century wore on. This chapter looks at the processes by which scientific and folk ideas on human origins and variability converged in midcentury and buttressed the autonomy of race as a generic natural category.

This period saw an acceleration in the amount and quality of scientific works, with advances particularly in the botanical, zoological, and geological sciences. Fossil remains and artifacts unearthed by the exploitative and extractive activities of the Industrial Revolution fostered a flurry of research, speculations, and interpretations and generated numerous questions about the antiquity of the earth, especially the theologically accepted dates of human origin.[1]

During the previous century, ideas about relationships between similar living forms, their developmental sequences, and institutions changing through time had been proposed and were already in the air. European savants such as Joseph Lafitau, Ann Robert Jacques Turgot, Adam Ferguson, and William Robertson had published theories on universal human history, postulating stages by which civilization as they knew it had grown. In the nineteenth century, historical changes manifest in material remains in Europe were better documented by new evidence. But civilization itself was increasingly perceived on both sides of the Atlantic as a product of specific races.

Nineteenth-century scientific contributions to ideologies about human differences were critical not only to the affirmation of the existence of races and race differences as natural and inborn, but also to the formulation of public policies and to the treatment of various immigrant groups still to come. Scientists constructed definitions and characterizations of each racial population, focusing especially on the identification of "the Negro" in the context of what had come to be defined as white civilization.[2] The implications of the social acceptance of innate inequalities seemed to require their documentation. Some turned to science because it was the one institution that could claim neutrality, or, at minimum, an absence of biased interest in keeping the Negro subservient. Science was objective and detached, at least by reputation, and people looked to science for those truths that resonated unsullied by politics or religion. Because the elements in the idea of race were so largely compounded of myths, there was a need for their persistent reiteration. Most important, due to the strength of the countervailing pressures of abolitionists and the growing humanitarian sentiments associated with democratic ideology, it was necessary to continuously seek ways of magnifying the differences presumed between races, thereby underscoring both their scientific validity and their inequality.

We have seen that the dominant view of human origins until the midnineteenth century accorded with the biblical vision of a single creation. All species were created in their present forms by an omnipotent being who fixed their characteristics from the beginning. Because of their known interfertility, all human groups belonged to a single species whose design emanated from the maker himself. Two explanatory paradigms operated as philosophical guidelines for the comprehension of the great intraspecies diversity. One was *degeneration*, which was compatible with biblical history in that it can be interpreted as a consequence of the "Fall from Grace." The other was the *Great Chain of Being*, which served as a model of God's hierarchical plan for the world.

In 1799 Charles White, a noted physician from Manchester, England, published a volume important for claiming scientific support for existing race ideas but contradicting the theory of origins. Entitled *An Account of the Regular Gradation in Man*, it proposed the evidence for the differential status on the Great Chain of Being accorded by the supreme being to Africans, Asians, Indians, and "white Europeans." White concluded that the Negro was an intermediate form between true human beings (white Europeans) and apes. Other races were assigned positions intermediate between the Negro and the European. Like Lord Kames and Edward Long before him, White rejected the Christian and Enlightenment notion of the unity of the human species. He found differences between geographically separated races to be sufficiently great as to counter the idea of a single species. White postulated instead that each race was a separate species, products of separate creations, specifically preadapted by God for the geographic area in which it was found.

With the early attention that taxonomists and systematists had focused on human diversity and the unremitting moral and ethical problems of slavery, the search for a scientific authentication of folk beliefs about human differences was a rational option. But to pose an answer in terms of separate species as products of separate creations was a remarkable position for a scientist to take, especially in light of the unsuccessful history of polygenist ideas over the previous two centuries and of commonly held understandings of what species were all about. The strength of the theologically based idea of a single creation, or monogenesis, was of such a nature as to be considered almost unassailable. The vast majority of scientists, even most of those who identified themselves as deists, adhered to the powerful principle of human unity. Whether for romantic, idealistic, or religious reasons, or those based entirely on rational considerations of empirical data, the idea of multiple creations was anathema to most learned people.

Yet, given the ever-expanding focus on human differences in the late eighteenth century and the potent motives of the proslavery establishment, White's position should not have been totally unanticipated. There were earlier precedents, as we observed; and it seems quite clear that polygenesis had remained a subdued minority viewpoint throughout the several centuries since Paracelsus. Earlier it had been promoted by such influential men as Voltaire and Lord Kames. But the most important factor about White's publication, which brought it exalted recognition among the educated population, was that it signified a new development. It took the question of the Negro's place in the natural scheme so widely held by Europeans and placed it unambiguously in the realm of science. His conclusions were based on comparative studies that he had made on the anatomical features of Negroes, Europeans, and apes, and they were presented in a seemingly objective, erudite fashion. White demonstrated what he thought were unvarying constitutional differences between black and white races in skeletal structure, muscles, tendons, cartilages, skin, hair, size of sex organs, and brains. He also claimed differences in sweat and odor, and in reason, speech, and language. Most important, he declared that the different gradations of human beings "were endued with various degrees of intelligence" (Greene 1954b, 390).

White's learned disquisition brought considerable reaction, in part because he made significant use of Thomas Jefferson's descriptions and evaluations of Negroes in Virginia. It promoted a curious phase in the history of the concept of race in the form of a major intellectual controversy.[3] The question, simply put, was, Were Negroes a product of the same act of creation as whites and thus members of the same species, but an inferior variant, or were they the result of a separate act of creation? It should be stated, however, from the outset that, contrary to most historical accounts, the debate that ensued was only superficially a debate about origins. At bottom, it was a debate about the meaning of race, especially about the place of "the Negro" in the context of racial ideology and about the magnitude of the differences between black and white that the dominant society had already decreed and accepted.

Polygeny Versus Monogeny: The Debate over Race and Species

The convenience of the taxonomic usage of the term "race" cannot be considered apart from the concept of "species." In the early eighteenth century, before the term "species" came into widespread general use by naturalists and taxonomists, it was sometimes used interchangeably, as we have seen, with "race," and both had much the same connotations as "type" or "kind." But the essential meaning of "species" in biological thought, even before the term itself became fixed as the significant semantic unit in taxonomic language, was understood in modern Europe certainly as early as the sixteenth century. Montaigne, for example, in his conclusion that all men were of one species, based his inference on the presumptive understanding of the ability of all known human populations to interbreed (Slotkin 1965, 61).

Where two contiguous populations that are otherwise similar physically and morphologically do not intermate naturally and produce viable offspring, they are identified as separate species. "Reproductive isolation," as this is now designated, was widely acknowledged, both implicitly and explicitly in the works of the ancient Greeks, as a critical divider separating species, and this still prevails. Moreover, it is likely that many (perhaps all) of the so-called "tribal" or preliterate peoples have a cognitive understanding of the significance of reproductive isolation, and they use this knowledge as a diagnostic criterion for the kinds of perceptual discriminations that inform native systems of classification (cf. Berlin, Breedlove, and Raven 1973).

Until the advent, and acceptance, of Darwin's *The Origin of Species* (1859), the predominant view was that species were created in their present state at the beginning of time and were fixed and unchanging. This was consonant with prevailing theological beliefs about the origin of all living phenomena and with the existing state of knowledge about the immutability of all natural forms. Linnaeus accepted the doctrine of "fixity of species" and engaged in what were the general goals of the biology of his time—the search for and identification of new species. There is no doubt but that, after at least several hundred years of solid work by systematists, the idea of species as animal (or plant) breeding populations clearly distinguishable from one another on the basis of reproductive isolation was well understood in the scientific and literate world.

Yet Charles White's assertion that the races of humans were created as separate species was not dismissed out of hand, nor was it ignored as nonsense contradictory to well-known facts. On the contrary, it polarized much of scientific opinion on the issue of human origins. The polygenists, on the one hand, who argued for multiple creations generally started with the enumeration of differences between racial groups. The monogenists, on the other hand, acknowledged and accepted most differences, but cited biblical sources for their adherence to belief in a single creation followed by diverging descent. With over three hundred years of "racial" intermixture on the American continents and throughout the world, during which viable "hybrids" had been produced and reproduced, there should have been no doubt anywhere in the world as to the inclusion in the species *Homo sapiens* of any known human population. How then do we account for the seeming retrogresssion in scientific thought and development represented by the sometimes virulent debates of the midnineteenth century over whether or not blacks were of the same species as whites?

The enormous waste of scientific energy, time, and money that accompanied this controversy set back the study of human biology for generations. That this debate should have taken place in the context of a society highly steeped in biblical theology and in the light of the tremendous power of biblical beliefs in the unity and oneness of humankind is an interesting development. That people of great eminence in the sciences should contradict one of the well-established tenets of biology, and without an empirical basis, was and is extraordinary.

To understand this development, we have only to realize that this period was characterized by intensification of efforts to maximize the number of scientific ways by which races could be differentiated. This was the "central theoretical concern of pre-Darwinian anthropology" (Stocking 1968, 40). That these efforts were aimed specifically at setting apart the Negro population is readily ascertained by the circumstances, the men involved, and the contents of the debates themselves. The focus on the one issue, that is, the Negro's place in nature, was overwhelming. There should be no doubt that such intensity of attention was a besieged culture's response to the rise of militant abolitionism, the threat of emancipation, and white fear of irrevocable social changes.

The major figures in this controvery for the pluralists (polygenists) were several men of impeccable scientific credentials. Dr. Samuel G. Morton was a Philadelphia physician and teacher of anatomy who had contributed some interesting insights into germ theory and who was widely known as a collector of human skulls. Dr. Josiah Nott, trained by Morton in cranial studies, was a well-known medical man in Mobile, Alabama. And Louis Agassiz was considered among the most brilliant of Harvard's scientists, whose legacy is memorialized in his name on buildings, streets, statues, prizes, and honors in the sciences. Associated with them, or concurring with them philosophically, were a host of other men of lesser stature such as George R. Gliddon, William Pickering, Charles Caldwell, J. Aitken Meigs, and Samuel Cartwright. Their counterparts in Europe, beginning with Lord Kames, included Dr. Charles White, Charles Hamilton Smith, Robert Knox, president of the Anthropological Society of London, Paul Broca, a professor of medicine, famous craniometrist, and founder of the Anthropological Society of Paris, and many others.

Opposing these men were the monogenists who held to the fundamental theorem of the unity of humankind in a single species. Samuel Stanhope Smith was president of the College of New Jersey (later Princeton) and a Presbyterian minister whose major work on human variation was reissued early in the nineteenth century. The Reverend John Bachman of St. John's Lutheran Church in Charleston, South Carolina, was also a learned scholar and a professor of natural history. Supporting them were a large number of European scholars, such as James Cowles Prichard and Sir William Lawrence, and, ironically, the whole weight of Southern Christian opinion. For these Southerners and their sympathizers the theory of multiple creations contradicted their biblical faith. They had long accepted the "Fall from Grace," and subsequent "degeneration" as sufficient explications for the dehumanized status of the Negro.

Reverend Smith, a contemporary of Dr. Charles White, was convinced that Negroes were potentially equal to whites. Following intellectual precedents set in the early Enlightenment, he argued that climate and other environmental factors were the cause of their unique physical and behavioral traits. His views were in turn criticized by Dr. Charles Caldwell, a physician from North Carolina, in an 1830 publication that "presented, with all the appearance of scientific objectivity, the case for ... the separate creation of the races as distinct species" (Fredrickson [1971] 1987, 73).

Shortly after the radical abolitionist movement gained momentum and national recognition, and, significantly, after Nat Turner and Denmark Vesey inspired infamous slave revolts, Samuel Morton produced his major contributions to the controversy. In two publications, *Crania Americana* (1839) and *Crania Aegyptiaca* (1844), he set forth his views on the nature of racial differences and their possible origins. Working initially within the limits of accepted biblical chronology, he did not at first claim species distinctions. But he based his conclusions about the enormity of the differences between the races on quantitative studies of human crania, for the measurements of which he himself had worked out sophisticated scientific techniques.[4] For these developments he became known as the founder of the science of craniometry and of the first American school of anthropology.

Morton became interested in skulls in the 1820s and started a collection of crania that came to be recognized internationally as the largest in the world (Gould 1981). He requisitioned these materials from all over the world, an operation not too difficult to fulfill because of the tremendous interest in skulls stimulated by the phrenology movement that was then rising in the United States (see Chapter 11). And precedents had been set by earlier scientists who collected and studied crania.

Morton devised thirteen ways of measuring features of skulls and concluded from the results that the different races of humans had distinctive skull shapes and sizes. He developed various means of measuring cranial capacity and found that the brains of the five races, beginning with the large-brained caucasoid, became successively smaller with the mongoloid, Malay, American (Indian), and the Negro in that order. He argued that these racial characteristics were permanent, pointing out that each race had been adapted for its peculiar habitat from its origin. Opposing Samuel Smith, he denied the possible effects of climate and geography in affecting physical changes, even in the long range. The evidence he offered for this was his studies of Egyptian crania that suggested (at least to him) that racial groups had not changed over four thousand years, that is, since presumably the origin of humans. He went on to describe not only the physical traits but also their moral and intellectual concomitants. Acting on the presupposition that brain size directly correlated with intelligence, Morton asserted an idea already on its way to orthodoxy in science: a natural superiority of white races over all others. The "joyous, flexible and indolent" Ethiopian was contrasted to the Caucasian with his "highest intellectual endowments" (Stanton 1960, 33).

Although Morton defended Indians against some of the stereotypes popularly conferred on them, he agreed that they were lacking in intelligence and the capacity for "a continued process of reasoning on abstract subjects" (Stanton 1960, 34). It is fair to point out that Morton's interpretation of the internal qualities of the mind, judged solely from the skull, was well in keeping with the increasingly popular tendencies toward embracing beliefs about innate sources for all talents and abilities that became widely disseminated with the phrenology fad.

Among the more important conclusions in Morton's books, noted in many journal articles in the latter half of the century, was his claim that the ancient Egyptians were not Negroes, merely dark-skinned Caucasians. This assertion was necessary because prior to and during the Napoleonic years French scholars, some of whom had accompanied Napoleon on his conquest of Egypt in 1798, had previously described the peoples associated with the ancient ruins recently discovered as "noires" (blacks) and their cultures as "les civilizations Negres."[5]

By 1817 the great French zoologist Baron von Cuvier, who had corresponded with Jefferson and no doubt was influenced by Jefferson's views on blacks, had concluded that the ancient Egyptians could not have been Negroes. The Negro with his low cranial capacity was incapable of creating such a great civilization (Stocking 1968, 35). Morton based his argument on the same premise. He was later influenced in its confirmation by George R. Gliddon, a British adventurer and opportunist who had lived in Egypt as U.S. vice-consul, had provided Morton with skulls, and had subsequently made a fortune lecturing on Egyptology, mostly to Americans. In his later work, *Crania Aegyptiaca* (1844), Morton retreated a bit from this position and claimed that the ancient Egyptians were neither Caucasian nor Negro, but a blend of "several distinct branches of the human family."[6] But he maintained that Egyptian slaves were all Negroes, which was intended to prove the constancy of their lowly status from the beginning of history.

Toward the end of his career, Morton became convinced that the races represented "primordial" differences and had been created separately in different environments. But in order to advance this argument of separate species status, he had to deal with the problem of "hybridity," the ability of the several races to mate and produce "mixed" offspring. Morton intuited that human hybrids somehow contradicted the law of nature. Eventually he concluded that interfertility did not prove the unity of the human species. On the contrary, he argued, since fertile hybrids had been produced by the crossing of two species in the animal and plant worlds, interfertility was not a valid test of species status or distinction between species. He finally arrived at what Louis Agassiz was to praise as a "true philosophical definition of species, the first to bless the world of science." A species, said Morton, was a "primordial organic form" (Stanton 1960, 141).

Morton's works were read and widely applauded in the Southern states. When he died in 1851, the *Charleston Medical Journal* published a biographical memoir stating, "We can only say that we of the South should consider him as our benefactor, for aiding most materially in giving to the negro his true position as an inferior race" (Stocking 1968, 144). No firmer statement or more open and unequivocal recognition of science's role in the construction and affirmation of folk beliefs can be found.[7]

Dr. Josiah Nott of Alabama was another well-known medical man who took up the cudgels of the polygenist cause, pushing his theories at a time when proslavery forces were most vigorous in their reaction against the abolitionists. In numerous talks and publications, beginning in the 1840s, Nott promoted the belief in the debilities and the degeneracy of Negroes and especially of "hybrids" (mulattoes), arguing that the latter were unnatural offspring of two species and analogous in their nature to mules. He agreed with Morton on the permanence and unvarying nature of species as products of adaptation to their original specific environments. Nott carried the argument further, however, emphasizing the degree to which the Negro experienced well-being under slavery. Like children, he argued, Negroes required care, direction, and control. If manumitted, they would soon perish because of their inability to endure the "ravages" of freedom. This theme was embraced and widely perpetuated by many members of the educated populace during and after the Civil War.

Nott lectured extensively in the South and his published works were frequently quoted. In 1854, the year of the formation of the Republican party, he collaborated with the notorious Gliddon to publish a work, *Types of Mankind*, which "was designed as a compendium of all anthropological evidence that had been brought forward in support of the specific diversity of mankind" (Stanton 1960, 163). One of the most popular works of its time, *Types* had ten editions by the end of the century. Although some theologians condemned it for its apparent negation of revealed religion, few criticized its arguments on behalf of the inequality of the races. It brought together all of the data of the polygenists, Morton (to whom it was dedicated), Nott, Gliddon, and others, and included a chapter by Agassiz. Numerous tables of statistical data collected by Morton, both previously published and some unpublished, were included in its contents.

This was perhaps the single most important book that set for the public the issue of race into a peculiarly scientific context. It was the culmination of a trend begun in the latter part of the eighteenth century and was spurred on by the tremendous growth in the reputation of science. For the next few generations, *Types of Mankind* was used by students and lay people alike as a major source of descriptive, statistical, and other quantitative data on the different kinds of human beings. Presented as the fruit of extensive, objective research, it succeeded in backing, with the awesome prestige of science, what were actually folk views of the Negro in the nineteenth century, expanded into racial ideology.

Louis Agassiz, a Swiss naturalist, whose fame as an ichthyologist derived from his major investigations on fossil fish, had been invited to come to Harvard in 1846 from Switzerland and Paris to pursue research on the fish of the New World. Until that time he held the monogenist position of most European naturalists—that all humankind comprised one original species. But in the United States between 1846 and 1850, he underwent a remarkable conversion to polygenism, to which several elements contributed. One had to do with his strong adherence to creationism, the idea of independent creations of all animal species and their immutability through time. Before his immigration to the states, he did little speculation on how the various kinds of humans fit within this paradigm. But, recognizing the geographic spread and diversity of humankind, he held open the possible interpretation that human types could be likened to animal species occupying clearly demarcated zoological zones. Lord Kames had suggested a similar theme in the eighteenth century, and Baron von Cuvier advanced the idea some four decades prior to Agassiz. Another element was the influence of Morton. Visiting the craniologist in Philadelphia, Agassiz was impressed with his collection of skulls, his apparently careful, precise, and objective methods of measurement, as well as his cogent arguments on the significance of these metrical differences.

The final element in Agassiz's conversion was not related to his religious convictions, the scholarly evidence and arguments, or the academic milieu. In Philadelphia, Pennsylvania, and later in Charleston, South Carolina, the site of most of the pluralist-monogenist debates, Agassiz saw Negroes for the first time, having contact with them as domestics in his hotel. A letter to his mother (resuscitated from Harvard's Houghton Library by recent scholars) expressed his shock at their features, their black skins, thick lips, and "grimacing teeth," their peculiar limbs, the "wool" on their heads instead of hair. He admitted that when the Negro waiter approached him in his hotel dining room, he wanted to flee. "What unhappiness for the white race," he exclaimed, "to have tied their existence so closely with that of negroes in certain countries! God preserve us from such a contact!" (quoted in Gould 1981, 45).

The experience convinced him, he wrote, that though Negroes were human, they were not of the same species as whites. "I experienced pity at the sight of this degraded and degenerate race, and their lot inspired compassion in me in thinking that they are really men" (Gould 1981, 45). This was, as Gould has commented, a visceral judgment, one that had no basis in reason or objective examination of fact. It is curious that Agassiz should have had such a reaction of personal repulsion, linked with an instant perception of the "ugliness" of the Negro. He had spent much of his life studying and identifying thousands of species of fossil fish, an animal form not generally lauded in Western cultures for its beauty.

Within months, Agassiz was lecturing in both the South and the North that the Negro and white races were morphologically and physiologically so distinct as to constitute separate species. He also published numerous articles in which he elaborated the argument. In the chapter contributed to *Types of Mankind*, Agassiz identified eight primary human types that "inhabited specific zoological provinces." He argued for the primordial qualities of their differences, as determined by the will of their creator. "I am prepared to show that the differences existing between the races of men are of the same kind as the differences observed between the different families, genera, and species of monkeys or other animals ... nay, the differences between distinct races are often greater than those distinguishing species of animals one from the other" (Nott and Gliddon 1854, lxxiv).

Thus it was that Agassiz lent the weight of his scientific reputation and status to the likes of Nott and Gliddon, and to the championing of the Southern cause. In these activities, however, he believed that he was supporting the cause of scientific freedom against dogmatic theology. Agassiz was also personally opposed to developmental or evolutionary theory, as was Cuvier, particularly criticizing the Lamarckian notion of the inheritance of acquired characteristics. Following the publication of Darwin's *The Origin of Species* in 1859, Agassiz became one of the most important leaders of the opposition to evolutionism (much to the pain and embarrassment of some of his students and colleagues).

Within a few years, Agassiz, who as an impecunious young student had been partially supported in Paris by his great friend and mentor, Cuvier, became one of the most famous professors and scientists at Harvard. He revolutionized teaching methods in the natural sciences, founded the Museum of Comparative Zoology, and raised large amounts of money for buildings, collections of natural phenomena, and publications. He also married into the wealthy and prestigious Cabot family after the death of his first wife. More importantly, he passed on his racial views and theories on human species to generations of students. According to one source, "Every notable teacher of natural history in the United States for the second half of the nineteenth century was either a pupil of Agassiz or of one of his students."[8] Two of his students, Nathaniel Shaler and Joseph Le Conte, also became outstanding late nineteenth-century promoters of the idea of the inequality of human races. All subsequent generations have revealed some degree of Agassiz's influence.

The midnineteenth century was a period of major new discoveries of new species and of extinct animal forms. An enormous amount of attention and resources was focused on the collection of new data and the establishment and refinement of new classifications and taxonomic methods. With Darwin's and Wallace's virtually simultaneous discovery of the chief mechanism of biological evolution, natural selection, attention was diverted from older issues and debates. Evolutionary theory raised the question of diachronic relationships among animal forms, and one effect of this was greater preoccupation with phylogeny. The debate over single or multiple origins of human groups soon languished with the acceptance of evolutionary theory and the dynamic perspective that it fostered.

As George Stocking (1968) has demonstrated, however, polygenist beliefs persisted long after Darwin because of their grounding in fundamental social values and because of a deeply rooted racial worldview. He observed that "the external forces which nourished a broadly polygenist point of view were if anything intensified: the gap between civilized white and savage black men, and the need to justify the white man's imperial dominion, were both becoming greater than ever before" (47). Both the biological and social sciences reflected attitudes that Stocking saw as survivals of the polygenists' perspective, implicitly if not explicitly, and regardless of whether their practitioners were theoretical monogenists or not. Indeed, for certain sectors of the scientific establishment, Darwinism provided an even more potent vehicle for arguing that black and white races had *evolved* as separate species.

It is now clear that the warfare that A. D. White ([1896] 1965) adduced between science and theology was, in this case, over false issues. At best, it involved the engineers of social values in what the purists claimed should be the sacred arena of science. The irony is that neither side maintained a rational position in view of known empirical realities, nor did they equivocate on the presumption of human inequality. With a few exceptions among some of the monogenists, virtually all involved in the controversy accepted fully the prevailing belief in the inferiority of "the Negro." Haller (1971) characterizes the era with this statement: "Almost the whole of scientific thought in both America and Europe in the decades before Darwin accepted race inferiority, irrespective of whether the races sprang from a single original pair or were created separately" (77).

What seemed to be at issue for the scientists was (1) the magnitude of the differences between races, and (2) the scientific explication of the inequality of the races. But the debate was spurious. Races and the differences between them had been so magnified by both popular and scientific characterizations that the argument over the taxonomic levels was redundant and irrelevant. *Race in the American collective consciousness had already assumed the same dimensions of differentiation as "species," even without a change in the terminology.*[9] It really did not matter at what taxonomic level scientists saw fit to allocate the differences.

The evidence for this, in retrospect, is overwhelming. It is revealed in the scholarly writings of learned men and women, in the images expressed in popular media and literature, and in social practices and public policies. Scientists expressed it in their continuing concern, down through the first half of the twentieth century, to ascertain the "Negro's place in nature." Their publications and speeches had powerful influences on other scholars, popular writers, educators, politicians, and others. James Paulding, author of the major historical work *Slavery in the United States* (1835), described, as did others, a litany of negative attributes of "the Negro." Referring to scientific works, he claimed that "anatomists and physiologists have classed the negro as the lowest in the scale of rational beings" (quoted in Tise 1987, 248). Colonizationists frequently called upon the expertise of science writings, and even Abraham Lincoln before the Civil War accepted the idea that whites and blacks were biologically suited to inhabit different regions, thus could never live together as equals (Fredrickson [1971] 1987, 151).

Fredrickson has observed that polygenism, although overtly decried by Christians in the South, "did speak to certain Southern needs. ... [It] raised prejudice to the level of science; thereby giving it respectability" ([1971] 1987, 89). Not only was the South affected; he noted that "A substantial segment of Northern opinion was prepared to welcome the biological theory that the Negro belonged to a separate and inferior species" (90). Thus was laid the groundwork for the racial exclusion and segregation that we inherited in the twentieth century.

After the Civil War and emancipation, numerous scholars continued to propose theories on whether Negroes could survive as free people. But now the theories were couched in Darwinian terms. A derivative postulate, widely believed, was that "the Negro" had not evolved to the same degree as had white men.[10] Thus, stunted in development, their natural inferiority did not equip them for success in the "struggle for existence." An inherent inclination toward crime, debauchery, and sloth would cause them to degenerate even further. Extinction was obviously to be their lot, just as other species had disappeared due to "lack of fittness." Darwinian evolution was thus made compatible with the ideological components of race, with a vocabulary that "reflected the country that bred it and, in reflecting it, wore the prejudices of the land that gave it birth" (Haller 1971, 94).

Clergymen, scholars, educators, and publicists justified their calls for total segregation of blacks from whites out of fear that the inherent degradation and barbarism of blacks might contaminate white society. Following the brief and anomalous Reconstruction era, state and local legislatures responded with segregation laws and statutes that aimed to isolate this inferior species from all unnecessary access to white institutions. Gossett (1965) tellingly summed up the sense of race differences in the decades that spanned the turn of the twentieth century. "American thought of the period 1880–1920," he noted, "generally lacks any perception of the Negro as a human being with potentialities for improvement" (286).

The Unnatural Mixture

Perhaps the clearest and most obvious example of the degree to which subhuman species status had been conferred on blacks was the now widespread belief that interracial sex or marriage was not only wrong socially, but was sinful and unnatural. One of the strongest advocates of this position, as we have seen, was Josiah Nott. One would have thought that a physican from Mobile, Alabama, where intermarriage was illegal but where there was a long history of creating "mulattoes" both on and off plantations, would have been highly knowledgeable about such matters. But he gave expression to beliefs that seemed, especially in that context, awkwardly unreal. He joined a number of polygenists in arguing that the mulatto was a degenerate and abnormal hybrid. This hybrid might be slightly superior intellectually to the full-blooded Negro, but still remained much inferior to the true white. Physically and morally, hybrids lacked the vigor of the pure types and, if left to themselves, would soon become extinct. The fame and fortune that attended Nott's lectures were indicative of public concurrence on this matter.

Louis Agassiz was even more certain of the degeneracy of the hybrids. His assertions that they were either sterile or suffered from diminished fecundity as a result of their unnatural ancestry should have evoked some shocked reaction, but there is little evidence that it did. For the wider public, as well as for declared polygenists and most of the monogenists, the mulatto was a tragic product of the unrestrained lust of black men or of white morals gone awry. Even more forbidding was the possibility that some black "blood" might contaminate the white race and cause the deterioration of all that was noble, pure, and superior.

Antipathy toward interracial unions was not new. We have seen evidence that some colonists expressed this sentiment quite early. For example, in 1691 Virginia attempted by legislative acts to restrict intermarriage; this was followed by similar laws in other colonies or counties. By the mideighteenth century, legislation designed to prohibit interracial unions had been passed in all of the Southern colonies and several Northern ones, at various times covering both fornication and marriage (Jordan 1968, Chapter 4). Such prohibitions did not totally prevent interracial liaisons, but did prevent or restrict intermarriages.

Public aversion to such unions and the imposition of such sanctions as social ostracism for white women who married black men no doubt expanded during the eighteenth century. Ridicule or scandal may have surrounded these marriages in many places, although there are examples of what seemed to be stable and happy unions. After blacks had been reduced to slavery, virtually no marriages took place between white men and black women, although the slave/master relationship spawned large numbers of "colored" slave children. In the nineteenth century, sexual congress between black and white underwent even greater castigation and vilification; its sinfulness and unnaturalness became part of public consciousness and values on matters of race.

Children of such unions were sometimes called "spurious issue," but antagonism toward them seems to have been minimal or moderate during the colonial period. It was not until the nineteenth century that public hostility to interracial sex and the resulting offspring became virulent, emotional, and malevolent as the statistical and other documentation of Negro inferiority increased. One has only to read some of the hundreds of publications on the subject from midcentury on to realize the perversity of the charges against miscegenation and of the many newly invented beliefs about the abnormality of the offspring.

That an accentuated degree of attention was paid in the nineteenth century to those persons regarded as mulattoes was signaled by the fact that they began to appear in the censuses in 1850. They were also differentiated in the studies done by the United States Sanitary Commission and the Provost Marshal-General's Bureau during and after the Civil War.[11] However, the general currents of the time were against the establishment of a "mixed-race" classification, as occurred in South Africa. Historically, as we have seen, such a category of people had had no separate social role to play in the North American colonial situation, as they had for example in the West Indian islands and in Latin America (see Chapter 6). Although in the late nineteenth and early twentieth centuries laws in some Southern states attempted to ascertain varying degrees of mixture, from one-half to one thirty-seconds black "blood," such refinements were socially useless to whites. They were overshadowed by the more fundamental dichotomy revealed in the debate over the race versus species question. The use of hypodescent (see Chapter 6) not only militated against the creation of a special "mixed" category, but had the added feature of better preserving the value of "pure" white "blood" that became such an obsession in Anglo-Saxon America.

Scientific Race Ideology in the Judicial System

Other evidence of the degree to which whites had now accepted the belief in a vast gulf between black and white, one tantamount to the level of species differences, can be seen in some of the legal decisions regarding blacks before and after the Civil War. Many judicial decisions and legislative acts reflected a general public consensus on certain deeply held racial values. And we have seen that many laws during the colonial and early republican periods not only applied differentially to Negroes, but protected the property rights of slave-owners at the expense of black human rights.

Yet long before the codification in law of what came to be accepted as a policy of official segregation of freedmen (Black Codes of 1865–1866 and Jim Crow laws of the 1890s) an important judicial decision had become a symbol of white attitudes toward blacks and of their conception of race differences. The well-known *Dred Scott* decision of 1857 was ostensibly about a fugitive slave who, having twice been taken to free territory, sued in the courts for his freedom. Scott received conflicting decisions at the state and lower federal courts. Since a number of constitutional issues were perceived to be involved and the issue of federal versus state control of slavery was crucial among these, Scott's lawyers, backed by moderate abolitionists, took the matter all the way to the Supreme Court.

The case was argued twice before the Court in 1856 before a final decision was rendered. It was written and presented in March 1857, by Chief Justice Roger B. Taney, a Jacksonian democrat and a man known to have proslavery sentiments. Taney was joined by six other justices, each of whom wrote opinions clarifying their points of concurrence. Taney posed the major issue in its broadest context, going beyond the more limited problem of fugitive slaves. He dealt with the whole matter of the constitutional right to the maintenance and perpetuation of slavery itself. And, expanding the scope, he examined the more profound issue of the social and legal status of all Negroes.

His decision first addressed the question of whether or not blacks could be citizens:

> The question is simply this: Can a negro, whose ancestors were imported into this country, and sold as slaves, become a member of the political community formed and brought into existence by the Constitution of the United States, and as such become entitled to all the rights, and privileges, and immunities, guarantied by that instrument to the citizen? One of which rights is the privilege of suing in a court of the United States." (quoted in Bell 1980, 1)

Taney went on to point out that the case applied to "that class of persons only whose ancestors were negroes of the African race, and imported into this country, and sold and held as slaves ... and the descendants of such slaves." He answered the question of citizenship by asserting that "people of the United States" and "citizens" are synonymous terms that apply only to those (whites) who were citizens of the several states when the Constitution was adopted. Negroes, he claimed, were seen only as property (they "were never thought of or spoken of except as property" [Bell 1980, 9]) and were not intended by the framers of the Constitution to be included in the category of citizen. "On the contrary, they were at that time considered as a subordinate and inferior class of beings" (3), and it did not matter whether or not they later obtained freedom.

Stretching history, Taney continued by arguing that Negroes "had for more than a century before been regarded as beings of an inferior order, and altogether unfit to associate with the white race, either in social or political relations; and so far inferior, that they had no rights which the white man was bound to respect. ... This opinion was at that time fixed and universal in the civilized portion of the white race" (Bell 1980, 6).

To support his position, Taney cited two laws of the early eighteenth century (from Maryland and Massachusetts) that showed in his words

> that a perpetual and impassable barrier was intended to be erected between the white race and the one which they had reduced to slavery, and governed as subjects with absolute and despotic power, and which they then looked upon as so far below them in the scale of created beings, that intermarriages between white persons and negroes or mulattoes were regarded as unnatural and immoral, and punished as crimes, not only in the parties, but in the person who joined them in marriage (Bell 1980, 7).

This stigma, he went on to say, "was fixed upon the whole race." Taney's use of such language as "scale of created beings" here indicates that he was familiar with the arguments of the biological sciences regarding human differences, and he assumed the same for his audience.

Taney cited other laws in the nonslave states that suggested to him that the Negro was not a citizen or considered the same order of human being even when ostensibly free. He also noted that there are two clauses in the Constitution "which point directly and specifically to the negro race as a separate class of persons" who were "not regarded as a portion of the people or citizens of the Government then formed" (10). The framers of the Constitution had in fact used the word "persons" (after much debate) to avoid inserting the word "slave" and thereby institutionalizing slavery itself in the Constitution.

The *Dred Scott* decision strengthened the idea that the property rights of white men superseded in importance the human rights of nonwhite individuals. But Justice Taney in effect declared a great deal more than that. He concluded that Negroes, either free or slave, were not citizens and could not be made citizens by either the state or federal government. And he formulated in legal terms what the folk beliefs and scientific pronouncements had expressed very clearly; the Negro was not fully human, but a separate and distinct class of beings, isolated from whites by an "impassable barrier."

Although the issue in the *Dred Scott* case was without question a matter pertaining only to blacks who were slaves, Taney had made a sweeping declaration about the status of *all* blacks. The most important phrase in the text of the decision is "[The Negro] had no rights which the white man was bound to respect." In this statement Taney went beyond affirming that slaves were mere property; he asserted a social value about a whole category of people that was an unambiguous statement about their status in the larger racial scheme of things. This was a far more meaningful conclusion than the actual decision about Dred Scott's slave status or about the legal standing of the Missouri Compromise, which was upset by this decision. This statement was not even pertinent to the legal decision; indeed, it was irrelevant for the testing of the legitimacy of the fugitive slave laws. It was a far more powerful reflection, and ultimate denouement, of prevailing social beliefs and practices. Going beyond slavery or the concept of property rights, it captured the essence of the American perspective on race differences between blacks and whites. Thus it was perfectly consonant with, indeed a product of, the racial cosmology that had been evolving during the past century, illuminating the exaggerated sense of difference that the term race then conveyed.

In midcentury, the United States had become in world forums the citadel of democracy. It had seen for the first time in the history of Europeans the rise of the common man to standards of individual rights and liberties unmatched by any previous sociopolitical system. As Irving Bartlett (1967) has reminded us, Americans fervently embraced beliefs in moral laws and justice and religious-based ideas about human worth and made them part of the American dream. But, as we have seen, they also had an unremitting drive for worldly success, and worldly success was most often accomplished by the exploitation of slaves and other poor labor. By diminishing the Negro to nonhuman status in their cognitive perceptions of the world, Americans declared that democracy, freedom, opportunity, and justice were not to be made available to blacks. They had placed the Negro beyond the moral and ethical parameters that ostensibly guided what was appropriate and acceptable behavior between human beings, especially in a democracy.

It is of telling interest that the Fugitive Slave Act of 1793 made no mention of race or racial categories, using only the term "person" (Ten Broek [1965] 1969, 57). Yet the unmistakable concern of the act was to protect the property rights of those who owned slaves, permitting them to reclaim fugitives without impediments, legal or otherwise. More than fifty years later, in the *Dred Scott* case, Justice Taney made "race" the specific arbiter of human, legal, and property status, overshadowing the status of slave. In so doing, he introduced and institutionalized the components of the idea of race in the law, giving legal stature to both the scientific presumptions and the folk ideology.

To the comfort of many, there was strong reaction to the *Dred Scott* decision and not only on the part of abolitionists. Justice Curtis in his dissent denied that the Constitution was made exclusively by and for the white race. He pointed out that free blacks were citizens and voters in at least five states at the time of its adoption. He quoted a case from North Carolina in which the state supreme court "rejected the proposition that free Negroes were less than citizens and laid emphasis on the commonly held doctrine that there was no intermediate class between citizens and slaves" (Miller 1966, 78). He also disagreed with the majority view that persons of African descent could not become citizens of the United States. Justice McLean, the other dissenter, opined that the Constitution did not protect slavery, merely tolerated it. And, he proclaimed, slaves were not simply chattel, but men made in God's image. Not everyone subscribed to the view that "the Negro" was a separate and inferior species.

Several Northern legislatures passed resolutions denying the legitimacy of the *Scott* decision. The antislavery press was vehement in its anger and rejected the implications of the decision. It was clear that Justice Taney's position had brought the new nation closer to civil war. But it should also be clear that most Americans were little disturbed by the Taney declarations on race. The differences connoted by the term were deeply and solidly established in the American psyche. And the majority of Americans, including those who were opposed to slavery, were attuned to the real implications of these differences. One inescapable fact of this century was that many whites profited in a great many ways, from economic opportunities to mere psychic satisfaction, from the seemingly indelible barrier created between black and white. This was especially true after the Civil War and Reconstruction when blacks were systematically eliminated from skilled and unskilled employment to make room for white labor, particularly the new immigrants from Europe. Moreover, with the recession of the 1880s and a severe depression in the 1890s, whites were economically embattled, bitter, and enraged, and they were more than willing to flay a scapegoat. The Negro became that scapegoat and for the next four decades endured an era of intimidation, torture, lynching, gross discrimination, and unheralded psychological brutality. If in the white mind blacks had not been transformed into beasts before the 1830s, they certainly were so after the 1890s.

White Supremacy

To a great degree, the debates between the monogenists and the polygenists were an anachronistic diversion, a subtle obfuscation of the fact that a qualitatively new form of social differentiation had taken place in the human experience that superseded "class" and even "nationality" differences in its impact and significance. The logical outcome of the racial idiom in which human diversity was now being expressed was the distillation of a corollary ideology, white supremacy. Fed by a rampant Anglo-Saxonism that was to become transformed in Europe as Nordism or Aryanism and by the fear of miscegenation at home, white Americans were exhorted to preserve the purity and sanctity of the race. For many, this became an obsession.

The sociopolitical conditions of the midnineteenth century lent credence to the belief in the innate superiority of Europeans. In the 1850s the illegal slave trade flourished in the United States as never before, with such a strength that some of the proponents of slavery suggested a return to legalization of the trade. This decade also saw the first significant penetration of Africa by the explorers Barth, Speke, Burton, and Livingstone, which was to presage the eventual conquest of the last of the overseas continents to succumb to European domination. In Asia the Opium Wars of 1839–1841 had led to the weakening of the dynastic leadership of China, and the British now literally handled the trade and foreign affairs of that sleeping giant. In the 1850s the long drawn out process of the conquest of India and Burma was completed. By 1859 all of the colonies and provinces of Australia had been founded and settled; from then on it was spoken of as a white man's land. In the ten years between 1851 and 1861, the white population doubled.[12] In 1854 Faidherbe began the fateful French penetration up the Senegal River in West Africa. In 1851 the British invaded Lagos Island, in Nigeria, and effectively exercised power in this port city with a titular ruler as a front. In 1859 the construction of the Suez Canal was begun and by the time Ismail came to power in Egypt in 1863, British and French presence and influence in eastern Africa and the Middle East was already ineradicable.

In the 1850s, then, it was painfully apparent that Europeans (or some of them) were rapidly becoming dominant forces nearly all over the world, and for most there was no other explanation for it but their "obvious" racial superiority. Thus, when in 1854 Robert Knox proclaimed "race is everything: literature, science, art—in a word, civilization depends on it" (Gossett 1965, 95), he was expressing this new dimension of social differentiation, as well as a new mode of interpreting history and new forms of power relationships that he and his contemporaries perceived as natural and universal. The "truth" of the ordering system denoted by race had been proved by science.

During the latter part of the nineteenth century an elaborate edifice of social philosophy and theory was developed around the theme of white racial superiority. Theories of racial history were transformed into theories of world history. Facts that did not fit the racial worldview of white superiority and black degradation were ignored, deleted, or obfuscated. Typical was the widely read book by John Van Evrie, *White Supremacy and Negro Subordination* ([1861] 1969). Explaining the "magnificent structures" of the ancient cultures of Mexico, Guatemala, Yucatan, and Peru, he reasoned that such high cultures were due to Caucasian adventurers or shipwrecked mariners who settled in these areas, became "undisputed masters, built cities, organized governments, framed laws and laid the foundations of a civilized society" ([1861] 1969, 46–47). Likewise in Asia, Van Evrie continued, all of the great leaders were white—Attila the Hun, Genghis Khan, Tamerlane, all "pure" Caucasians. Confucius was also white, as were all the more progressive portions of Chinese society. Explications for advanced social systems in Africa, discovered or rediscovered in the late nineteenth century, were predicated on ascertaining the degree of Caucasian mixture in the aristocratic or ruling elements. Thus the Hamites, once the burnt-faced sons of Ham and lineage-founder of blacks, were reinterpreted to be archaic caucasoids who conquered Negro tribes and provided them with whatever aspects of order, law, and civilization were discernible among them (Sanders 1969). According to Van Evrie, "Progress and indefinite perfectibility are the specific attributes of the Caucasian" ([1861] 1969, 79).

From the anthropologist Daniel Brinton in America to Herbert Spencer in England, writings poured forth expounding the values of racial purity and particularly the need to preserve that of the Aryans or Nordics, those English and other Germanic peoples whose intellectual prowess and qualities of character had become the sources of all civilization.[13]

The wedding of scientific and folk beliefs was now complete. From midnineteenth century on, science provided the bases for the ideological elements of a comprehensive worldview summed up in the term "race." Numerous scholars of the late nineteenth and early twentieth centuries occupied themselves in tedious research not only into the nature of human differences but also into the interpretation of how these differences reflected the inequality of the races.

But it was also the activities and findings of scientists that were to create the impetus for the contemporary rebellion against the idea of race. We shall turn to this seeming paradox after we take a look, in the next chapter, at the diffusion of race ideas in Europe and at some of the ways by which European and American scientists influenced one another in the documentation of race differences.

Notes

1. Early Christian savants had placed the origin of the world at 6,000 years before the Christian era. This date was diminished by later scholars, such as Isidore of Seville and Rabbi Moses Maimonides in the twelfth century, who placed creation at 4,000 years before the Christian era. Under Pope Urban VIII, the Roman Catholic church declared in 1640 that creation took place 5,199 years before Christ. In 1658, Archbishop Ussher, a Professor of Divinity at Dublin and scholar of Hebrew scriptures, published the first biblical chronology, *Annals of the World*, dating the creation at 4,004 B.C. This became the best known and most widely accepted date and was adhered to up through the nineteenth century by a great many biblical scholars.

2. Alfred Haddon in his *History of Anthropology* ([1934] 1959) identified "The Negro's Place in Nature" as one of the important anthropological controversies in the nineteenth century, showing that it was directly related to the debate over human origins.

3. Stocking (1968) holds that the speculations of the Scottish jurist and philosopher Lord Kames (*Sketches of the History of Man*, 1774) may be seen as the beginning of the debate between the polygenists and monogenists (45). Kames, however, did not have the "scientific" data that White had developed to support his theories.

4. See Stephen Jay Gould's (1981) review of Morton's works and documentation of his errors, omissions, distortions, and questionable techniques.

5. See Baron Denon, *Travels in Upper and Lower Egypt* (N.Y.: Heard & Foreman, 1803); and Count Constantin Volney, *Travels Through Egypt and Syria* (N.Y.: J. Tiebout, 1798). Volney is quoted in Diop (1981), along with de Rienzi and Champollion. See also Sanders (1969).

6. Quoted in Stanton 1960, 51. The debate over the "racial" identification of ancient Egyptians was renewed in the twentieth century and continues to have periodic efflorescence, as in the recent two-volume *Black Athena* by Martin Bernal.

7. For those who find it of interest to speculate on cycles in history, it might be useful to compare Morton's role with that of a modern-day scientist, Arthur Jensen. Both men published scholarly works promoting the idea of black inferiority. In both cases, their major publications came in the wake of dramatic events that tended to advance the cause of racial equality: Morton in the wake of the abolitionist movement; Jensen following the civil rights movement of the 1950s and 1960s. Both were impeccable scholars, having established their reputations in fields other than racial biology. Both were esteemed for their probity by their colleagues and had not previously been known for harboring racist beliefs. Yet both achieved widespread fame for their support of popular race ideology. Such patterns in history should provide stimulating research for some young scholars.

8. See volume one of *Encyclopaedia Britannica* (1971), p. 290. See also Lurie (1954).

9. Long after I had come to this conclusion, I discovered a footnote in John C. Greene (1959), p. 371, that confirms this position. Writing about the midcentury debates, he states, "Although the racial intepretation of history was by no means confined to the polygenist camp, it is perhaps significant that the qualities of purity, permanence, and divine contrivance which later came to be associated with the idea of a 'pure race' were qualities which the eighteenth century attributed to species rather than to varieties."

10. For discussion of late nineteenth-century scientific speculations on the evolutionary position of the Negro, see Haller (1971), Fredrickson ([1971] 1987), and Gould (1981).

11. See Haller (1971), especially Chapters 1 and 2 for a description of the role of these agencies in the study of racial differences.

12. In that same period 40,000 Chinese arrived in Australia, having been recruited to work in the gold mines, and the first serious race riot occurred in 1861 between the Chinese and white populations.

13. Of the considerable literature on the origins and development of white supremacy, the reader is referred to two seminal ones, George Fredrickson (1981) and John W. Cell (1982), both of which have the added dimension of contrasting South Africa and the United States.

11

Science and the Interchange of Race Ideology Between Europe and America

T HE CULTURAL CONSTRUCTION of the ideology of race culminated in its institutionalization as a worldview in the nineteenth century. At its developmental peak, in the latter half of the century, it had achieved systemic autonomy and uniqueness as a mechanism for the hierarchical structuring of society and as a rationalization for imposed inequalities. The degree to which economic competition could be thwarted and access to privilege and power limited to members of a "superior race" were lessons available to all. The components of race ideology had potential applications that transcended group relations in the North American setting. Allegations of racial superiority and inferiority could satisfy the private interests of some powerful groups in Europe. And European scholars were prepared to substantiate theories of racial inequality with measurement techniques and arguments similar to those in the United States.

This chapter briefly locates European race thinking in the evolving spectrum of racial attitudes, but focuses specifically on how European science complemented the developing ideology. Evidence of the appearance of race as a generic, autonomous, and essentialist idea with universal application is shown in the proliferation of arbitrary racial classifications in Europe during the nineteenth century. Ideas from Europe diffused back and forth to the United States, further nourishing racial thought, and helped to condition American reactions to the massive immigrations of "inferior" southern and eastern European "races" beginning in the latter part of the century.

By the midnineteenth century race had emerged in European consciousness as a worldview that affirmed the division of Europeans into "racial" groups and the inherent superiority of certain of these "races"

255

over others. But the ideology was refashioned for quite different social circumstances, with the result that a peculiarly intra-European version of race was created out of what traditionally had been class and ethnic differences. That is, Europeans began to interpret their internal group differences in terms of permanent, innate endowments, ignoring and dismissing the historically deep awareness of such cultural distinctions as manifestations of learned (acquired) behavior.[1] Simultaneously, it provided rationalization and justification for further conquests abroad, satisfying the elevated imperial ambitions of politicians, military adventurers, and those with commercial interests.

Not surprisingly, many Europeans turned their racial imagery toward those minority ethnic groups within their own borders with whom there had been conflict or competition. Defining such groups as separate races became the new raison d'être for imposing harsh restrictions and repressive practices. This was particularly hard on such largely endogamous groups as the Jews who in many areas suffered the ignominy of being defined as racial inferiors. The power politics within European nations took on a whole new spectrum of racial incompatibilities. By taking ethnic or class stereotypes and making them biological givens, Europeans transformed the complexion of political realities, structures, and processes and exacerbated existing conflicts, regardless of their origin or source.

Race became a worldview that was extraordinarily comprehensive and compelling in its explanatory powers and its rationalization of social inequality. It is little wonder that it spread so rapidly among European nations and into the overseas territories where many of them had expanded. Its basic components left little or no room for doubt. To identify these internal "racial" types, Europeans paid close attention to such physical features as hair color, eye color, shape of head, chin, and nose, and stature as signifiers of race identity. In the process, scholars invented a variety of techniques to measure miniscule variations in such features. Although European race thinking took on a quite different cast as it was adapted to the exigencies of life there and abroad, it retained the fundamental ideological elements bound together at its origin, that is, exclusive group categories, hereditary inequality, the linkage of biology and behavior, and the notions of permanence and immutability.

European Contributions to the Ideology of Race

We saw in Chapter 8 that some of the French began to use the term race to refer to those groups, discernible in the social system of eighteenth-century France, who had long had differential access to power, privilege, high status, and vital resources. In their examination of the different ethnic groups that historically were thought to have composed the French population, a few intellectuals sought to identify a natural order by which certain groups were seen as recipients of a divine right to superordinate status. But the divine right was no longer couched in theological terms; it became identified in terms of the inherent biological superiority of those groups in power. According to Boulainvilliers, weaker classes owe obedience to the stronger. His racial theory was essentially rooted in the class conflicts of his time but carried the invidious notion that each class had distinct and unalterable qualities derived from separate origins.

Race was a particularly useful term, it is important to emphasize, when a rationale based on descent, unequal rank, and heritability of social status was sought. And aristocratic, upper-class elements in human societies tend to have a penchant for thinking of themselves as innately superior, if not divinely endowed. Defenders of the rights of the aristocracy during the revolutionary eighteenth century in France found in the ideological components of race a perfect, and expedient, paradigm for their entrenched class structures, interests, and beliefs.

Nurtured by the growing glorification of Germanic origins among English writers and historians, French writers began to extol the virtues of the Franks, the Germanic tribe that defeated the Gauls. There came into the consciousness of the French people of the nineteenth century the notion that they were composed of three separate racial strains, Nordics, Alpines, and Mediterraneans. Each had different physical characteristics and correlative differences in traits of temperament, mental acumen, and natural abilities, such as those of leadership, of economic resourcefulness, of progress and inventiveness, and of moral and aesthetic sensitivity. The tall blond Nordics, descendants of ancient Germanic tribes, were the originators of all civilization and the only ones capable of effective and efficient leadership in a rapidly changing world.[2]

This French upper-class conception of internal racial divisions was vividly expressed in the famous work of Count Arturo de Gobineau, "Essay on the Inequality of the Human Races" (1853–1855). Although this nobleman divided all of the world's people into three races, the white, yellow, and black, Gobineau was especially concerned with the peoples of Europe and the decline in its "high civilizations." He was a major advocate of the natural superiority of the aristocratic or noble classes. Using the premise that such classes were responsible for all great works of civilization, he proposed what he thought was a natural law of the decline of great nations: Civilizations fall when the aristocratic classes intermarry with the lower classes and dilute their superior blood (Chase 1980, 91).

Gobineau's publications were among the most well known of numerous other writings on racial populations in Europe at a time when the anthropological sciences were becoming consolidated in learned societies and academies. More important, they influenced the nationalistic racial theories of many Germans. According to Hannah Arendt ([1951] 1968), German race thinking differed from that of the French in that its purpose was to unify, rather than to divide, the nation (45). It appealed to nationalism rather than to class interests. Its advocates sought to awaken the peoples of disparate German states to a "consciousness of common origin" (45). After the Franco-Prussian War (1870–1871), such consciousness was fully developed in the form of a new dogma of Aryanism. It was the composer Richard Wagner who introduced Gobineau to the German public by whom "he was revered as a prophet and as the great forerunner of the truths of racialism" (Snyder 1962, 49). After 1890 Wagner's British-born son-in-law, Houston S. Chamberlain, who brought a religious fanaticism to his beliefs in Germanic dominance (he believed that Jesus was a Teuton, not a Jew), became the chief proselytizer of German racial superiority (Gossett 1965, 330).

Chamberlain developed a virulent anti-Semitism, like many of his compatriots, claiming that Jews had a moral defect as part of their racial character. Hatred of the Jews increased out of opposition to what was thought to be their liberal political ideas and the growing belief that they were dominating German culture. Theories about the purity of the German race and about their destiny in history flourished into the early twentieth century under the influence of the writings of these men. They had a major impact on Adolf Hitler and the National Socialist party. But they also deeply influenced American writers, such as Madison Grant and William Z. Ripley, who extolled the virtues of Nordics and opposed the immigration of southern Europeans.

Measurement of Human Differences: Anthropometry and Somatometry

Like their American counterparts, many of the French writers invoked the techniques and findings of science to reveal the specific qualities of each racial group, qualities that had already been incorporated into a popular worldview. Thus it was that French scientists were among the first to develop techniques for measuring differences between any human groups to whom they had applied the classification of "race" and to use these measurements to justify social inequality.

It is useful to recall that, as early as 1784, Peter Camper had devised a method of measuring the degree of prognathism, that is, the jutting of the lower jaw in relation to the incline of the forehead. His offhand suggestion, not an assertion, that human groups could be evaluated in terms of their distance from ape forms by using the objectively determined facial angle was the result of comparisons of a limited number of skulls for artistic (and thus subjective) reasons. To him, those populations with a high degree of prognathism, with snouts like apes, represented clear manifestations of inferior racial stocks. At the other extreme, the "orthognathous" types were not only superior because of their enlarged forebrain but also aesthetically the most beautiful. Camper made no claim that Negroes were of a separate species from other humans, but as John Greene (1959) noted, his use of measurements and his comparisons, regardless of intent, were "destined to exert a profound influence on the development of physical anthropology" (190). According to Haller (1971), by 1869 the facial angle had become the most frequent means of explaining the gradation of species to which, I have argued, racial differences had been elevated (11).

Camper's findings opened the way for a proliferation of new techniques for defining and measuring biological differences. His work was followed by that of such men as Jean Daubenton, an anatomist who had collaborated with Comte de Buffon. Daubenton identified variations in the position of the foramen magnum, the hole where the spinal cord enters the skull, and its relationship to posture, which reflects a definitive difference between humans and nonhuman primates. He also invented new techniques for measuring anatomical differences.

In the nineteenth century, Camper's intellectual heirs continued the tradition of devising ways of measuring human anatomy and morphology. Anders Retzius invented the cephalic index, which differentiated people with round heads (those with high ratios of skull width to length) from those with long heads (those with low ratios of skull width to length). Long-headed (dolichocephalic) populations were interpreted to be more advanced than round-headed people (brachycephalic). This latter trait Retzius attributed to both the Stone Age ancestors of Europeans and to modern primitives, suggesting an evolutionary trajectory from round-headedness to elongated heads. Many saw this finding as a major breakthrough in the effort to discover techniques of calculating racial differences. It was widely used until the discovery that the cephalic indices of many "savages," like some black Africans, were similar to the long-headed measurements of Scandinavians. The cephalic index was used also by one of the major racial determinists of the nineteenth century, Paul Broca, the great French anthropologist who, it turned out, was round-headed (Gould 1981, 99).

What occasioned such attention to the skull were a number of currents running through European and American cultures early in the nineteenth century. One was the increasing discoveries of fossil materials, primarily skulls, beginning in the late eighteenth century. Among these finds were skulls that had obvious humanlike features. In 1833 William Buckland had examined a human cranium found with bones of extinct animals at Liege. During the next two decades Boucher de Perthes discovered and examined a number of ancient sites containing fossils associated with flint implements, including the famous Abbeville site. In 1857 the first Neanderthal skeleton was found. The strange characteristics of this skull, particularly the teeth formation and size, attracted a great deal of attention. Accelerated interest in the comparative study of fossils and in the significance of the apparent sequential transformations observed when comparisons were made of many of these fossils provided evidence for theories about the evolution of modern humans from more "primitive types."

Undoubtedly more significant, however, was a popular synthesis of ideas about human mental processes and certain associated features of the skull or cranium that led to the so-called science of phrenology. First conceived by Franz Joseph Gall and much publicized by his colleague, Jacob Spurzheim, phrenology purported to demonstrate "that different parts of the brain each had their own mental function, and that the relative size of these parts determined the degree of development of their respective faculties. Observations and measurements of 'bumps' on skulls and heads could thus provide rather accurate estimates of personality and character" (Malefijt 1974, 260). Phrenology thus inspired scientists to study skulls for the purpose of assessing the personality traits and talents of individuals and the national character of ethnic populations.

Gall had concluded that the human mind was composed of thirty-seven different faculties expressed in the configurations of the brain. The strengths or weaknesses of each faculty could be ascertained by measuring the corresponding regions of the skull. Everything from aesthetic sensitivity to mathematical ability, musical and other talents, moral character, criminality, frugality, and other personality traits became measurable products of the mind. The potential usefulness of this approach for establishing or demonstrating racial distinctions was obvious. During the 1830s phrenology as a faddish form of scientism, as well as an interesting parlor game, found its way into the United States via

Jacob Spurzheim and George Combe, a student of Gall's who greatly influenced Morton (Bakan 1966).

It remained only for someone to apply statistical methods to the quantitative information acquired through the various measuring techniques. Such an activity had been initiated by Lambert A. J. Quetelet (1796–1874), a Belgian statistician who published his principal work in 1835. Applying his statistical techniques to the biological data and the findings from some psychological tests, he produced what was to become a fundamental concept of later typologists, the notion of the "average man," an abstraction that could be calculated for each racial population. Quetelet's statistical theories laid the foundation for the massive data analyses of the American Civil War anthropometric investigations. His procedures became known and used by nearly every biologist of the late nineteenth century. Such seemingly objective techniques, regardless of the accuracy or integrity of the data, produced a kind of typological thinking about races and racial differences that was to characterize most of anthropology until long after World War II.

It was Paul Broca, however, who made the most extensive use of quantitative methods for classifying races as well as for promoting phrenological assumptions in the sciences. Broca, like Morton a polygenist and founder of the Anthropological Society of Paris in 1859, invented a number of instruments used by craniometrists, and himself accumulated over 180,000 measurements on different populations. Anthropometry (the science of measuring human bodies) and anthropometrists proliferated in Europe and America. According to John S. Haller, Jr., "the hallmark of anthropology in the 19th century was anthropometry" (1971, 71), and its primary objective was to clarify, document, and measure physical differences among human groups. The greater the number of variables that could be quantified and measured, the stronger the argument for a vast gulf between the races. Those who argued that the Negro was nearer to the ape than to Caucasians found much support in anthropometry.[3]

The instruments of the growing fields of anthropology and human biology came to be employed abundantly, from the middle of the nineteenth century on, to support the principles of racial determinism and racial separation. Marvin Harris summed up the significance of these endeavors: "Prior to the nineteenth century, nations had never rewarded their wise men to prove that the supremacy of one people over another was the inevitable outcome of the biological laws of the universe" (1968, 81).

During the latter part of the century, many claims to the scientific verification of the inferiority of all nonwhite peoples, and of some whites to others, rested upon the wide-ranging anthropometric studies of Civil War soldiers and sailors. Two agencies, the U.S. Sanitary Commission and the Provost Marshal-General's Bureau, had been charged at various times with investigating the physical and moral conditions of soldiers in the Union army, captive subjects for such researches. After President Lincoln authorized the use of Negroes in the military and naval services in 1862, the Sanitary Commission commenced large-scale studies of military recruits to determine the extent of differences between the races.[4] For each group represented in the study the commission investigators "sought to construct Quetelet's average man" (Haller 1971, 22).

Using the increasingly more sophisticated techniques of anthropometry (calipers, andrometers, dynomometers, measuring tapes, spirometers), some of which were refined for the purpose by Louis Agassiz, the commission tested and measured thousands of white soldiers, white sailors and marines, "full-blooded" Negroes, and several hundred "mulattoes" and Indians. They took measurements of body dimensions throughout, from head size to toe lengths. They tested physical strength, vision, respiration, and pulmonary capacity. Their conclusions, and later interpretations of these data, were published over a period of several decades following the war. Explicit in these works was the preordained conclusion that, in virtually all ways that mattered to a civilized world, "the Negro" was inferior to whites and so were his mulatto offspring. He had a smaller brain, being closer phylogenetically to the apes, although his good physical endowment made him a capable soldier and worker (Haller 1971, 191).

The Provost Marshal-General's Bureau also published the findings from a series of questionnaires that had been distributed to military doctors inquiring into the relative capacities of black and white soldiers. Following the Civil War, some southern physicians continued studies on the Negro. Their conclusions "reflected not only the section's appeal for reappraisal of Reconstruction politics but also mirrored the race ideology of the ante-bellum South" (Haller 1971, 39). A plethora of anthropometric studies until the end of the century helped to convince a wider public that Negroes could not survive as freedmen. Early census data showing a decline in the black population seemed to confirm the growing suspicion that, without the benign and beneficial conditions of slavery, the Negro was about to become extinct. According to Haller (1971), "The belief in the Negro's extinction became one of the most pervasive ideas in American medical and anthropological thought during the late nineteenth century" (41). In the "struggle for existence," it was proclaimed, only the superior white races would prevail. This extraordinary example of wishful thinking thus appealed to natural laws as expressed in Spencerian terms. Often confused with Darwin's theory of natural selection, which related only to reproductive success, Spencer's ideas referred specifically to the exploitation of the poor and weak by the wealthy and powerful.

Even though the varied findings of these commissions and physicians were questioned by other scientists and census data were shown to be erroneous, continued interest in the measuring of racial differences persisted well into the twentieth century. Some scientists, dissatisfied with the apparent subjectivity and inaccuracies of older anthropometric work, proposed innovative new mechanisms for measuring and differentiating races. Elaborate techniques for observing and reporting skin color, for example, were developed early in the century; the tintometer (1908), the color top (1912), color blocks (1918), color standards (1916), and the photometer in the late 1920s and early 1930s (Guthrie 1976). For a while somatometry and somatotyping (classifications based on bodily dimensions) became the vogue, especially under psychologist-cum-anthropologist W. H. Sheldon of Harvard, though ultimately such classifications proved not very useful as diagnostic criteria for discrete races.

Typological Models of Race

Anthropometric, morphological, and somatometric pursuits in the late nineteenth and early twentieth centuries, as already suggested, fostered typological thinking in the biological sciences. The new typological models, however, ostensibly based on rigorous scientific methodology, once again proved indistinguishable from popular stereotypes (Allport 1972).

The essential elements in the typological scheme were large numbers of statistics derived from external measurements of individuals, often within an arbitrarily identified population. Quantitative measurements were supplemented by morphological observations, or, in other words, purely visual impressions. From the quantitative data, means, averages, and standard deviations were computed, which gave a statistical profile of the population. This profile was purported to represent, in objective and quantitative terms, the type characteristics of that population as abstracted from the real data. That the completed profile may not have corresponded to any individual in the population was irrelevant. The profile of each group conveyed the important point that each was a distinct morphological type. When profiles of different groups were compared, the differences between them would be interpreted as the degree of their racial differences (Hunt 1959, 66).

Concomitant with these abstractions, there developed the notion of "pure" and "intermediate" types (Bean 1926; Hooton 1926, 1936). It was assumed that all races were originally pure and unmixed, that is, without genetic infusion from other races. It was also assumed that racial histories of whole populations, manifest in terms of migration, contact, and isolation with independent development, could be reconstructed on the bases of statistical similarities and differences among the various abstractly conceived types.

The notion of "racial type" also carried another implicit ingredient; this was the idea that "races" could be classified on the basis of the invariable association of a limited number of specific and unique characteristics presumably transmitted together. The problem was to discover those clusters of traits that made each race, or at least each "pure" race, distinct. "In the idealistic typological approach, every race consists of members who possess characteristics that are typical of that race but different from those of all other races. Each member conforms to the ideal type ... and each representative is separated morphologically by a distinct gap from the members of all other races" (Bennett 1969, 413).

The procedures and the findings validated the image of races as discrete and internally homogeneous, obscuring all of the variability in the original data. By extrapolation and creative interpretations, some scholars used such data to confirm the assumption that some races were more developed than others. Frequent assertions were made that some races actually constituted primeval primitive types that had not evolved, or at least not as rapidly as the more advanced races.[5] Lending a theoretical framework to the absolutism inherent in this perspective were the late nineteenth-century generalized theories of evolution, both biological and social, especially those proposed by Spencer and his ideological compatriots. Clearly, if some people were able to evolve more complex and sophisticated social and political institutions, laws, and technologies, this was indicative of their superior intellectual endowments.

Americans and many Europeans of the nineteenth and early twentieth centuries were even more convinced that there were fundamental and ineradicable differences between racial populations, equivalent, as we have seen, to those used to identify separate species. However, a new element soon evolved in the racial cosmology on both continents that held that every race has a distinct "racial essence." This idea was necessary in Europe because populations there were not so easily distinguished from one another on physical grounds alone. And North Americans required the concept because of the presence of persons of mixed ancestry who were phenotypically white. Racial essence is based on the presupposition that distinctive temperament and character, moral proclivities, and intellectual prowess were bound together as part of God's ordained plan and were inherited together regardless of superficial features. Despite the lack of empirical evidence, these abstracted qualities of racial uniqueness persisted in the mental imagery. It was presumed that such qualities were also amenable to measurement; it was up to science to discover, measure, and document these realities.

In a general sense the distance between races as expressed by the measurements of physical features were compounded (metaphorically) in the interpretations of psychological and intellectual differences that the metrical evidences were thought to mirror. At bottom, the real key to the differences that denoted a race's ranking and capacity for civilization rested in ascertaining these mental, psychological, and intellectual traits. By the end of the century, new modalities were operating that attempted to isolate the psychodynamic aspects of race differences and to calculate and measure these independently of the anthropometric findings.

The Measurement of "Race" Differences: Psychometrics

Most scientists became disenchanted with phrenology by the 1860s largely because of the faddish, mystical, and increasingly discredited associations of special virtues and vices with arbitrarily defined sites on the skull. But measurement of the contents of the skull, the presumed racial variables in size and weight of the brain, and the success of craniometric endeavors spurred the development of a new field, psychometrics, or the measuring of mental, intellectual, and/or psychological processes.

We must recall that the concept of race from its inception presumed hereditary inequality among human groups. The unshakable sway of this "factual" truth escaped no one, not even learned blacks, as Haller has pointed out (1971, 207). Although the knowledge of genes and chromosomes was not yet part of the repertoire of science, commonly held views about individual heredity combined with statistical data and techniques (e.g., Malthus's population studies, Quetelet's "normal distribution" of body measurements and the notion of the "average man") had already provided the philosophical tools and strategies for large-scale psychometric studies.

At the font of these studies was Sir Francis Galton's demonstration that extraordinary skills and talents ran in family lines. A half-cousin of Charles Darwin, Galton came out of the same aristocratic British background that had produced a disproportionate number of scientists and intellectuals in nineteenth-century England. In 1869 he published *Hereditary Genius*, a landmark volume designed to convince all but the most irascible skeptics of the superior hereditary endowment of certain eminent British families. His proof was provided by complex statistical methods, some of which had been derived from the works of Quetelet. Arguing that there is a physiological basis for psychological traits, he invented techniques for measuring what he thought was intelligence, along with the bell-shaped curve for demonstrating its "normal distribution." Galton also introduced such concepts as "regression toward the mean" as a way of explaining the stability of the normal distribution curve in the light of the flux found within a population and even among individual members of the same family. These are still basic models for twentieth-century psychology.

Although he never fathered a child, Galton had an almost fanatical concern with "superior" heredity, as evidenced in two of his other famous books, *Human Faculty* (1883) and *Natural Inheritance* (1889). He is especially remembered for having coined the term "eugenics" to denote efforts to improve racial stock by selective mating, thus founding the first scientific movement to overtly implement racist hereditarian beliefs (see Chapter 12). Additionally, Galton wrote much on mental defectives, the criminal mind, color blindness, and other traits that he believed were differentially inherited in inferior races. More importantly, Galton discovered the hereditary significance of the study of twins and is thus the intellectual predecessor of Sir Cyril Burt, the recently discredited twin expert in England, and Edward Lee Thorndike, the originator of the first important American study on twins. Galton suggested the need to observe not only the differences between fraternal and identical twins, but also recommended the study of twins reared together as distinct from those reared apart.

At approximately the same time that Galton persuaded the British Association for the Advancement of Science to conduct a survey of the mental abilities of English schoolchildren, Alfred Binet, director of the Sorbonne psychology laboratory in Paris, was requested by the French government to establish some means of testing and discriminating among the differential capabilities of Parisian schoolchildren. Both Galton and Binet thought that they were measuring intelligence. But neither ever defined it, nor did they approach an operational characterization of what they thought they were measuring. However, unlike

Galton, Binet never argued that intelligence was a single, innate, unitary entity. Since his main concern was to improve the performance of schoolchildren, he advanced no determination as to the cause of poor performance. According to Gould, "Not only did Binet decline to label IQ as inborn intelligence; he also refused to regard it as a general device for ranking all pupils according to mental worth" (1981, 152). Thus, Gould continues, Binet avoided the fallacies of reification and hereditarianism.

In the early twentieth century, such Americans as Lewis Terman, Henry Goddard, and Carl Brigham adopted Binet's mental testing techniques, revised them, and proceeded to develop "intelligence" testing on a grand scale in the United States. During World War I the Army Alpha and Stanford-Binet tests were instituted and used on nearly two million recruits. Revised for civilian use, they became virtually universal instruments for measuring racial differences in mental processes. Jack Fincher (1976) points out that these men all held personal views on heredity that justified inequities not only of racial treatment, but also of class differences (176ff). But it is Gould's indictment that penetrates to the proverbial bottom line:

> American psychologists perverted Binet's intention and invented the hereditarian theory of IQ. They reified Binet's scores, and took them as measures of an entity called intelligence. They assumed that intelligence was largely inherited, and developed a series of specious arguments confusing cultural differences with innate properties. They believed that inherited IQ scores marked people and groups for an inevitable station in life. And they assumed that average differences between groups were largely the products of heredity, despite manifest and profound variation in quality of life (1981, 157).

The main legacy, then, of the nineteenth-century science of raciology (as it was called) as it redounds to us in the twentieth century is not merely the penchant for measuring differences between groups called "races." It was the whole engorged mind-set that sought to explicate differences in behavior, real and imagined, in terms of heredity. The hereditarian component in the worldview of race has become the major argument of those who continue to adhere to the ideology of race and race differences; IQ became the idiom of its expression. The emphasis on differential intelligence, and the array of inferences about innate qualities of which this was the center, are the direct outgrowth of a late eighteenth-century concoction that contradicted and distorted a fundamental human reality, the extrinsic, nonbiological causes of human behavior.

The Clothing of Immigrants in the Garment of Race

Although the phenomenon of slavery and the black/white social polarization were basic ingredients out of which the ideology of race was most visibly generated, it is clear that other peoples could also be fitted into the scheme. Wherever there were overt physical and/or cultural differences among new immigrants to the United States, the potential for the now acknowledged stigma of racial inferiority could be, and usually was, applied.

Americans became even more conscious of having multiple racial populations with the immigration of the Chinese that began in the 1850s following the 1848 discovery of gold in California. During the 1860s the Chinese provided the major labor for the building of the Central Pacific Railroad. When this was completed in 1869 thousands of Chinese were out of work and thrown into an already depressed labor force, mostly in California (Daniels [1962] 1977). But antagonism toward the Chinese began as early as 1852, and by 1870 organized protests against the "Mongolian hordes" were taking place in San Francisco.

Protests, demonstrations, even massacres against the Chinese increased in many areas after the Civil War. Gossett (1965) points out that the supreme court of California barred Chinese people from testifying in court cases involving whites for a reason that was incontrovertibly racial. The court claimed that since Indians were not allowed to testify against whites and the Chinese were of the same race as the Indians, the law should also apply to them (290). Arguments about the inferiority of the Chinese and fear of hordes of Asians taking over the Western states were rampant. By 1882 Congress had passed the first of several Chinese exclusion laws designed to prevent further immigration. Throughout this time, violence against the Chinese left untold numbers murdered, and "incidental brutality and casual assault" were their "daily lot" (Daniels [1962] 1977, 17).

Japanese immigrants began to arrive gradually in the United States during the last quarter of the century. After 1890 their numbers increased rapidly in the next two decades. Although initially perceived by Americans as more acceptable than other Asians, opposition to the Japanese did not lag, however, and it became so strong that by 1909 an executive order, the famous Gentlemen's Agreement, was promulgated in order to restrict immigration. By 1924 Japanese immigration was effectively terminated. But anti-Japanese sentiment increased between the two world wars, reaching a crisis in 1945 (see Daniels 1975).

In the case of both the Chinese and the Japanese, objections to their presence in the United States were overwhelmingly racial. Although many employers accepted them as laborers during periods of heightened demand, organized labor unions, especially in the West, vigorously opposed their presence. Through their leaders, unions expressed the dominant themes of hostility toward, and fear of, "the yellow peril." From their point of view, the Asians as a racially distinct population were not assimilable. They were expected to live separate and, indeed, segregated lives, with their own habits, customs, and institutions. Their inherent inferiority prevented their accommodation to the American (white) way of life. Most important, their presence was a threat to the "racial purity" of white Americans. This was translated as a threat to democratic institutions, since only Anglo-Saxons (Nordics, Teutonics, Aryans) had the innate capability for preserving democracy. The Asians with their high birthrate and incorrigible habits could only contribute to the demise of white civilization. Count de Gobineau surely must have agreed.

In 1913 and again in 1920, Congress passed two Alien Land laws designed to exclude "the yellow peril" from white territories. Such groups as the California Oriental Exclusion League and numerous other anti-Japanese organizations, including the American Legion, lobbied to exclude all Asians from citizenship.

The irrational hatred and fear of these peoples also helped to establish a precedent for the treatment of others, not so visibly distinct but, nevertheless, unwanted. In the late nineteenth century Italians, Jews, Greeks, Slavs, and others from eastern and southern Europe began to arrive in increasingly larger numbers, outnumbering eventually even the immigrants from northern Europe. Concern over these foreign elements led in 1894 to the organization, by a group of Harvard alumni, of the Immigration Restriction League. The platform of this and many other such organizations to come aimed to restructure immigration policy solely on racial grounds. As is well known, by 1924 they were eminently successful. And their success was due in large part to the arguments that they could adduce from a large repertoire of scientific literature on race differences.

It would have been tantamount to a form of perversion had any reputable scientist in America at the turn of the century promoted the idea that the races were equal in their endowments. The social and intellectual currents of the time mandated conformity to a racial worldview resolutely fixed in American culture and consciousness. It was a cosmological perspective that was compatible with European and American industrial and commercial dominance and with the accelerating exploitation of non-European lands and peoples.[6] With the start of the Spanish-American War in 1898, a conflict permeated with racial elements, America entered into the colonial world and took upon itself some of the "white man's destiny" and "burden" in the form of the "little brown peoples" of the Philippines. After the Berlin Treaty of 1885, nearly the entire continent of Africa came under at least nominal European control, and the mantle of providing contrasting images of savagery and civilization fell almost exclusively to its indigenous population. Thus the sixteenth- and seventeenth-century "savages" yielded in the nineteenth century to an even more invidious portrayal of the "wild men" of Africa (Curtin 1964).

Scientists, scholarly and popular writers, and other people of letters directly reflected general folk perceptions and fears of Negroes, Chinese, native Americans, and the southern European "types" who flooded the United States during the latter half of the nineteenth and early twentieth centuries. Science writers synthesized and articulated the hatreds, fears, and frustrations emanating from explosive and unprecedented experiences, such as race riots, labor conflicts, and the like. Race was the social doctrine that permeated them all.

In bringing to bear the "objectivity," the knowledge, the methodologies, the logic, and the authority of science, these experts advanced the racial worldview (1) by certifying and validating, often obliquely, the incredulous beliefs of lay people, and (2) by providing material evidence and arguments on which public policies, such as the immigration laws, segregation laws, and discriminatory employment practices came to be based. Mark Haller (1963) observed that "Between 1870 and 1900 educated Americans took giant strides toward a fairly wide acceptance of varying forms and degrees of racism" (50). These educated Americans were contemporaries, or social offspring, of Herbert Spencer and the Social Darwinists. They were students of Louis Agassiz, such as Joseph Le Conte and Nathaniel Shaler who thought race prejudice was innate and who defended the lynch laws of the South (Haller 1971, 184–185). They were often persons of wealth who also controlled the public media, such as Edward Drinker Cope, editor of the *American Naturalist*. And they frequently published in the leading journals and popular magazines of the time, *DeBow's Review, North American Review, Atlantic Monthly, Science, Popular Science, Nineteenth Century, Arena, Nation, McClure's Magazine, Scientific Monthly,* and *Sewanee Review.*[7] John S. Haller, Jr., grasped the situation astutely when he noted, "The subject of race inferiority was beyond critical reach in the late nineteenth century" (1971, 132). He might have added, until well into the twentieth century.

During the first half of the twentieth century, Americans were barraged with images of the otherness and bestiality of "the Negro," and the horror of miscegenation. Separateness and exclusiveness of the races were stamped upon the American psyche. For African-Americans particularly, the convenient stereotyped images that Americans created to deal with "inferior" races functioned as the alternative to recognizing and treating them as human beings. All of the components of the racial worldview now dominated American thought and actions.

Yet, as we see in the next chapter, gradual modifications began to occur in race ideology during the first half of the twentieth century. With the rise of Hitler's Germany, even the term "race" itself took on nuances for the first time that conveyed to an increasingly receptive public its malignant and corrosive influences on human society.

Notes

1. Because of their proximity to one another, Europeans have always been aware that individuals, families, and even larger groupings often migrate and change their language and culture; in other words, changes in ethnicity, nationality, and even class are unrelated to the biophysical characteristics that an individual or family may have. The components of the ideology of race transform this kind of consciousness in subtle ways.

2. There has been a stubborn persistence of this triadic paradigm and of stereotypes in European racial myths. H.F.K. Gunther in a 1927 publication entitled *The Racial Elements of European History* described the characteristics of these three presumed races without equivocation as to their innateness. The Nordic, he believed, has a strong urge toward "truth and justice, prudence, reserve, steadfastness," and exhibits calm judgment, fairness, and trustworthiness. The Mediterranean, in contrast, is "strongly swayed by sexual life." He is not as continent as are Nordics, for whom "passion has little meaning." Alpines are "petty criminals, small-time swindlers, sneak thieves and sexual perverts." Nordics are "capable of the nobler crimes." See Tobias (1972, 27).

3. Gould (1981) has examined the original data of many of the outstanding nineteenth-century anthropometrists involved in race and gender studies. He has shown how their blind commitment to race and other hereditarian differences led these scientists to fudge, finagle, and misconstrue their own data in order to support the fundamental assumptions and myths of their culture.

4. Information on the results of these activities during the Civil War and later can be found in Haller (1970, 1971).

5. One of the great popularizers of the belief that the Negro was lower in the scale of evolution was Joseph Le Conte, a professor of natural history and geology at the University of Georgia and Columbia University. Although a student of Agassiz, he became a prominent evolutionist and a follower of Herbert Spencer. Le Conte felt that Negroes had evolved as far as they could under slavery and that any further development would have to be under the aegis and control of whites since blacks lacked a natural impetus for development. For accounts of this and of other scientists, see Chase (1980) and Haller (1971).

6. For discussions and analyses of the relationship between racism and colonialism, see Bolt (1971), Curtin (1964), Davis (1966), Hammond and Jablow (1970), Robinson, Gallagher, and Denny (1968), Ross (1982), and Williams ([1944] 1966).

7. During the two decades of the 1850s and 1860s, S. A. Cartwright dominated the pages of *DeBow's Review* with numerous articles dealing with the peculiarities and diseases of the Negro, the question of Negro inequality, and the impossibility of Negro freedom. Throughout the latter half of the century, the *Atlantic Monthly* made much of the "Negro problem" and, among many others, Thomas Nelson Page forcefully expressed the Southerner's view of Reconstruction and the ineducability of the Negro.

12

Dismantling the Cultural Construction of Race: Twentieth-Century Transformations in Science

R ACIAL ATTITUDES BEGAN to fluctuate and change during the first half of the twentieth century. Popular thought was affected by two world wars involving Americans in Europe and in parts of the Third World. It was also affected by the Great Depression, extensive demographic changes, the growth in education and experiences of the American public, the presence of new immigrants, and internal migrations as restless Americans began to traverse the land looking for jobs and opportunities. Millions of African-Americans relocated from the South to urban centers in the North and West. Labor unions consolidated a working-class agenda, gained in power and legitimacy, and slowly (albeit reluctantly) incorporated black labor. Many blacks and native Americans served in the armed forces, returned, and sought education and economic betterment. Others obtained employment in the growing auto, manufacturing, and defense industries.

African-Americans and the newer European immigrants were now involved more than ever in the national economy and national purpose. By midcentury, genetically heterogeneous, culturally distinct, Spanish-speaking populations began to expand on both coasts, increasing the complexity in the melting pot. Most of all, the racial component in Nazi beliefs and the atrocities committed in the name of racial purity had shocked nearly everyone into rethinking fundamental values. During and after World War II, Americans widely propagandized antiracist sentiments, and many came to believe in them themselves.

Science increased in stature and strength as a major source of opinion and thought about race during the twentieth century, as the disciplines

273

of physical anthropology, biology, genetics, physiology, chemistry, and various subfields experienced rapid growth in knowledge, resources, and research techniques. Findings in these fields were not easily accessible to the lay public, but various trends and positions held by scientists on issues of race attained widespread publicity, awakening and encouraging transformations in popular thought in their wake.

This history is instructive as it demonstrates not only the expansion of the influence of science but also the degree to which advances in science often entail struggles between the power of popular beliefs and the researchers' need for some level of independence, if not complete neutrality and objectivity, in acquiring and assessing new information. It was in the field of anthropology that accelerating changes in knowledge and opinion and the drive for objectivity in understanding and evaluating human differences were most dramatically focused. This chapter will discuss the rise of the science of mankind (now transformed to "humankind"), the emergence of new scientific positions on race that conflicted with older views, and the influences of a new liberal perspective in the educational establishment. Historians and social scientists began to recognize the separate social reality and functions of race. And experts in the biological sciences began to question its usefulness to science.

The Rise of Physical Anthropology

Anthropology materialized as an academic discipline connected with universities in the closing decades of the nineteenth century. In the United States it was considered a unitary science covering all aspects of the human condition. The first professionals were trained to be experts in all of what were later delineated as subfields: archaeology, linguistics, ethnology/ethnography (cultural anthropology), and physical anthropology. Researches in the latter subfield complemented other growing disciplines, human biology, genetics, anatomy, and paleontology, but physical anthropology evolved a uniqueness of its own in its focus on race.

Two men were primarily responsible for the growth of physical anthropology in early twentieth-century North America, E. A. Hooton and Ales Hrdlicka (Brace 1982). Both had a major interest in race and the study of racial differences, and both inherited the tradition of anthropometry, whose foundation had been laid by Samuel Morton. Hooton taught at Harvard for nearly forty years, preserving the legacy of racial and polygenist thought that we saw so vividly expressed by Agassiz. He transferred his views to hundreds of students, who later composed the first professorate ranks of physical anthropology.

Hrdlicka was central to the founding of the *American Journal of Physical Anthropology* and helped to organize the American Association of Physical Anthropologists. Reflecting the very strong influence of race thinking, both men emphasized the racial identity of living and extinct populations through measurement techniques, the refinement of racial taxonomies, and the historical reconstruction of population movements and interrelationships through the study of skeletal remains. Several authors have pointed out that, even in the face of contradictory evidence appearing at that time, the typological approach toward race fostered by these men and the perception of racial populations as discrete biological entities persevered.[1]

Nevertheless, specialists in these fields began moving in a number of different directions as their attitudes toward human diversity began to shift. One direction of change was toward a redefinition of the term "race" that would transform and limit its meaning. It was a direction that attracted many anthropologists who were uncomfortable with what they thought was the diffuse and imprecise way in which the term had been used in the past. Impetus was given to this change by Franz Boas, then the most influential leader of the field in America.

Franz Boas and Attempts to Transform the Meaning of Race

In the early decades of the twentieth century a number of individuals from the newly structured field of anthropology began to promote the idea that race was (or should be) a taxonomic term referring to classifications of human groups based solely on biophysical and morphological characteristics. The distinctive physical traits of different races, it was argued, have not been demonstrated to be intrinsically related to a group's language, religion, customs, morals, traditions, art, laws, knowledge, or beliefs. Thus anthropologists sought to divorce the physical features of diverse humankind (calling the resulting clusters "races") from language and culture, which is learned behavior. Their success would have meant a radical transformation of the meaning of race, for, as we saw in earlier chapters, physical and cultural/behavioral elements had been cognitively and integrally fused in the term from its origin.

Although this principle of separating biology from culture came to be seen in twentieth-century anthropological circles as a radically new idea, in fact it was a perspective that had a long history. It was reflected in the writings of ancient Greek and Roman historians who had been well aware that social behavior, language, and beliefs were learned phenomena, external to the physical characteristics of their bearers. It appeared in early Enlightenment ideas about the power of education and socialization. Among nineteenth-century evolutionists, the first "school" of sociocultural anthropology, E. B. Tylor's famous definition of culture, now widely quoted in nearly every introductory textbook, implicitly incorporated this principle (see Introduction). Simply stated, human behavior is learned and a group's inherited physical characteristics have nothing to do with its people's capacity to acquire any cultural behavior.

As early as 1897 Franz Boas began to question some of the elements of nineteenth-century thought on race. He argued, while reviewing a book by Paul Ehrenreich, that races should not be characterized by linguistic criteria because "the laws according to which anatomical types are preserved are not the same as those according to which languages are preserved" ([1897] 1940a, 153). He persisted in this stance in other articles and reviews ([1899] 1940b, [1899] 1940c, [1902] 1940d, [1915] 1940h, [1931] 1940l, [1932] 1940m). But his most significant contribution to the crystallization of this view of race stems from his anthropometric studies of children and adults. Following the then customary activities of his discipline, Boas conducted anthropometric studies on schoolchildren in such places as Worcester, Massachusetts; Puerto Rico; Oakland, California; New York; and New Jersey. He studied the children of Italian and Jewish immigrants and the offspring of French-Italian "mixed" marriages, native Americans, "half-blood Indians," and mulattoes, among others. His concerns were with mental and physical growth patterns and the influences of heredity and environment on growth. What he discovered was to startle the scientific and intellectual communities and to dislodge many of the basic assumptions of anthropometry.

Boas found that children of immigrants in a single population varied significantly from their parents in anthropometric measurements, that head form (cephalic index) could change in one generation from round heads to long heads, and that stature, facial width, and a number of other features thought to have been fixed, stable, and unvarying due to heredity underwent sometimes drastic changes in different environments ([1910–1913] 1940e, [1912] 1940f). These findings challenged and eventually undercut the notion of fixity and permanence of physical racial characteristics as measured by anthropometric techniques and demonstrated the plasticity of the human skeleton (within limits). Boas reintroduced the importance of environmental influences, particularly nutrition and climate, as major determinants of the final expression of many physical traits. Until then, such external influences had been largely ignored. Under the Social Darwinists, "nature," or biological inheritance, had been promoted over "nurture" as the causative agent of human racial potential. By insisting on the notion of a rigid and unalterable nature, those oriented to this type of race thinking had hitherto precluded consideration of modifications of physical characteristics through responses to environmental forces.

Finally, Boas's findings also helped to demote the concept of "averages" as a way of describing whole populations ([1897] 1940a, 176) and thereby much of the reified typological approach to racial identification. His works and those of his students and colleagues paved the way for the eventual recognition of the limits to the meaning and interpretation of anthropometric data as a way of describing racial populations. Although scholars may not have been fully aware of it then, such findings were also an early first step challenging certain components of the folk idea of race in anthropology.

Boas dominated American anthropology for half a century. His students and all those influenced by the "Boasian milieu" advocated the principle of the separation of race (biology) from language and culture as one of the fundamental pillars of American anthropology. The idea gradually spread, even beyond scientific circles and into the social and political consciousness of many people in the West, especially during World War II. The social and historical context in which it proliferated helps us to comprehend the importance of this attempt to construct a new, purely biological, meaning of race.

At the time of Boas's initiation into the field of anthropology, its practitioners had begun focusing much of their attention on "primitive races" in attempts to comprehend their customs, beliefs, and practices and the workings of their minds. The racial worldview dominated virtually all scholarly attitudes toward non-Europeans, and efforts were geared to ascertaining the fundamental ("racial") nature of different groups. It was widely assumed that cognitive processes differed among the "lower" races, whose mental development was presumed stultified.

Certain popular works perpetuated this theme. Charles Carroll's book *The Negro a Beast* (1900) continued the polygenist tradition and enlarged upon the now widely accepted argument that the Negro was in reality an ape. And Thomas Dixon's popular novels terrorized their readers with their portrayals of animallike black males attacking virgin white women. As Fredrickson ([1971] 1987) reveals, a great deal of literature written during the first quarter of the century consciously exaggerated black bestiality, degeneracy, crime, and sexuality, especially the lust for white women. Such stereotypes help to explain the increasingly extreme white avoidance of contact with African-Americans even in northern cities and the burgeoning hatred of blacks, a prime condition fostering the emergence of urban black ghettos. Exclusion and keeping the Negro in the lowest-ranked position was the goal, reflecting the racial worldview.

The period between the two world wars was punctuated in the United States by outbursts of intense racial hatred that took various forms. Some of the most violent resulted from the reinvigoration of the Ku Klux Klan under a dogmatic leadership that was relentlessly committed to the preservation of "Anglo-Saxon civilization." Klan leaders saw the restlessness of African-Americans emigrating from the South and the onrush of different immigrant peoples from southern and eastern Europe as threats to the dominance of the older white Anglo-Saxon establishment. Throughout the South and in many regions of the West and North, the Klan turned to intimidation and threats to maintain the subordination of the undesirable groups. Anti-Jewish and anti-Catholic sentiment also thrived throughout the country.

In the context of a society pervaded by such virulent racism, Franz Boas and his students had begun their research and publications, many of which expressed fundamental antagonism to all forms of racism. Much of Boas's own attitude was summed up in an early book, *The Mind of Primitive Man* (1911, later revised), which laid the philosophical groundwork for the even more famous social critiques of some of his most eminent students, Ruth Benedict, Margaret Mead, Melville Herskovits, and others.

As Leslie Spier (one of Boas's students) has claimed, several of the themes of this book are now axiomatic in anthropology. He identifies them as (1) there is no such phenomenon as hereditary racial purity; (2) races are not stable, immutable entities, but undergo changes due to domestication, selection, mutation, and other environmental influences; (3) "the average differences in physical traits between races is small in contrast to the great overlapping of range and duplication of types among them"; (4) there is no evidence that any race is "incapable of participating in any culture or even in creating it";[2] (5) "there is no identity of race, language, and culture such that physical heredity can be credited with the formulation of languages and the achievements of civilizations"; and finally, (6) Boas held that some groups "are not primitive by reason of hereditary inferiority but because the circumstances of their life were more static than those of civilized men, the differences being products of their variant history and traditional equipment" (Spier 1959, 147).

Major influences on Boas and his contemporaries and students were the disturbing circumstances surrounding the growth of fascism under Hitler and the horror of extreme racism manifested before and during World War II. Boas grew up in Germany at a time when European race ideas were still evolving. Although he was in the United States and teaching at Clark University (later at Columbia) by 1888, as a Jew he was well aware of developing racial thinking in Germany and its relationship to American race ideology and its many supporters.

In 1916, for example, Madison Grant, who held leadership positions in the American Eugenics Society and the Immigration Restriction League, published *The Passing of the Great Race*, a notorious book that, like its nineteenth-century predecessors, explicated the rise and fall of great civilizations on the basis of the amount of Nordic "blood" in the population. He warned that America, and Europe in general, was facing decline because of the dilution of the blood of the superior race. Both Grant and Houston Stewart Chamberlain before him (*Foundations of the Nineteeth Century,* 1899), emphasized the varied mental and other heritable qualities of the different races of Europe. Although Grant had once argued that the Germans were not really Nordics, it was from works like these that the nineteenth-century ideology of racial determinism began receiving renewed impetus in Germany. By the time of the Third Reich, an elaborate variation of the ideology of race had been embroidered for Nazi consumption.

With Adolf Hitler's rise to power in 1932, the race doctrine of the National Socialist party (Nazis) raised to its zenith the Germanic race aristocracy theory. Hitler took the myth of superior and inferior races to a logical extreme, proclaiming the Germans as a "master race" destined to rule the world. From his point of view, it was also logical that inferior races, the destroyers of civilization, should be exterminated; and this he systematically began to accomplish. When Europeans began to treat one another as subhuman, in much the same manner as they had treated non-Europeans, and to rationalize brutality in the name of racial purity, or racial inferiority, reaction against ideas of race and racism were inevitable. Boas and his students were part of that reaction, projecting a liberal scientific and social philosophy that opposed and refuted Nazi race ideology.

Perhaps the high point of the liberal doctrines on race to emerge from the Boasian era was Ruth Benedict's *Race: Science and Politics* ([1940] 1947). It was a supreme attempt to present a progressive scientific view of race and to argue that racism was a vicious and brutal impediment to human progress, brotherhood, and understanding. A pamphlet that Benedict coauthored with Gene Weltfish in 1943 became the major forum through which these ideas were disseminated to the public via schools, churches, news media, and private organizations. It also caused somewhat of a storm of controversy when conservative advocates of race determinism objected to it, claiming that it represented "communist propaganda."

An important consequence of the liberal assertions about race was, in effect, the posing of a challenge to raciologists to undertake the kind of definitive research that would prove once and for all the inequality of the races. The avenue through which this could be achieved now resided in mental tests, especially those, such as the IQ test, that purported to measure intelligence. Some of the country's most outstanding scholars, principally psychologists and geneticists, became involved in efforts to counteract the liberal trend and to demonstrate racial differences in intelligence. Since World War I, this has been the major strategem employed by those whose hereditarian values ascribe inferior status to nonwhite races, particularly to blacks.[3]

There is a peculiar and somewhat ironic twist to these efforts of liberal-thinking anthropologists and other scientists to expunge the causal link of biology and behavior/culture from the idea of race. Both Boas and his colleagues in early anthropology recognized some of the fused cultural components in popular notions of race, but they seemed unaware of its history as a folk concept that had become assimilated to science. We have seen in this volume that at no time in the history of its use for human beings was the term "race" reserved for groups based solely on their biophysical characteristics. From the start it was a cultural construct composed of social values and beliefs synergistically related in a comprehensive worldview, integral to the cognitive perceptions that Europeans and white Americans had of themselves and of the rest of the world. The question must arise: How does science extricate a singular component from a total folk worldview and transform it into the realm of objective, neutral science?

In retrospect, the Boasians could not at that time perceive that race was a culturally constructed way of looking at and interpreting human variation that was deeply rooted in historical circumstances. Moreover, they themselves were not totally immune to the social conditioning of a culture that reflected so negatively on obvious variations in skin color, hair form, and physiognomy. Even some of those who argued that race, language, and culture were not intrinsically related held personal views and were conditioned to certain emotional responses to different human groups that tacitly qualified their scientific proclamations.[4]

The attempt in the early twentieth century to transform the meaning of race, even if only in the scientific lexicon, was bound to have limited success, perhaps in part because the premises were too radical and ahead of their time. It was concomitant, however, as we shall see below, with rising specializations in the biological sciences in which the concentration on genetics tended to support, for reasons of relevance, the separation and isolation of biogenetic factors.

In the wider society, however, the folk sense of race and race differences was far too deeply ingrained in the American psyche and culture. Despite the well-intentioned efforts of anthropologists, the fundamental folk belief in the reality of race persisted. As C. Loring Brace has recently contended, "The assumption that contemporary human variation can be understood in terms of 'racial' variation, despite some pointed critiques, ... sails on without any substantial change from the time when Hrdlicka and Hooton were shaping the field into its subsequently recognizable form" (1982, 12).

Inevitably, there was a paradox not perceivable in academic circles at the time. To argue, as the Boasians did, that science had not proved that the races were unequal in their abilities, intellectual and otherwise, is to argue a contradiction in terms. The central meaning of race has from its origin historically been that of inherently unequal human groups. In terms of folk understandings and attitudes, to claim that races were equal was tantamount to transforming black into white.

There is another irony in the Boasians' attempts to modify the meaning of race. Both H. S. Chamberlain and Madison Grant, among others, were engaged in the same enterprise. Like the Boasians, they wanted to separate physical characteristics from their linkage with culture and language. But they had a quite different perspective, and obviously different purposes. Adhering to firmly established racial hierarchies, which had no referents in the real world, both came to believe that race was a matter of innate "inner essences" and not necessarily reflected in outward physical characteristics. Thus Grant argued that Nordics need not be tall, blond, blue-eyed, and pale. Some true Nordics are short with brown eyes and hair and olive skins, clearly a belief that later accommodated Italian fascists. But their Nordicism, and thus their racial superiority, were manifest in other forms, in their intellectual prowess, physical vigor, love of liberty, and domineering temperament (Gossett 1965, Chapter 14).

Part of the irony lies in the fact that these proponents of racial superiority were operating with an understanding of race, and race differences, that was closer in many respects to its late eighteenth-century original meaning than were the Boasians. Their conception of racial divisions made it possible for them to engage in the arbitrary assignment of race status, irrespective of biophysical realities. In this matter, they took the concept of race to its logical end, rendering it as a true political device justifying one group's domination of others.

The Boasians were combating another very powerful factor, the conservative scientific establishment that persisted in attempts to discover measurable ways of differentiating races. As we saw earlier, scientists turned to the measuring of "intelligence" to document established beliefs about racial superiority and inferiority. Despite some anomalies that were largely ignored, IQ tests showed superior performance by whites.[5] Black inferiority thus seemed absolutely verified and the results were widely publicized.

The entire society in the early twentieth century was permeated with such a strong sense of racial differences that Jim Crow laws, and the social customs that set the stage for them, were now nearly ubiquitous (see Woodward 1974). Segregated residential areas and distinctive institutions in the North matched the emergent "separate but equal" conditions of the South. Laws, customs, and social practices were aimed at maintaining the separateness and exclusiveness that the term "race" conveyed. Efforts to preserve for blacks the society's servile roles were largely successful in keeping the vast majority of them underemployed and uneducated, if not immobile. Native Americans continued to be pushed back onto reservations where the tragic problems of tuberculosis, alcoholism, lack of education and opportunity, and especially lack of jobs intensified and exacerbated cultural idiosyncracies. In both groups, crime, drink, hopelessness, despair, and lassitude were often the only culturally available options. These and the behavior associated with them became part of public stereotypes. It should come as no surprise that American scientists, like the rest of the population, were conditioned to a worldview that seemed to be constantly reaffirmed by the very conditions of society itself. Under the circumstances, the segregation of racial populations in national and community life was seen as natural and desirable.

Nevertheless, the Boasians' efforts to restrict the idea of race to purely biophysical characteristics was paralleled, and perhaps inadvertently bolstered, by developments in various fields of human biology. New discoveries in genetics by the midtwentieth century inspired biological researchers to concentrate on identifying the precise mode of inheritance of specific physical features. Although these discoveries suggested few direct implications for the inheritance of intelligence or moral behavior, one consequence, perhaps unintended, was that they often firmly enhanced the scientific underpinnings of the idea of race by their inordinate focus on biogenetic differences rather than similarities among human groups.

The Rise of Population Genetics

With the rediscovery of Gregor Mendel's experiments on heredity at the beginning of the twentieth century and the enlarged understanding of the roles of genes and chromosomes, a new biological conception of race began to emerge in science. The classificatory goals of pre-Mendelian biology began to yield to modifications brought on by a new dynamic perspective on the nature of heredity. This was reflected in a rekindled interest in evolution and the processes by which variations appear.

This new interest claimed the attention of a number of scholars, many of whom had mathematical and statistical backgrounds. Under their aegis much of the research activities of biologists during the first half of the century were aimed at (1) identifying the mode of heredity of specific known genetic traits, and (2) comprehending the evolutionary processes of natural selection, isolation, mutation, genetic drift, and gene flow as these have operated to bring about variation and change.

Population genetics ironically had its origins in the works of Sir Francis Galton and his student Karl Pearson, founders of the biometrical school, who attempted to develop quantitative techniques for describing the characteristics of different populations, each comprising individuals of unique heredity. Unfortunately, those characters that Galton sought to study included such complex and nonquantifiable traits as artistic ability, intelligence, and good and bad temper. He believed that intelligence was a unitary and segregative trait inherited in much the same manner as was (he thought) eye color, hair color, and stature. He did not recognize or even contemplate that the characteristics he chose reflected the values of his own cultural background, nor that the questions he raised were predicated on certain assumptions shaped by his own social class interests. Despite such flaws, which were not then so readily recognized, Galton's statistical methodologies continued as major ingredients of the new field of genetics. And so did many of his presuppositions about the nature of heredity.

The new understanding of heredity also helped to inspire the eugenics movement, whose influence rose during the first third of the century. The generalized philosophy and abstract goal of the movement, dating back to Galton (who coined the term "eugenics"), were to improve the race by selective breeding.[6] Members relied for scientific support on a very rudimentary field of genetics. At that time the only traits amenable to study by the techniques known were those determined by single genes, expressed in a number of allelic variations. The majority of known hereditary traits were various types of abnormalities

(Ludmerer 1969, 46). Concentration on such traits tended to retard theoretical interest in "normal" traits, to maintain focus on a small range of variation and limited generational depth, and to emphasize the evaluation of a few characters for "fitness" within a single generation. Eugenicists advocated sterilization of those individuals who carried "defective" genes (which could include any imagined hereditary trait, such as criminality, feeblemindedness, epilepsy, various mental diseases, and poverty). Even members of the U.S. political system adhered to eugenical beliefs and supported policies of sterilization (Chase 1980).[7]

Between 1914 and 1917 a number of scientists interested in the effects of close inbreeding (brother-sister mating) had discovered that the results led to diminished heterozygosity (variability). This stimulated interest in other theoretical problems of variation and eventually prompted the development of one of the fundamental principles of population genetics, random genetic drift. Often called the "Sewall Wright effect," after one of its founders, it introduced the element of chance or accident into the evolutionary process through which isolated populations, prevented from outbreeding, evolve hereditary characteristics distinct from the other populations in the species.

Theories of population genetics began to be consolidated in the 1930s, after a number of advances had been made in cytology, the study of the structure of cells, and in the discovery that mutations could be induced by external forces such as heat and radiation. Knowledge of the structure and functions of genes increased rapidly, forcing realization of the enormous genetic complexity of humans and other living forms (Dunn 1965a).

Between 1930 and 1950 the fundamental tenets of population genetics were established and outlined in such publications as T. Dobzhansky's *Genetics and the Origin of Species* (1937). Central to these tenets was the concept of a gene pool, all the genes and allelic variations extant in a given population.[8] Populations, which were the unit of study and analysis, were defined in terms of breeding behavior. In the laboratory plant and animal populations could be clearly delineated, since what constituted a breeding population was a consequence of artificial intervention. Although it was obvious that human breeding habits could not be so controlled, the gene pool model was still thought to be scientifically valid when applied to humans, especially where isolating mechanisms (geographic barriers) could be identified.

The basic features that came under examination in the study of population genetics were an increasingly wide variety of genetic elements found in the blood. After the discovery of the ABO blood group system, many other studies of human blood group patterns were undertaken. The first was done by two physicians, L. and H. Hirschfeld, serving with the allied forces during World War I. Their work, showing how populations could be identified by the frequencies of ABO alleles as manifest in the phenotypes, was the first suggestion that a new and more scientific way of identifying racial populations was now possible.[9] In 1927 Lansteiner and Levine discovered another blood factor, which they called the MN blood group. And between 1939 and 1941 the Rhesus (Rh) factor was isolated by several geneticists, who also identified the association between this system and hemolytic disease in newborn children in which the mother and child are incompatible for Rh (erythroblastosis).

Since those early days, a great many more inherited elements of the blood have been identified, primarily antigens, serum proteins, hemoglobins, and a wide variety of other proteins. Scientists have identified the structure of genetic material (DNA) in the cell nucleus, and they have calculated mathematically the mode of inheritance for numerous allelic variations in certain traits. For some physical anthropologists and human biologists serology research became one of the major instruments for differentiating human populations according to the expressions of hereditary factors that presumably are stable, or are not directly affected by environmental influences. Coincident with the new technology, the language of racial definitions in science rapidly became the quantitative theorems of population genetics (i.e., expressing population differences in terms of the proportions of genetic expressions of given traits). As a result, the morphological and typological conceptions of race were supplemented in the midtwentieth century by (some would say replaced by) a new genetic conception of race. This was reflected in definitions appearing in textbooks as late as the 1970s, as seen in these examples:

- "[A race is] a population within a species which can be readily distinguished from other such populations on genetic grounds alone" (Hulse 1971, 509).
- "a conceptual term meaning a variety reproductively partly isolated from other members of the species. Formally applied to groups of people who resemble each other in appearance, but now when used by anthropologists, confined to meaning a breeding population whose members share a higher degree of common inheritance than they share with other members of the species" (Lasker 1973, 384).
- "Mendelian populations; ... a population distinguished from another by demonstration of differences in allele frequencies" (Buettner-Janusch 1973, 551).

- "a human population whose members have in common characteristics that distinguish them from others. ... A race is a breeding population that differs from others in the frequency of certain genes" (Barnouw 1971, 123).
- "an interbreeding population whose gene pool is different from all other populations" (Birdsell 1972, 487).

The fundamental assumption was that each breeding population will have distinctive proportions (frequencies) of genetic alleles for any given trait or set of traits. Because most humans select their mates according to some degree of propinquity, distinctive breeding populations should be ascertainable from a study of the distribution of these Mendelian traits. Race differences were thus conceptualized in the scientific community as differences in the relative frequencies of hereditary traits found in all populations.

Some scientists soon concluded that the blood groups could also be employed, from a dynamic perspective, to study genetic changes and adaptation in the human species. Since 1924, when Felix Bernstein demonstrated that one could deduce certain conclusions about hereditary transmission from the proportions of phenotypes in a random breeding population, it was thought that blood groups would be useful for calculating historical relationships between groups. Experts also noted the possibility that blood group differentials might reflect changes in the genetic structure of a population due to natural selection, mutation, and gene drift, the mechanisms of evolutionary change.

Works by Boyd (1950), Mourant (1954), and Race and Sanger ([1958] 1975) were among the first publications to attempt worldwide or regional classifications of racial populations using the blood groups, which were seen as objective, clear-cut, measurable ways of classifying human groups. However, a number of problems beset such attempts at classification. From the standpoint of racial taxonomy, the major problem was that the blood-group patterns did not correlate with conventional racial classifications, except in very gross ways and for certain isolated peoples such as the Lapps.[10]

After the 1950s a more dynamic, evolutionary perspective surfaced, one of whose major tenets was that the breeding population represented the primary unit of analysis for evolutionary change (Thieme 1952). The theory was that each breeding population undergoes adaptation to a given set of environmental circumstances or constraints. The selection pressures of each environment occasion the manifestation of those traits (or allelic variations) that best promote group survival and reproduction. From the standpoint of evolutionary theory, then, races could be interpreted as products of the adaptive interaction of genetic systems in particular environmental contexts. Over time, changes in the environment would introduce new selection pressures. Along with other mechanisms of change, such as gene drift, mutations, and differential fertility, these would indirectly help bring about changes in the gene pool. Thus races were seen as episodes in the evolutionary process, displaying characteristics subject to modification over long ranges of time (Hulse 1962). This was a new way of looking at biophysical variation among human groups, as dynamic and changeable entities rather than as static, fixed categories.

Among the problems with the concept of race as breeding populations that the biologists and physical anthropologists themselves have recognized is the question, What constitutes a breeding population?[11] What level of fertile endogamous marriage (or matings) must be maintained in order for scientists to agree to construe a group as a breeding population? Should it be expressed in terms of a percentage of all actual fertile matings? If so, what percentage should be definitive, 90 percent, 60 percent, a simple majority (51 percent)? If, in a long stable community most people marry within a twenty-block area of their homes, is this population a race? If it were shown that over several generations 70 percent of all marriages took place among people who attended the same high school, does the high school constitute a racial population? How does one ascertain breeding populations when social barriers prevent intermarriage, but not intermating? Is a small relatively endogamous town in Colorado racially distinct from a small endogamous town in Vermont? How long, or how many generations of intramating does it take to produce a race? Underlying these questions is a more fundamental one: If races are breeding populations, are all breeding populations races?

In light of the contemporary knowledge of genetics, it is clear that no two breeding populations can ever be precisely alike. If breeding populations must differ "significantly" from one another in their genetic structures in order to be designated as racially distinct, what degree of genetic difference is "significant"? If races are particular types of breeding populations, then the diagnostic criteria for them must be specified. Such a reformulation of diagnostic criteria clearly must alter the genetic definition of races.

There were other problems, some of which have to do with the failure of the genetic model to accord with the conventional identification of races. Traits whose genetic bases are known do not manifest variations concordantly so that they cluster in a manner that makes for clear delineation of different groups (Boyd 1971, 221; Hiernaux [1964] 1969, 43). Instead, they display one of the fundamental Mendelian laws, that of independent assortment. This means that people who are grouped together on the basis of one or two genetic traits would have to be grouped very differently for other traits. The distribution of the ABO system does not correspond on a worldwide or regional basis with the frequency distribution of MNS, or the Rhesus system, and none of these correspond with the distribution of skin color or hair form or body size. From this, we can infer that some selection of traits for relevancy in the classification process would be necessary. The question then becomes, Which traits are taxonomically relevant? We know comparatively little about the mode of inheritance of such polymorphic traits (determined by more than a single gene or position on the DNA) as skin color, hair form, nose shape, and so forth. But these are the observable features used popularly and traditionally to identify races. Analyses of blood groups and serum proteins have been of little help in identifying or specifying members of customary race groupings.[12]

It would seem then that the breeding population conceptualization of race is cumbersome and without much substance or meaning if any given set of individuals can be called a race who display certain mating habits along with different frequencies of expression of known genetic traits. Moreover, it fails to confirm the expected large differences between populations that have conventionally been identified as distinct races. What has occurred in nearly all studies is that the investigator has operated with the traditional categories of race based usually on visible physical (phenotypic) differences and sought to describe these populations in terms of whatever different frequencies are found among specific blood-group genes, PTC tasters, red-green color blindness, midphalangeal hair, and other genetic features. From such studies and their attendant problems, scientists have generally concluded that there is greater variation among peoples within a geographical race (negroid, mongoloid, caucasoid) than there is between them (Lewontin, 1970; Nei and Roychoudhury 1972, 1974). Indeed, some experts have discovered that only a minor amount of variation in known genetic traits exists between the major "racial" groups (Nei and Roychoudhury 1974).

The genetic conception of race has had a wide appeal, and most experts feel that the older typological race concept, with each member conforming more or less to an ideal, has been thereby totally discredited (Bennett 1969; Birdsell 1972; Dobzhansky 1973). These developments have helped to foster an orientation toward viewing human variations in terms of their adaptive significance or other evolutionary processes. They have also tended to deflect interest away from traditional racial studies and toward a more dynamic and eclectic comprehension of human variability, both individual and group.

Yet the attention devoted to biogenetics has not precluded continuation of the older folk conception of human differences. The genetic construction of race so far has had little impact on contemporary social usages and beliefs about race differences in ordinary affairs. Indeed, for some experts and lay persons the genetic concept of race tends to preserve certain components of race ideology. For one thing, the concentration on differences (no matter how minute) as opposed to similarities between human groups retains, perhaps innocently, the underlying philosophy and belief in polarizing barriers between visibly and not-so-visibly different humans. The statistical manipulations not only continue to provide scientific legitimacy for the search for racial differences, but also tend to magnify the nature of whatever differences are found. They tend to affirm not only the obvious contrasts in external appearance but also the existence of inner submicroscopic differences whose significance may be trivial or nonexistent.

An example of the ongoing versatility of the race concept in science is found in the work of Stanley Garn (1965), which is still promoted as textbook reading in some courses. He attempted to wed the populationists' concept of breeding unit with an older classificatory system based on visible physical variation and the geographic distribution of morphological types. He defined three levels of racial subdivisions: geographical race, local race, and micro race. A geographical race is a major subdivision of humankind that is inclusive of the other two. It is a large collection of "similar races" and conforms to the differences represented by populations in the continental land masses. Local races are subdivisions of a geographic race that are largely endogamous. In other words, they constitute breeding populations, at some level, and can be conceived as independent evolutionary units. Micro races are regional manifestations of relatively minor genetic differences brought about by selection, drift, or random mutations. According to Garn, there are nine geographical races, hundreds of local races (he identifies thirty-two), and perhaps thousands of micro races. Thus the attempt has been made to render traditional racial classifications compatible with the new images of dynamic variability.

Enduring also is that cardinal quality in the idea of race—heritability, presumptive common ancestry, and the incalculable nuances of separateness that this conveys. Some scholars have thought it a firmly established principle, for example, that racial categories could be reconstructed on the basis of the ABO blood types. But to claim that two populations are separate races because one has ABO allele frequencies of A=10 percent, B=8 percent, AB=2 percent, and O=80 percent and the other has frequencies of A=10 percent, B=24 percent, AB=6 percent, and O=60 percent, requires one to totally ignore that the majority of persons in both groups are more like one another for this trait (O) than they are different. Similarly, the complex permutations that appear when more than one trait is investigated belies the subjective calculation of what constitutes "real" differences between human groups.

That hereditarian attitudes have not been limited to only physically measurable features is clearly demonstrated in the materials that provide insight into the social beliefs of some of the proponents of genetic theory. Those who are inclined to see races as distinct breeding isolates and who preserve the use of the term also tend to hold that there are potential behavioral correlates. Such racial differences in behavior are rarely specified other than as manifest through performances on IQ tests. Some adherents of this position have embraced new subfields in the various sciences, such as sociobiology, still seeking biogenetic bases for behavior.

Like others of his generation, Henry Fairfield Osborn, a leading eugenicist and paleontologist, who believed that interfertility should not bar the races from being classified as species, held that each race was "distinguished by innumerable differences of character and predispositions, spiritual, intellectual, moral and physical" (1926, 4). His explanation for the inferiority of the Negro was that this stock evolved first, was the most ancient, and therefore the most primitive.[13] As we reach the turn of the twenty-first century, there are many who retain such beliefs and who are actively seeking their proofs.

The link between mental qualities and other modes of behavior on the one hand, and biophysical characteristics, on the other, is well preserved by the ambiguities in the concept of race as "breeding populations." It implicitly connotes a continuity of behavior that is belied by history and the entire American experience. Through socialization, breeders as parents pass on to their children their customs, beliefs, habits, knowledge, and so forth. "Inherited" culture, by analogy, assumes the same magnitude and quality of difference as do physical traits. The "cultural" personalities of breeding populations, including "qualities of the mind" and "moral temperament," become as unalterable and as permanent in the minds of some scientists as are presumably the genetic materials.

The notion that social behavior, intelligence, character, and moral temperament are innate was integral to the folk concept of race, a truth that cannot be too often emphasized. Nor has it been suspended by the discovery of the mode of inheritance of blood hemoglobins. If anything, some proponents of the heritability of intelligence have been buoyed by the findings of geneticists. Every new discovery of hereditary proteins, haptoglobins, hemoglobins, and biochemical reactions of all sorts strengthens their conviction in the eventual identification of the gene loci that determine intelligence. "Moral temperament," no doubt, will not be far behind.

The Rise of a Liberal Social Position on Race

Between the two world wars, academicians in both the biological and social sciences turned their foci to the study of the social problems of races and race relations. Publications on "racial conflict," "racial attitudes," "race relations," and "racial histories" became part of a vogue. Liberal social scientists particularly, in reaction against the rising tide of fascism in Germany and other parts of Europe, expanded the political thrust for equality. The need to combat the racial ideology being forced on contemporary Europe and its colonial extensions inspired noble statements and publications on racial equality. Ironically, the movement for racial toleration and justice, with its emphasis on understanding others (their cultures, values, beliefs, and so forth), tended to support the notion that races existed, that they have different cultures, and that they would continue as permanent, separate communities in the American experience and in science.

By the 1950s a liberal point of view was dominant among perhaps the majority of contemporary scientists, although elements of race ideology still restrained the more conservative members of the profession. Many scientists saw race as an innocent term that was first used within a scholarly context for the purpose of classifying physical diversity in the human species. They assumed that it was taken from zoological taxonomy, endowed by society with a number of fallacious and prejudicial adhesions, then subsequently transformed into the basis and explanation for systems of gross social inequality.

With some exceptions, contemporary scientists deplore racism as an abominable by-product of the lay person's confused misconception of the "true" or "real" meaning of race. They naively believe that if people were only made cognizant of the actual scientific understandings of biological differences, then the irrational prejudice upholding racism would disappear. Many people optimistically assume that the causal linkage in the racist mind between phenotypic characteristics and behavioral differences can be eradicated by greater and more sustained contact among members of the polarized racial groups. Familiarity with each others' values and life-styles, it is thought, will lead to greater appreciation of racial differences. As one of the first lines of defense against racism, this position is relatively weak in its inability to distinguish biophysical features from cultural behavior and to recognize class and status differences in all populations.

It also fails to take into consideration the fact that race is a way of looking at the world that has deep and tangled roots. It functioned, and continues to function, to the benefit of particular individuals and groups. The fact is that the lay understanding of race, however hesitant, inarticulated, and diffuse, continues as a more accurate reflection of the sociohistorical meaning of race than that of modern science. The ideological components persist as part of a fixed conception of the world. What has declined in the United States since the 1960s has been the magnitude and virulence of racism, that is, the strength with which the ideological components are played out. The degree of subscription to the elements of race has also been declining as the subject matter of race waxes and wanes in the public eye. It is popular to protest against racism; it is even more common to deny its existence primarily because we fail to understand its historical, and contemporary, meaning.

Yet the disintegration of the components of the idea of race in American intellectual life may have already begun. The influences of liberal anthropological ideas have penetrated many aspects of American culture with unanticipated, and yet uninvestigated, consequences. Great advances in science have, perhaps inadvertently, challenged the constituent components of race ideology and set in motion a possible irreversible trend in new thinking about human differences. We will take a look at some other factors responsible for this in the last chapter.

Notes

1. See Brace (1982), and Armelagos, Carlson, and Van Gerven (1982).

2. Mark Haller (1963, 145) and Dwight Hoover (1976, 233) both underscore the fact that Boas was by no means oblivious to the racial conditioning of his time and place. Boas did not deny inequality of mental traits among individuals and races, and he thought that Negroes' physical traits were indicative of their greater degree of primitiveness. In the late nineteenth century Boas expressed the view that races could possibly deteriorate due to admixture, but there is no evidence that he continued with this view after the second decade of the twentieth century. (See also Stocking 1968.)

3. So much has been recently published on intelligence tests that even a brief review would be beyond the scope of this work. Fincher (1976) has a good summary of the history, but see also Davenport (1929), Dobzhansky (1973), Herrnstein (1973), Kagan (1982), Lewontin (1970), Sanday (1972), Spuhler and Lindzey (1967), and Wober (1971).

4. Refer to note 2 above.

5. The most obvious anomaly was the differential in performance between white students from the northern states and whites from the South where sup-

port for education was much lower. Northern whites have been found to be more "intelligent" via IQ scores than Southern whites on all national tests. This should have suggested environmental determinants of test performance but was generally ignored. See Chase (1980), Chapters 18–22.

6. For a history of the eugenics movement, which continues to have a substantial group of adherents, see Haller (1963), Ludmerer (1969), and Pickens (1968).

7. The idea of ridding a population of inferior and/or deleterious traits by selective breeding and of improving the "racial stock" by controlling the reproduction of only those individuals with superior inheritance appeals to a great many racists. Although the logic is misplaced and the ideas have no basis in facts, there are still a great many adherents and advocates of producing a "super" race through special breeding. See Chase (1980), King (1981), and Ludmerer (1969), among others.

8. Alleles were defined as variations in the phenotypic expression of single gene traits.

9. See Gates (1939), Davis (1935), Ottenberg (1926), and Snyder (1930), among many others.

10. A useful introduction to population genetics can be found in Morris (1971).

11. For some discussion of the problems see Baker (1967), Boyd (1971), Cavalli-Sforza and Bodmer (1971), Hiernaux ([1964] 1969), and Morris (1971), among others.

12. There are certain traits, such as some of the dozen or so Rhesus alleles, which are rarely or never found in certain regions of the world, making possible educated guesses about a person's or group's origin. But in a world of increasingly "mixed" people, these can never be absolute. New technology, such as electron microscopy, has enabled the mapping of DNA so that the genetic patterns of individuals can now be compared and matched. Such techniques have allowed experts to view in intricate detail the complexity of presumed hereditary patterns. But the techniques have not been used, to my knowledge, to establish racial taxonomies. Experts have known for some time that, although superficial similarities such as skin color, hair form, and nose shape have caused earlier scholars to classify together such groups as pygmies in Africa and New Guinea, these groups differ dramatically in the hereditary components of their blood.

13. One should compare this theory to that of Carleton S. Coon (1962), a reknowned anthropologist and student of Hooton, who explicated the same phenomenon with a totally opposing theory, that Negroes evolved to *sapiens* state last. See Gould's (1977) treatment of the irreconcilable logic of these contradictory positions.

13

New Perspectives on Human Variation and Some Tentative Conclusions

IN THE INTRODUCTION I referred to a 1982 study that revealed decreasing use of the term "race" in physical anthropology textbooks and the tendency of recent scholars to eschew categorization of humans in racial terms. This does not mean that there is less interest in the subject of human biophysical variation. On the contrary, the discovery of the structure of the genetic code (DNA) has unveiled the complexity of human heredity and generated infinite new scientific queries about our diversity. A major question was and is whether the homogenization of individuals into racial categories is the best vehicle for comprehending this diversity. Some experts have obviously found the idea of race, even when used in a purely biological sense, not adequate for the task. In this final chapter we explore further sources of dissatisfaction with the use of the term race, delineate some of the controversy over its use, and briefly outline new perspectives on human variation that threaten the components of folk ideology. We then speculate on some of the implications of the trend away from the term race in science.

The Decline of the Idea of Race in Science

Lest it be thought that American and other Western scientists represented a uniform sameness in their attitudes toward race, it should be noted that skepticism, even over such fundamentals as the presumed inferiority of the Negro, was alive and well, though somewhat attenuated, during the late nineteenth and early twentieth centuries. In the growing field of anthropology there was also some discomfort with the term race when used for human populations as early as the 1890s.

Paul Topinard exemplified this in his development. The first to write a general work on anthropology, in 1876, he formulated one of the earliest and most widely used definitions of the science: "the branch of natural history which treats of man and the races of man," (Haddon [1934] 1959, 2). Later (1891), however, Topinard questioned the use of the term "race," especially for intracontinental populations in which more or less random matings of heterogeneous peoples have confused lines of descent and discrimination. He also noted that "the word 'race' is hardly used by naturalists when speaking of wild animals and plants. They prefer the term 'variety,' which leaves unsettled the question of permanence, the condition *sine qua non* for race" (quoted in Count 1950, 175). Although he still conceded the possible use of the term for large general divisions of humankind, he maintained that "race is only a subjective notion" (176). Like Boas, Topinard early on was thus questioning one of the central components in the meaning of race, the notion that traits are permanent and immutable, but he carried the argument no further, perhaps because of the overwhelming strength of this worldview.

Some of Topinard's learned contemporaries deplored the various associations of the term race with language or linguistic groups, as in the case of "Aryan," "Hebrew," or "Latin." Some also criticized as unscientific what they saw as the stereotyping of group behavior. These critics reflected the increasing growth, independence, sophistication, and specialization of anthropology and the concentration of numerous studies on biophysical characteristics alone. Anthropometry was responsible for some of this development, albeit without the conscious intent of its practitioners.

Perhaps it was the imprecision of definition, the arbitrariness of classificatory schemes, or the sheer absurdity of trying to establish a scientific definition for an ideological conception of exclusiveness that did not exist empirically. In any case, some individual scientists were galvanized to dispute either the use of the term race or the concept itself. As early as 1900, the French anthropologist Joseph Deniker indicated objections to the use of the term among scientists because it had not been demonstrated that human groups represented subdivisions of the species in the same manner as other zoological forms.

In April 1936 an editorial appeared in *Nature* magazine under the title "The Delusion of Race." Among other things, the author (anonymous) criticized the definitions of race proposed by a committee of the Royal Anthropological Institute and the Institute of Sociology that were intended to serve as guidelines for the general public. The definitions themselves contained the latest scientific information, identifying races as breeding populations, each with distinguishable genetic characteristics. However, the author went on to say:

> In so far as the races of man are concerned, these definitions, far from being generalisations from concrete realities and empirical, are no more than logical concepts, postulated for purposes of classification and investigation. In face of the actual facts of the distribution of physical characters among the population groups of the world, as they exist at the present moment, *race is a pure abstraction*. The races or types into which the anthropologist groups the varieties of Homo sapiens are ideal types built up to explain congeries of characters in individuals and groups derivative from a variety of strains, in some sort of a phylogeny. Man seems to be almost infinitely variable within a wide range, and since upper palaeolithic times in the course of world-wide migration has interbred freely, with the result that the ideal types of anthropological classification, if they ever existed at all in any degree of purity, have become a matter of faith rather than of evidence. Characters on which classifications have been based are found everywhere to overlap, and both individual and population groups bear witness to their inextricably mixed descent (636).

The author completed the editorial with the statement that the significance attached to race is a delusion.

That same year Julian Huxley and A. C. Haddon published *We Europeans*, essentially a book on race, a term that they viewed as taxonomically interchangeable with subspecies. Yet in it they asserted that "the existence of ... human sub-species is purely hypothetical. No where does a human group now exist which corresponds closely to a systematic sub-species in animals. ... The essential reality of the existing situation ... is not the hypothetical sub-species of race, but the mixed ethnic groups which can never be genetically purified into their original components" (quoted in Montagu 1969, 17). It was from this source, Ashley Montagu informed us, that he himself adopted the term "ethnic group." In 1941 Montagu presented a now famous lecture, "On the Meaninglessness of the Anthropological Conception of Race" (reprinted in Montagu 1969). Since then he has consistently argued that race is a myth, "the Phlogiston of our time" (xii).

Montagu has been joined in his abnegation of the race concept in science by others who believe the concept is outmoded or has lost its usefulness for describing human physical variability. They agree with Montagu that "the very notion of 'race' is antithetical to the study of population genetics, for the former traditionally deals with fixed clearcut differences, and the latter with fluid or fluctuating differences" (19). Frank Livingstone, in an article entitled "On the Non-Existence of Human Races" (first published in *Current Anthropology* in 1962), pointed out that there is a fundamental incompatibility between race and natural selection, which is the basic determinant of biological variation. One cannot study the causes of physical variations in the human population and still retain the belief in races, taken as fixed, permanent forms based on nonadaptive traits.

The positions taken by these scholars helped to generate a spritely debate in the midtwentieth century between those who would retain the use of the term and those who would eliminate it. Much of the controversy arose from the fact that the contemporary record showed enormous ambiguity on the matter of race and little common agreement among experts on what is meant by the term. In some circles, the debate continues.

The Scientific Debate over Race: The Splitters and the Lumpers

In an earlier article, Lieberman (1968), using a simple but revealing dichotomy (first formulated by zoologist Cedric Dover in an issue of *MAN* in 1951), represents this controversy in the form of two opposing camps, the *splitters* and the *lumpers*, that have polarized around two related issues, the question of whether or not races exist and the question of the heuristic value of the term as a biological concept in modern science. Both splitters and lumpers operate with a presumed biological conception of race, but there are disagreements in both camps over definitions.

The splitters are a collection of scholars (physical anthropologists, biologists, geneticists, ethologists, and others) whose elemental or working hypothesis is that races are (or should be) in some sense taxonomic subdivisions of the human species. Some proponents hold that races are in reality subspecies, or incipient species. They argue that the taxonomic categories, however defined, correspond in some manner to natural phenomena. Thus, "there are valid races but biology is only beginning to properly discern and define them."[1]

Alice M. Brues expresses the views of a number of splitters who want to recognize the differences in genetic characteristics among populations that usually mate and marry only among themselves, that is, "breeding populations." Although she notes that race is not easily defined, she poses a genetic definition that, as we saw in the last chapter, has been widely held: A race is "a division of a species which differs from other divisions by the frequency with which certain hereditary traits appear among its members" (Brues 1977, 1). For all of the splitters, race is a useful term for expressing genetically based differences among populations, although neither the level of mating behavior that identifies a breeding population nor the magnitude of the differences are specified.

Splitters also argue for the increasing collection of new data, plus the development of more refined techniques for using such data to identify races, although classification alone is not necessarily their principal interest.[2] Their stated objectives are to understand the ways by which human populations differ and to ascertain the significance of these differences in various arenas of scientific inquiry (ecological, and/or environmental, evolutionary, behavioral, intellectual, immunological, etc.).

Manifest physical differences, especially those of populations originating in widely separated geographical regions, are demonstrably important to Western conceptions of race. Evolutionists see the migrations of populations and subsequent isolation and adaptation in different environments as part of the basic processes responsible for the emergence of new species. To this extent, for the splitters, isolated and differentiated human populations are, or were at one time, tantamount to subspecies. It is believed that they were evolving differences that, theoretically, would eventually reach a state in which the disparate groups could no longer interbreed should they later resume contact with one another.

As we have seen earlier (Chapter 1), many scholars believe that it is natural for human beings to separate and to categorize this multiplicity of diverse populations according to some or all of their differing physical attributes. An aphoristic quality marks the apparently widely prevailing point of view that there are universal perceptual and cognitive processes that lead to the treatment of human physical variation in terms of distinct categories. Thus, for many splitters, the term race is not only useful but represents naturally identifiable taxonomic units.

Some of the more extreme splitters of the twentieth century still reflected earlier polygenist views. The British geneticist R. Ruggles Gates, for example, argued that the differences among the major geographic clusters of human populations are of such magnitude as to require their classification not as races but as separate species. He not only identified five species, but added that "the primary so-called races of living men have arisen independently from different ancestral species in different continents at different times."[3]

Most theorists among the splitters, however, are today more moderate. They recognize that there is no clear definition of race that would serve all purposes and that the classifications are often arbitrary.[4] In their publications, many of them eschew the social connotations associated with the term race and firmly declare that the term should only be used in its biological sense. Some have further argued that even if we could eliminate the term race from the lexicon of science, the social meanings and attendant social problems would still exist (Dobzhansky 1973, 68; Loehlin, Lindzey, and Spuhler 1975, 19).

The other camp, the "lumpers," comprise a diverse group of scientists who for various reasons object to the term race. Some, who may occasionally concur with the need for a taxonomic means of identifying subunits of the human species, object to the term because (1) it is ambiguous; (2) it carries a burden of offensive and invidious social connotations; (3) there is no consensus among the experts on its definition; (4) the criteria for establishing racial classifications are not consistent; and (5) thus, it is arbitrarily used and too often used on the basis of nonbiological characteristics, such as language, religion, nationality, and so forth. These were some of the arguments that inspired the first dissenters and helped to ignite the controversy. In its place, many of these scientists would substitute "breeding populations" or "ethnic groups."

A more extreme view found among the lumpers is the idea that human races, in any kind of biological sense, do not really exist.[5] Human variation, it is argued, is extraordinarily complex. Most traits are not inherited in discrete units, but their ranges of expression are continuous and overlapping from one population to another. There are virtually no traits that can be scientifically used in an absolute way to distinguish separate populations, especially where there is any degree of propinquity. Even the frequencies of independently assorted genetic traits are discordant. (These facts are admitted by even those who would retain the use of the term race, as, for example, Brues 1977, 2, 3.) Moreover, unlike other animal species that manifest geographic variation in localized populations, humankind undergoes adaptation within a cultural context. Cultural, or learned, factors influence not only the nature of the selective forces that affect the survival of certain genetic features, but they also affect human mating and reproductive habits. Since the emergence at least of *sapiens* forms, mating customs have ceased to be random. The biological expressions of genetic transmission have been heavily imprinted by migration and by social preferences and taboos. The so-called human races are thus not clear-cut, homogeneous, or uniform groupings bounded by absolute, natural lines of demarcation.

Another powerful argument advanced against using race is that the effort to establish racial classifications and to fit all human populations into one or another category obscures and/or distorts the reality of biological variation so that it is useless for the study of human evolution (Hiernaux [1964] 1969). For one thing, racial classifications as an end in themselves cannot provide us with *explanations* as to how such variations originated. And the very act of attempting to compress all peoples into limited categories tends to prevent full recognition and comprehension of existing variability—that is, the ranges and gradations of specific physical features. Additionally, they argue, the race concept in biology is a static one, suited to rigid typological thinking but not to modern understanding of the dynamics of genetic processes or the evolutionary significance of human diversity.

What this controversy reveals about the nature of "race" is the inability of science to agree on its definition or to establish its credibility as a scientific entity with consensus on its meaning. This is the backdrop to the present-day trend away from the use of the term in all scientific fields, including zoology where it did not fully attain legitimate taxonomic status.

The Ecological Perspective

One of the chief developments associated with population genetics has been the recognition of the importance of natural selection in the production of biophysical variation. This presupposes a dynamic process by which a population interacts with and adapts to its environment by gradual physiological changes. By the 1960s a new mode of interpreting variations, on the basis of the adaptive significance of their expression, had come into vogue. The demonstration that many biophysical traits, once thought adaptively neutral, are quite probably the consequences of natural selection operating on existing variations produced by bisexual reproduction and mutations was a major stimulus to research in human ecology. The basic premise is that human groups, like all other animal forms, are subject to pressures from the natural forces of our environments. In the process of adapting to such forces as climate, disease, food supply, and so forth, we experience minute changes in our phenotypic and genetic makeup, some of which permit us greater reproductive, and therefore adaptive, success.

The ecological perspective is reminiscent of eighteenth-century Enlightenment environmentalism in that it links gross physical features of different populations to long residence in certain climatic conditions. For example, researchers have shown that skin color variations correspond to temperature and amount of sunlight. They have also demonstrated an association between body size and shape and habitation of certain regions of the world. Once scientists had connected the sickle-cell trait to natural selection because in its heterozygous form it confers resistance to a malarial environment, they sought other adaptive linkages. Physiological adaptation to cold temperatures in the form of increased vasodilation and/or vasoconstriction, additional layers of body fat, and higher metabolic rates has been shown to be adaptively significant among Eskimos, native Australians, and Norwegians. Theoretical speculations have been offered about the adaptive significance of pygmy body size in a tropical forest environment or thin, linear body forms in a hot desert environment. Through DNA mapping techniques, researchers have plotted immunological responses that correspond to the prevalence of certain disease organisms. Speculations about the adaptive advantage of variations in hair form, nose shapes, and stature have stimulated wide-ranging research on the adaptive aspects of other physical characteristics.[6]

Scientists today focus not so much on the clustering of traits that might discriminate racial populations, but on specific features and their manifestations in given ecological settings. These scholars are finding that race (and certainly the establishment of racial taxonomies) is no longer of any relevance in these studies because the incidences of traits studied transcut population boundaries and may in fact span several of the conventional races. The variations are independent of other genetic traits, but correspond to the pressures or influences of geographic, climatological, topographical, and pathological disease phenomena.

For many scholars, then, the manifestation of biophysical diversity in *Homo sapiens* is expressed most accurately in the form of clines (Brace 1964; Brues 1977; Livingstone 1969). Clines are variations in the intensity of expressions of known hereditary traits over wide geographic regions. Skin color represents a prime example of such a cline since its gradations are continuous and can be plotted on a map showing its correspondence to latitude and temperature variations. Human skin color variability reflects the adaptive responses of a relatively hairless primate to the forces of natural selection; or, to put it in another way favored by scholars, it is the product of the interaction of a complex multiple gene system with differing environments or ecological settings.

The proponents of evolutionary explanations whose theories tend to be directional and adaptive have detractors among some recent scholars who propose an alternative theory. For them, much, if not most, of human biophysical variation is not so much a product of natural selection as of random mutations, accidents, and other stochastic processes not necessarily related to adaptation. They use simulated models and computer techniques to demonstrate their non-Darwinian theories. These proposed nonadaptive evolutionary processes, which include genetic drift, sexual selection, and gene flow with migration, are thought to explain much minor variability in fairly delimited populations.

It is significant that the research of both groups can and does proceed without reference to the term race. "Breeding unit" or some similar concept is used to describe populations in which certain limited variations with respect to specific traits are found, as for example, hereditary baldness. Other traits, examined independently of social or political boundaries, can be studied in situational contexts. Race classifications neither explain nor describe the nature or significance of this variability.

Even while biologists, anthropologists, and geneticists were trying to reconceptualize human variability, avoiding the use of the term race, the ideological components of the folk worldview remained essential to the social system. Beginning in 1969 with a publication in the *Harvard Educational Review* by Arthur Jensen, some recent scholars, deeply steeped in the folk race tradition, have reinvigorated the arguments for race inferiority. Jensen, William Shockley, Hans Eysenck, and others garnered enormous public attention with their arguments for innate intellectual differences between blacks and whites. Although often met with opposition or skepticism, they toured the universities, fed their ideas frequently to the media, published many books and articles, and gave numerous talks proselytizing their beliefs. The extent of their influence has not been fully studied, but it is no accident that their publications appeared in the wake of the civil rights movement and the revolutions of the 1960s.

Monogeny Reconsidered: The Nonproblem of Race Mixture

There has been another transformation in scientific attitudes toward race that appears even more profound and subtle and has proceeded in tandem with these developments. In an article in *Science* magazine in 1973, William Provine revealed a change in attitude among British and American scientists on the subject of race mixture. Tracing briefly some of the attitudes about interracial mating that we have already explored, Provine noted that, early in this century, such geneticists as Charles B. Davenport and Edward M. East, continuing the polygenist views of the late nineteenth century, argued against race crossing. These men felt that mixture between two very different races, such as blacks and whites, produced disharmonies in hybrids of "physical, mental and temperamental qualities," and diminished the qualities of the superior race. Two other experts, Paul Popenoe and Roswell Johnson, who wrote a widely used textbook on eugenics, "suggested that racial antipathy was a biological mechanism to protect races from miscegenation" (Provine 1973, 791). Provine observed that "published opposition from geneticists and other biologists to these arguments on race crossing was nonexistent before 1924" (792).

In the mid-1930s, Provine continued, the attitude of geneticists changed from condemnation of race mixture to a position of agnosticism, indifference, or neutrality. Yet another shift in thinking occurred during World War II. Scholarly literature following this period almost unanimously expressed the view that race mixture was harmless or possibly even beneficial to the species. This reversal in attitude, Provine notes, was accompanied by little new scientific data. He feels that the change was due to the revulsion that scientists and other educated people had to Nazi race theories and their consequences. With this transformation, the species-level (or polygenist) sense of differences seems to have been eliminated from the concept of race in science. Logically, it should also challenge the ideological component of exclusiveness in the folk race idea.

Provine ends this article with the following candid observation:

> It is necessary and natural that changing social attitudes will influence areas of biology where little is known and the conclusions are possibly socially explosive. The real danger is not that biology changes with society, but that the public expects biology to provide the objective truth apart from social influences. Geneticists and the public should realize that the science of genetics is often closely intertwined with social attitudes and political considerations (1973, 796).

Summary and Conclusions

Historical evidence shows that race as it originated and evolved in the American experience was not a mere objective sorting of human physical diversity into convenient categories, nor was it a scientific term invented and defined by scholars. Race was a folk concept that was elevated to the ranks of scholarly discourse when scientists began developing rationalizations and justifications for existing social realities. I have argued that, from the beginning, race reflected a set of attitudes toward human differences generated out of the special circumstances of the rise of some European states to world commercial and political dominance. These attitudes encompassed judgments about the human worth of different groups involved in unequal power relationships. It was only accidental, perhaps incidental, that the conquered and enslaved peoples were physically distinct, for this permitted social status to be linked with biophysical differences. At bottom, race was a social mechanism for concretizing and rigidifying a universal ranking system that gave Europeans what they thought was to be perpetual dominance over the indigenous peoples of the New World, Africa, and Asia.[7]

In trying to ferret out the origins of this attitude toward, or way of thinking about, human differences, I have had to refer back to English society before the founding of the American colonies. It was pointed out that the English and other northern Europeans had been historically isolated from the areas of extensive contact between heterogeneous groups and the social and technological developments that had centered on the Mediterranean. Here populations of great diversity in physical features and in cultures had interacted and developed a familiarity with one another that was not shared with northerners. With little knowledge or experience of human heterogeneity before coming to the New World, the only precedents that the English had when they became technologically able to traverse the globe were those provided by extreme chauvinism and hostility with neighboring groups, especially with the Irish.

Out of a prolonged and anguishing conflict with the Irish, the English developed the consummately negative image of a people as savages and thus unsuited for and incapable of behavior that the English saw as civilized. The first tentative expressions of Irish inferiority gave an early warning of the potential in English culture and worldviews for dehumanizing "the other." This phenomenon of extreme ethnic chauvinism was certainly not unique in human history, but the ultimate outcome of this trajectory of development represented an unprecedented reality.

A related material factor influencing perceptions and behavior of the English at the time of New World exploration and settlement was their extreme obsession with property, particularly as a measure of human worth and a symbol of personal identity. This was at the root of the expressed need of young Englishmen to explore and exploit new territory for the production and private accumulation of wealth. From the Spanish they learned of the use of forced (slave) labor, particularly on large plantation estates, and they subsequently set out to emulate what they thought was a profitable economic pattern.

Attempts to establish slave plantations in Ireland and in the New World with native labor were failures. Certain circumstances made it necessary for the English to develop their enterprises exclusively with a population, the Africans, that was visibly different from any of the others in the New World, and one that had to be imported. The institution that the English created was unlike the systems of Old World slavery that the Spanish and Portuguese had inherited. In time, the English constructed a system of slavery whose most exceptional feature was that it legally gave priority in all matters to the property rights of slave-owners, while simultaneously demoting the Africans and their descendants to subhuman status.

But there was present in American culture another reality, one of powerful import, that also devolved from English social norms, but one that collided with the philosophy of enslavement and oppression for gain. This was that vibrant humanitarian force, rooted in Judeo-Christian morality and propelled to the sociopolitical forefront by many Enlightenment thinkers and their philosophical descendants. It was a force that insisted that individual human rights, liberty, justice, and equality (quite apart from property rights) were proper English values; it promoted the worth of all human beings in the sight of God, the brotherhood of man, and concern about the oppression of the poor. It was a force that ultimately helped to doom slavery in the United States and the Caribbean.

Countering this force were those interests that held to a hierarchical view of human groups, forces that derived advantages from an ideology that justified human oppression and exploitation. Representatives of these interests turned to the growing authority of science to provide a seemingly unassailable justification for the prevailing system. In the nineteenth century, scientists, who generally reflected the class interests of people of property, responded sympathetically, affirming the reality of the folk idea of race, and thus the existence of inferior beings. We should understand the significance. In the wider context of flourishing Christianity, with its doctrines on human goodness, and of broadened sensitivities to the values of human liberty, equality, justice, and opportunity, the creation of the idea of race was an instrument that provided for a guilt-free structuring of economic, political, and social inequality.

Scientists substantiated and strengthened the ideology of race, reifying it as part of a natural ordering system. It was an ordering system that reflected the reality, and the rigidity, of the hierarchy that conquest and the institutionalization of chattel slavery had helped to create. Race assumed an identity and autonomy of its own, exceeding slavery in its hegemonic grip of the social system, so that it survived even the termination of slavery. Race bore its own ranking and inequality of status, its own prescriptions for behavior.

Nevertheless, the roots of democratic and humanitarian ideals run deep in Western culture, despite the duplicity and hypocrisy that often mar them. Even as they used violence throughout the nineteenth and early twentieth centuries to keep "inferior races" in their socially decreed places, Americans perpetuated the myth of a classless society and a social dream about true democracy. They were committed to the ideals of justice, equality, and the preservation of the inalienable human rights of all people as no other society has ever been before. It was an adventure and an undertaking from which there was no turning back, for the imagery of such a perfect society provided its own momentum. White Americans soon realized that these ideals could not be restricted forever only to males of European background. The rhetoric of the Declaration of Independence and the Bill of Rights would return incessantly to haunt them.

A critical point came when some Europeans, in part under American influence, extended the ideology of race to other Europeans, attempting to reduce them to subhuman status. The subsequent ruthless and brutal debasement of millions of people in Europe during World War II and a policy of deliberate extermination of Jews and others under the guise of their racial inferiority revealed to many thinking Europeans and Americans the intolerable extremes to which the ideology of race and racial differences could lead human beings. An expanded consciousness accompanied this conflict as men and women learned that Nazi racial ideas were wrong and dangerous and evil.

Two powerful and contradictory forces have thus characterized the evolution of the race idea in North America—one intolerant, chauvinistic, rigid, given to religious dogmatism, and simultaneously associating the rightness and pursuit of property and wealth as God-ordained. The people who represented this facet of American culture were those who from the beginning identified the inferior savage and met him with violence and oppression. Their philosophical descendants in the twentieth century still use violence as a way of relating to the world, while often still carrying in one hand the Bible, with its endearing stories about a God of love.

Another powerful force, guided by a more fine-tuned consciousness and a more sophisticated understanding of world realities, and itself born out of Judeo-Christian ideals, has consistently formed a countering agent in the American and Western experience. It holds tantalizingly before us the image and hope of a more perfect society characterized by the realization of equality and full human rights for all. It shames us in our self-serving quests for personal aggrandizement at the price of human suffering. And it provides us with the moral weapons that can be used to combat the truculently violent and repressive urges that diminish our humanity.

In the twentieth century these humanitarian themes have been buttressed by the expanding knowledge and consciousness of advanced science. It is indeed ironic that the very scientific establishment that was so instrumental in the rationalization and perpetuation of the idea of race seems to be presiding over its eventual decline and demise as a biological concept.

*   *   *

It is too early to tell whether developments in the treatment of human biophysical variation in physical anthropology textbooks represent any real or sustainable transformation in scientific views and understandings of human differences. What we should understand, however, is that the sociocultural context in which the folk idea of race emerged has changed drastically. There are newer social, economic, ideological, and political factors, arising in the midtwentieth century, that have begun to influence the ways by which we view human differences.

The breakup of the older colonial empires and the creation of new nation-states in Asia, Africa, and South America, responding to the propaganda of freedom, have changed the contours of international relations. Though there remains a debilitating economic dependency between the West and the Third World, the political impact, especially in the United Nations, of non-European peoples has been considerable in an age of increased travel and immigration. Businesspeople and educators, politicians and diplomats, students and tourists from these once colonized worlds have become a part of the reality that we view frequently through television and other news media or experience directly in the major cities.

The civil rights movement of the 1960s and political pressure from African-Americans and their supporters brought into sharp relief the differences between American democratic ideology and the values and practices that so strongly contradict it. For the first time, many Americans confronted openly the contradictions—the moral duplicity and hypocrisy—to which we had been conditioned. This has led to the opening of many sectors of American society slowly but perceptibly and the integration of some African-Americans into the middle-class mainstream. The breakdown of public barriers and the eradication of laws that called for or buttressed public segregation have had an impact on the perception of differences. The appearance of African-Americans in film and frequently on television to the degree that their portrayals depart from customary stereotypes, has had an unmonitored and therefore unknown effect on the broader public mind. We should not underestimate the power of the popular media, films, literature, and especially television to influence both our values and our behavior.

Americans and Europeans are becoming increasingly familiar with people of color whom they have long considered inferior. This includes especially the rise of the Japanese to full and equal competitiveness in the industrial world during the latter part of the twentieth century. It also includes the numerous Asian and African populations, and the many peoples of Latin America, Central America, and the Caribbean who reflect in their ancestry a mixture of Indian, African, and European elements. They do not fit easily within our conventional racial categories. Moreover, military personnel from many nations have been relocated around the world and in the process have contributed to the genetic variability in numerous populations. Increasing mixtures of peoples have created a state of uncertainty about the "racial" identities of large numbers of individuals.

American receptivity to Asian immigrants, despite some community conflicts, has generally been without much rancor. The emergence of some newly immigrant Asians to positions in which they are performing as intellectual leaders in high schools, colleges, and universities, particularly in science, mathematics, and "high technology" fields, was bound to have a disquieting effect on white Americans who have previously accepted scores on intelligence tests as documentation of the innate superiority of Caucasians. The superior academic performance of some of these Asian students provides clear evidence of the external nature of the factors—high motivation, self-discipline, perseverance, willingness to make sacrifices, respect for knowledge—that generate excellence in all academic fields. They also provide contrasts with many contemporary American students and the often self-indulgent, leisure-loving manner in which so many are socialized. Published explanations for the success of these Asian students are notably lacking in references to "superior" genetic or hereditary qualities.

The great American experiment, involving the intermingling of people in a heterogeneous society that sociologists used to call the "melting pot," is the best evidence for contradicting folk race ideology. Yet it is strange that few Americans have been conscious of the fact that people of all physical variations and cultural backgrounds have come to the United States and been transformed in the process of assimilation to that nebulous reality called American culture. Chinese, Russians, Africans, East Indians, Polynesians, South Asians, Eskimos, and peoples indigenous to the Amazon River valley have learned to walk, talk, eat, drink, and think like Americans. So many of us seem unaware of this transformation in outlook and behavior and its demonstration of the extrinsic, learned nature of cultural behavior.

Yet another potential direction of development in our interpretations of human differences has presented itself in the latter part of the twentieth century. In the 1970s we saw the rise of concern for "ethnicity" and "ethnic groups." Group values, group interests, group traditions of common ancestry (the "roots" phenomenon) may emerge as precepts of new forms of social relationships and interactions. The notion of "ethnic group" may well be wedded to hereditarian beliefs explicit in the concept of "breeding populations" and become a new formulation of race, containing all of the social connotations of conventional race status but applied to whatever new group permutations the public (and publicists) care to devise. Moreover, Herrnstein's (1973) "meritocracy" preserves the hereditarian element in his explanation of class differences.

The willingness of Americans, then, to relinquish belief in the elements subsumed in the idea of race, particularly the belief in natural inequality and group inheritance of innate behavior, will determine the degree to which race and its ideological elements can be eliminated from our worldview and our vocabulary. But relinquishing a belief system that has been so critical to our social structure and to our interpersonal relationships will not come easily.

The fundamental question is, If the concept of race loses its validity, credibility, or substantive usefulness to science, does it follow that its force and meaning will be diminished in the larger society? Baxter and Sansom (1972) insightfully observe that scientific writings about race "cannot remain merely descriptive statements but become calls to social action" (11). Increasingly, science and scientists are providing us with models not only of what the world is like in a mechanistic and material sense, but also of moral and ethical belief systems. We have already entered a stage in human cultural development in which reliance on science for providing the basis for policy alternatives as well as new ideologies-cum-myths is a reality. This expanded role of science is a product of immense technological changes that have broadened our knowledge of the universe and co-opted for many much of religious mythology and explanations. There is the possibility that someday, perhaps in the far future, it will also refashion for us our perceptions and understandings of human diversity. In this case, the disintegration of the ideological components of race may well become a reality.

Notes

1. M. T. Newman (quoted in Lieberman 1968, 131).
2. See Spuhler and Lindzey (1967). Although there has been much disagreement among the splitters on the number of races thought to exist (see for example Molnar [1975] 1983, Chapter 1, and Snyder 1962, Chapter 1), most concur on at least three major races: negroid, mongoloid, and caucasoid. Dobzhansky has

pointed out that "hardly any two independently working classifiers have proposed identical sets of races" (1973, 68). For further readings see Boyd (1950), Coon (1962), Garn (1960), Newman (1963), and Washburn (1963).

3. Quoted in Tumin (1949).

4. See, among others, Boyd (1950, Chapter 11), Brues (1977, Chapter 1), Dobzhansky (1973, Chapter 2), Dunn (1965a, Chapter 5), Loehlin, Lindzey, and Spuhler (1975, Chapter 2), and Molnar ([1975] 1983, Chapter 1).

5. For literature embracing this position, see articles by Barnicot, Brace, Hiernaux, Livingstone, and Montagu in Montagu (1969) as well as numerous other works by Montagu (e.g., [1964] 1971).

6. A good review of some of the literature on evolution and ecological adaptation is found in Little (1982).

7. For a very similar position see Banton and Harwood (1975), and Fredrickson (1988).

Bibliography

Ackerman, Bruce A. 1977. *Private Property and the Constitution*. New Haven: Yale University Press.

Alland, Alexander, Jr. 1973. *Human Diversity*. Garden City, N.Y.: Anchor Books.

Allport, Gordon W. 1972. "Stereotype Defined." In *Race and Social Difference*, edited by P. Baxter and B. Sansom. Middlesex: Penguin.

Altschuler, Glenn C. 1982. *Race, Ethnicity and Class in American Social Thought, 1869–1919*. Arlington Heights, Ill.: Harlan Davidson.

Anchor, Robert. 1967. *The Enlightenment Tradition*. Berkeley: University of California Press.

Arendt, Hannah. [1951] 1968. *Imperialism*. New York: Harcourt, Brace and World.

Armelagos, G. J., D. S. Carlson, and D. P. Van Gerven. 1982. "The Theoretical Foundations and Development of Skeletal Biology." In *A History of American Physical Anthropology, 1930–1980*, edited by F. Spencer. New York: Academic Press.

Aston, Trevor, ed. 1965. *Crisis in Europe, 1560–1660*. London: Routledge & Kegan Paul.

Bakan, David. 1966. "The Influence of Phrenology on American Psychology." *Journal of the History of the Behavioral Sciences* 2, no. 2: 200–220.

Baker, Paul T. 1967. "The Biological Race Concept as a Research Tool." *American Journal of Physical Anthropology* 27, no. 1: 21–27.

Baker, William. 1970. "William Wilberforce on the Idea of Negro Inferiority." *Journal of the History of Ideas* 30, no. 3: 433–440.

Banton, Michael. 1967. *Race Relations*. New York: Basic Books.

———. 1977. *The Idea of Race*. London: Tavistock.

———. 1983. *Racial and Ethnic Competition*. Cambridge: Cambridge University Press.

———. 1988. *Racial Consciousness*. London and New York: Longman.

Banton, M., and J. Harwood. 1975. *The Race Concept*. New York: Praeger.

Barnouw, Victor. 1971. *An Introduction to Anthropology*. Vol. 1. Homewood, Ill.: Dorsey Press.

Barrow, R. H. 1928. *Slavery in the Roman Empire.* New York: Barnes & Noble.

Bartlett, Irving H. 1967. *The American Mind in the Mid-Nineteenth Century.* New York: Thomas Y. Crowell.

Barzun, Jacques. 1965. *Race: A Study in Superstition.* New York: Harper & Row.

Baxter, P., and B. Sansom, eds. 1972. *Race and Social Difference.* Middlesex: Penguin.

Bean, Bennett B. 1926. "Types of the Three Great Races of Man." *American Journal of Anatomy* 37, no. 2: 237–270.

Bell, Derrick A., Jr., ed. 1980. *Civil Rights: Leading Cases.* Boston: Little, Brown & Co.

Benedict, Ruth. [1940] 1947. *Race: Science and Politics.* New York: Viking Press.

Bennett, K. A. 1969. "Typological vs. Evolutionary Approach in Skeletal Population Studies." *American Journal of Physical Anthropology* 30, no. 3: 407–415.

Bennett, Lerone, Jr. 1964. *Before the Mayflower: A History of the Negro in America, 1619–1964.* Chicago: Johnson.

Berger, P. L., and T. Luckman. 1966. *The Social Construction of Reality.* New York: Doubleday.

Berkhofer, Robert F., Jr. 1978. *The White Man's Indians.* New York: Alfred A. Knopf.

Berlin, B., D. Breedlove, and P. Raven. 1973. "General Principles of Classification and Nomenclature in Folk Biology." *American Anthropologist* 75, no. 1: 214–242.

Bidney, David. 1954. "The Idea of the Savage in North American Ethnohistory." *Journal of the History of Ideas* 15, no. 2: 322–327.

Birch, Herbert G. 1945. "Psychological Differences Among Races." *Science* 101, no. 2,610: 16.

Birdsell, J. B. 1963. "The Origin of the Human Races." Review. *Quarterly Review of Biology* 38, no. 2: 178–185.

——— . 1972. "The Problem of the Evolution of Human Races: Classification or Clines." *Social Biology* 19, no. 1: 136–162.

Blassingame, John W. 1979. *The Slave Community.* New York: Oxford University Press.

Blauner, Robert. 1972. *Racial Oppression in America.* New York: Harper & Row.

Bloch, Marc. 1961. *Feudal Society.* London: Routledge & Kegan Paul.

Boas, Franz. [1897] 1940a. "Review of Paul Ehrenreich's 'Anthropogische Studien Ueber die Ureinwohner Brasiliens.'" In *Race, Language and Culture.* New York: Free Press.

——— . [1899] 1940b. "Review of William Z. Ripley's 'The Races of Europe.'" In *Race, Language and Culture.* New York: Free Press.

——— . [1899] 1940c. "Some Recent Criticisms of Physical Anthropology." In *Race, Language and Culture.* New York: Free Press.

_____ . [1902] 1940d. "Statistical Study of Anthropometry." In *Race, Language and Culture*. New York: Free Press.

_____ . [1910–1913] 1940e. "Changes in Bodily Form of Descendants of Immigrants." In *Race, Language and Culture*. New York: Free Press.

_____ . [1912] 1940f. "Remarks on the Anthropological Study of Children." In *Race, Language and Culture*. New York: Free Press.

_____ . [1913] 1940g. "Influence of Heredity and Environment on Growth." In *Race, Language and Culture*. New York: Free Press.

_____ . [1915] 1940h. "Modern Populations of America." In *Race, Language and Culture*. New York: Free Press.

_____ . [1916] 1940i. "New Evidence in Regard to the Instability of Human Types." In *Race, Language and Culture*. New York: Free Press.

_____ . [1922] 1940j. Report on the Anthropometric Investigation of the Population of the United States." In *Race, Language and Culture*. New York: Free Press.

_____ . [1923] 1940k. "Review of Roland B. Dixon's 'The Racial History of Man.'" In *Race, Language and Culture*. New York: Free Press.

_____ . [1931] 1940l. "Race and Progress." In *Race, Language and Culture*. New York: Free Press.

_____ . [1932] 1940m. "Race and Character." In *Race, Language and Culture*. New York: Free Press.

Bober, M. M. [1927] 1965. *Karl Marx's Interpretation of History*. Reprint. New York: W. W. Norton.

Bodmer, W. F., and L. L. Cavalli-Sforza. 1976. *Genetics, Evolution and Man*. San Francisco: W. H. Freeman.

Bohannan, P. 1963. *Social Anthropology*. New York: Holt, Rinehart & Winston.

Bolk, L. 1929. "Origins of Racial Characteristics in Man." *American Journal of Physical Anthropology* 13, no. 1: 1–28.

Bolt, Christine. 1971. *Victorian Attitudes to Races*. London: Routledge & Kegan Paul.

Borden, Phillip. 1970. "Found Cumbering the Soil." In *The Great Fear: Race in the Mind of America*, edited by G. B. Nash and R. Weiss. New York: Holt, Rinehart & Winston.

Boskin, Joseph. 1972. "Race Relations in Seventeenth-Century America: The Problem of the Origin of Negro Slavery." In *The Origins of American Slavery and Racism*, edited by Donald L. Noel. Columbus, Ohio: Charles E. Merrill.

Bowser, Frederick P. 1974. *The African Slave in Colonial Peru, 1524–1650*. Stanford: Stanford University Press.

_____ . 1975. "The Free Person of Color in Mexico City and Lima: Manumission and Opportunity, 1580–1650." In *Race and Slavery in the Western Hemisphere*, edited by S. L. Engerman and E. D. Genovese. Princeton: Princeton University Press.

Boyd, W. C. 1950. *Genetics and the Races of Man*. Boston: D. C. Heath & Co.

_____ . 1971. "Four Achievements of the Genetic Model in Physical Anthropology." In *Human Populations: Genetic Variation and Evolution*, edited by L. N. Morris. San Francisco: Chandler.

Brace, C. L. 1964. "On the Race Concept." *Current Anthropology* 5, no. 4: 313–314.

——— . 1982. "The Roots of the Race Concept in American Physical Anthropology." In *A History of American Physical Anthropology, 1930–1980*, edited by F. Spencer. New York: Academic Press.

Bradley, K. R. 1984. *Slaves and Masters in the Roman Empire.* Brussels: Latomus Revue D'Etudes Latines.

Brodie, Fawn. 1974. *Thomas Jefferson: An Intimate History.* New York: Bantam.

Brown, Leon C. 1968. "Color in Northern Africa." In *Race and Color*, edited by J. H. Franklin. Boston: Houghton Mifflin Co.

Brues, Alice M. 1959. "The Spearman and the Archer." *American Anthropologist* 61, no. 3: 457–469.

——— . 1972. "Models of Race and Cline." *American Journal of Physical Anthropology* 37, no. 3: 389–400.

——— . 1977. *People and Races.* New York: Macmillan.

Buckland, W. W. 1908. *The Roman Law of Slavery.* Cambridge: Cambridge University Press.

Buettner-Janusch, J. 1973. *Physical Anthropology: A Perspective.* New York: J. Wiley.

Burke, John G. 1972. "The Wild Man's Pedigree: Scientific Method and Racial Anthropology." In *The Wild Man Within*, edited by E. Dudley and M. Novak. Pittsburgh: University of Pittsburgh Press.

Burns, H. 1971. "Racism and American Law," In *Amistad.* Vol. 2, edited by C. Harris. New York: Random House.

Campbell, Leon. 1973. "Racism Without Race." In *Racism in the Eighteenth Century*, edited by E. Pagliaro. Cleveland, Ohio: Case Western University Press.

Campbell, Mavis. 1974. "Aristotle and Black Slavery: A Study in Race Prejudice." *Race* 15, no. 3: 283–301.

Canny, Nicholas P. 1973. "The Ideology of English Colonialization: From Ireland to America." *William and Mary Quarterly*, 3d Ser. 30: 575–598.

Castro, Americo. 1971. *The Spaniards.* Berkeley: University of California Press.

Cavalli-Sforza, L. L., and W. F. Bodmer. 1971. *The Genetics of Human Populations.* San Francisco: W. H. Freeman.

Cell, John W. 1982. *The Height of White Supremacy.* Cambridge: Cambridge University Press.

Chase, Allen. 1980. *The Legacy of Malthus.* Urbana: University of Illinois Press.

Clagett, M., ed. 1962. *Critical Problems in the History of Science.* Madison: University of Wisconsin Press.

Cohen, William. 1969. "Thomas Jefferson and the Problem of Slavery." *Journal of American History* 56, no. 3: 503–526.

Cohen, Yehudi, ed. 1974. *Man in Adaptation.* Chicago: Aldine.

Conrad, Earl. 1969. *The Invention of the Negro.* New York: Paul S. Erikson.

Coon, Carlton S. 1962. *The Origin of Races.* New York: Alfred A. Knopf.

Costa, Emilia V. da. 1977. "Slave Images and Realities." *Annals, New York Academy of Sciences* 292: 293–310.

Count, E. W. 1946. "The Evolution of the Race Idea in Modern Western Culture During the Pre-Darwinian Nineteenth Century." *Transactions of the New York Academy of Sciences:* 139–165. New York: New York Academy of Sciences.

———. ed. 1950. *This is Race.* New York: Henry Schuman.

Covarrubias Horozco, Sebastian. [1611] 1943. *Tesoro de la Lengua Castellana O Espanola.* Barcelona: S. A. Horta.

Cox, Oliver C. [1948] 1959. *Caste, Class, and Race.* Reprint. New York: Monthly Review Press.

Cuffel, Victoria. 1966. "The Classical Greek Concept of Slavery." *Journal of the History of Ideas* 27, no. 3: 323–342.

Curtin, P. D. 1964. *The Image of Africa: British Ideas and Action, 1780–1850.* Madison: University of Wisconsin Press.

———. 1977. "Slavery and Empire." *Annals, New York Academy of Sciences* 292: 3–11.

Curtis, L. P., Jr. 1968. *Anglo-Saxons and Celts.* New York: New York University Press.

———. 1972. "Anglo-Saxonism and the Irish." In *Race and Social Difference,* edited by P. Baxter and B. Sansom. Middlesex: Penguin.

Dalton, George., ed. 1967. *Tribal and Peasant Economies.* Garden City, N.Y.: Natural History Press.

Daniels, Roger. 1975. *The Decision to Relocate the Japanese Americans.* Philadelphia: J. B. Lippincott.

———. [1962] 1977. *The Politics of Prejudice.* Reprint. Berkeley: University of California Press.

Darnell, Regna, ed. 1974. *Readings in the History of Anthropology.* New York: Harper & Row.

Davenport, C. B. 1929. "Do Races Differ in Mental Capacity?" *Human Biology* 1, no. 1: 70–89.

Davis, Allison. 1935. "The Distribution of the Blood Groups and Its Bearing on the Concept of Race." Parts 1 and 2. *Sociological Review* 27, no. 1: 19–34, no. 2: 182–200.

Davis, David Brion. 1966. *The Problem of Slavery in Western Culture.* Middlesex: Penguin.

———. 1969. "A Comparison of British American and Latin American Slavery." In *Slavery in the New World,* edited by L. Foner and E. Genovese. Englewood Cliffs, N.J.: Prentice-Hall.

———. 1975. *The Problem of Slavery in the Age of Revolution.* Ithaca, N.Y.: Cornell University Press.

———. 1984. *Slavery and Human Progress.* New York: Oxford University Press.

Degler, Carl N. 1959–1960. "Slavery and the Genesis of American Race Prejudice." *Comparative Studies in Society and History* 2, no. 1: 49–66.

——— . 1970. "Slavery in Brazil and the United States: An Essay in Comparative History." *American Historical Review* 75, no. 4: 1,004–1,028.

——— . 1971. *Neither Black Nor White.* New York: Macmillan.

Deniker, Joseph. 1900. *The Races of Man.* London: Walter Scott.

Dickason, Olive P. 1979. "Europeans and Amerindians: Some Comparative Aspects of Early Contact." *Papers of the Canadian Historical Association.* Ottawa: The Association.

Dietz, F. C. 1932. *A Political and Social History of England.* New York: Macmillan.

Diop, Cheikh Anta. 1981. "Origins of the Ancient Egyptians." In *Ancient Civilizations of Africa.* Vol. 2 of UNESCO General History of Africa, edited by G. Mokhtar. Boston: Heinemann Educational Books.

Dobzhansky, T. 1944. "On Species and Races of Living and Fossil Man." *American Journal of Physical Anthropology,* New Series 2, no. 3: 251–265.

——— . 1950. "The Genetic Nature of Differences Among Men." In *Evolutionary Thought in America,* edited by S. Persons. New Haven: Yale University Press.

——— . 1967. *Mankind Evolving.* New Haven: Yale University Press.

——— . 1973. *Genetic Diversity and Human Equality.* New York: Basic Books.

Dover, Cedric. 1951. Letter to the editor, *MAN,* no. 95, April.

Drake, St. Clair. 1987. *Black Folk Here and There.* Vol. 1. Los Angeles: Center for Afro-American Studies, University of California.

Drescher, S. 1986. *Capitalism and Antislavery.* New York: Oxford University Press.

——— . 1989. "Manumission in a Society Without Slave Law." *Slavery and Abolition* 10, no. 3: 85–101.

DuBois, W.E.B. [1935] 1985. *Black Reconstruction in America.* Reprint. New York: Atheneum.

——— . 1965. *The World and Africa.* Rev. ed. New York: International Publishers.

Dudley, E., and M. Novak, eds. 1972. *The Wild Man Within.* Pittsburgh: University of Pittsburgh Press.

Dumond, Dwight L. [1961] 1966. *Antislavery.* Reprint. New York: W. W. Norton.

Dunn, L. C. 1958. *Race and Biology.* Paris: UNESCO.

——— . 1965a. *Heredity and Evolution in Human Populations.* New York: Atheneum.

——— . 1965b. *A Short History of Genetics.* New York: McGraw- Hill.

Dyson-Hudson, R., and N. Dyson-Hudson. 1980. "Nomadic Pastoralism." *Annual Review of Anthropology,* vol. 9. Palo Alto, Calif.: Annual Reviews.

Edmonson, Munro S. 1965. "Measurement of Relative Racial Difference." *Current Anthropology* 6, no. 2: 167–198.

Elkins, Stanley M. [1959] 1963. *Slavery.* New York: Grosset & Dunlap.

Ellis, R., and A. Wildavsky. 1990. "A Cultural Analysis of the Role of Abolitionists in the Coming of the Civil War." *Comparative Studies in Society and History* 32, no. 1: 89–116.

Engerman, S. L., and E. D. Genovese, eds. 1975. *Race and Slavery in the Western Hemisphere: Quantitative Studies.* Princeton: Princeton University Press.

Evans, W. Mc. 1980. "From the Land of Canaan to the Land of Guinea: The Strange Odyssey of the Sons of Ham." *The American Historical Review* 85, no. 1: 15–43.

Faust, Drew G., ed. 1981. *The Ideology of Slavery.* Baton Rouge: Louisiana State University Press.

Fields, Barbara. 1982. "Ideology and Race in American History." In *Region, Race and Reconstruction,* edited by J. M. Kousser and J. M. McPherson. New York: Oxford University Press.

Fincher, Jack. 1976. *Human Intelligence.* New York: G. P. Putnam.

Finley, Moses I. 1968a. "Slavery." *Encyclopedia of the Social Sciences.* New York: Macmillan and Free Press.

_____ , ed. [1960] 1968b. *Slavery in Classical Antiquity.* Reprint. Cambridge: W. Hepper and Sons.

_____ . 1980. *Ancient Slavery and Modern Ideology.* New York: Viking Press.

Fleure, H. J. 1936. "Racial Theory and Genetic Ideas." *Nature* 138: 1,042.

Foner, L., and E. D. Genovese, eds. 1969. *Slavery in the New World.* Englewood Cliffs, N.J.: Prentice-Hall.

Fontaine, Pierre-Michel, ed. 1985. *Race, Class and Power in Brazil.* Los Angeles: Center for Afro-American Studies, UCLA.

Fowler, H. W. [1926] 1962. *A Dictionary of Modern English Usage.* 3d ed. Oxford: Clarendon Press.

Fox-Genovese, Elizabeth. 1988. *Within the Plantation Household: Black and White Women of the Old South.* Chapel Hill: University of North Carolina Press.

Franklin, John H. 1969. "History of Racial Segregation in the United States." In *The Making of Black America,* edited by A. Meier and E. Rudwick. New York: Atheneum.

_____ ., ed. 1968. *Color and Race.* Boston: Houghton Mifflin.

Franklin, J. H., and A. A. Moss, Jr. 1988. *From Slavery to Freedom.* 6th ed. New York: Alfred A. Knopf.

Fredrickson, George M. 1971. "Toward a Social Interpretation of the Development of American Racism." In *Key Issues in the Afro-American Experience,* Vol. 1, edited by N. I. Huggins, M. Kilson, and D. M. Fox. New York: Harcourt Brace Jovanovich.

_____ . 1977. "White Images of Black Slaves in the Southern United States." *Annals of the New York Academy of Sciences* 292: 368–375.

_____ . 1981. *White Supremacy.* New York: Oxford University Press.

_____ . [1971] 1987. *The Black Image in the White Mind.* Middletown, Conn.: Wesleyan University Press.

_____ . 1988. *The Arrogance of Race.* Middletown, Conn.: Wesleyan University Press.

Gabriel, J., and G. Ben-Tovim. 1978. "Marxism and the Concept of Racism." *Economy and Society* 7, no. 2: 118–154.

Garn, Stanley N. 1957. "Race and Evolution." *American Anthropologist* 59, no. 2: 218–224.

―――, ed. 1960. *Readings on Race.* Springfield, Ill.: Charles C. Thomas.

―――. 1965. *Human Races.* 2d ed. Springfield, Ill.: Charles C. Thomas.

Garn, S. M., and C. S. Coon. 1955. "On the Number of Races of Mankind." *American Anthropologist* 57, no. 4: 996–1,001.

Garrett, H. E. 1945a. "Facts and Interpretations Regarding Race Differences." *Science* 101, no. 2,610: 173–174.

―――. 1945b. "Psychological Differences Among Races." *Science* 101, no. 2,610: 16–17.

―――. 1973. *IQ and Racial Differences.* Cape Canaveral, Fla.: Howard Allen.

Gates, R. Ruggles. 1939. "Blood Groupings and Racial Classification." *American Journal of Physical Anthropology* 24, no. 3: 385–390.

Genovese, Eugene. 1967. *The Political Economy of Slavery.* New York: Random House.

―――. 1969. "Materialism and Idealism in the History of Negro Slavery in the Americas." In *Slavery in the New World,* edited by L. Foner and E. D. Genovese. Englewood Cliffs, N.J.: Prentice- Hall.

―――. 1976. *Roll, Jordan, Roll: The World the Slaves Made.* New York: Vintage Books.

Genovese, E., and E. Fox-Genovese. 1983. *Fruits of Merchant Capital.* New York: Oxford University Press.

George, Katherine. 1958. "The Civilized West Looks at Primitive Africa: 1440–1800, A Study in Ethnocentrism." *Isis* 49: 62–72.

Gergen, Kenneth. 1968. "The Significance of Skin Color in Human Relations." In *Race and Color,* edited by J. H. Franklin. Boston: Houghton Mifflin Co.

Geschwender, James A. 1978. *Racial Stratification in America.* Dubuque, Ia.: William C. Brown Co.

―――. 1987. "Race, Ethnicity and Class." In *Recapturing Marxism,* edited by R. F. Levine and J. Lembcke. New York: Praeger.

Glasco, Lawrence. N.d. "The Mulatto: A Neglected Dimension of Afro-American Social Structure." Unpublished manuscript.

Glass, Bentley. 1953. "The Dynamics of Racial Intermixture: An Analysis Based on the American Negro." *American Journal of Human Genetics* 5, no. 1: 1–20.

Gluckman, Max. 1965. *Politics, Law and Ritual in Tribal Society.* Chicago: Aldine.

Godilier, M. 1977. *Perspectives in Marxist Anthropology.* Cambridge: Cambridge University Press.

Goldsby, R. A. 1971. *Race and Races.* New York: Macmillan.

Goldschmidt, W. 1965. "Theory and Strategy in the Study of Cultural Adaptability." *American Anthropologist* 67, no. 2: 402–434.

Gossett, Thomas F. 1965. *Race: The History of an Idea in America.* New York: Schocken.

Gould, Steven Jay. 1977. *Ever Since Darwin.* New York: W. W. Norton.

―――. 1981. *The Mismeasure of Man.* New York: W. W. Norton.

_____ . 1983. "Bound by the Great Chain." *Natural History* 92, no. 11: 20–24.

Graham, Richard, ed. 1990. *The Idea of Race in Latin America, 1870–1940.* Austin: University of Texas Press.

Greene, John C. 1954a. "Some Early Speculations on the Origin of Human Races." *American Anthropologist* 56, no. 1: 31–41.

_____ . 1954b. "The American Debate on the Negro's Place in Nature, 1780–1815." *Journal of the History of Ideas* 15, no. 3: 384–396.

_____ . 1959. *The Death of Adam: Evolution and Its Impact on Western Thought.* Ames, Ia.: Iowa State University Press.

_____ . 1981. *Science, Ideology, and World View.* Berkeley: University of California Press.

_____ . 1984. *American Science in the Age of Jefferson.* Ames, Ia.: Iowa State University Press.

Grove, Ella F. 1926. "On the Value of the Blood-Group Feature as a Means of Determining Racial Relationships." *Journal of Immunology* 12: 251–261.

Guthrie, R. V. 1976. *Even the Rat Was White.* New York: Harper & Row.

Gutman, H. G. 1976. *The Black Family in Slavery and Freedom, 1750–1925.* New York: Vintage Books.

Haas, Jere. 1982. "The Development of Research Strategies for Studies of Biological Variation in Living Human Populations." In *A History of American Physical Anthropology, 1930–1980,* edited by F. Spencer. New York: Academic Press.

Haddon, Alfred D. [1934] 1959. *History of Anthropology.* Reprint. London: Watts and Co.

Haller, John S., Jr. 1970. "Civil War Anthropometry: The Making of a Racial Ideology." *Civil War History* 16: 309–325.

_____ . 1971. *Outcasts from Evolution: Scientific Attitudes of Racial Inferiority, 1859–1900.* Urbana: University of Illinois Press.

Haller, Mark H. 1963. *Eugenics: Hereditarian Attitudes in American Thought.* New Brunswick, N.J.: Rutgers University Press.

Hallowell, A. I. 1960. "The Beginnings of Anthropology in America." In *Selected Papers from the American Anthropologist, 1888–1920,* edited by F. de Laguna. Evanston, Ill.: Row Peterson Co.

Hammond, D., and A. Jablow. 1970. *The Africa That Never Was.* New York: Twayne Publishers.

Handlin, Mary, and Oscar Handlin. 1972. "The Origins of Negro Slavery." In *The Origins of American Slavery and Racism,* edited by D. Noel. Columbus, Ohio: Charles E. Merrill Co.

Handlin, Oscar. [1948] 1957. *Race and Nationality in American Life.* Reprint. Boston: Little, Brown.

Harris, Marvin. 1964. *Patterns of Race in the Americas.* New York: W. W. Norton.

_____ . 1968. *The Rise of Anthropological Theory.* New York: Thomas Y. Crowell.

_____ . 1970. "Referential Ambiguity in the Calculus of Brazilian Racial Identity." *Southwestern Journal of Anthropology* 26, no. 1: 1–14.

Harris, M. 1983. *Cultural Anthropology.* New York: Harper & Row.

Havens, George. 1955. *The Age of Ideas.* New York: Free Press.

Heine-Geldern, R. 1964. "One Hundred Years of Ethnological Theory in the German-Speaking Countries." *Current Anthropology* 5, no. 5: 407–416.

Herrnstein, R. 1973. *IQ in the Meritocracy.* Boston: Little, Brown & Co.

Herskovits, M. J. 1958. *The Myth of the Negro Past.* Boston: Beacon Press.

Hiernaux, J. [1964] 1969. "The Concept of Race and the Taxonomy of Mankind." In *The Concept of Race,* edited by A. Montagu. Reprint. London/New York: Collier-Macmillan.

Hitti, Phillip. 1953. *History of the Arabs.* London: Macmillan.

Hodgen, Margaret. 1964. *Early Anthropology in the Sixteenth and Seventeenth Centuries.* Philadelphia: University of Pennsylvania Press.

Hooton, Earnest A. 1926. "Methods of Racial Analysis." *Science* 63, no. 1,621: 76–81.

―――. 1936. "Plain Statements About Race." *Science* 83, no. 2,161: 511–512.

Hoover, Dwight. 1976. *The Red and the Black.* Chicago: Rand McNally.

Hopkins, Keith. 1978. *Conquerors and Slaves: Sociological Studies in Roman History.* Vol. 1. Cambridge: Cambridge University Press.

Horsman, Reginald. 1976. "Origins of Racial Anglo-Saxonism in Great Britain Before 1850." *Journal of the History of Ideas* 37, no. 3: 239–262.

―――. 1981. *Race and Manifest Destiny.* Cambridge: Harvard University Press.

Howells, W. W. 1942. "Fossil Man and the Origin of Races." *American Anthropologist* 44, no. 2: 182–183.

Huggins, N., M. Kilson, and D. M. Fox, eds. 1971. *Key Issues in the Afro-American Experience.* New York: Harcourt Brace Jovanovich.

Hulse, F. S. 1962. "Race as an Evolutionary Episode." *American Anthropologist* 64, no. 4: 929–945.

―――. 1971. *The Human Species.* New York: Random House.

Hunt, E. E. 1959. "Anthropometry, Genetics and Racial History." *American Anthropologist* 61, no. 1: 64–87.

Hunwick, John O. 1978. "Black Africans in the Islamic World." Extract of *Tarikh* 5: 20–40.

Husband, Charles, ed. 1982. *"Race" in Britain: Continuity and Change.* London: Hutchinson & Co.

Huxley, Julian, and A. C. Haddon. 1936. *We Europeans.* New York/London: Harper.

Jefferson, Thomas. [1787] 1955. *Notes on the State of Virginia,* edited by W. Peden. Chapel Hill: University of North Carolina Press.

Jensen, Arthur. 1969. "How Much Can We Boost IQ and Scholastic Achievement?" *Harvard Educational Review* 39, no. 1: 1–123.

Johnston, F. E. 1964. "Racial Taxonomies from an Evolutionary Perspective." *American Anthropologist* 66, no. 4: 822–827.

Jones, Howard M. 1942. "Origins of the Colonial Idea in England," *American Philosophical Society* 85, no. 5: 448–465.

―――. 1964. *O Strange New World.* New York: Viking Press.

Jordan, Winthrop D. 1968. *White over Black: American Attitudes Toward the Negro, 1550–1812.* Baltimore: Penguin.

―――. 1977. "Planter and Slave Identity Formation: Some Problems in the Comparative Approach." *Annals of the New York Academy of Sciences* 292: 35–40.

Kagan, Jerome. 1982. "IQ: Fair Science for Dark Deeds." *Radcliffe Quarterly.* 3–5.

Keesing, R. M., and F. M. Keesing. 1971. *New Perspectives in Cultural Anthropology.* New York: Holt, Rinehart & Winston.

Kincaid, L. 1970. "Two Steps Forward, One Step Back: Racial Attitudes During the Civil War and Reconstruction." In *The Great Fear,* edited by G. Nash and R. Weiss. New York: Holt, Rinehart & Winston.

King, James C. 1981. *The Biology of Race.* Rev. ed. Berkeley: University of California Press.

Klass, M., and H. Helman. 1971. *The Kinds of Mankind.* Philadelphia: J. B. Lippincott.

Klein, Herbert. 1971. "Anglicanism, Catholicism and the Negro Slave." In *The Debate over Slavery,* edited by A. J. Lane. Chicago: University of Chicago Press.

Knight, F. W. 1970. *Slave Society in Cuba During the Nineteenth Century.* Madison: University of Wisconsin Press.

Knollenberg, B. 1965. *Origin of the American Revolution: 1759–1766.* Rev. ed. New York: Free Press.

Kolchin, Peter. 1982. "Comparing American History," pp. 64–81. *Reviews in American History.* Baltimore: Johns Hopkins University Press.

Kovel, Joel. 1970. *White Racism: A Psychohistory.* New York: Pantheon.

Kuhn, Thomas. 1962. *The Structure of Scientific Revolutions.* Chicago: University of Chicago Press.

Kupperman, Karen O. 1984. *Roanoke: The Abandoned Colony.* Totowa, N. J.: Rowman and Allanheld.

Lane, Ann J., ed. 1971. *The Debate over Slavery: Stanley Elkins and His Critics.* Chicago: University of Chicago Press.

Lasker, G. W. 1973. *Physical Anthropology.* New York: Holt, Rinehart & Winston.

Lauber, Almon W. [1913] 1970. *Indian Slavery in Colonial Times Within the Present Limits of the United States.* Reprint. Williamstown, Mass.: Corner House Publishers.

Lewis, Bernard. 1971. *Race and Color in Islam.* New York: Harper & Row.

―――. 1990. *Race and Slavery in the Middle East.* New York: Oxford University Press.

Lewontin, Richard C. 1970. "Race and Intelligence." *Bulletin of the Atomic Scientists* 5, no. 1: 2–8.

―――. 1974. *The Genetic Basis of Evolutionary Change.* New York: Columbia University Press.

Lieberman, Leonard. 1968. "The Debate over Race: A Study in the Sociology of Knowledge." *Phylon* 29: 127–141.

Liggio, Leonard P. 1976. "English Origins of Early American Racism." *Radical History Review* 3, no. 1: 1–36.

Lincoln, C. Eric. 1967. *The Negro Pilgrimage in America.* New York: Bantam.

Little, Michael. 1982. "The Development of Ideas on Human Ecology and Adaptation." In *A History of American Physical Anthropology, 1930–1980,* edited by F. Spencer. New York: Academic Press.

Littlefield, Alice, Leonard Lieberman, and Larry Reynolds. 1982. "Redefining Race: The Potential Demise of a Concept in Physical Anthropology." *Current Anthropology* 23, no. 6: 641–656.

Livingstone, Frank B. 1969. "On the Non-Existence of Human Races." In *The Concept of Race,* edited by A. Montagu. New York: Free Press.

Loehlin, J. D., G. Lindzey, and J. N. Spuhler. 1975. *Race Differences in Intelligence.* San Francisco: W. H. Freeman.

Lovejoy, Arthur. 1936. *The Great Chain of Being.* Cambridge: Harvard University Press.

Lovejoy, P. E. 1983. *Transformations in Slavery: A History of Slavery in Africa.* Cambridge: Cambridge University Press.

Ludmerer, Kenneth. 1969. *Genetics and American Society.* Baltimore: Johns Hopkins University Press.

Lurie, Edward. 1954. "Louis Agassiz and the Races of Man." *Isis* 45: 227–242.

Lutz, Donald. 1984. "The Relative Influence of European Writers on Late Eighteenth-Century American Political Thought." *American Political Science Review* 78, no. 1: 189–197.

Lyman, S. M. 1972. *The Black American in Sociological Thought.* New York: Capricorn.

McDermott, W. C., and W. Caldwell, eds. 1951. *Readings in the History of the Ancient World.* New York: Rinehart & Co.

Macfarlane, Alan. 1978. *The Origins of English Individualism.* Oxford: Basil Blackwell.

MacPherson, C. B. 1962. *The Political Theory of Possessive Individualism.* Oxford: Clarendon Press.

Malefijt, A. deWaal. 1974. *Images of Man: A History of Anthropological Thought.* New York: Alfred A. Knopf.

Malone, Dumas. 1962. *Jefferson and the Ordeal of Liberty.* Boston: Little, Brown & Co.

———. 1970. *Jefferson the President: First Term, 1801–1805.* Boston: Little, Brown & Co.

———. 1981. *The Sage of Monticello.* Boston: Little, Brown & Co.

Marshall, Gloria. 1968. "Racial Classifications: Popular and Scientific." In *Science and the Concept of Race,* edited by M. Mead et al. New York: Columbia University Press.

Mason, Phillip, ed. 1960. *Man, Race and Darwin.* London: Oxford University Press.

Mathews, D. G. 1980. "Religion and Slavery: The Case of the American South." In *Antislavery, Religion and Reform: Essays in Memory of Roger Anstey,* edited by C. Bolt and S. Drescher. Folkstone, England, and Hamden, Conn.: Dawson/Archon.

Mead, M., T. Dobzhansky, et al., eds. 1968. *Science and the Concept of Race*. New York: Columbia University Press.

Mendelsohn, Isaac. 1949. *Slavery in the Ancient Near East*. New York: Oxford University Press.

Merriam-Webster, G. & C. 1971. *Webster's Third New International Dictionary of the English Language*. Chicago: Encyclopaedia Britannica.

Miers, S., and I. Kopytoff, eds. 1977. *Slavery in Africa*. Madison: University of Wisconsin Press.

Miller, John C. 1977. *The Wolf by the Ears*. New York: Free Press.

Miller, C. Loren. 1966. *The Petitioners: The Story of the Supreme Court of the United States and the Negro*. New York: Pantheon.

Miller, William. 1962. *A New History of the United States*. Rev. ed. New York: Dell Publishing.

Mintz, Sidney W. 1961. "Review of Stanley Elkin's 'Slavery.'" *American Anthropologist* 63, no. 4: 579–587.

―――. 1975. "History and Anthropology: A Brief Reprise." In *Race and Slavery in the Western Hemisphere*, edited by S. L. Engerman and E. D. Genovese. Princeton: Princeton University Press.

―――. ed. 1974. *Slavery, Colonialism and Racism*. New York: W. W. Norton.

Molnar, Steven. [1975] 1983. *Human Variation: Races, Types and Ethnic Groups*. Reprint. Englewood Cliffs, N.J.: Prentice-Hall.

Montagu, Ashley. [1964] 1971. *Man's Most Dangerous Myth: The Fallacy of Race*. Reprint. New York: World Publishing.

―――, ed. 1969. *The Concept of Race*. London: Collier-Macmillan.

Morgan, Edmund S. 1972. "Slavery and Freedom: The American Paradox." *Journal of American History* 57, no. 1: 5–29.

―――. 1975. *American Slavery, American Freedom*. New York: W. W. Norton.

Morner, Magnus. 1967. *Race Mixture in the History of Latin America*. Boston: Little, Brown & Co.

―――. 1978. "The Impact of Regional Variety on the History of the Afro-Latin-Americans." *Secolas Annals* 9.

Morner, M., J. F. de Vinuela, and J. D. French. 1982. "Comparative Approaches to Latin American History." *Latin American Research Review* 17, no. 3: 55–89.

Morris, Laura N., ed. 1971. *Human Populations, Genetic Variation, and Evolution*. San Francisco: Chandler.

Morrison, L. R. 1980. "Nearer to the Brute Creation: The Scientific Defense of American Slavery Before 1830." *Southern Studies* 19, no. 3: 228–242.

Mourant, A. E. 1954. *The Distribution of Human Blood Groups*. Oxford: Blackwell.

Myers, James P., ed. 1983. *Elizabethan Ireland*. Hamden, Conn.: Archon Books.

Nash, Gary B. 1972. "Red, White and Black: The Origins of Racism in Colonial America." In *The Origins of American Slavery and Racism*, edited by D. Noel. Columbus: Charles E. Merrill.

_____ . 1982. *Red, White and Black: The Peoples of Early America.* Rev. ed. Englewood Cliffs, N.J.: Prentice-Hall.

_____ . 1986. *Race, Class, and Politics.* Chicago: University of Illinois Press.

Nash, G. B., and R. Weiss, eds. 1970. *The Great Fear: Race in the Mind of America.* New York: Holt, Rinehart & Winston.

Nature. 1936. "The Delusion of Race," vol. 137, no. 3467: 635. April.

Nature. 1936. "Genetics and Race," vol. 138, no. 3502: 988. December.

Nature. 1937. "Racial Doctrines and Social Evolution," vol. 140, no. 3553: 945–946. December.

Nature. 1940. "Disease and Race," vol. 145, no. 3664: 98. January.

Nature. 1943. "Race Theories," vol. 151, p. 220. February.

Nei, M., and A. K. Roychoudhury. 1972. "Gene Differences Between Caucasian, Negro and Japanese Populations." *Science* 177, no. 4,047: 434–435.

_____ . 1974. "Genetic Variations Within and Between the Three Major Races of Man, Caucasoids, Negroids and Mongoloids." *American Journal of Human Genetics* 26: 421–443.

Newman, Marshall T. 1963. "Geographic and Microgeographic Races." *Current Anthropology* 4, no. 2: 189–192.

Noel, Donald L. 1972. "Slavery and the Rise of Racism." In *The Origins of American Slavery and Racism,* edited by D. Noel. Columbus, Ohio: Charles E. Merrill.

Nott, Josiah, and George R. Gliddon. 1854. *Types of Mankind.* Philadelphia: Lippincott, Grambo & Co.

Oakes, James. 1990. *Slavery and Freedom: An Interpretation of the Old South.* New York: Alfred A. Knopf.

O'Farrell, Patrick. 1971. *Ireland's English Question.* New York: Schocken Books.

Ortner, Sherry B. 1984. "Theories in Anthropology Since the Sixties." *Comparative Studies in Society and History* 26, no. 1: 126–166.

Osborn, Henry F. 1926. "The Evolution of Human Races." *Natural History* 26, no. 1: 3–13.

Ottenberg, R. 1926. "The Relationships of Races as Shown by Blood Characteristics." *Natural History* 26, no. 1: 80–84.

Oxford English Dictionary of Historical Principles, 1933.

Pagden, A. 1982. *The Fall of Natural Man.* Cambridge: Cambridge University Press.

Page, Thomas N. 1896. "The Negro: The Southerner's Problem." *McClure's Magazine.*

Pagliaro, H. E., ed. 1973. *Racism in the Eighteenth Century.* Cleveland, Ohio, and London: Case Western Reserve University Press.

Palmer, Colin. 1976. *Slaves of the White God.* Cambridge: Harvard University Press.

Patterson, Orlando. 1982. *Slavery and Social Death.* Cambridge: Harvard University Press.

Pearce, Roy H. 1953. *The Savages of America.* Baltimore: Johns Hopkins University Press.

Penrose, Boies. 1955. *Travel and Discovery in the Renaissance, 1420–1620.* Cambridge: Harvard University Press.

Pessen, Edward. 1985. *Jacksonian America.* Rev. ed. Urbana: University of Illinois Press.

Peterson, Merrill. 1962. *The Jefferson Image in the American Mind.* New York: Oxford University Press.

———. 1970. *Thomas Jefferson and the New Nation.* New York: Oxford University Press.

Pickens, Donald. 1968. *Eugenics and the Progressives.* Nashville, Tenn.: Vanderbilt University Press.

Pierson, D. 1942. *Negroes in Brazil.* Chicago: University of Chicago Press.

Pirenne, Henri. [1925] 1952. *Medieval Cities.* Reprint. Princeton, N.J.: Princeton University Press.

Pole, J. R. 1978. *The Pursuit of Equality in American History.* Berkeley: University of California Press.

Poliakov, Leon. 1982. "Racism from the Enlightenment to the Age of Imperialism." In *Racism and Colonialism,* edited by R. Ross. The Hague: Martinus Nijhoff.

Popkin, R. H. 1973. "The Philosophical Basis of Eighteenth-Century Racism." In *Racism in the Eighteenth Century,* edited by H. Pagliaro. Cleveland, Ohio: Case Western Reserve University Press.

Provine, William. 1973. "Geneticists and the Biology of Race Crossing." *Science* 182, no. 4,114: 790–796.

Puzzo, Dante. 1964. "Racism and the Western Tradition." *Journal of the History of Ideas* 25, no. 4: 579–586.

Quarles, Benjamin. 1969. *The Negro in the Making of America.* Rev. ed. New York and London: Collier-Macmillan.

Quinn, D. B. 1958. "Ireland and Sixteenth-Century European Expansion." *Historical Studies.* New York: Hilary House.

———. 1966. *Elizabethans and the Irish.* Ithaca, N.Y.: Cornell University Press.

Race, R. R., and R. Sanger. [1958] 1975. *Blood Groups in Man.* Reprint. Philadelphia: F. A. Davis.

Real Academia Española. [1726–1739] 1737. *Diccionario de la Lengua Castellana.* Madrid: Francisco del Hierro.

Reed, T. E. 1969. "Caucasian Genes in American Negroes." *Science* 165, no. 3,895: 762–768.

Reichenbach, H. 1951. *The Rise of Scientific Philosophy.* Berkeley: University of California Press.

Robinson, R., J. Gallagher, and A. Denny. 1968. *Africa and the Victorians.* Garden City, N.Y.: Anchor Books.

Rodney, Walter. 1974. *How Europe Underdeveloped Africa.* Washington, D.C.: Howard University Press.

Ross, Robert., ed. 1982. *Racism and Colonialism.* The Hague: Martinus Nijhoff.

Rotberg, Robert. 1965. *A Political History of Tropical Africa.* New York: Harcourt, Brace & World.

Roth, Cecil. 1964. *The Spanish Inquisition.* New York: W. W. Norton.

Rout, Leslie B., Jr. 1976. *The African Experience in Latin America.* Cambridge: Cambridge University Press.

Rowe, John H. 1965. "The Renaissance Foundations of Anthropology." *American Anthropologist* 67, no. 1: 1–20.

Rubin, V., and A. Tuden. 1977. "Comparative Perspectives on Slavery in New World Plantation Societies." *Annals, New York Academy of Sciences,* vol. 292.

Ruchames, Louis, ed. 1969. *Racial Thought in America.* Vol. 1. Amherst: University of Massachusetts Press.

Sanday, Peggy R. 1972. "On the Causes of IQ Differences Between Groups and Implications for Social Policy." *Human Organization* 31, no. 4: 411–424.

Sanders, Edith R. 1969. "The Hamitic Hypothesis: Its Origin and Functions in Time Perspective." *Journal of African History* 10, no. 4: 521–532.

Sanders, Ronald. 1978. *Lost Tribes and Promised Lands: The Origins of American Racism.* Boston: Little, Brown & Co.

Sauer, Carl O. 1971. *Sixteenth-Century North America.* Berkeley: University of California Press.

Scheidt, Walter. 1950. "The Concept of Race in Anthropology and the Divisions into Human Races, from Linnaeus to Deniker." In *This Is Race,* edited by E. Count. New York: Henry Schuman.

Segal, Bernard E., ed. 1966. *Racial and Ethnic Relations.* New York: Crowell Co.

Seigel, B. J. 1945. "Some Methodological Considerations for a Comparative Study of Slavery." *American Anthropologist* 47, no. 34: 357–392.

Service, Elman. 1975. *Origins of the State and Civilization.* New York: W. W. Norton.

Shapiro, Harry L. 1944. "Anthropology's Contribution to Inter-Racial Understanding." *Science* 99, no. 2,576: 373–376.

Sherwin-White, A. N. 1970. *Racial Prejudice in Imperial Rome.* Cambridge: Cambridge University Press.

Shils, Edward. 1968. "Color, the University Intellectual Community and the Afro-Asian Intellectual." In *Race and Color,* edited by J. H. Franklin. Boston: Houghton Mifflin.

Sio, Arnold A. 1964–1965. "Interpretations of Slavery: The Slave Status in the Americas." *Comparative Studies in Society and History* 7: 289–308.

Skidmore, Thomas E. 1972. "Toward a Comparative Analysis of Race Relations Since Abolition in Brazil and the United States." *Journal of Latin American Studies* 14, no. 1: 1–28.

Skidmore, Thomas. 1990. "Racial Ideas and Social Policy in Brazil, 1870–1940." In *The Idea of Race in Latin America,* edited by R. Graham. Austin: University of Texas Press.

Slotkin, J. S. 1944. "Racial Classifications of the Seventeenth and Eighteenth Centuries." *Transactions of the Wisconsin Academy of Sciences* 36: 459–467.

_____ , ed. 1965. *Readings in Early Anthropology.* London: Methuen and Co.

Smith, Page. 1976. *Jefferson: A Revealing Biography.* New York: American Heritage Publishing Co.

Snowden, F. M., Jr. 1970. *Blacks in Antiquity: Ethiopians in the Greco-Roman Experience.* Cambridge: Harvard University Press.

_____ . [1970] 1983. *Before Color Prejudice.* Rev. ed. Cambridge: Harvard University Press.

Snyder, L. H. 1925. "Human Blood Groups and Their Bearing on Racial Relationships." *Proceedings of the National Academy of Sciences* 11: 406–407.

_____ . 1930. "The Laws of Seriologic Race Classification Studies in Human Inheritance." *Human Biology* 2, no. 1: 128–134.

Snyder, Louis L. 1939. *Race: A History of Modern Ethnic Theories.* New York: Longman, Green & Co.

_____ . 1962. *The Idea of Racialism: Its Meaning and History.* Princeton, N.J.: D. Van Nostrand Co.

Soderlund, Jean R. 1985. *Quakers and Slavery: A Divided Spirit.* Princeton: Princeton University Press.

Spencer, Frank. 1982. *A History of American Physical Anthropology.* New York: Academic Press.

Spier, Leslie. 1959. "Some Central Elements in the Legacy." *American Anthropological Association Memoirs* 61, no. 89.

Spitzer, Leo. 1948. *Essays in Historical Semantics.* New York: S. F. Vanni.

Spuhler, J. N., and G. Lindzey. 1967. "Racial Differences in Behavior." Bobbs-Merrill Reprint. From *Behavior-Genetic Analysis,* edited by J. Hirsch. 1967. New York: McGraw-Hill.

Stamp, Kenneth M. 1956. *The Peculiar Institution.* New York: Vintage Books.

Stanton, William. 1960. *The Leopard's Spots: Scientific Attitudes Toward Race in America, 1815–1859.* Chicago: University of Chicago Press.

Staples, Robert, ed. 1971. *The Black Family.* Belmont, Calif.: Wadsworth Publishing Co.

Steinberg, Stephen. 1989. *The Ethnic Myth.* 2d. ed. Boston: Beacon Press.

Stocking, George. 1968. *Race, Culture, and Evolution.* New York: Free Press.

Sutch, Richard. 1975. "The Breeding of Slaves for Sale and the Westward Expansion of Slavery, 1850–1860." In *Race and Slavery in the Western Hemisphere,* edited by S. Engerman and E. Genovese. Princeton: Princeton University Press.

Swartz, M., and D. K. Jordan. 1976. *Anthropology.* New York: John Wiley & Sons.

Sweet, Louise. 1965. "Camel Raiding of North Arabian Bedouin: A Mechanism of Ecological Adaptation." *American Anthropologist* 67, no. 4: 1,132–1,150.

Takaki, Ronald, ed. 1987. *From Different Shores: Perspectives on Race and Ethnicity in America.* New York: Oxford University Press.

Tannenbaum, Frank. 1946. *Slave and Citizen: The Negro in the Americas.* New York: Knopf.

Ten Broek, J. [1965] 1969. *Equal Under the Law.* 2d ed. London: Collier Books.

Thieme, F. 1952. "The Population as a Unit of Study." *American Anthropologist* 54, no. 4: 504–509.

Thomas, G. E. 1975. "Puritans, Indians and the Concept of Race." *New England Quarterly* 48, no. 1, (March): 3–27.

Thompson, V. B. 1987. *The Making of the African Diaspora in the Americas, 1441–1900.* New York: Longman.

Tildesley, M. L. 1953. "The Significance of Racial Difference." *Nature* 171, no. 4,346: 292.

Tindall, George B. 1988. *America: A Narrative History.* 2d ed. New York: W. W. Norton.

Tise, Larry E. 1987. *Proslavery: A History of the Defense of Slavery in America.* Athens: University of Georgia Press.

Tobias, Phillip V. 1972. "The Meaning of Race." In *Race and Social Difference,* edited by P. Baxter and B. Sansom. Middlesex: Penguin.

Tocqueville, Alexis de. [1831] 1945. *Democracy in America.* Vol. 2. Reprint. New York: Vintage Books.

Trevor, J. C. 1951. Letter to the Editor, no. 96, *MAN* (April).

Tumin, Melvin J. 1949. "The Idea of Race Dies Hard." *Commentary* 8 (July): 80–85.

Turner, D., and J. M. Bright., eds. 1965. *Images of the Negro in America.* Lexington, Mass.: D. C. Heath & Co.

Tylor, E. B. [1881] 1946. *Anthropology.* Reprint. London: Watts.

——— . [1871] 1958. *Primitive Culture.* New York: Harper & Row.

Van den Berghe, P. L. 1967. *Race and Racism.* New York: John Wiley & Sons.

——— . 1971. *Race and Ethnicity.* New York: Basic Books.

Vander Zanden, J. W. 1959. "The Ideology of White Supremacy." *Journal of the History of Ideas* 20: 385–400.

Van Evrie, John H. [1861] 1969. *White Supremacy and Negro Subordination.* New York: Negro Universities Press.

Vaughan, Alden T. 1965. *New England Frontier: Puritans and Indians, 1620–1675.* Boston: Little, Brown.

Voget, Fred W. 1967. "Progress, Science, History and Evolution in Eighteenth- and Nineteenth-Century Anthropology." *Journal of the History of the Behavioral Sciences* 3, no. 1: 132–155.

Wagatsuma, H. 1968. "The Social Perception of Skin Color in Japan." In *Color and Race,* edited by J. H. Franklin. Boston: Houghton Mifflin Co.

Walvin, James. 1980. "The Rise of British Popular Sentiment for Abolition, 1787–1832." In *Anti-Slavery, Religion and Reform,* edited by C. Bolt and S. Drescher. London: Dawson-Archon.

Washburn, S. L. 1963. "The Study of Race." *American Anthropologist* 65, no. 3, part 1: 521–531.

Watson, Alan. 1987. *Roman Slave Law.* Baltimore: Johns Hopkins University Press.

Watson, James L., ed. 1980. *Asian and African Systems of Slavery.* Berkeley: University of California Press.

Weaver, P.R.C. 1972. *Familia Caesaris: A Social Study of the Emperor's Freedmen and Slaves.* Cambridge: Cambridge University Press.

Westermann, W. L. 1955. *The Slave Systems of Greek and Roman Antiquity.* Philadelphia: American Philosophical Society.

White, A. D. [1896] 1965. *The History of the Warfare of Science with Theology in Christendom.* New York: Free Press.

Wiedeman, T.E.J. 1987. *Slavery.* Oxford: Oxford University Press.

Williams, Eric. [1944] 1966. *Capitalism and Slavery.* New York: Capricorn Books.

Williamson, Joel. 1984. *The Crucible of Race.* New York: Oxford University Press.

Wober, Mallory. 1971. "Race and Intelligence." *Transition* 40 (December): 17–26.

Woodward, C. Vann. 1974. *The Strange Career of Jim Crow.* 3d ed. New York: Oxford University Press.

Wright, Louis B. 1965. *Religion and Empire.* New York: Octagon.

Yavetz, Zvi. 1988. *Slaves and Slavery in Ancient Rome.* New Brunswick, N.J.: Transaction Books.

About the Book and Author

FEW TOPICS IN THE Western intellectual tradition have been subjected to as much scrutiny and analysis as the subject of race. In the eighteenth century, a prevailing belief in biologically exclusive and permanently unequal human groups, each with distinctive behavioral, moral, spiritual, and intellectual characteristics, led people to see biophysical and behavioral features as innate and immutable. In the nineteenth century, differences between whites, Indians, and Africans were magnified in the popular mind and in scholarly writings to the point that these groups were seen as separate species, justifying the preservation of "racial" slavery and the subsequent dehumanization of freed blacks. With the application in the late nineteenth century of the racial worldview to European peoples, and the subsequent twentieth-century inhumanity and brutality of Nazi race ideology, the concept of race came under attack. Liberal ideology coupled with advances in science prompted criticism of "race" and efforts to eliminate the term from the lexicon of science.

In a sweeping work that traces the idea of race through three centuries of North American history, Audrey Smedley shows race to be a cultural construct used variously and opportunistically throughout time, although the scientific record shows little common agreement on its meaning. Tracing the social and historical processes that helped shape the idea of race, Smedley argues that race was and is a folk worldview, fabricated as an existential reality out of elements of English cultural history and the conquest and enslavement of physically distinct populations. The schism between science and popular thought on race, which appeared in the mid-twentieth century, continues today. If progressive scientists no longer accept the biological idea of race, will society eventually also reject it?

Audrey Smedley is associate professor of anthropology at the State University of New York–Binghamton. She teaches the history of anthropological thought, social anthropology, and the ethnography of Africa in addition to her course titled "The Concept of Race in Western Thought." She received a B.A. and M.A. in history and anthropology from the University of Michigan and a Ph.D. from the Victoria University of Manchester in England.

330

Index

Abolitionists, 193, 205, 206, 211, 212, 236.
  See also Antislavery movement
*Account of the Regular Gradation in Man,
  An* (C. White), 232–233
Adair, James, 158
Adaptation, 286, 288, 299, 300–301
Africa/Africans, 43, 44, 55, 57, 61, 73, 89,
  92–110, 124, 134, 135, 149(n25), 181,
  259, 270, 271, 307, 308
  and European domination, 251
  and exploration period, 92–93, 132
  See also African-Americans; Bozales;
  Negroes; North Africa; Slavery
African-Americans, 7, 9, 28, 32, 139, 307
  colonization proposal concerning, 217–
  218
  relations with whites, 222, 223–224, 226
  urban culture, 229(n2)
  See also Negroes
Agassiz, Louis, 26, 236, 239, 240–242, 245,
  262, 274
Alexander the Great, 24
Al-Idrisi, 43
Alien Land laws, 269
Al-Masudi, 43
Almoravids, 92, 110(n3)
American Anti-Slavery Society, 215
American Association of Physical
  Anthropologists, 275
American Colonization Society,
  218American Legion, 269
American Slavery As It Is (Weld), 215
Ancient world, 33, 121, 124, 125, 126, 128,
  129, 154, 275. *See also* Rome
Anglo-Saxonism, 62, 102, 188–192, 199, 223,
  251, 269, 278
Animals, 37, 38, 161–162, 200, 240, 241,
  242, 295
  breeding of, 39, 40
  See also Pastoralism
Anthropological Society of Paris, 261
Anthropology, 3, 6, 29, 67, 203(n8), 219, 231,
  236, 237, 258, 261, 292, 294, 295

physical, 2, 20, 274–275, 307
  sociocultural, 178, 276
Anthropometry, 261, 262, 274, 276–277, 295
Anti-Catholicism, 278
Anti-Semitism, 258, 278
Antislavery movement, 145, 205–229, 250
  decline of, 214–215
  history, 206–216
  proslavery response to, 216–219, 239
  sources of thought, 205–206
  See also Abolitionists
Apes, 162, 164–165, 181, 182, 183, 233, 259,
  261, 262, 277. *See also* Primates
Apprentices, 100
Arabia/Arabs, 43, 44, 55
  language, 37
Arendt, Hannah, 189, 258
Aristocracy, 257–258
Aryanism, 251, 252, 258
Asia/Asians, 24, 61, 221, 252, 268–269, 307,
  308
Asia Minor, 124
Astronomy, 4
Australia, 18, 251, 254(n12), 301
Average man, 262

Bachman, John, 236
Bacon, Nathaniel, 174
Banton, Michael, 34(n7)
Baptism, 67, 208, 209. *See also* Religion,
  conversions
Bartlett, Iring, 249
Barzun, Jacques, 189
Baxter, Paul, 309
Beauty, 259
Behavior, 164, 275, 276, 280, 291, 295, 307,
  308. *See also under* Heredity issues
Benedict, Ruth, 278, 279–280
Benezet, Anthony, 207
Ben Israel, Menassah, 158
Berkhofer, Robert, Jr., 71(n13), 80, 87
Berlin Treaty of 1885, 270
Bernier, Francois, 163, 187

Bernstein, Felix, 286
Biblical texts, 153, 155–157, 210
Binet, Alfred, 266–267
Biology, 6, 20, 29, 261, 275, 280, 282, 303.
    See also Blood groups; Genetics;
    Heredity issues; genetic variability
Black Death, 63
Black Folk Here and There (Drake), 34(n4)
Blackness, 97, 150(n32)
Bloch, Marc, 46
Blood groups, 284–285, 286, 289–290,
    293(n12)
Blumenbach, Johann, 166, 167
Boas, Franz, 275–282, 292(n2)
Bodin, Jean, 162
Bohannan, Paul, 120
Boucher de Perthes, Jacques, 260
Boulainvilliers, Henri de (Count), 189–190,
    257
Bowser, Frederick P., 132, 135, 138, 150(n30)
Bozales, 133, 150(n29)
Brace, C. Loring, 281
Brakenridge, Hugh H., 179
Brazil, 34(n3), 44, 136, 137, 139, 146(n4),
    150(nn 32, 33)
Brigham, Carl, 267
Brinton, Daniel, 252
Bristol, 102
British Abolition Society, 212
British Association for the Advancement of
    Science, 266
Broca, Paul, 260, 261
Brodie, Fawn, 194, 197
Brown, John, 216
Brues, Alice M., 297
Bruno, Giordano, 157, 159, 163
Buckland, William, 260
Buffon. *See* Louis LeClerc, Comte de Buffon
Bunyan, John, 37
Burma, 61, 251
Burt, Sir Cyril, 26, 266

Cabot, John, 72, 85, 90(n1), 93
Cabot, Sebastian, 72, 90(n1)
Cadamosto, Alvise, 153
Caldwell, Charles, 237
Calhoun, John, 218
California, 268
Calvinism, 88
Cambrensis, Giraldus, 57
Campbell, Leon, 135, 137
Camper, Peter, 183, 259
Campion, Edmund, 37, 58
Cannibalism, 60, 71(n10), 76, 159
Canny, Nicholas P., 76, 84, 85, 86
Capitalism, 45–52, 70(n2), 83, 111(n12), 121,
    174, 207, 225
Caribbean area, 85, 95, 99, 104, 308
Carroll, Charles, 277
Cartwright, S. A., 272(n7)
Castas system, 134, 135
Castro, Americo, 66
Catherine of Aragon, 59
Catholicism, 44, 59, 62, 65, 81, 84, 105, 125,
    131, 159–160, 278

Caucasians, 167, 238, 252, 308
Central America, 44, 94, 308
Central Pacific Railroad, 268
Cephalic index, 259–260, 276
Chamberlain, Houston Stewart, 190, 279,
    281
Charleston Medical Journal, 239
Chauvinism, 61, 102, 189. *See also*
    Ethnicity, ethnocentrism
Chesapeake colony, 77, 86
Chicago, 93
Chiefdoms, 121
Children, 34(n7), 49, 55, 57, 68, 79, 98, 102,
    104, 117, 120, 122, 124, 129, 135, 141,
    148(n10), 207, 266, 276
    of slave and master, 139, 140, 151(nn 36,
    38), 198–199, 204(n14), 245–246
China/Chinese, 23, 43, 251, 254(n12), 268–
    269
Christianity, 143–144. *See also* Catholicism;
    Judeo-Christian morality; Protestants;
    Religion
Cimarrons, 73, 94, 111(n11)
Cities. *See* City-states; Urban areas
Citizenship, 247, 248, 250, 269
City-states, 120–121, 126
Civil rights, 83, 99, 212, 228, 302, 307
Clarendon (Lord), 58
Clarkson, Thomas, 212
Classification. *See under* Science
Class issues, 28, 51, 89, 160, 206, 224–229,
    230(nn 10, 11, 12), 256, 257, 309. *See
    also* Middle class; Poverty/poor people;
    Upper classes Clergy, 81–82
Climate, 165, 237, 276, 300, 301
Clines, 301
Colonialism, 8–9, 16, 18, 22, 47, 57, 69, 82,
    307. *See also* England, North American
    colonists; Spain, colonies
Color. *See* Skin color
Columbian Magazine, 182
Columbus, Christopher, 44, 75, 90(n3), 92,
    153
Combe, George, 261
Common man, 218, 228, 249
Common Sense (Paine), 213, 230(n5)
Comtaeus, Robert, 158–159
Comte de Buffon. *See* Louis LeClerc, Comte
    de Buffon
Confucius, 252
Conquest, 83, 101, 121, 222, 256
Conquistadores, 44, 131, 148(n21)
Constitutional Convention, 213–214
Continental Congress, 179
Conversos, 65–66. *See also* Religion,
    conversions
Coon, Carleton S., 293(n13)
Cooper, David, 207
Cotton gin, 215
Count, Earl, 16
Cox, Oliver, 12(n2)
Crania Americana/Crania Aegyptiaca
    (Morton), 237, 238
Craniometry, 237
Creationism, 240

Creation of world, 253(n1)
Crevecoeur, Hector St. Jean, 91(n8)
Cromwell, Oliver, 58, 103
Cruelty, 117, 127, 222, 224, 250
Crusades, 42
Culture(s), 29, 30, 31, 32, 116, 178, 185, 187, 188, 199, 224, 229(n2), 275, 280, 290, 299
Curtin, P. D., 148(n17)
Curtis, Benjamin Robbins (Supreme Court Justice), 249–250
Curtis, L. P., Jr., 189
Cuvier, Baron von, 238, 240, 241, 242
Cyprus, 72
Cytology, 284

Da Costa, Emilia Viotti, 136, 137
"Dance of the Sevin Deidly Synnis, The," 37
Darwin, Charles, 235, 241, 242, 243, 244, 266
Daubenton, Jean, 259
Davenport, Charles B., 302
Davis, David Brion, 110(n4), 125, 147(n9), 193, 205, 221
DeBow's Review, 272(n7)
Debtors, 99
Decision-making, 17
Degeneration. *See under* Differences
Degler, Carl, 96–97, 97–98, 136
De Gobineau (Count), 190, 269
Dehumanization, 84. *See also* Slavery, human status of slaves
Democracy, 189, 218, 249, 269, 305
Deniker, Joseph, 295
De Pauw, Cornelius, 184
Desmond rebellion, 60
Determinism, 186–188
Devil, 63–64, 87. *See also* Witchcraft
Diccionario de la Lengua Castellana, 38
Dictionaries, 37, 38
Dietz, F. C, 47
Differences, 6, 21, 22, 24–25, 29, 31, 32, 39, 64–65, 90, 106–107, 109, 145, 177, 222, 241, 249, 265, 278
  attitudes toward, 114, 141, 167, 181, 184, 205, 210, 217, 221, 226, 275, 287
  and degeneration, 166, 232, 236
  ethnic, 66
  explanations for, 153, 155, 165–166, 188, 232, 233–234, 267, 286, 294, 298, 300. *See also* Polygenesis
  measuring, 256, 258–263, 265–267, 275. *See also* Anthropometry
  vs. similarities among people, 159, 211, 282, 289
  See also Heredity issues, genetic variability; Skin color
Disease, 63, 77, 81, 104, 106, 132, 300, 301
Dixon, Thomas, 277
DNA, 5, 285, 293(n12), 294, 301. *See also* Genetics; Race, genetic conception of
Dobzhansky, T., 283, 309(n2)
Dover, Cedric, 37
Downing, Emanuel, 220
Drake, Francis, 73, 85, 93, 94

Drake, St. Clair, 34(n4)
Dred Scott decision, 247–250
DuBois, W.E.B., 230(n11)
Dumond, Dwight, 211, 215
Dunbar, William, 37

East, Edward M., 302
Ecological perspective, 300–302
Economic issues, 26, 108, 119, 195, 206, 214, 215, 217. *See also* Capitalism
Education, 21, 101, 160
Edward III (English king), 46
Egalitarianism, 3, 4, 27, 88, 174, 176, 228, 230(n12)
Egypt/Egyptians, 23, 237, 238, 253(n6)
Elites, 3, 108, 135, 140, 175, 230(nn 11, 12)
Elizabeth I (English queen), 52, 61, 73, 93
Elkins, Stanley, 115
Emancipation, 226
Enclosure movement, 46, 50
Endecott, John, 79
England, 41, 44, 45–50
  and Africa, 251
  antislavery in, 215
  cultural values, 56, 84, 185
  Glorious Revolution, 173
  and Indians, 74–80, 84, 85–88, 94, 101, 102, 106, 140, 141, 185
  and Irish, 24, 52–53, 57–59, 59–61, 70(n10), 78, 80, 83, 84, 85, 87, 94, 101, 102–103, 106, 141, 143, 181, 185, 304
  North American colonists, 8–9, 16, 40, 49, 52, 72–90
  Parliament, 212
  precolonial, 10
  royalty, 40(n), 50
  and self-doubt, 186
  and slavery, 72–73, 77, 89–90, 93, 94–95, 97–98, 137–142, 304
  social order, 50–52, 88–89
  and Spain, 40(n), 41, 59, 62, 64–65, 73
  superiority of English, 102
  uniqueness of, 49, 137–142
Enlightenment period, 61, 154, 155, 195, 197, 206, 211–216, 217, 237, 276, 300, 305
Equality/inequality, 26, 27, 28, 47, 109, 111(n5), 120, 136, 141, 146, 159, 166, 168, 176, 191, 209, 210, 213, 217, 223, 226, 242, 243, 256,265, 281, 291, 305, 306. *See also* Egalitarianism
Eskimos, 301
"Essay on the Inequality of the Human Races," 257
Essex (Lord), 86
Ethiopians, 238
Ethnicity, 9, 66, 256, 308
  ethnocentrism, 29, 31, 41, 52–61, 102, 126, 143, 167, 187, 189, 304
  See also under Race
Eugenics, 266, 283
Eunuchs, 149(n23)
Europeans, 24, 62, 70(n3), 91(n8), 140, 152, 153, 167, 187, 191, 227–228, 271(n1), 306

immigrants, 250, 258, 269, 278
northern, 43, 44, 269, 304
race issues, 255–256
southern, 42, 258, 269, 278. *See also*
Mediterranean world
travelers from, 42
Evangelists, 211. *See also* Great Awakening
Evolution, 241–242, 243, 244, 264, 283, 286,
298, 299–300. *See also* DNA; Genetics;
Natural selection
Exclusiveness. *See* Separateness
Exploration period, 15, 26, 36, 41–44, 92–93,
152, 157
Eysenck, Hans, 302

Farmers, 54, 56, 101, 122, 180, 227
Fascism, 279, 281, 291. *See also* Nazis
Fatherhood, 67–68, 120, 135. *See also*
Children, of slave and master
Faust, Drew G., 219
Feudalism, 46, 62, 104
Fincher, Jack, 267
Finley, Moses I., 112(n14), 149(n24)
Food, 77, 300
Fossils, 260
Fowler, H. W., 37
Fox, George, 209
Fox-Genovese, Elizabeth, 47
France/French people, 16, 40, 44, 46, 75, 95,
105, 140, 159, 189, 212, 215, 258–259,
266
and Africa, 251
French Revolution, 215, 230(n5)
and race issues, 256–258
Franco-Prussian War (1870–1871), 258
Franklin, Benjamin, 202(n5)
Franklin, John Hope, 92, 110(n1), 196
Franks, 257
Frazier, E. Franklin, 12(n2)
Fredrickson, George, 99, 218, 230(n11), 244,
277
Freedom, 48, 48, 49, 51, 56, 57, 62, 89, 98,
99, 101, 138, 147(n6), 173, 189, 192,
213, 222, 239, 307
Freemasonry, 189
Free-Soilers, 218
Freudianism, 23, 24
Frontier areas, 174, 227
Fugitive Slave Act (1793), 249
Fugitive Slave Law (1850), 216

Gall, Franz Joseph, 260–261
Galton, Sir Francis, 266, 283
Garn, Stanley, 289
Garrison, William Lloyd, 215
Gates, R. Ruggles, 298
Genetic drift, 283, 301
Genetics, 282, 283–291
gene pool model, 283, 287
Genetics and the Origin of Species
(Dobzhansky), 283
Genocide, 28, 57, 61, 91(n6), 279, 306
Genovese, Eugene, 47, 147(n6)
Gentlemen's Agreement (1909), 268
Geography, 43, 300, 301

Geography (Ptolemy), 43
Geology, 231
Georgia, 220
Gergen, Kenneth, 23
Germany/Germans, 16, 124, 148(n19), 189,
190, 257, 258, 271, 279, 291. *See also*
Nazis
Gilbert, Humphrey, 57, 73, 85, 90(n6), 94
Gliddon, George R., 238, 239, 240
Gobineau, Arturo de (Count), 257–258
Goddard, Henry, 267
Godwyn, Morgan, 181, 208
Gossett, Thomas, 16, 23, 244, 268
Gould, Stephen Jay, 177, 241, 267, 271(n3)
Grant, Madison, 258, 279, 281
Great Awakening, 174, 209, 211
Great Chain of Being, 27, 143, 177, 178,
202(n4), 232
Greed, 174, 180
Greeks, 23, 119, 124, 126, 217, 234
Greene, John, 26, 165, 200–201, 202(n1),
254(n9), 259
Grenville, Richard, 73, 85, 90(n6)
Grotius, Hugo, 158, 159
Gunther, H.F.K., 271(n2)

Haddon, A. C., 296
Haiti, 215
Haller, John S., Jr., 243, 259, 261, 262, 265,
270
Haller, Mark, 270, 292(n2)
Ham (biblical), 158, 216–217, 252
Hammurabi, codes of, 128, 151(n36)
Handlin, Oscar and Mary, 98
Harpers Ferry, 216
Harris, Marvin, 141, 188, 261
Harvard Educational Review, 302
Harvard University, 242, 269
Havens, George, 197
Hawkins, John, 73, 80, 93
Heathenism, 59, 107, 187, 196, 211
Hemings, Sally, 203(n10), 204(n13), 204(nn
13, 15, 16). *See also* Jefferson, Thomas,
slave mistress of
Henry II (English king), 53
Henry VII (English king), 57
Henry VIII (English king), 57, 59, 62
Herders. *See* Pastoralism
Hereditary Genius (Galton), 266
Heredity issues, 265, 276, 283
abnormalities, 283–284
behavior, 27, 30, 31–32, 39, 72, 167, 168,
188, 202(n5), 208, 256, 267, 290, 309
genetic variability, 5, 7, 12(n1), 14, 20, 22,
23, 27, 206, 283, 288, 297, 301. *See also*
Differences
and social status, 66, 67, 68
Herodotus, 33
Herrnstein, R., 309
Herskovits, Melville, 278
Hierarchies, 27, 41, 50, 56, 109, 135, 136,
168, 177–185, 223. *See also* Great Chain
of Being; Ranking
Hirschfeld, L. and H., 285

History, 188, 217, 231–232, 252, 253(n7)
historians, 16–17, 80, 84, 102, 229(n2), 275
History of Jamaica (Long), 182
Hitler, Adolf, 258, 279
Hodgen, Margaret, 42, 186
Holy Wars (Islamic), 44
Home, Henry (Lord Kames), 169, 183, 233, 240, 253(n3)
Homogeneity, 68–69, 71(n13)
Hooton, E. A., 274–275, 281
Hoover, Dwight, 77, 82, 87, 180, 197, 292(n2)
Horsman, Reginald, 62, 189
Hrdlicka, Ales, 274–275, 281
Humanitarian ideals, 305, 306
Human rights, 192
Humans
and apes, 164–165
genus "Homo," 163–164
origins, 153, 155–157, 160, 166, 168–169, 183, 231, 232. *See also* Polygenesis
universal history, 231–232
Hume, David, 184
Hundred Years' War, 46
Huxley, Julian, 296
Hybrids, 235, 238–239, 245, 302. *See also* Mulattoes
Hypo-descent, 141, 145, 246

Iberian Peninsula, 129–130. *See also* Portugal/Potuguese; Spain/Spanish people
Ibn Battuta, 43
Ideas, 10, 17, 221
history of, 15
Identities, 7, 25, 52, 62, 67, 88, 119–120, 150(nn 30, 34), 185, 188, 256, 304
Ideology, 6, 9, 17, 18, 26–27, 31, 108–109, 116, 139, 185–188, 191, 221
Ignatius of Loyola, 159–160
Immigrants, 32, 268–269, 309. *See also under* Europeans
Immigration Restriction League, 269
Inbreeding, 283
India, 23, 43, 61
Indian Removal Act (1830), 180
Indians, 9, 61, 90(n2), 91(nn 6, 7, 8), 104, 105, 134–135, 150(n30), 220, 268
Christian, 79
Civilized Tribes, 179
lands in South, 180
mounds, 180, 200
origins, 158–159
population decline, 132–133, 178
views concerning, 75–76, 148(n21), 160, 176, 178–181, 191, 200, 211, 221, 238
See also Native Americans; *under* England; Language; Spain
Individualism, 45, 89, 175, 227
possessive, 48, 49, 173–174
Industrialization, 225
Inquisition, 38, 63, 66, 69
Intelligence, 238, 264, 265, 266–267, 283, 290–291, 302
testing, 267, 280, 282, 290, 293(n5), 308

Intermarriage, 21, 40(n), 65, 99, 100, 114, 134–135, 141, 145, 185, 199, 228, 244, 245, 248, 258. *See also* Miscegenation
International relations, 307
Ireland/Irish people, 24, 28, 37, 56, 71(n11), 98
conflict with English, 24, 56–61
Irish immigration in 19th century, 218–219
servitude in New World, 102–103, 105
See also England, and Irish
IQ tests. *See* Intelligence, testing
Islamic peoples. *See* Muslims
Italy, 16, 44, 126, 153, 281
Italian language, 37, 38

Jackson, Andrew, 180, 218, 228
Jamestown, 75, 95
Japan/Japanese, 34(n4), 268–269
Jefferson, Thomas, 112(n13), 180, 191, 192–202, 202(n4), 207, 224, 238
biographies, 203(n10)
slave mistress of, 194, 203(n13). *See also* Hemings, Sally
Jensen, Arthur, 253(n7), 302
Jesuit Relations, 160
Jesuits, 159–160
Jews, 23, 38, 64, 65–66, 67, 71(n12), 134, 158, 159, 256, 258, 278, 306
Jews in America (Thorowgood), 158
Johnson, Roswell, 302
Johnston, Sir Harry, 146(n4)
Jones, Howard Mumford, 76, 86
Jordan, Winthrop, 84, 94, 97, 99–100, 107, 110(n4), 128, 145, 181, 184, 186, 192, 196, 202(n4), 210
Judeo-Christian morality, 305, 306

Kames (Lord). *See* Home, Henry
Kansas-Nebraska Act, 216
Kinship, 46, 47, 49, 67–68, 70(n3), 119–120, 121, 122, 123–124, 148(n16), 203(n8)
Klein, Herbert, 130
Knox, Robert, 251
Kolchin, Peter, 115
Kovel, Joel, 19
Ku Klux Klan, 226, 278
Kupperman, Karen, 76

Labor, 26, 53, 58, 82, 132, 143, 194, 250
advantages of African, 106
coerced, 121, 144
demand for, 89, 102, 104, 133, 149(n26), 219–220
as property, 48
unions, 228, 269
wage, 46, 50, 51, 62, 121, 122, 207
Laetius, 159
Lafitau, Jean, 203(n8), 231
Land, use of, 83
Lane, Ralph, 73, 74–75
Language, 16, 29, 31, 33, 36–40, 102, 140, 142, 156–157, 191, 275, 276, 277, 278, 295
English, 97

of Indians, 153, 158, 180
Latin, 37, 126
Romance, 38
Las Casas, Bartolomé de (Bishop), 148(n21), 149(n26)
Las Siete Partidas, 130–131, 138
Latin America, 9, 107, 113, 114–115, 129, 150(nn 32, 33), 209, 246
Le Conte, Joseph, 242, 271(n5)
Legal issues, 28, 53, 58, 60, 62, 84, 95–96, 98–99, 100, 101, 107, 115, 122, 138, 245, 268, 269
natural law, 128
and scientific race ideology, 246–250
segregation laws, 244, 282
See also Slavery, laws
Lewis, Bernard, 23
Liberalism, 279–280, 291–292
Liberator, The, 215
Library of Congress, 200
Lieberman, Leonard, 2, 297
Life styles, 54, 108, 140, 173, 175, 195, 219, 291. *See also* Pastoralism
Liggio, Leonard, 52, 58, 85, 91(n6), 99, 105
Lima, Peru, 149(n27)
Limpieza de Sangre, Certificates of, 66
Lincoln, Abraham, 243, 262
Linnaeus, Carolus, 163–164, 167, 177, 178, 235
Literacy, 210
Literature, 277
Littlefield, Alice, 2
Liverpool, 102
Livingstone, Frank, 296–297
Locke, John, 48, 173, 175, 197
Long, Edward, 182, 233
Louisiana Purchase, 180
Louis LeClerc, Comte de Buffon, 165–166, 167, 178, 183, 200, 259
Lovejoy, Arthur, 177

Macfarlane, Alan, 49, 50
McLean, John (Supreme Court Justice), 250
MacPherson, C. B., 48
Malefijt, A. deWaal, 157
Maleria, 300
Mali, 43
Malone, Dumas, 197, 204(n13)
Manifest Destiny doctrine, 191
Manumissions, 100, 114, 125, 129, 131, 138, 208, 213, 239. *See also* Slavery, freed slaves
Marriage, 58, 86, 122, 124, 138, 149(n23). *See also* Intermarriage
Martyr, Peter, 153–154
Marx, Karl, 70(n2)
Marxists, 47, 225, 230(n10)
Mary I (daughter of Henry VIII), 59
Maryland, 98, 100, 107, 248
Mason, John, 79
Massachusetts, 248
Massachusetts Bay colony, 78
Massacres, 58, 91(n6), 268. *See also* Genocide
Matacom's War of 1675, 79

Mating customs, 299
Mead, Margaret, 278
Media, 21, 250, 307
Mediterranean world, 42–43, 44, 124, 125, 129, 149(n25), 304
Merchants, 50
Mestizos, 9, 134, 135, 140, 150(n30)
Methodists, 174–175
Mexico, 44, 131, 133, 134, 135–136
Middle Ages, 38, 43, 125, 177
Middle class, 45, 47, 173, 212, 307
Middle East, 24, 61, 129, 251
Military forces, 125
Miller, John Chester, 192, 204(n13)
Miller, Loren, 214
Mind of Primitive Man, The (Boas), 278
Miscegenation, 135, 137, 139, 145, 199, 204(n15), 246, 251, 270, 302
Missionaries, 75, 159
Missouri Compromise, 216, 249
Mita system, 132
Mobility, 50, 54–55, 56, 62
Monarchies, 45
Money, 47, 49, 218
Monogeny, 234–244, 245, 250, 253(n3), 302–303
Montagu, Ashley, 296
Montaigne, Michel Eyquem de, 234
Montesquieu, Baron de, 195
Moors, 38, 44, 64, 65, 66, 67
Morality. *See under* Slavery
Morgan, Edmund, 73, 77, 80, 84, 99, 107, 110(n3), 175–176
Morner, Magnus, 131, 136
Morton, Samuel G., 236, 237–239, 240, 253(n7), 261, 274
Moss, A. A., Jr., 92
Mulattoes, 100, 130, 134, 135, 136, 138, 139, 140, 204(n14), 239, 244–246, 262
Muslims, 24, 42, 43, 44, 64, 65, 67, 124, 125, 126, 129, 134, 148(n19), 149(n22), 151(n36)
Mutations, 283, 300, 301
Myers, James, 57
Mystic Fort, 79, 86

Nash, Gary, 75, 76, 78, 80, 84, 85, 101, 116, 140, 141, 142, 143, 199
Nationalism, 61–64, 258
Nationality, 30
Nation-state building, 69, 189
Native Americans, 7, 28, 282. *See also* Indians
Natural selection, 242, 283, 297, 300, 301
Nature magazine, 295
Nazis, 11, 28, 190, 273, 279, 303, 306
Neanderthals, 260
Negro a Beast, The (Carroll), 277
Negroes, 272(n7)
belief in extinction of, 262–263
natural inferiority of, 172, 176, 181–185, 196–197, 219, 232, 233, 239, 243, 244, 248, 261, 262, 271(n5), 282, 290, 294. *See also* Polygenesis

and primitiveness, 292(n2)
rights, 248–249
Negro in the New World, The (Johnston), 146(n4)
Netherlands/Dutch people, 16, 45, 75, 95
New Christians, 65
New England, 78, 81, 100–101, 208
New Spain, 149(n28)
Nigeria, 251
Nine Years' War, 57
Niño, Pedro Alonzo, 92
Noah (biblical), 155, 156, 158, 216–217
Noel, Donald L., 144, 205
Nomads, 60, 86. *See also* Pastoralism
No-race position. *See under* Science
Nordics/Nordicism, 251, 252, 257, 271(n2), 279, 281
North Africa, 42, 64, 97
North Carolina, 100, 250
Norwegians, 301
Notes on the State of Virginia (Jefferson), 196, 200, 202(n4)
Nott, Josiah, 236, 239–240, 244–245
Nudity, 86, 156

O'Farrell, Patrick, 85, 86
Oglethorpe, James, 220
O'Neill, Hugh, 52, 60
"On the Meaninglessness of the Anthropological Conception of Race," 296
"On the Non-Existence of Human Races," 296–297
Origin of Species (Darwin), 235, 241
Osborn, Henry Fairfield, 290
Overpopulation, 82
Oxford English Dictionary of Historical Principles, 37

Paine, Thomas, 193, 213, 230(n5)
Palmer, Colin, 110(n3), 131, 134
Panama, 44, 73, 132
Park, Robert, 12(n2)
Passing, 12(n3)
Passing of the Great Race, The (Grant), 279
Pastoralism, 54–56, 70(n7), 104
Patterson, Orlando, 147(n8)
Paulding, James, 243
Paul III (Pope), 148(n21)
Pearce, Roy H., 80, 179
Pearson, Karl, 283
Peasants, 50, 67, 68, 120
Peculiam, 138
Pedro de Alvarado, 132
Pequot War of 1637, 79
Persians, 23
Peru, 131, 132, 133, 135–136, 137, 138, 149(n27)
Peterson, Merrill, 197, 203(n13)
Pets, 117
Petty, William, 38, 163, 186
Philippines, 270
Phillip II (Spanish king), 40(n), 59, 133
Phoenicians, 124, 158
Phrenology, 237, 238, 260–261, 265

Pierson, D., 136
Pilgrim's Progress, 37
Piracy, 73, 93
Pirenne, Henri, 51
Pizzaro, 132
Plantations, 60, 71(n11), 103, 111(n9), 137, 145, 175, 187, 210, 304. *See also* Sugar plantations
Poliakov, Leon, 169
Polygenesis, 168–169, 233, 234–244, 245, 250, 253(n3), 274, 277, 298, 302
advocates of, 236
Popenoe, Paul, 302
Population genetics, 283–291, 296
Portugal/Portuguese, 16, 40, 44, 59, 72, 89, 93, 97, 115, 130, 133, 139, 140, 220, 304
Poverty/poor people, 47, 50–51, 68, 82, 111(n10), 174, 176, 208, 230(n11)
Power, personal, 219, 223–224, 226
Prejudice, 25, 34(nn 3, 4)
Press, antislavery, 250
Prester John (black king), 42
Primates, 162, 165, 178, 182, 183. *See also* Apes
Primogeniture, 45, 49
Primordialists, 14–15, 22–25
Private property, 45, 46, 47, 49, 51, 52, 54, 86, 304
property rights, 48, 56, 142–143, 175, 179, 194, 201, 213, 214, 225, 246, 248, 304–305
Prognathism, 183, 259
Prosser, Gabriel, 215
Prostitution, 122
Protestants, 62, 63, 111(n10), 209, 210
Protestant ethic, 51
Reformation, 42, 81, 160
See also Puritans
Provine, William, 302–303
Psychometrics, 265–267
Ptolemy, 43
Purchas, Samuel, 77
Puritans, 52, 58, 62, 75, 78–80, 81, 83, 89, 227
virtues, 82
Puzzo, Dante, 15
Pygmies, 293(n12), 301

Quakers, 209, 212
Queen Ann's War, 87
Quetelet, Lambert A. J., 261, 262, 266
Quinn, David B., 57, 59, 85

Race
antiracism, 273
beliefs concerning, 185–188, 190–191
as breeding populations, 287–288, 290, 297–298, 299, 302, 309
categories, 115–116, 221, 257, 271(n2), 281, 286, 289, 296, 297, 299–300, 309(n2)
definitions. *See* Race, meaning of
as essence, 32, 109, 145, 264–265, 281. *See also* Race, as unchangeable
and ethnicity, 15, 29–33, 299

etymology of term, 36–40
as exclusive groups, 185–186. *See also*
  Separateness
as folk idea, 6, 7, 19, 25, 26, 171, 221, 277,
  280, 290, 303, 305
genetic conception of, 285–289. *See also*
  Genetics
and historical reconstruction, 181
history of idea, 6, 10, 13, 14, 165
and human status, 119
as knowledge system, 15, 20
meaning of, 275–282, 295–296, 297, 298,
  300
priority over class, 224–229
race relations, study of, 291
romantic racialism, 221
as sociocultural construct, 6–7, 13–14, 16,
  19, 21, 28, 280
as species equivalent, 11, 234, 243, 290,
  298
typological models, 263–265, 275, 288,
  300
as unchangeable, 9, 21, 27, 39–40, 237,
  256, 295. *See also* Race, as essence
as worldview, 9, 11, 15, 18, 21, 25–29, 32,
  109, 171, 172, 201, 242, 255, 256, 269,
  270, 278. *See also* Ideology
See also Racism; Science, no-race position
  of
Race: Science and Politics (Benedict), 279
Racial Elements of European History
  (Gunther), 271(n2)
Racism, 3, 20, 205, 270, 278, 279, 291, 292
as modern idea, 15–16
Raleigh, Walter, 73, 74–75, 85, 90(n6), 94
Randolph, Thomas Jefferson, 198–199
Ranking, 27, 39, 72, 109, 134, 141, 146, 166,
  176, 178, 195, 200, 221, 303
Rape, 183
Rathlin Island, 86
Ray, John, 162
Reason, 212, 238
Rebellions, 60, 104, 174, 215, 223, 237
Reconstruction period, 226, 244
Regression toward the mean, 266
Religion, 28, 31, 41, 47, 52, 62, 63, 64, 68,
  80–85, 86, 101, 106, 129, 201, 206, 208–
  211
  conversions, 65–66, 67, 69, 75–76, 78, 88,
    208, 209, 210, 211
  revivalist movements, 174. *See also* Great
    Awakening
  See also Biblical texts; Catholicism;
    Christianity; Heathenism; Protestants
Renaissance, 42, 153, 157
Reproductive isolation, 234, 235
Republicanism, 175, 176, 228
Retzius, Anders, 259
Reynolds, Larry, 2
Rich, Barnabe, 58
Rights, 79, 99, 100, 148(n17), 173, 192, 228,
  305, 306
  natural vs. civil, 83. *See also* Civil rights
  rights-in-persons, 122–123

See also Private property, property rights;
  under Negroes; Slavery
Riots, 219, 254(n12), 270
Ripley, William Z., 258
Rivalry, 31
Roanoke Island, 73, 74, 76, 94
Robertson, William, 203(n8), 231
Rome, 119–120, 124, 126, 127, 128, 129,
  149(n24), 190, 217
Rousseau, Jean Jacques, 230(n4)
Rout, Leslie, Jr., 130, 131
Rowe, John H., 153
Rush, Benjamin, 210
Rut, John, 72

Sanders, Ronald, 71(n12), 74
Sansom, B., 309
Santo Domingo, 72
Satan. *See* Devil
Sauer, Carl, 74
Savages, 60, 61, 69, 86, 87, 101, 102, 106,
  107, 143, 145, 154, 164, 168, 176, 179,
  181, 186, 187, 221, 259, 270, 304, 306
  noble savage, 75, 109, 160, 190
Scandinavians, 259
Scapegoats, 29, 103, 250
Scheidt, Walter, 165
Science, 3, 26, 116–117, 146, 152–170, 171,
  200–201, 219, 305, 306–307
  classification, 161–170, 242, 262, 263, 286,
    288
  and cultural context, 4, 5, 11, 28, 167, 177,
    178, 307, 309
  debate over race, 297–300
  and ideology of race, 6, 192
  and measurement. *See* Differences,
    measuring
  nineteenth-century, 231–252, 255–271,
    305
  no-race position of, 2, 4–5, 6, 19, 20, 28–
    29, 296–297, 299–300
  as substitute for religion, 201
  and supernatural knowledge, 154–155
  twentieth-century, 273–292
  works concerning, 6
Science magazine, 302
Scorched-earth policy, 70(n10), 103
Scotland/Scotsmen, 102, 212
Segregation, 244, 246, 282, 307
Separateness, 26, 33, 69, 72, 78, 98, 109, 137,
  140, 180, 227, 270, 289, 298. *See also*
  Segregation
Serfdom, 128
Servants, 98, 99, 100, 103–104, 104–105,
  111(n4), 208
  freed, 103–104
  indentured, 95, 98, 103, 105–106, 227
Sewall Wright effect, 284. *See also* Genetic
  drift
Sexuality, 58, 86, 122, 134, 135, 140, 141,
  151(n39), 181, 183, 204(n13), 277. *See
  also* Miscegenation
Shakespeare, William, 37
Shaler, Nathaniel, 242
Sharp, Granville, 212

Sheldon, W. H., 263
Shils, Edward, 23
Shockley, William, 302
Sickle-cell traits, 300
Sio, Arnold, 97
Sketches of the History of Man (Lord Kames), 169
Skin color, 23, 34(n4), 78, 97, 106, 107, 111(n8), 136, 162, 163, 165–166, 263, 300, 301
Skulls, 237, 259–260, 276
Slavery, 15, 22, 47, 48, 50, 69, 79
  as booty, 121
  debt slavery, 124, 125
  dependence on, 219–220
  freed slaves, 99, 132, 149(n24), 151(n38), 203(n10). *See also* Manumissions
  human status of slaves, 116, 117, 118, 119, 127, 128–129, 131, 142, 143, 144, 145, 151(n35), 182–183, 186, 193–194, 196, 198, 210, 211,215
  Indian, 98, 102
  industrial, 125, 127
  laws, 115, 128, 130–131, 143, 194
  morality of, 127–128, 172, 174, 208
  natural slaves, 126–127
  nature of, 118–119, 147(n8), 148(n17)
  Old World, 116, 119–131, 149(n22)
  and Old World customs and habits, 138–142, 151(n38)
  origin of term, 148(n1)
  permanent, 100
  and property, 115, 118, 128, 142, 193–194, 247
  racial, 96–106
  raids, 124
  rights, 115, 128, 129, 131, 142–143. *See also* Negroes, rights
  runaways, 104
  skilled laborers, 194
  slave ships, 80
  and status of owners, 122
  systems compared, 113–146
  types of, 124–125
  voluntary, 124
  women slaves, 129, 138, 139–140, 151(nn 36, 39)
  See also under England; Spain/Spanish people
Slavery in the United States (Paulding), 243
Slotkin, J. S., 166
Smallpox, 81
Smith, John, 76
Smith, Page, 200, 204(n16)
Smith, Samuel Stanhope, 167, 191, 210, 236–237
Snowden, F. M., Jr., 130
Snyder, Louis, 16
Social Darwinists, 277. *See also* Spencer, Herbert
Social death, 120, 147(n8)
Social structures, 108
  stratification, 22, 176, 221–222, 227
Society for the Propagation of the Gospel in Foreign Lands, 209

Soderlund, Jean R., 209
Somatometry, 263
South Africa, 18
  apartheid, 9, 28
South Carolina, 100, 107, 220
Southern Baptists, 174–175
Spain/Spanish people, 16, 38, 40, 64–69, 71(n12), 93, 97, 105, 273
  colonies, 44, 60, 69, 72, 149(n28), 150(n29), 220. *See also* Spain/Spanish people, and slavery
  and Indians, 61, 132
  royalty, 40(n)
  and slavery, 89, 95, 110(n3), 115, 126, 130–137, 139, 304
  Spanish Armada (1588), 62
  Spanish language, 37, 38, 162
  See also England, and Spain; Inquisition
Spanish-American War (1898), 269
Species, 11, 39, 162–163, 166, 168–169, 232, 239, 242, 246, 254(n9), 264
  subspecies, 296, 297, 298
  See also Polygenesis; Race, as species equivalent
Spencer, Herbert, 252, 263, 264
Spier, Leslie, 278
Spitzer, Leo, 37
Spurzheim, Jacob, 260, 261
Standish, Miles, 78
Statistics, 261, 263, 265, 266
Statutes of Kilkenny, 53, 141
Steinberg, Stephen, 32
Stereotypes, 168, 179, 183, 210, 221, 256, 263, 271, 271(n2), 277, 282, 295
Sterilization, 284
Stocking, George, 242, 253(n3)
Stone, John, 79
Stowe, Harriet Beecher, 215
Suez Canal, 251
Suffrage, 218. *See also* Voting
Sugar plantations, 95, 102, 126
Sutch, Richard, 151(n35)
Sweden, 34(n7)
Systemae Naturae (Linnaeus), 163–164

Tacitus, 33, 190
Takaki, Ronald, 33
Taney, Roger B., 247–249
Tannenbaum, Frank, 114–115
Tartars, 159
Taxation, 214
Technology, 43
Terman, Lewis, 267
Tesoro de la Lengua Castellana o Espanola (Cobarruvias), 38
Third World, 16, 307
Thomas, G. E., 78, 80
Thomas, William, 57
Thorndike, Edward Lee, 266
Thorowgood, Thomas, 158
Tise, Larry, 216, 217, 219
Tobacco, 89, 95, 175, 195
Tocqueville, Alexis de, 96, 111(n5)
Topinard, Paul, 295

Trade, 43, 45, 46, 49, 50, 75, 76, 94, 104, 121, 130, 195, 209
Treaties, 79, 104, 180
Trevor, J. C., 37
Tucker, William, 77
Turkey, 130
Turner, Nat, 215, 237
Twins, 266
Tylor, E. B., 30, 276
Types of Mankind (Gliddon), 239–240
Tyson, Edward, 162, 178

Uncle Tom's Cabin (Stowe), 215
Unemployment, 82
United Nations, 307
United States, 18
    Chinese/Japanese Americans in, 34(n7)
    Civil War, 261, 262
    Congress, 216, 268, 269
    Constitution, 248, 250. *See also* Constitutional Convention
    educated Americans in 19th century, 270
    Indian Department, 202(n2)
    Provost Marshal-General's Bureau, 246, 262
    race system in, 9, 20–21, 26, 28, 32, 33
    Sanitary Commission, 246, 262
    Southern, 144, 179–180, 206, 209, 211, 217, 219, 224, 226, 228(n2), 236, 245, 246, 262, 282, 292(n5)
    Supreme Court, 247–250
Upper classes, 212, 257–258, 270
Urban areas, 45, 46, 47, 50, 133, 137, 219, 228(n2), 278
Utopianism, 94

Vagabonds, 51, 82, 89, 98, 103, 111(n7)
Values, 3, 4, 22, 29, 50–52, 81, 89, 90(n4), 116, 144, 167, 173–176, 205, 242, 243, 291, 307
    value judgments, 39. *See also* Ranking
    See also England, cultural values
Van den Berghe, Pierre, 23–24
Van Evrie, John, 252
Varen, Bernard, 162
Vaughan, Alden, 75
Verrazzano, Giovanni da, 75
Vesalius, Andreas, 162
Vesey, Denmark, 215, 237

Violence, 59, 76–80, 85, 86, 105, 117, 118, 144, 223, 230(n11), 268, 305,306. *See also* Cruelty; Genocide; Massacres
Virginia, 89, 95–96, 98, 100, 103, 107, 111(n4), 140, 174, 175, 176, 245
Virginia Company, 85
Virtues, 52, 82, 144
Voltaire, 169, 170(n2), 183–184, 233
Vosmaer, Arnout, 183
Voting, 99, 100, 228, 250. *See also* Suffrage
Vulnerability, 76, 107

Wagner, Richard, 258
Warfare, 91(n7), 121
Wealth, 45, 46, 47, 48, 49, 52, 63, 84, 106, 111(n12), 113, 121, 132, 144, 175, 176, 227
Weber, Max, 70(n2)
Webster, Noah, 180
Webster's New International Dictionary, 30
We Europeans (Huxley and Haddon), 296
Weld, Theodore, 215
Wessagusset, 78
West Indies, 58, 80, 95, 102, 104–105, 106, 151(n39), 212, 246
Weston, Thomas, 78
White, A. D., 243
White, Charles (Dr.), 232–233, 233–234, 235
White, John, 73–74
Whitefield, George, 220
Whiteness, 97, 135, 142, 183, 222, 245, 246
    white supremacy, 191, 250–252
White Over Black (Jordan), 192
White Supremacy and Negro Subordination (Van Evrie), 252
Wilberforce, William, 212
Williams, Eric, 111(nn 6, 12)
Williams, Roger, 80
Williamson, Joel, 204(n14), 226
Winthrop, John, 81, 83
Witchcraft, 63–64, 89
Women, 34(n4), 55, 56, 57, 79, 102, 121, 122, 132, 135, 167, 192
    Indian, 98
    See also Slavery, women slaves
Woolman, John, 207
Working class, 3, 226, 228
Worldviews, 17–18. *See also* Race, as worldview
World Wars I/II, 267, 273, 277, 303, 306
Wright, Louis B., 81, 82

Young, Andrew, 12(n4)